FATHERLAN

State-building and Nationhood in Ninete

Fatherlands is an original study of the nature of identity in nineteenth-century Germany, which has crucial implications for the understanding of nationalism, German unification and the German nation state in the modern era.

The book approaches these questions from a new and important angle, that of the non-national territorial state. It explores the nature and impact of state-building in non-Prussian Germany. The issues covered range from railway construction and German industrialisation, to the modernisation of German monarchy, the emergence of a free press, the development of a modern educational system, and the role of monuments, museums and public festivities.

Fatherlands draws principally on extensive primary research focusing on the three kingdoms of Hanover, Saxony and Württemberg. It is an attempt to 'join up the dots' of German history – moving beyond isolated local, regional and state-based studies to a general understanding of the state formation process in Germany.

ABIGAIL GREEN is Tutor and Fellow in History, Brasenose College, Oxford

1

NEW STUDIES IN EUROPEAN HISTORY

Edited by

PETER BALDWIN, University of California, Los Angeles
CHRISTOPHER CLARK, University of Cambridge
JAMES B. COLLINS, Georgetown University
MIA RODRÍGUEZ-SALGADO, London School of Economics and
Political Science
LYNDAL ROPER, Royal Holloway, University of London

This is a new series of scholarly monographs in early modern and modern European history. Its aim is to publish outstanding works of research, addressed to important themes across a wide geographical range, from southern and central Europe to Scandinavia and Russia, and from the time of the Renaissance to the Second World War. As it develops the series will comprise focused works of wide contextual range and intellectual ambition.

FATHERLANDS

State-Building and Nationhood in Nineteenth-Century Germany

ABIGAIL GREEN

PUBLISHED BY THE PRESS SYNDICATE OF THE UNIVERSITY OF CAMBRIDGE
The Pitt Building, Trumpington Street, Cambridge, United Kingdom

CAMBRIDGE UNIVERSITY PRESS
The Edinburgh Building, Cambridge CB2 2RU, UK
40 West 20th Street, New York NY 10011–4211, USA
477 Williamstown Road, Port Melbourne, VIC 3207, Australia
Ruiz de Alarcón 13, 28014 Madrid, Spain
Dock House, The Waterfront, Cape Town 8001, South Africa

http://www.cambridge.org

First published 2001
First paperback edition 2004

Typeface Monotype Baskerville 11/12.5   *System* QuarkXPress™   [SE]

A catalogue record for this book is available from the British Library

Library of Congress cataloguing in publication data

Green, Abigail.
Fatherlands : state-building and nationhood in nineteenth-century Germany / Abigail Green.
p.   cm. – (New Studies in European history)
Includes bibliographical references and index.
ISBN 0 521 79313 0 hardback
1. Nationalism – Germany – History – 19th century.   2. Nationalism – Germany – Hanover
(Province) – History – 19th century.   3. Nationalism – Germany – Saxony – History – 19th
century.   4. Nationalism – Germany – Württemberg – History – 19th century.   5.
Monarchy – Germany – History – 19th century.   6. Germany – Cultural policy.   7.
Industrialization – Germany – History – 19th century.   8. Germany – Intellectual life – 19th
century.   I. Title.   II. Series.
DD204.G692   2001
943′.07–dc21   00–069796

ISBN 0 521 79313 0 hardback
ISBN 0 521 61623 9 paperback

Contents

Illustrations

Maps

Tables

Acknowledgements

I would like to take this opportunity to thank the many people who have made this book possible.

First, I would like to thank the archives I used for their cooperation in this project: the Hauptstaatsarchiv (Stuttgart), the Niedersächsisches Hauptstaatsarchiv (Hanover) and the Sächsisches Hauptstaatsarchiv (Dresden). In particular I would like to thank HRH Ernst August, Prince of Hanover, for allowing me to use the royal archive. I would like to thank the staff of all three archives for their good advice, for their willingness to help wherever possible and for the time and trouble they devoted to my very numerous requests. My thanks are also due to the staff at the numerous libraries I have used: Cambridge University Library, the British Library, the German Historical Institute, and the *Landesbibliotheken* in Dresden, Hanover and Stuttgart.

Secondly, I would like to thank the various institutions which supported me financially during this project: the British Academy, the German Academic Exchange Service, Gonville and Caius College, Cambridge, and the Kurt Hahn Foundation. Without their help this book would never have been written.

Thirdly, I would like to thank my Ph.D. supervisors, Tim Blanning and Jonathan Steinberg in Cambridge and Dieter Langewiesche in Tübingen, for their advice, support and encouragement, for their helpful comments on my work and for the many useful discussions we had. I am very grateful too, to the fellows of St John's College, Cambridge and Brasenose College, Oxford for providing such a supportive and friendly environment to live and work in. More generally, I would like to thank the wider community of German historians in Cambridge for providing such a stimulating working environment. Special thanks are due to Jo Whaley for the dedication with which he read my work, and for his help with many small things – both academic and practical – which went far beyond the call of duty. Likewise, I would like to thank Chris Clark for his unfailing helpfulness and for his ideas about my more recent work, which have proved invaluable in pointing me in the right direction. Many thanks are due, too, to Brendan Simms for his help with the 'Tübingen connection'. I would also like to thank those who taught me at Oxford and have remained interested in my progress: Michael John, for his advice on things Hanoverian, and Niall Ferguson for his faith in me, and for his support and inspiration over the years.

Fourthly, I would like to thank the many others who have helped me with this project. Special thanks are due to Sibylle Mager for her help in editing the first draft of my manuscript, and to Emma Winter for her comments on the second draft. In particular, I would like to thank those whose hospitality and friendship made my time researching in Germany so enjoyable: Gabrielle, Danielle, Cedric and Martin in Stuttgart; Mathias, Andy and Dirk in Dresden; Phaula and Marita in Hanover, and last but not least Berit in Cologne. All these people put themselves out for me again and again as I dragged my suitcases around Germany.

On a more personal note, I feel that a special vote of thanks is due to Natasha, for supporting me through the final moments of my Ph.D., and to Morwena for writing to me so faithfully over the years. I am very grateful, too, to Boaz for listening so patiently to my thoughts on nineteenth-century Germany – a subject in which he has no interest whatsoever. Finally, I would like to thank my parents, for their love and support through my difficult years as an eternal student. This book is dedicated to them. With love.

Introduction

'What is the German Fatherland?' This question, posed by the poet Ernst Moritz Arndt, was to prove one of the most intractable problems in nineteenth century Germany. For Arndt, a passionate German nationalist, the answer was easy: not Austria or Prussia, not Bavaria or Saxony but all of these together – the whole of Germany, with no exceptions. For many of his contemporaries, however, the question was more problematic. In the early nineteenth century, most Germans were Austrians or Prussians, Bavarians or Saxons, first and foremost.

The complexities of the situation were neatly encapsulated by another early nineteenth-century German nationalist, the poet Heinrich von Kleist. In his 'German Catechism', Kleist envisages a confrontation between a Saxon father and his German son.[1] 'I am a German,' the son declares. 'A German?' his father cries. 'You must be joking. You were born in Meissen, and Meissen is in Saxony!' 'I was born in Meissen,' the son replies, 'and Meissen is indeed in Saxony; but my Fatherland, the country to which Saxony belongs, is Germany – and your son, my father, is a German.' But the father remains unconvinced. 'Where is this Germany?' he asks. He cannot find it on the map. Had the father asked this question a hundred years later, his son would have found it easier to answer. By that time the state of Germany was very much on the map and German nationalism was an important force in the new Germany. How did this change come about? How far did the nationalism of the new nation state displace older loyalties to the German states and their rulers?

First, these developments need to be understood in terms of the wider European context. Nationalism emerged as a political creed throughout Europe during the nineteenth century. By 1900 it had become a serious

---

[1] Heinrich von Kleist, *Katechismus der Deutschen abgefasst nach dem Spanischen zum Gebrauch für Kinder und Alte* (1809).

force to be reckoned with. European history is littered with examples of this development: the unifications of Germany and Italy; the Polish revolts against Russia in 1830–1 and 1863; the nationalist uprisings throughout the Habsburg Empire during the 1848–9 revolution, notably in Hungary; the 'national' struggle of the French and the Germans in 1870–1; the birth of Zionism in the 1880s; the mushrooming of nationalist organisations in Britain, France and Germany in the decades before the First World War. How can we understand the emergence of this new ideology?

Theorists of nationalism are generally in agreement over its central tenets: the belief that political and national units should be congruent, and the belief in the nation as a supreme value.[2] Theorists of nationalism differ, however, in their definition of a nation and in their explanations of how and why nationalism emerged.[3] On the one hand, theorists of nationalism have sought to do justice to what Anthony Smith has termed 'the ethnic origins of nations' – that is the cultural roots of nationhood: a collective name, language, myth of descent, religion, history and so on.[4] This approach inevitably emphasises the extent to which modern nationalisms have drawn on existing ethnic and political units and the loyalties they evoke. On the other hand, most theorists of nationalism have understood it to be a modern political phenomenon, whose origins are usually associated with French mobilisation of the political nation during the revolutionary era.[5] In this context, theorists of nationalism are concerned with how far nationhood can be stimulated or created within a given political unit (the state), as a result of government activity (state-building) and of popular participation in shared political institutions (democratisation). Moreover, awareness of nationalism as a modern phenomenon has led theorists of nationalism, like Ernest Gellner, to examine its growth in terms of the relationship

---

[2] For instance, Peter Alter, *Nationalism* (London, 1989), pp. 4–5, p. 11; Ernest Gellner, *Nations and nationalism* (Oxford, 1983) p. 1; John Breuilly, *Nationalism and the state* (Manchester, 1993, 2nd edn) p. 2.

[3] Tellingly, these issues are the focus for the recent anthology John Hutchinson and Anthony D. Smith (eds.), *Nationalism* (Oxford, 1994).

[4] Anthony D. Smith, *The ethnic origins of nations* (Oxford, 1986).

[5] For instance, Breuilly, *Nationalism and the state*, p. 1, describes nationalism as 'an essentially appropriate form of political behaviour in the context of the modern state and the modern state system'. Eric Hobsbawm sees the basic characteristic of the nation as modernity. See Hobsbawm, *Nations and nationalism since 1780. Programme, myth, reality* (Cambridge, 1990), p. 14. Although Benedict Anderson also sees nationalism as a modern phenomenon, he traces it back to the eighteenth century and sees the Creole nationalisms of America as the earliest manifestation of the nationalist phenomenon. Anderson, *Imagined communities* (London, 1983), pp. 47–65.

between nationalism and socio-economic change – that is, in the context of the modernisation process as a whole.[6] More recently, however, the modernist view of nationalism has been called into question by the work of Adrian Hastings.[7] Hastings has pointed out the ancient character of the word 'nation', as well as the existence in England of hybrid sentiments of political and cultural identification, similar to nationalism, as early as the medieval period.[8]

In many ways, this debate over the modernity of the nation, and the relative importance of cultural and political elements in nationalism, is a diversion from more important issues. Of course, many people did feel a sense of collective identity – whether cultural, political or both – long before the French Revolution and the onset of 'modernity'. This feeling of collective identity certainly had something in common with nationalism and, in many cases, subsequently formed the basis of a modern nation. Nevertheless, the emergence of nationalism as an ideology was indeed a nineteenth-century phenomenon. In this sense, it is important to distinguish between nationalism and the nations that inspired it. Individual nations often pre-dated the age of nationalism, but belief in the primacy of nationhood over other values and loyalties did not. The idea that we need to know what a nation is in order to understand nationalism – and not vice versa – stems from a readiness to accept nationalist ideas at face value for, as John Breuilly has pointed out, nationalists use the same word (nation) to mean quite different things (cultural or political units) and then claim that these things are, or should be, identical.[9] As a result, the 'nation' is a fluid concept that changes its meaning in accordance with the particular variant of nationalism it endorses. Inevitably, therefore, it is impossible to fix on a definitive definition of the word 'nation'. The attempt to find such a definition is in many ways a red herring, a case of historians taking on board the obsessive preoccupation of nationalists with the idea of nationhood. If we shift the focus from the nation itself to the ideology of nationalism, a different series of questions arises. Instead of seeking to define the nation, we need to understand the relationship between nationalism and 'pre-national' loyalties and identities. How and why did nationhood

---

[6] Gellner, *Nations and nationalism*. Gellner argues that, in industrial society, mankind is committed to a productive system based on cumulative science and technology in order to sustain itself and that this in turn enforces a degree of cultural homogeneity, which eventually 'appears on the surface in the form of nationalism'. Thus 'the age of transition to industrialism was bound . . . also to be an age of nationalism', pp. 40–1.

[7] Adrian Hastings, *The construction of nationhood: ethnicity, religion and nationalism* (Cambridge, 1997).

[8] Ibid., pp. 14–19, 35–51.   [9] Breuilly, *Nationalism and the state*, p. 62.

came to be adopted as a supreme value in places like Germany, where cultural identity had coexisted for centuries with multiple regional, local and religious identities?

In the past, the German nation has been taken both as a classic example of the cultural nation and as a text-book example of nation state formation and, by extension, of political nationalism. This demonstrates the extreme incongruity of the German nation as a political and cultural entity through history. On the one hand, the existence of the German nation as a cultural entity for many centuries before German unification is undisputed. On the other hand, at no time (except under Hitler) did political structures in German Europe bring all the Germans together in a single state, of the kind which we would recognise today. Nevertheless, the discrepancy between cultural and political nationhood was not absolute. Recent historians have acknowledged the 'statehood' of the Holy Roman Empire, despite the many ways in which it failed to conform to the modern understanding of a state.[10] Moreover, Peter Krüger and others have emphasised the attachment of Germans to the Holy Roman Empire as a political unit, as well as their pride in its achievements and its constitution.[11] In this sense, the German nation before 1800 had political as well as cultural attributes. This has important implications for our understanding of nineteenth-century German nationalism in the period before unification, since it enabled nationalism to coexist with more local loyalties. Just as the Holy Roman Empire had remained a meaningful political unit, despite the existence within it of hundreds of different German states, so many nationalists believed that a German nation state could incorporate existing political units without destroying them altogether. Yet the political and cultural legacy of the Holy Roman Empire is of only limited relevance to our understanding of German nationalism after 1871, for the new German Empire was heir to the Holy Roman Empire in name only. In fact, the 'unification' of Germany in 1871 really marked the division of the historic German nation, both as a cultural and as a political entity – excluding those Germans who later became Austrian from the new 'nation state'.

---

[10] On this, see Peter Krüger, 'Auf der Suche nach Deutschland – ein historischer Streifzug ins Ungewisse' in Peter Krüger (ed.), *Deutschland, deutscher Staat, deutsche Nation. Historische Erkundungen eines Spannungsverhältnisses* (Marburg, 1993), pp. 41–70 (48–53).

[11] Ibid. For an analysis of these views in the late eighteenth and early nineteenth centuries, see Joachim Whaley, 'Thinking about Germany, 1750–1815: the birth of a nation?', *Transactions of the English Goethe Society* NS 66 (1997), 53–72.

For most of the nineteenth century Germany was a patchwork of states ranging from the very large to the very small, which were joined from 1815 until 1866 in a loose but indissoluble union: the German Confederation (see Map 1, p. 24). The Emperor of Austria was titular head of the new Confederation, although in practice it was dominated by an alliance of the German great powers, Austria and Prussia. This alliance was largely founded on the desire of both states to maintain the *ancien régime* in Germany and to clamp down on subversive and revolutionary forces. Membership of the German Confederation in 1815 marked a new beginning for most German states. For the first time they were truly sovereign, no longer nominally dependent on the Holy Roman Empire. Many of these states had, furthermore, either gained or lost land and subjects during the Napoleonic era and in this sense too they bore little resemblance to their former selves. The onus on many German governments was to reinvent the state for this new context, reforming its institutions, refining its relations with its neighbours, and redefining the identity of its inhabitants.

Yet 1815 did not merely mark the beginning of a period of sovereign statehood for the German states. Countervailing tendencies were at work. The Napoleonic era also saw the dawn of a new kind of German nationalism, which moved beyond a sense of German cultural identity to a more political understanding of the German nation (although the precise nature of this political vision remained unclear). This politicised and ideological German nationalism emerged as a response to Germany's humiliation in the Napoleonic wars and reached a climax in the wars of national liberation against the French. The new German Confederation failed, however, to fulfil the nationalist aspirations aroused by these events. The faint stirrings of German political nationalism subsided in the 1820s, but re-emerged spasmodically during the decades which followed, in 1830–2, 1840, 1848/9 and 1859 – each time with greater force and a clearer political vision.

These nationalist stirrings exacerbated the existing tensions between Austria and Prussia over power within Germany and threw the dualist alliance at the heart of the German Confederation into disarray. This disarray first became apparent during the revolution of 1848/9, subsided to some extent during the reactionary 1850s and re-emerged permanently after 1859, as Prussia sought to force Austria to abandon her claims for hegemony in Germany and was increasingly ready to exploit the nationalist movement for her own ends. These tensions culminated in the divisive Austro-Prussian war of 1866, which created a new Germany dominated by Prussia. Popular identification with the new Germany was initially hesitant. In 1870–1, however, German victory in the Franco-Prussian War acted as a national catharsis, paving the way for German unification in 1871 and providing a basis for national identity in the new German Empire.

German 'unification' has traditionally been portrayed in part as a victory for German nationalism as a political movement. More recently, however, many historians have emphasised the weakness of German nationalism before unification and the limited nature of its appeal.[12] Instead, they have stressed the strength of other kinds of loyalty and identity in Germany – confessional, regional, state-based, social.[13] Indeed, the German Empire has been described as an uncompleted nation state. Historians have therefore turned their attention to the process of national integration within this state after 1871 – a process completed by 1914 at the latest.[14] In this sense, German nation state formation represented the

---

[12] See Breuilly, *Nationalism and the state*, pp. 96–114; John Breuilly, 'The national idea in modern German history' and William Carr, 'The unification of Germany' in John Breuilly (ed.), *The state of Germany. The national idea in the making, unmaking and remaking of a modern nation state* (London/New York, 1992), pp. 1–29, 80–102; Geoff Eley, 'State formation, nationalism and political culture in nineteenth century Germany' in Ralph Samuel and Gareth Stedman Jones (eds.), *Culture, ideology and politics* (London, 1982), pp. 277–301; Julius H. Schoeps, 'Die Deutschen und ihre Identität. Zwischen Kyffhäusermythos und Verfassungspatriotismus' in Krüger (ed.), *Deutschland, deutscher Staat, deutsche Nation*, pp. 85–99. Michael Hughes, *Nationalism and society, Germany 1800–1945* (London, 1988), pp. 115–16, qualifies this view. He argues that nationalism was certainly a growing force by the 1860s, but that it remains important not to over-estimate it. Hagen Schulze, *The course of German nationalism, from Frederick the Great to Bismarck 1763–1867* (Cambridge, 1991) does not support this consensus. He dates nationalism, as a mass phenomenon capable of influencing political events, to the Rhine crisis of 1840, ibid., pp. 66–7. Equally, historians of the national gymnastic, singing and shooting movements stress the existence of a mass nationalist base. See Dietmar Klenke, 'Nationalkriegerisches Gemeinschaftsideal als politische Religion: Zum Vereinsnationalismus der Sänger, Schützen und Turner am Vorabend der Einigungskriege', *Historische Zeitschrift* 260:2 (April 1995), 395–448.

[13] Notably James J. Sheehan, 'What is German history? Reflections on the role of the *Nation* in German history and historiography', *Journal of Modern History* 53 (February 1981), 1–23. Of course, this was not merely the case in Germany. For instance, Eugen Weber has demonstrated the persistence of such particular loyalties and identities in nineteenth-century France, in his study of nation-building in the Third Republic. See Weber, *Peasants into Frenchmen, the modernisation of rural France 1870–1914* (London, 1977).

[14] On this, see Eley, 'State formation, nationalism and political culture'; Peter Gay, 'Probleme der kulturellen Integration der Deutschen 1849 bis 1945', and Jürgen Kocka, 'Probleme der politischen Integration der Deutschen 1867 bis 1945', in Otto Büsch and James J. Sheehan (eds.), *Die Rolle der Nation in der deutschen Geschichte und Gegenwart* (Berlin, 1985), pp. 181–92, 118–36; Schoeps, 'Die Deutschen und ihre Identität'; Hans-Ulrich Wehler, *The German Empire 1871–1918* (Leamington Spa, 1985). See also Celia Applegate, *A nation of provincials. The German idea of Heimat* (Berkeley/Oxford, 1990); Alon Confino, *The nation as a local metaphor. Württemberg, Imperial Germany and national memory 1871–1918* (Chapel Hill/London, 1997); Werner Hartung, *Konservative Zivilisationskritik und regionale Identität. Am Beispiel der niedersächsischen Heimatbewegung 1895 bis 1919* (Hanover, 1991).

triumph of new state structures over an existing 'cultural nation', rather than the triumph of emancipatory nationalism over pre-modern state structures. It is worth noting, however, that the persistence of strong particular identities during the unification period did not necessarily preclude outbursts of nationalist feeling, of the kind which swept Germany during the Franco-Prussian war. Internal differences did not prevent Germans from uniting as a nation in the face of a common foe.

This analysis of the unification process prompts serious questions concerning the states that preceded the German Empire and the kinds of political loyalty that they inspired. What was the relationship between these states and the German Empire which succeeded them? The longstanding influence of the prussophile Borussian School of historians has meant that these issues have already been examined fairly exhaustively in the case of Prussia. Yet Prussia only made up some two-thirds of the new Germany. What of the other states incorporated in the German Empire? How did these states and the loyalties they inspired relate to German nationalism and to the German nation state?

Fatherlands addresses these questions from two important angles. First, it asks how state-based identity coexisted with national identity before unification. Secondly, it asks how this relationship developed after unification, as states became integrated in the new German Empire. In other words, the book attempts to establish how national Germany was before unification and how federal it remained thereafter.

These issues are of crucial importance, not merely for our understanding of modern German history, but also for our understanding of nationalism and nation state formation in the modern world. The complex relationship between statehood and nationalism in nineteenth-century Germany illuminates the role of territorial borders and political institutions in fostering nationalism at this time. The study of state building and identity formation in the pre-unification German states helps us to understand how far state-building activities within a subnational territorial state could create state-based political loyalty and identity. Important parallels can be drawn between this process and the nature of state-building and identity formation in the German nation state after 1871.

The relationship between federalism and nationalism in Germany is so intimately connected with particularist statehood and particular identities that it cannot simply be studied in a general way. I have chosen, therefore, to approach the subject primarily through a comparative study of three German states (Hanover, Saxony and Württemberg), although the book will also consider the experiences of other states, such as Bavaria.

The study of nineteenth-century Germany has traditionally focused on Prussia. This reflects the long shadow cast by Borussianism, and by the work of historians like Droysen, Ranke and Treitschke. During the unification period and its aftermath, Borussian historians reinterpreted the German past in the light of contemporary politics. They chose to see German history in terms of a Prussian mission to unite the German nation and so enable it to fulfil its unique historic potential. Recent historians have consciously rejected this tradition. Instead, they have turned their attention to local and regional studies, which explore the diversity and specificity of the German experience before unification. These studies have tended to concentrate on the so-called 'Third Germany' – the Germany that was neither Prussia nor Austria. Most studies of the Third Germany have focused on particular states or, where they cover several states, on particular regions.[15] All this has greatly enriched our understanding of nineteenth-century Germany, but it remains important not to lose sight of the general picture. It is clearly right to realise that Prussian history is not German history. We should remember, however, that the history of regions and states like the Rhineland, Hesse and Bavaria is not German history either. The very wealth of German diversity and the specific nature of most local, regional and state-based studies makes it difficult to draw wider conclusions either about Germany in general, or about the Third Germany in particular.

In this book I have attempted to avoid the short-comings of both approaches. *Fatherlands* takes a comparative approach, which combines a general awareness of developments and issues in nineteenth-century Germany with a more specific focus on three important case studies, the Kingdoms of Hanover, Saxony and Württemberg. On one level, the book is a study of three German states and as such it is concerned with

---

[15] Some examples of this are Werner K. Blessing, *Staat und Kirche in der Gesellschaft. Institutionelle Autorität und mentaler Wandel in Bayern während des 19. Jahrhunderts* (Göttingen, 1982); Lothar Gall, *Der Liberalismus als regierende Partei. Das Großherzogtum Baden zwischen Restauration und Reichsgründung* (Wiesbaden, 1968); Hans-Werner Hahn, *Wirtschaftliche Integration im 19. Jahrhundert. Die hessischen Staaten und der Deutsche Zollverein* (Göttingen, 1982); Manfred Hanisch, *Für Fürst und Vaterland. Legitimitätsstiftung in Bayern zwischen Revolution 1848 und deutscher Einheit* (Munich, 1991); Nicholas Martin Hope, *The alternative to German unification: the anti-Prussian party in Frankfurt, Nassau and the two Hessen 1859–1867* (Wiesbaden, 1973); Dieter Langewiesche, *Liberalismus und Demokratie in Württemberg zwischen Revolution und Reichsgründung* (Düsseldorf, 1974).

the specific experience of these states and their distinctive characteristics. It therefore forms part of the new body of work on German diversity, regionalism and the Third Germany. Fundamentally, however, the book is a comparative study. As such, it is concerned more generally with the tensions between federalism and nationalism in Germany, and with the role of lesser German states in the unification process. Indeed, *Fatherlands* is to some extent a comparative study with a difference, for it focuses on the similarities between developments in Hanover, Saxony and Württemberg rather than on the differences between them. In a way, it is an attempt to 'join up the dots', moving beyond isolated local, regional and state-based studies to a wider understanding of the Third Germany.

Hanover, Saxony and Württemberg are good subjects for a comparative study of this kind because they had much in common in terms of size (populations of about two million), status (kingdoms) and confessional orientation (Protestant majorities). These three states can therefore be seen to represent the Third Germany in two important ways. First, after Prussia and Bavaria, they were the largest states to be incorporated in the new German Empire. Consequently, the experience of statehood in Hanover, Saxony and Württemberg was fairly typical for the Third Germany, in that it affected a relatively high proportion of its population. After 1871, roughly a third of those Germans not originally of Prussian origin had been inhabitants of these three states. Second, the experience of statehood in these three states was representative in geographical terms. Each state was situated in a different part of Germany (the North, the Centre, the South-West) and subject to different geographical, socio-economic and political influences as a result.

All three states were politically important within Germany. Before unification they had been, after Bavaria, the most important of the medium-sized German states, known to contemporaries as *Mittelstaaten* – literally, 'middle states'. The *Mittelstaaten* were neither tiny principalities nor great powers, like Prussia and Austria.[16] Consequently, they were large enough to exercise political influence within and through the German Confederation, but too small to exercise this influence beyond it. Unlike the smaller German states, the *Mittelstaaten* were not resigned to losing their sovereignty. In 1849/50 most of the German states agreed to participate in Prussia's plans for a 'little German' (*kleindeutsch*) national union excluding Austria. Crucially, however, the four non-Prussian German kingdoms did not. This concern with sovereignty, and the belief

---

[16] Other, less important *Mittelstaaten* were Baden, Hesse-Kassel, Hesse-Darmstadt and Nassau.

in their viability as independent states, renders the *Mittelstaaten* good subjects for a study of particularist state building.

Bavaria was certainly both larger and more important than either Hanover, Saxony or Württemberg – indeed almost a third of non-Prussian Germans were Bavarians in 1871. In fact, the Bavarian experience was highly distinctive in terms of size, status and confessional orientation. The greater size and importance of Bavaria has led historians to take it as representative of the Third Germany.[17] Yet precisely because it was significantly larger, Bavaria was in fact atypical and far less representative of the Third Germany than the three states studied here. Bavaria was over double the size of the next most populous state in the German Confederation, Saxony. Consequently, the Bavarian government claimed special status, refusing to accept that Bavaria should be placed in the same category as other states in the Third Germany. Bavaria aspired at the very least to a leadership role among the lesser German states. Indeed, Bavaria aspired to quasi-great-power status on the basis of this role. The Bavarian government hoped to attain such status through a seat alongside Austria and Prussia in a putative German executive. Moreover, the existence of a Catholic majority, and the traditional strongly Catholic identity of state and dynasty, meant that the Bavarian experience of German unification and integration in the new German Empire was unique.

Particularism and the persistence of state-based loyalties have been primarily seen as South German and Catholic phenomena, in part because historians have tended to study Bavaria rather than other parts of the Third Germany. This view of particularism reflects the independence of the South German states from 1866 to 1871, the strong South German anti-Prussian vote in the *Zollparlament* elections, the impact of the *Kulturkampf* and the emergence of a powerful Catholic Centre Party during the 1870s. The association of particularism with Catholics and South Germans is valid up to a point. Nevertheless, the strength of particularism among these groups should not blind us to the persistence of state loyalties elsewhere in Germany. *Fatherlands* establishes the importance of state-based identity in three largely Protestant states, two of which were in North Germany. This substantially qualifies our view of particularism, demonstrating that state loyalties remained important throughout Germany after unification. Confession and geography may

---

[17] As in Richard Kohnen, *Pressepolitik des Deutschen Bundes. Methoden staatlicher Pressepolitik nach der Revolution von 1848* (Tübingen, 1995). Kohnen's study focuses on the two great powers (Austria and Prussia) and Bavaria (representing the Third Germany).

have coloured the nature of particularism in some German states, such as Bavaria. Elsewhere, particularism focused on other factors, such as the dynasty or the state's constitutional traditions. Interestingly, religion played little part in the state-based identities of Hanover, Saxony or Württemberg, although it was, of course, an important factor in domestic politics and confessional orientation certainly influenced the balance between particularist and national allegiances. The relative insignificance of religion in state-based identity here is unsurprising: although traditionally and predominantly Protestant, two of these states had substantial Catholic minorities and the third was ruled by a Catholic dynasty.

Fatherlands covers the whole of the 'long nineteenth century', from the fall of Napoleon and the creation of the German Confederation in 1815 to the outbreak of the First World War in 1914. How did the German states respond to the contradictory challenges of state-building and German nationalism at this time? Particularist state-building in nineteenth-century Germany has usually been studied in the context of the Napoleonic era and its aftermath.[18] At this stage, state-building was motivated by largely domestic concerns, notably the need of recently enlarged states to integrate new territories with their traditional heartlands. Studies of particularist state-building in this period have therefore focused on administrative and constitutional reform, rather than religious, cultural and education policy.[19]

In fact, particularist state-building was not restricted to this early period, as Manfred Hanisch's solitary study of state-building in Bavaria after 1848–9 demonstrates.[20] Consequently, I have chosen in this book to focus in particular on the middle years of the century. These years saw the development of the German Confederation in its second incarnation, from its restoration in 1850/1 until its collapse in 1866 – or, more pertinently, from the failure of the German revolutions in 1848/9 to German unification in 1871. These years, traditionally condemned as a period of reaction, are arguably the most under-researched period in

---

[18] For instance Helmut Berding, 'Staatliche Identität, nationale Integration und politischer Regionalismus', *Blätter für deutsche Landesgeschichte* 121 (1985), 371–93; Karl Bosl, 'Die historische Staatlichkeit der bayerischen Lande', *Zeitschrift für bayerische Landesgeschichte* 25:1 (1962), 3–19; Walter Demel, *Der bayerische Staatsabsolutismus 1806/8–1817. Staats- und gesellschaftspolitische Motivationen und Hintergünde der Reformära in der ersten Phase des Königreichs Bayern* (Munich, 1983); Lawrence J. Flockerzie, 'State-building and nation-building in the Third Germany: Saxony after the congress of Vienna', *Central European History* 24 (1991), 268–92; Gerhard Schmidt, *Reformbestrebungen in Sachsen in den ersten Jahrzehnten des 19. Jahrhunderts* (Dresden, 1969).

[19] The earlier chapters of Blessing, *Staat und Kirche in der Gesellschaft*, pp. 23–57, are an exception here.

[20] Hanisch, *Für Fürst und Vaterland*.

nineteenth-century German history.[21] Recently, however, some historians have turned their attention back to the 1850s and 1860s, reassessing the importance of the period in both political and socio-economic terms. They now recognise that the 1848/9 revolution fundamentally changed the face of Germany and that the restoration of the German Confederation did not bring with it a return to *Vormärz* conditions. As Hans-Ulrich Wehler has argued, the 1850s and 1860s were the breakthrough years for Germany's twin national and industrial revolutions.[22] Wolfram Siemann has portrayed the period similarly, as one of both political and socio-economic turmoil, encapsulated in his phrase 'Gesellschaft im Aufbruch'.[23]

The general reassessment of the period has led to a reinterpretation of German government policy and the role of the state. Historians continue to recognise the repressive elements of government policy, particularly during the so-called decade of 'reaction' in the 1850s. Indeed, the study of government repression in the shape of the *Polizeiverein* has provided an important focus for Siemann's work.[24] Siemann argues that Prussia and Austria formed a counter-revolutionary alliance within the German Confederation, which remained fully operative until 1859 – despite the foreign policy differences between the two powers, which have obscured historians' awareness of this understanding.[25] On the other hand, the picture now painted of the 'reaction' differs significantly from older interpretations of the period. Thus recent historians have stressed the innovative approach to counter-revolution taken by some – though not all – German governments. Siemann underlines the unprecedented nature of non-diplomatic inter-governmental cooperation over domestic policy in the *Polizeiverein*.[26] Interest shown by Richard Kohnen and others in government press policy reflects a similar awareness that the German governments were breaking new ground in their approach to public opinion and news management after 1848/9.[27] Moreover,

---

[21] Wolfram Siemann, *Gesellschaft im Aufbruch. Deutschland 1849–1871* (Frankfurt, 1990), p. 11, notes the extent to which this period has traditionally been ignored by historians.

[22] Hans-Ulrich Wehler, *Deutsche Gesellschaftsgeschichte*, Vol. III, *Von der 'Deutschen Doppelrevolution' bis zum Beginn des Ersten Weltkrieges 1849–1914* (Munich, 1995), pp. 4–5. In fact, Wehler dates the beginnings of this revolution back to 1845.   [23] Siemann, *Gesellschaft im Aufbruch*.

[24] See Wolfram Siemann, *Der 'Polizeiverein' deutscher Staaten: eine Dokumentation zur Überwachung der Öffentlichkeit nach der Revolution von 1848/9* (Tübingen, 1983).

[25] Siemann, *Gesellschaft im Aufbruch*, pp. 32–44, 62–5.   [26] Ibid., pp. 44–52.

[27] Kohnen, *Pressepolitik des Deutschen Bundes*; Wolfgang Piereth, 'Propaganda im 19. Jahrhundert. Die Anfänge aktiver staatlicher Pressepolitik in Deutschland 1800–1871' in Wolfram Siemann and Ute Daniel (eds.), *Propaganda, Meinungskampf, Verführung und politische Sinnstiftung 1789–1989* (Frankfurt, 1994), pp. 21–43.

Manfred Hanisch's study of 'nation-building' policies in Max II's Bavaria demonstrates that here government press policy formed part of a wider propaganda campaign designed to reinforce Bavarian identity and to strengthen the state.[28] Finally, there has been greater recognition of the role played by German governments in determining the parameters for economic take-off, through economic legislation and through sponsoring railway construction and other kinds of state industry.[29]

The middle of the nineteenth century was a period of crucial importance in the relationship between state-building and nationhood in Germany. First, the period proved decisive in determining the outcome of the 'national' revolution. The experiences of 1848/9 had raised the German question in a new and acute form. The revolution revealed the existence of pressures for national reform among significant sectors of public opinion and clarified the nature of the problems this reform entailed, notably the vexed question of Austria's role in a new national settlement. Neither the Frankfurt assembly (1848/9), the Erfurt parliament (1849/50) nor the Dresden conferences (1851) managed to provide such a settlement. The German question therefore remained unresolved. Consequently, questions about the future shape of Germany – and its component parts – were most insistently raised and finally answered during the years that followed the revolution.

Second, the period saw renewed government interest in state-building measures. The experiences of 1848/9 had increased the interdependence of domestic and national politics in Germany. On the one hand, the revolutions of 1848/9 were domestic revolutions, which aimed to overthrow traditional and conservative political systems within the German states. On the other hand, they were also a single national revolution, since the creation of a liberal political order at national level was seen as a precondition of the desired domestic changes. The failure of

---

[28] Hanisch, *Für Fürst und Vaterland*. See especially pp. 304–20, on the role of press policy in Max's wider policy 'zur "Hebung des bayerischen Nationalgefühls"'.

[29] In particular, relatively liberal economic policy is no longer seen as a peculiarly Prussian phenomenon. Hubert Kiesewetter, *Industrialisierung und Landwirtschaft. Sachsens Stellung im regionalen Industrialisierungsprozeß Deutschlands im 19. Jahrhundert* (Cologne/Vienna, 1988), pp. 166–96, argues that in practice the Saxon government allowed economic structures and conditions to develop which furthered the industrialisation process, despite the persistence of guild legislation in Saxony until 1861. Similarly, Richard J. Bazillion, *Modernizing Germany, Kurt Biedermann's career in the Kingdom of Saxony 1835–1901* (New York, 1990), pp. 299–300, argues that the Saxon *Gewerbeordnung* was a model of moderate reformism, liberalising the economy in a regulated fashion designed to minimalise the social costs of industrialisation. Bazillion argues that Saxony later provided a model for Bismarck, demonstrating the viability of a conservative state with a modern economy.

the revolution led to the apparent restoration of pre-revolutionary political institutions and practices at both state and national level. Dissatisfaction with the political order at both levels persisted and so pressures for national and domestic political change remained interrelated after 1848/9. The role of the German Confederation in domestic repression after 1850 encouraged a belief that liberalisation at state level was impossible without national reform. Continued pressures for national reform after 1848 – and particularly after 1859 – further intensified the level of interdependence between state and national politics. In order to face the national challenge, German governments needed to respond successfully to domestic pressures for change – hence the innovative nature of government reactionary policies and the governments' concern with state-building.

By this stage, state-building was not merely a response to domestic concerns, as it had been after 1815. Instead, state-building was a response to nascent nationalist pressures and the threat to state sovereignty. This new context influenced the kind of initiatives adopted at this time. Earlier state-building activities had already resolved many administrative issues, and the impact of the revolution prevented renewed constitutional reform. The cultural and, to a lesser extent, economic aspects of state-building were therefore particularly apparent during the later period. These aspects of state-building form the major focus of this book, which examines four areas of government policy: the official press, education, state-based culture and railway construction.

The search for a domestic response to the national challenge was partly a recognition of the failure of the *Mittelstaaten* to respond to this challenge at German Confederation level. The *Mittelstaaten* were large enough to hope that they could influence the outcome of the German question in their favour. Up to a point, the failure of Prussia's *kleindeutsch* plans in 1849–50 showed this to be true: at this stage the *Mittelstaaten* were still able to block Prussia's national ambitions. Thereafter, however, they repeatedly proved unable to influence German policy at German Confederation level, which continued to be dictated by Prussia and Austria. The impotence of the *Mittelstaaten* was demonstrated during the Crimean war, the Italian war of 1859, the Schleswig-Holstein crisis and, conclusively, the collapse of the German Confederation in 1866. Both the attempts of the *Mittelstaaten* at collective action and German Confederation reform (the Würzburg and Bamberg conferences) and the initiatives of individual *Mittelstaaten* (Saxony's German Confederation reform proposals) proved equally ineffectual. These failures are usually attributed to division and jealousy among the *Mittelstaaten*, due to their differing interests and consequent mutual mistrust. Together with the dualism of the German great powers, the inability of the *Mittelstaaten* to form a united front is seen as a major obstacle to German Confederation reform.

Nevertheless, historians have begun to question the traditional assumption that *kleindeutsch* German unification was inevitable. Instead, the trend has been to re-evaluate the German Confederation, both as a viable solution to the German question and as a functioning institution in its own right. Lothar Gall and, more recently, Andreas Kaernbach have emphasised the willingness of both Prussia and Bismarck to accept a divide-and-rule settlement within the German Confederation – provided that this acknowledged the parity between Austria and Prussia, allowing the former to dominate the South and the latter the North.[30] Helmut Rumpler and others have argued that the German Confederation itself was a far from moribund institution and that the impact of efforts by the *Mittelstaaten* at reform has been underestimated.[31] Rumpler cites the General German Commercial Code as an instance of the German Confederation evolving to meet the needs of a new era.[32] Conversely, Hans-Werner Hahn has concluded that economic integration within the *Zollverein* did not render *kleindeutsch* unification inevitable, although it facilitated this process.[33] With time the *Zollparlament* might have increased pressures for political unification, but it might equally have reduced them by satisfying the need for economic integration and rendering a political counterpart unnecessary. Moreover, inner German state borders remained important in other respects, as Andreas Fahrmeir has recently demonstrated with respect to citizenship laws.[34] As yet, this reassessment of the unification process in

---

[30] Lothar Gall, *Bismarck, the white revolutionary*, Vol. 1, *1851–1871* (London, 1986), for instance pp. 217–18, on Bismarck's readiness to contemplate a Greater Prussian solution after the *Frankfurter Fürstentag*; Andreas Kaernbach, *Bismarcks Konzepte zur Reform des deutschen Bundes. Zur Kontinuität der Politik Bismarcks und Preußens in der deutschen Frage* (Göttingen, 1991), especially in conclusion pp. 238–44.

[31] For a revisionist view of the German Confederation, see Helmut Rumpler (ed.), *Deutscher Bund und deutsche Frage 1815–1866* (Munich/Vienna, 1990).

[32] According to Rumpler, 'Das Allgemeine Deutsche Handelsgesetzbuch als Element der Bundesreform im Vorfeld der Krise von 1866' in Rumpler (ed.), *Deutscher Bund und deutsche Frage*, pp. 215–234, the German Commerical Code introduced in 1861 demonstrated that the German Confederation was capable of evolving to meet the needs of a new era. The Commercial code was the product of a Bavarian initiative in the Confederal Diet, intended to prove the potential of the German Confederation as an institution. Ironically, Rumpler argues, the success of this initiative (which unleashed a flood of proposals for similar legislation) ensured that in fact the German Confederation's days were numbered.

[33] Hans-Werner Hahn, *Geschichte des deutschen Zollvereins* (Göttingen, 1984), p. 187.

[34] Andreas Karl Otto Fahrmeir, 'Citizenship, nationality and alien status in England and the German states, 1815–1870' (unpublished Ph.D. thesis, Cambridge, 1997).

general, and of the German Confederation in particular, remains somewhat one-sided because it fails to take proper account of developments
at state level.

There is certainly an awareness among historians of the crucial interplay between domestic and national politics in Germany at this time.[35]
Indeed, many studies of liberalism in the German states explore precisely this issue. Nicholas Hope has shown how divisions over the future
shape of Germany in Hesse and Nassau related to more fundamental
divisions between liberals and reactionaries.[36] Thus the popularity of
the *kleindeutsch* movement and the limited appeal of its opponents
reflected the ability of the former to tap into widespread dissatisfaction
with the governments of these states, whilst the opponents of *kleindeutsch*
unification suffered through their association with reactionary regimes.
Hans-Werner Hahn has argued that the failure of governments in
Hesse-Kassel and Nassau to liberalise both economically and politically
ensured the relatively painless absorption of these states by Prussia after
1866, although the situation in Hesse-Darmstadt was somewhat different.[37] Similarly, Michael John has related the unusual strength of
National Liberalism in Hanover, both before and after unification, to
Hanover's history of constitutional conflict, entrenched noble privilege
and hard-line monarchic government.[38] Conversely, Lothar Gall has
shown how the domestic policies of Baden's liberal government in the
1860s provoked a backlash among Catholics and the rural population,
which then contributed to the collapse of the *kleindeutsch* consensus in this
state.[39] Interestingly, divisions over national rather than domestic political issues appear to have been most important in Württemberg, where
Dieter Langewiesche has shown that they were central to the split
between liberals and democrats and to the resultant party-formation
process in the 1860s.[40] In general, these studies have demonstrated the
counter-productive effects of reactionary regimes. Where governments
were reactionary, the opposition tended to support a *kleindeutsch* solution
and to prioritise unity over freedom; where they were more liberal, the

---

[35] Historians of liberalism in particular have increasingly stressed the importance of local and
regional context to liberal politics. See, for instance, the essays in Lothar Gall (ed.), *Liberalismus
und Region. Zur Geschichte des deutschen Liberalismus im 19. Jahrhundert* (Munich, 1995).

[36] Hope, *The alternative to German unification*, especially pp. 17–18.

[37] Hahn, *Wirtschaftliche Integration im 19. Jahrhundert*, p. 2.

[38] Michael John, 'Liberalism and society in Germany, 1850–1880: the case of Hanover', *English
Historical Review* cii:402 (1987), 579–98, and Michael John, 'Kultur, Klasse und regionaler
Liberalismus in Hannover 1848–1914' in Gall (ed.), *Liberalismus und Region*, pp. 161–93.

[39] Gall, *Der Liberalismus als regierende Partei*, pp. 177–8.

[40] Langewiesche, *Liberalismus und Demokratie in Württemberg*, p. 447.

opposition was sceptical about the virtues of Prussian hegemony and inclined to prioritise freedom over unity.

This is obviously an important point, but it does not give a complete picture of the interplay between domestic and national developments. By and large, historians have neglected developments which strengthened rather than undermined the German states – notably the renewed interest in state-building shown by many German governments during this period. Yet particularist state-building clearly affected the process of national integration in Germany at this time. How?

Fatherlands opens with a wide-ranging comparative history of the three states which form the main focus of the book. It covers the period 1815–1871. This establishes a framework for further analysis, providing the socio-economic and political context for developments in each of the three states.

A second chapter looks more closely at the rulers of these states themselves. Monarchs were crucially important in developing state-building policies and in determining political developments within the German states. Hanover, Saxony and Württemberg were essentially dynastic units, and monarchs and their families therefore played a key role in government propaganda. The main body of the book is concerned with the nature of this propaganda and the development of policies designed to strengthen state identity. This chapter looks at the men behind the myths. How successfully did they modernise the institution of monarchy? How far did their priorities shape government concerns?

The analysis of government policy begins in Chapter 3 with a study of state-sponsored cultural activities designed to foster a sense of particular identity: historical associations, art galleries, historical museums, monuments and public festivities. The chapter explores the parallels between nationalist and particularist culture in Germany and the interaction between the German governments and civil society in promoting culture at state level.

Chapters 4 and 5 examine in more detail how the revolution of 1848 transformed government policy, prompting a series of state-building initiatives designed to shore up particularist loyalties. Chapter 4 focuses on the most obvious vehicle for government propaganda: the official press. The emergence of a substantially free press in Germany after 1848 was accompanied in all three states by the development of a 'positive' press policy designed to minimise the dangers posed by this new factor in German politics. The chapter relates government press policy to wider considerations, placing organisational developments in their immediate political context. It also examines the impact of these organisational developments and political considerations upon the nature of the government's appeal to the people, as presented in the official press.

Chapter 5 analyses education policy after 1848 and the efforts of German governments to rear a new generation of loyal patriots uncorrupted by revolutionary ideas. The chapter demonstrates that governments gradually abandoned the traditional emphasis on religious education and moral values, in favour of a more modern approach to education as a means of identity formation. This new approach placed greater emphasis on history, geography and nature studies (the *Realien*), in order to strengthen popular awareness of the characteristics of the particular Fatherland. The shift away from traditional schooling, which focused on the catechism, towards more comprehensive elementary education in the years immediately preceding unification was fundamental to the emergence of a modern education system in these states. Furthermore, it marked a shift in the basis of popular legitimacy in Germany – away from doctrines of religious and dynastic legitimacy towards an explicitly patriotic approach. These changes had long-term effects, since education remained the prerogative of state governments after unification in 1871. Consequently, they remained relevant in the post-unification era.

The impact of railway construction on cultural activities of this kind and on state identity in general is discussed in Chapter 6. State-based railway networks increased the impact of cultural initiatives by creating a more effective community. This was a dual process, whereby peripheral regions were rendered less isolated and the capital acquired a more central role in the transport network. State railways reinforced existing identities by emphasising the competing interests of neighbouring states both specifically, as regards border areas, and more generally, as regards competition for freight, passengers and profits. The chapter also explores the symbolic importance of railways, as manifested in related monuments, inaugural festivities and the ceremonial role of railway stations.

These threads are drawn together in Chapter 7, which examines how the various kinds of government propaganda actually depicted these states. There were important similarities in the portrayal of all three states, notably acceptance of the wider German context and the role of tribal origins and dynasty in state identity, as well as past and present economic and cultural achievements. Nevertheless, the images of these

states also reflected long-term historical developments and, more importantly, domestic political conditions. Cultural achievements and, crucially, constitutional traditions were therefore emphasised in Saxony and
Württemberg, but not in Hanover, where propaganda was more dynastically oriented. The relative success of government propaganda in the
three states partly reflected the different nature of these approaches. The
chapter casts new light on the nature of German identity during this
period, by investigating the self-image of the *Mittelstaaten* and the role
they were assigned within Germany as a whole.

Finally, Chapter 8 examines the legacy of particularist state-building
in the new German Empire, asking how far inhabitants of the Third
Germany adapted to or resisted integration in the new nation state. By
and large, particularism did come to terms with the new nation state in
time. Even so, the officially sponsored Prussocentric nationalism of the
German Empire made relatively little headway in non-Prussian
Germany, where older, more inclusive ideas of the German nation continued to coexist with particular loyalties.

Primarily, *Fatherlands* is concerned with the formulation and development of government policy. Consequently, it is based on research in the
main government archives of these states, and the most important
sources have been official documents relating to government policy at the
centre.[41] Where this policy involved the production of material intended
to influence public opinion, this material has also been consulted. In particular, Chapter 7, which looks at the nature of government propaganda,
is based almost exclusively on this material. Sources used here include
official and semi-official newspapers, school readers and history books,
royal obituaries and patriotic poetry. Where appropriate, the analysis of
government policy in earlier chapters also draws on this material. Thus
Chapter 4 relates the content of official and semi-official newspapers to
the development of government press policy, and Chapter 5 relates the
content of officially sponsored school books to education policy.[42] The
approach to these sources taken here is primarily quantitative, looking at
the numbers of newspaper articles and school reader passages devoted
to particular themes. The approach taken in Chapter 7 is qualitative,
examining what government propaganda actually said.

[41] Sächsisches Hauptstaatsarchiv (Dresden); Niedersächsisches Hauptstaatsarchiv (Hanover);
Hauptstaatsarchiv (Stuttgart). Records from the period covered here are well preserved in both
Dresden and Stuttgart, but patchier in Hanover due to flood damage.
[42] The mechanics of this analysis and the approach to newspapers as sources are discussed in this
chapter at greater length.

The book is not concerned with the mechanics of how these policies were implemented at a local level. Consequently, local archives have not been consulted. Nevertheless, the book is concerned with the impact of these policies. This raises the thorny issue of reception. It is, of course, almost impossible to assess the actual effect of newspaper articles on readers, school books on pupils, monuments on passers by, festivities on participants, or railways on passengers. The most that can be revealed with any certainty is the intentions of those behind them: journalists, educationalists, monument and festival committees, railway companies, or governments. The study of these intentions forms the core of this book. It is possible that a detailed study of police reports, diaries, letters and literary evidence might illuminate the impact of the official press, school books and other kinds of particularist cultural activity. Such a study would be a major undertaking in its own right and therefore falls beyond the scope of this book. Where evidence is available, however, the book does assess the effectiveness of government propaganda in terms of the number of people it actually reached – on the basis of newspaper circulation figures, the actual distribution of school books in schools, attendance figures at museums and festivities, and railway ticket sales. In this way it is at least possible to speculate on the impact of the policies studied here.

Fatherlands shows the extent to which the national challenge forced 'reactionary' governments to innovate and adapt in order to defend the status quo, demonstrating the interaction between state and society in Germany at this time. The book also approaches the question of the inevitability of *kleindeutsch* unification from a new angle, looking at the viability not of the German Confederation but of the member states. It examines the various ways in which governments attempted to strengthen state-based loyalties in the population, and concludes that they were fairly successful in so doing. Governments influenced the press at state and local level, instituted patriotic education in elementary schools, sponsored the flowering of particularist culture and built railway networks which reflected the interests of the territorial state unit. These achievements frequently contrasted starkly with the lack of such developments at national level during the period. This was not enough to prevent German unification, which was the product of military and diplomatic events beyond the control of the *Mittelstaaten*. Nevertheless, all three states retained distinctive political cultures and identities within the German Empire – even when annexed by Prussia, as was the case in

Hanover. This demonstrates the significant if limited impact of state-building policy on identity formation in territorial states of this kind at this time.

The persistence of these particular cultures and identities did not ultimately prove incompatible with the development of a national culture or a national identity in the new Germany. Partly, this was because the state-based political cultures and identities examined here always reflected an awareness that the states were part of a wider Germany and therefore never claimed exclusivity in the way that a truly national identity might. Particular and national cultures and identities had always coexisted within Germany before unification, and they continued to do so thereafter. This dualism was perhaps the most distinctive aspect of the new German nation.

CHAPTER ONE

Variations of German experience: Hanover, Saxony and Württemberg

For nineteenth-century European tourists, political fragmentation was an integral part of the German experience. No one travelling through Germany could fail to notice that the country was a patchwork of states, each of which stamped its own distinct identity on to the landscape and its inhabitants. When the writer Frances Trollope entered the tiny principality of Hohenzollern-Heckingen on her trip through Swabia in the 1830s, she knew at once that it was not part of neighbouring Württemberg 'by the black and white stripes which distinguish every hand-rail and sign-post upon the domain'.[1] Similarly, Charles Elliott, another Englishman to visit Germany during the 1830s, described how 'guard-houses, barrières, and other similar public buildings, are marked as property of government by broad stripes of paint in diagonal lines. In Prussia, black and white alternate with each other . . . our entrance into Saxony was manifested by an enormous barrière which stretched across the road its lengthened streaks of green and white.'[2] Symbolism of this kind was not restricted to the paintwork. The uniforms worn by postillions and, later, by railway officials were equally distinctive. Thus when Richard Smith, yet another Englishman abroad, arrived in Saxony, his postillion 'changed the blue and orange livery of Prussia for the long yellow coat and cocked hat of Saxony'.[3] Such differences were by no means incidental. In fact, as Elliott's and Smith's accounts indicate, they were an important way in which governments asserted their sovereignty over places and people.

Signposts and uniforms reflected more profound differences among the German states. To some extent, the shared German context meant

[1] Frances Trollope, *Vienna and the Austrians; with some account of a journey through Swabia, Bavaria, the Tyrol and Salzbourg* (London, 1838), p. 42.
[2] Charles Boileau Elliott, *Letters from the North of Europe, or a journal of travels in Holland, Denmark, Norway, Sweden, Finland, Russia, Prussia and Saxony* (London, 1832), p. 445.
[3] Richard Bryan Smith, *Notes made during a tour in Denmark, Holstein, Mecklenburg-Schwerin, Pomerania, the Isle of Rügen, Prussia, Poland, Saxony, Brunswick, Hannover, the Hanseatic territories, Oldenburg, Friesland, Holland, Brabant, the Rhine country and France* (London, 1827), p. 203.

that they were subjected to similar political and socio-economic pressures. At the same time, each state remained a separate political unit with a distinctive path of political development, reflecting the interplay of indigenous economic, social, geographical and historical factors. The particular experiences of Hanoverians, Saxons and Württembergers were variations on a nationwide process of state-building and industrialisation. They testify to a regional diversity that is too easily masked by more general histories of the German nineteenth-century.

Superficially, the states of Hanover, Saxony and Württemberg had much in common. To contemporaries, however, they would have felt like very different places. Partly this reflected geographical realities. Hanover, Saxony and Württemberg were situated in North, Central and South-West Germany respectively (see Map 1). Their different locations were crucially important in shaping the relationship of Hanoverians, Saxons and Württembergers with their fellow Germans and indeed with the wider world. Hanover was the most important German state on the North Sea coast. Consequently, travellers en route from Hamburg to the rest of Germany inevitably passed through it, even though few found much reason to stay. By contrast, both Saxony and Württemberg were land-locked. Saxony lay at the very heart of Germany, sandwiched between Austria and Prussia and easily accessible from Berlin, Prague and Vienna. Württemberg, however, was definitely off the beaten track. As a result, it was the most insular and provincial of the three. Relatively few foreigners bothered to visit an obscure state lacking any cultural attractions of note and tucked away in a corner of South-West Germany between Baden, Bavaria and the small principality of Hohenzollern.

Yet despite Hanover's relative accessibility, visitors from Hamburg invariably remarked on the desolate and empty countryside, and on the appallingly bad roads. Travelling through Germany shortly after the defeat of Napoleon, one such visitor, Henry Stutzer, reported: 'The country soon became sandy, and the ground was . . . so thin it could hardly repay for the trouble of sowing . . . I never, in all my life . . . met with so few people on any road.'[4] Writing ten years later, William Wilson found the population scanty, the landscape gloomy, barren and tedious and the road incomparably awful.[5] Only once Wilson had passed the city of Hanover itself did he detect any improvement,

---

[4] Henry Lewis Stutzer, *Journal of a five weeks' tour through Hanover, Westphalia and the Netherlands in July and August, 1818* (London, 1819), pp. 17, 29.
[5] William Rae Wilson, *Travels in Norway, Sweden, Denmark, Hanover, Germany, Netherlands &c* (London, 1826), pp. 493–6.

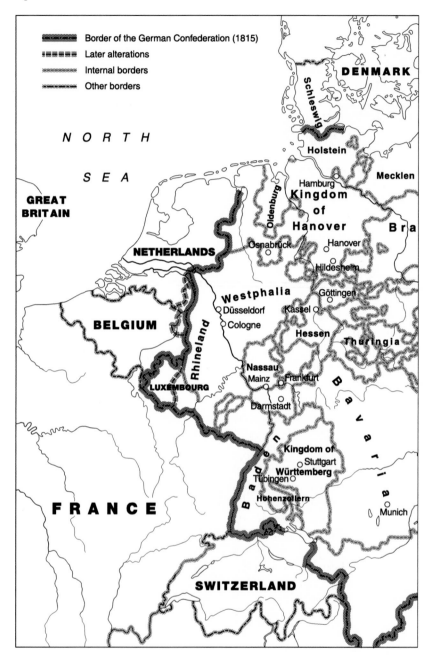

Map 1 The German Confederation 1815–66

Table 1.1. *Population density*[a]

State	Size (m^2)	Population Year: 1841	Inhabitants/m^2 1841	1870
Hanover	38,470.3	1,745,053	45	51
Saxony	14,972.2	1,716,300	115	168
Württemberg	19,508.3	1,653,000	85	93
German Confederation	522,467.2	31,514,117	60	75

Note:

[a] Wolfram Fischer, Jochen Krengel and Jutta Wietog (eds.), *Sozialgeschichtliches Arbeitsbuch*, Vol. 1, *Materialien zur Statistik des Deutschen Bundes 1815–1870* (Munich, 1982), pp. 40–1.

admitting the flocks in this part of the country to be numerous and the ground fertile.[6]

Even so, these accounts contrast strikingly with the experience of travellers in Saxony and Württemberg. Visitors to the picturesque 'Saxon Switzerland', like Richard Smith, found a countryside 'teeming with riches for the husbandmen, who, with all their household, were busily employed in securing the treasure'.[7] Some thirty years later, Walter White, an English schoolteacher on a walking holiday in the isolated Erzgebirge, listed the 'signs of numerous population: church spires and villages in the distance . . . and in little valleys . . . teeming with foliage, snug cottages thickly nestled; and as your eye wanders . . . it sees many wavy columns of smoke betraying the site of rural homes scattered beneath'.[8] Equally, the Frenchman Jacques Boucher de Perthes, visiting Württemberg at about the same time, described how 'To the left and right towns and villages follow one another, interrupted by plantations, streams and hills. An air of ease and gaiety prevails everywhere: it is a wonderful country!'[9]

These contrasting impressions reflected different demographic realities, as a comparison of rates of population density (Table 1.1) and population growth (Table 1.2) in each state demonstrates. The population explosion in the nineteenth century was perhaps the single most important element in Germany's transition from a traditional society to a

[6] Ibid, p. 499.   [7] Smith, *Notes made during a tour of Denmark*, p. 246.
[8] Walter White, *A July holiday in Saxony, Bohemia, and Silesia* (London, 1857), p. 44.
[9] Jacques Boucher de Perthes, *Voyage en Danemarck, en Suède, en Norvège, par la Belgique et la Hollande. Retour par les villes anséatiques, le Mecklembourg, la Saxe, la Bavière, le Wurtemberg et le Grand-duché de Bade, séjour à Bade en 1854* (Paris, 1858), p. 431.

Table 1.2. *Population growth*[a]

State	Year:	1816–36	1835–56	1856–70	Total % 1816–70
		Annual population growth in %			
Hanover		1.21	0.39	0.49	47.2
Saxony		1.56	1.18	1.44	110.4
Württemberg		0.61	0.25	0.59	28.8
German Confederation		1.16	0.79	0.88	64.8

Note:
[a] Figures from Fischer, Krengel and Wietog, *Sozialgeschichtliches Arbeitsbuch*, p. 42.

dynamic modern economy. Between 1816 and 1870 the population of Germany increased by some 65%, with a growth rate of between 60 and 80% in the most intensely affected areas.[10] Notwithstanding this general trend, rates of population density and population growth differed dramatically from state to state, as the experiences of Hanover, Saxony and Württemberg indicate. In 1841 all three states were similar in size, with populations of between 1.65 and 1.74 million. In Saxony, population growth was rapid and the pressures of population density were intense – far higher than the German average. No wonder, then, that both Smith and White found Saxony to be literally 'teeming' with life. In Hanover things were very different – hence the desolate emptiness of the Hanoverian countryside. The situation in Württemberg was more complex. Although levels of population density in Württemberg were higher than the German average, the rate of population growth here was even lower than in Hanover. All this meant that by the late nineteenth century Saxony was significantly more populous than either Hanover or Württemberg, with a population of 2.35 million inhabitants in 1865, as compared with 1.93 million and 1.75 million respectively.[11]

These demographic patterns reflected profound socio-economic differences. Broadly speaking, industrialisation was the dominant feature of the German economy at this time, bringing sustained economic growth, a large movement of labour away from agriculture towards urban industry, and a substantial increase in productivity and real incomes. In practice, this meant fewer peasants, larger towns, more

[10] Hans-Ulrich Wehler, *Deutsche Gesellschaftsgeschichte*, Vol. ii, *Von der Reformära bis zur industriellen und politischen 'Deutschen Doppelrevolution' 1815–1845/9* (Munich, 1987), p. 663.
[11] James J. Sheehan, *German History 1770–1866* (Oxford, 1989), p. 458.

artisans and more factory workers. Hubert Kiesewetter has found that levels of industrialisation in nineteenth-century Germany were related to a combination of both population density and population growth in a particular state or region.[12] According to this measure, industrialisation was far further advanced in Saxony than elsewhere in Germany. By contrast, the same criteria indicate that the Hanoverian economy was exceptionally backward at this time. The case of Württemberg is less clear cut. In fact, relatively high population density in Württemberg was not indicative of a high level of industrialisation, because the economy was not sufficiently dynamic to support high population growth. Consequently, historians have branded Württemberg a 'late-industialiser', whose economy did not take off until the second half of the nineteenth century.[13] Population density here was therefore very different in kind to the pressures experienced in Saxony, reflecting different degrees of urbanisation in the two states.

The two main towns in Saxony, Dresden and Leipzig, were both cities in the modern sense, with populations of between one and two hundred thousand. Yet each retained a distinctive identity. Despite its size, Dresden was in many ways a typical royal capital (*Residenzstadt*), which continued to be dominated by the monarch and his court. As late as the 1860s one French tourist, Arsène Legrelle, described how

twenty different signs recall at any moment the proximity of the palace . . . There are the officers who pass by, with their sabres tucked under their arms . . . Then the troupes of men in livery who come and go, invariably wearing . . . the royal crown, which image soon ends up incrusted in your retina, unless you take good care . . . It seems in truth that the whole town only lives off reproductions of the masterpieces in its museum and the beautiful vistas in the surrounding area.[14]

Other travellers agreed that Dresden was resting on its laurels. As the English tourist Charles Elliott noted regretfully, 'Dresden is not what Dresden was.'[15] Yet Elliott also pronounced it a 'handsomely built' city, and his contemporary Richard Smith described the newer suburbs as well-paved and spacious, with large and well-built stone houses that had 'a very substantial appearance'.[16] In this sense at least, Dresden

---

[12] Kiesewetter, *Industrialisierung und Landwirtschaft*, pp. 239–44.
[13] For instance, Klaus Megerle argues that industrialisation in Württemberg took off significantly later than in most of Germany. See Megerle, *Württemberg im Industrialisierungsprozeß Deutschlands. Ein Beitrag zur regionalen Differenzierung der Industrialisierung* (Stuttgart, 1982), p. 124.
[14] Arsène Legrelle, *A travers la Saxe. Souvenirs et études* (Paris, 1866), p. 330.
[15] Elliott, *Letters from the North of Europe*, p. 446.
[16] Smith, *Notes made during a tour of Denmark*, p. 205.

Table 1.3. *The five largest towns in Saxony and Württemberg*[a]

State	Town	Population	Date of figure
Saxony	Dresden	177,040	1871
	Leipzig	106,925	1871
	Chemnitz	68,229	1871
	Zwickau	27,322	1871
	Plauen	22,844	1870
Württemberg	Stuttgart	91,683	1871
	Ulm	26,290	1871
	Heilbronn	18,955	1871
	Esslingen	17,941	1871
	Reutlingen	14,237	1871

Note:
[a] Figures for Saxon towns from Erich Keyser (ed.), *Bibliographie zur Städtegeschichte Deutschlands* (Cologne/Vienna, 1969), pp. 309–18; figures for Württemberg towns from Langewiesche, *Liberalismus und Demokratie in Württemberg*, p. 45.

appeared to be a modern town. Nonetheless, visitors like Smith invariably remarked on the 'much greater appearance of life and bustle' in the thriving commercial city of Leipzig.[17] Leipzig combined 'very old and richly ornamented' houses with large modern buildings, 'many of which consist of five or six stories ... The ground floors are all fitted up as shops or stores, and let off at the great fairs held here.'[18] Leipzig was famous not for its paintings and palaces but rather for commerce and learning: for its annual trade fairs, the university and the book trade, which made it according to Legrelle 'the city of books *par excellence*'.[19] But elsewhere in Saxony, urbanisation brought industry not learning, factories not grand commercial houses. In this sense, Walter White's description of the road leading out of Zwickau 'between noisy factories, past vitriol works, smelting furnaces and thick with dust' was perhaps more typical of the country in general.[20]

In any event, the urban experience in Saxony was significantly more metropolitan and therefore qualitatively different from that of Württemberg. A comparison of the five largest towns in Saxony and Württemberg (Table 1.3) makes this point very clearly. In Württemberg, only the capital, Stuttgart, was remotely comparable in size with

[17] Ibid., p. 260.
[18] Elliott, *Letters from the North of Europe*, p. 464; Smith, *Notes made during a tour of Denmark*, p. 260.
[19] Legrelle, *A travers la Saxe*, p. 276.   [20] White, *A July holiday*, p. 41.

Dresden and Leipzig. Visiting in the 1830s, Frances Trollope commented presciently that 'the extraordinary activity perceptible in every part of the city in the construction of handsome edifices both public and private, shows that it is increasing in wealth and importance'.[21] Like Dresden, Stuttgart was a royal capital, and in 1854 the Frenchman Jacques Boucher de Perthes found it a pleasant little place, with its 'royal palace, court theatre, library, painting and natural history galleries'.[22] But Stuttgart was actually developing rather more dramatically than this account implies – indeed, it had a growth rate of 67% between 1855 and 1871, some 20% higher than that of the second fastest growing town in Württemberg.[23] This kind of urban growth was qualitatively new and clearly linked to social and economic change. By and large, however, population density in Württemberg was not caused by increased urbanisation as a facet of the modernisation process. High population density simply reflected the fact that there had always been a great many towns in Württemberg. Relatively speaking there were in fact more towns here than in any other major German state.[24] Mostly, however, these were traditional 'home-towns' dominated by guilds, shop-keepers and old-fashioned handicrafts, not cities in the modern sense at all. Indeed, the existence of occupational and residence restrictions – vigorously defended by their guilds and corporations – in these towns actively impeded the process of economic change. Certainly, old imperial cities like Reutlingen and Rottweil had little in common with metropolises like Stuttgart, Dresden and Leipzig, or with industrial towns like Zwickau and Chemnitz in Saxony. Fanny Trollope, for one, found little apart from the church to distinguish Reutlingen 'from any other large *Dorf*, [or] ordinary village'.[25] Moreover, she was positively astonished at the backwardness of Tübingen, the seat of Württemberg's ancient university, declaring: 'there is something almost inconceivable in the preservation of such buildings as constitute the chief part of some of the remote towns of Germany . . . One asks oneself, "Are they to last for ever thus?"'[26]

Yet even towns like Reutlingen and Tübingen would have seemed impressive in Hanover, where the urbanisation process was in its earliest

---

[21] Trollope, *Vienna and the Austrians*, p. 11.   [22] Boucher de Perthes, *Voyage en Danemarck*, p. 434.

[23] Langewiesche, *Liberalismus und Demokratie in Württemberg*, p. 44.

[24] In Württemberg there was on average one town per German square mile, compared with one town per 1.7 square miles in Saxony, 2.35 in Bavaria, 3.7 in Prussia and 3.9 in Hanover. Figures for 1821, from Mack Walker, *German home towns. Community, state and General Estate 1648–1871* (Ithaca, 1971), p. 32.   [25] Trollope, *Vienna and the Austrians*, p. 50.   [26] Ibid., p. 39.

stages. The city of Hanover was twice the size of any other Hanoverian town but was perhaps the size of the fourth largest town in Saxony. Nevertheless, visitors like Henry Stutzer pronounced the streets of the old town to be 'more spacious than one might expect, considering the age in which they were built, and still contain[ing] a great number of old houses with gable-tops . . . But there are likewise many handsome houses of modern architecture.'[27] The university town of Göttingen also received fairly favourable reports, but the same could not be said for smaller towns, like Munder, which Stutzer found 'barely superior to a large dirty village, and miserably paved.'[28] In any case, towns in Hanover were few and far between. Indeed, they were relatively scarcer than in any other German state – highlighting the essentially rural character of Hanover and its primarily agricultural economy.

Agriculture continued to occupy some 55% of the population in Hanover as late as 1861, in sharp contrast with the situation in Saxony, where the proportion of Saxons working in agriculture declined dramatically.[29] Indeed, by 1849 it was as low as 34%, by 1861 it had fallen to 29% and by 1871 it had plummeted still further to just 19%.[30] This was roughly 10% less than those working on the land in Württemberg. The relative decline of Saxon agriculture was directly correlated to the existence of well-developed proto-industrial activities in Saxony before 1815, and to the rapid pace of industrialisation in this state thereafter. Indeed, Kiesewetter has argued persuasively that Saxon agriculture became incapable of feeding the population, since in 1815 Saxony lost its most important agricultural lands to Prussia.[31] Saxony was therefore forced to industrialise quickly, financing the necessary agricultural imports through the export of manufactured goods. Consequently, manufacturing was unusually important in Saxony, where it occupied some 50% of the population by 1871.[32] Those working in Saxon manufacturing were both artisans and factory workers. In 1865 the proportion of factory workers in Saxony was twice as high as in any other

[27] Stutzer, *Journal of a five weeks' tour,* pp. 53–7.   [28] Ibid., p. 104.
[29] Figures from ibid., and from Wolfgang Köllmann (ed.), *Quellen zur Bevölkerungs-, Sozial- und Wirtschaftsstatistik Deutschlands 1815–1875,* Vol. III, *Norddeutsche Staaten,* pp. 191, 215.
[30] Figures from Köllmann (ed.), *Quellen zur Bevölkerungs-, Sozial- und Wirtschaftsstatistik,* Vol. IV, *Mitteldeutsche Staaten,* pp. 128, 150; and from Kiesewetter, *Industrialisierung und Landwirtschaft,* p. 253.
[31] This argument is made concisely in Hubert Kiesewetter, 'Bevölkerung, Erwerbstätige und Landwirtschaft im Königreich Sachsen 1815–1871' in Sidney Pollard (ed.), *Region und Industrialisierung. Studien zur Rolle der Region in der Wirtschaftsgeschichte der letzten zwei Jahrhunderte* (Göttingen, 1980), pp. 89–106.
[32] Figures from ibid.; Köllmann, *Quellen zur Bevölkerungs-, Sozial- und Wirtschaftsstatistik,* Vol. IV, pp. 128, 150; and Kiesewetter, *Industrialisierung und Landwirtschaft,* p. 253.

German state.[33] At the same time, the proportion of artisans was not significantly lower here than elsewhere in Germany, testifying to the continuation of traditional forms of manufacturing. Before 1848, however, the proportion of artisans in Saxony had actually been higher than elsewhere in Germany.[34] That this was no longer the case by 1865 indicates that the interim period saw a key transition from traditional to more modern manufacturing activity in Saxony.

Like Saxony, Württemberg had a relatively large manufacturing sector, which employed some 40% of the total labour force.[35] Here, however, manufacturing was traditional rather than industrial. The proportion of factory workers in Württemberg was significantly higher than in any other German state, apart from Saxony.[36] Nevertheless, although the proportion of workers in Saxony was double that in Württemberg, the proportion of factories in Saxony was half that in Württemberg.[37] Factories in Württemberg were far smaller and more closely resembled artisanal work-shops than in Saxony. The strength of traditional manufacturing in Württemberg is unsurprising given the number of home towns, which protected and fostered artisans through the guilds. The situation in both states contrasted sharply with that in Hanover, which had unusually low proportions of both artisans and factory workers in 1861.[38]

These occupational patterns had important implications for the social stability of the three states. Unrest in mid-nineteenth-century Germany has been related to the proletarianisation of artisans and handicraftsmen as a consequence of declining numbers of master artisans, relative to apprentices and journeymen.[39] This decline meant that increasing numbers of apprentices and journeymen failed to fulfil traditional expectations of making a respectable independent living in a trade or craft. Frustrated and disappointed, they attributed the uncertainties of their new position to the growth of factories and out-working, which had

[33] 96/1000 of the population, compared with 49/1000 in Württemberg, 37/1000 in Prussia, 25/1000 in Bavaria and 24/1000 in Hanover. Figures from Walker, *German home towns*, pp. 410–11.
[34] According to Bazillion, *Modernizing Germany*, p. 39.
[35] Figures from Kiesewetter, *Industrialisierung und Landwirtschaft*, p. 253.
[36] 49/1000 of the population. See n. 33 for full comparison.
[37] There were 11 factories per 1000 of the population in Württemberg, compared with 5/1000 of the population in Saxony. Figures from Walker, *German home towns*, pp. 410–1.
[38] The ratio of artisans to the general population in Hanover was 1:24.8, compared with 1:17 in Saxony, 1:16.1 in Prussia, 1:15.1 in Württemberg and 1:13.1 in Bavaria. There were only 24 factory workers per 1000 of the population in Hanover; for comparative figures see n.33. All figures from ibid.
[39] See for instance Wehler, *Von der Reformära bis zur industriellen und politischen "Deutschen Doppelrevolution" 1815–1845/9*, pp. 648–52.

Table 1.4. *Masters, apprentices, management and workers as a percentage of those engaged in trade and industry*[a]

State	Year	Masters	Apprentices/ journeymen	Management	Workers
Hanover	1831	64.7%	35.3%	0%	0%
	1861	44.7%	54.7%	0%	1%
Saxony	1849	42.2%	57.5%	0%	0.3%
	1861	28.4%	61.9%	1%	9.1%
Württemberg	1852	46.2%	53.8%	0%	0%
	1861	46.5%	53.4%	0.1%	0%

Note:
[a] Figures from Köllmann (ed.), *Quellen zur Bevölkerungs-, Sozial- und Wirtschaftsstatistik*, Vol. III, pp. 188, 213; Vol. IV, pp. 123, 146; Vol. V, pp. 563, 585.

undermined the guild system. The revolutions of 1848/9 allowed these disillusioned artisans to give full voice to their discontent. In the Prussian Rhineland, unruly mobs marched through the cities, stoning the residences of the rich and setting fire to the mills. In the Saxon town of Chemnitz, local weavers held a huge demonstration protesting at the introduction of weaving machinery and the construction of textile factories. Replicas of these local disturbances occurred throughout Germany. Meanwhile, at national level, the Congress of German Trades and Craftsmen in Frankfurt drafted 'a solemn protest against economic freedom . . . to which millions of unfortunates subscribe'.[40]

Unsurprisingly, perhaps, these social strains were particularly acute in Saxony, where the ratio of masters to apprentices and journeymen (Table 1.4) was lower than in either Hanover or Württemberg by 1849. Indeed, the proportion of masters in Saxony fell still further in the next ten years, from 42.2% in 1849 to 28.4% in 1861, when guild restrictions were finally removed. This decline of over 10% brought with it a corresponding increase in the number of factory workers, testifying to a particularly dramatic transformation of traditional working patterns in this rapidly industrialising state. In Württemberg the proportion of masters working in trade and industry barely altered during this period – a startling statistic, which highlights the fairly stagnant nature of the Württemberg

[40] Cited after Theodore S. Hamerow, *Restoration, revolution, reaction. Economics and politics in Germany 1815–1871* (Princeton, 1958), pp. 144–5.

economy before the removal of guild restrictions in 1861. By this bench-
mark, even Hanover appeared relatively dynamic. Here, the proportion
of masters fell from 65% to 45% between 1831 and 1861, whilst the proportion of apprentices and journeymen rose accordingly. Clearly, despite
the continued importance of agriculture in the Hanoverian economy,
other sectors were undergoing important changes. Even so, this only
brought the Hanoverian economy into line with that of other states, like
Württemberg, where the proportion of masters to apprentices and journeymen in 1861 was actually fairly similar. Hanoverian guilds were therefore unusual in successfully defending their privileges until annexation by
Prussia in 1866. Socially, the impact of economic changes in Hanover
had yet to become fully apparent.

   The impression that emerges both from travellers' accounts of life in
these three states and from more concrete social and economic data is of
three very different places and societies: rapidly industrialising Saxony,
teeming with people, towns and, increasingly, factories; over-crowded
and more backward Württemberg, with its quaint old towns; isolated,
empty and largely rural Hanover, which caused one English tourist to
remarked scathingly that it boasted 'few objects that are calculated to
arrest in a remarkable degree the attention of travellers; there being no
magnificent edifices, splendid demesnes, works of art, remarkable ruins
&c. or any of the splendid scenery which is to be met with in . . . other
countries'.[41] To some extent, these different presents also reflected different pasts.

By 1800 Hanover, Saxony and Württemberg were all well-established
states, each ruled by a distinguished dynasty: the Welfs, the Wettins and
the Württembergs. The Electorate of Hanover had emerged as a significant power in North-West Germany in the seventeenth century, although
the Welfs had long dominated the area known as Lower Saxony. After
1714 personal union with the British crown brought Hanover greater
influence within Germany, but also greater distractions, as the Welfs
themselves moved to London, taking their court and their cultural patronage with them.[42] Under these circumstances, it was hardly surprising
that visitors to Hanover in the early nineteenth century should have
found so little to admire there. The Electorate of Saxony, by contrast, had
been a major player in Germany since the Reformation. Saxon influence

---

[41] Wilson, *Travels in Norway*, p. 499.
[42] On the history of Hanover during this period, see Reinhard Oberschelp, *Politische Geschichte
Niedersachsens 1714–1803* (Hildesheim, 1983).

within Germany waned after Saxony lost her position at the head of Protestant Germany, when Augustus the Strong converted to Catholicism in 1697 in order to become King of Poland. Initially, the Polish crown more than compensated for this loss of influence. In the long run, however, a series of disastrous wars forced Saxon rulers to abandon territorial ambitions in Poland and led to a catastrophic decline within Germany itself.[43] Nevertheless – as many nineteenth-century visitors noted – Augustus the Strong's fabulous art collections and Baroque redevelopment of the capital, Dresden, proved a more enduring legacy. Compared with both Hanover and Saxony, the Duchy of Württemberg's development from unimportant dynastic unit to small but influential state had been slow and steady.[44] This long history was linked to a strong constitutional tradition, for the Württemberg Estates traced their rights back to 1516.

In their nineteenth-century incarnations, however, all three states were products of the Napoleonic era. Between 1803 and 1806 Napoleon and his victorious armies re-drew the map of Germany. These years saw the death throes of the Holy Roman Empire and the end of many of its more anachronistic principalities, as ecclesiastical princes, the imperial nobility and imperial cities lost their sovereign status when they were amalgamated into larger states.[45] Contemporaries called this process 'mediatisation'. Later, it would serve as a terrible warning for the smaller states that had survived Napoleon but continued to seem anomalous in the modern world. In the short term, however, the loss of sovereignty by smaller states often brought corresponding gains in land and status for their larger neighbours, as Margravates became Grand Duchies and Duchies became Kingdoms. Mediatisation was a boon for states like Württemberg, whose growth had been impeded by pockets of independent territory within its borders. In exchange for a timely alliance with Napoleon, Württemberg was made a Kingdom and swallowed up imperial cities like Esslingen and Reutlingen, ecclesiastical lands such as those

---

[43] The best general history of Saxony has recently been republished, reflecting renewed interest in Saxony following German reunification in 1989/90: Rudolf Kötschke and Hellmut Kretzschmar, *Sächsische Geschichte* (Augsburg, 1995, reprint). James Retallack, 'Society and politics in Saxony in the nineteenth and twentieth centuries. Reflections on recent research', *Archiv für Sozialgeschichte* 38 (1998), 396–457, provides an excellent review of the new wave of post-unification Saxon historiography.

[44] The history of Württemberg before 1815 is surprisingly well covered in English. See James Allen Vann, *The making of a state, Württemberg 1593–1793* (Ithaca, 1985) and Peter H. Wilson, *War, state and society in Württemberg, 1677–1793* (Cambridge, 1995).

[45] On the 'mediatised' nobility after 1815, see Heinz Gollwitzer, *Die Standesherren. Die politische und gesellschaftliche Stellung der Mediatisierten 1815–1918* (Göttingen, 1964, 2nd edn).

of the Grand Master of the Teutonic Order, and the myriad petty principalities of Upper Swabia. All in all, Württemberg gained some 120,000
new subjects and forty-one German square miles of territory during the
Napoleonic era. Saxony, too, initially did well out of the French wars.
Like Württemberg, Saxony became a Kingdom and briefly reacquired
much of Poland, in the shape of the Grand Duchy of Warsaw. By contrast, Hanover, as a British territory, was a victim of French success,
undergoing periods of Prussian, French and Westphalian rule.

Yet the defeat of Napoleon brought a swift reversal of fortune for
both Hanover and Saxony, whilst Württemberg successfully defended
its gains. German victories against Napoleon in 1813 prompted a
second wave of territorial and political reorganisation, enshrined in the
Treaty of Vienna of 1815. The Treaty of Vienna created a new political structure to replace the Holy Roman Empire, in the shape of the
German Confederation. This was a permanent and supposedly indissoluble alliance of thirty-nine states of varying size under the presidency of Austria, with a Confederal army and a Confederal Diet in
Frankfurt, at which each state was represented. Besides creating the
new German Confederation, the Treaty of Vienna also brought huge
gains for some states, particularly Prussia. During the wars of liberation, Prussia finally emerged victorious after its humiliating defeat by
Napoleon at Jena in 1806 and now expanded westwards into the
Rhineland and Westphalia. Hanover, too, was resurrected. Indeed,
Hanover became a Kingdom by virtue of its connection with Britain
and acquired large swathes of territory to go with its new status: the
former prince-bishoprics of Osnabrück and Hildesheim, the imperial
city of Goslar, Prussian East Friesland, the Emsland, Bentheim, Lingen
and the Lower Eichsfeld. To some extent, however, these gains were
undermined by Hanover's awkward geographical position in the new
Germany, sandwiched between the two halves of the Prussian state.
Inevitably, the Prussians saw Hanover as a thorn in their side and
Hanoverian foreign policy came to be dominated by the tense relationship with this over-weening neighbour. The humiliation of Saxony at
the hands of Prussia was more immediate than this. In 1815 Saxony
became the only state to suffer significantly as a result of its earlier alliance with Napoleon. States like Württemberg and Baden did not have
to pay the price of collaboration because they had been able to switch
allegiance from France to the Allies, but the immediate presence of
French armies on its territory prevented Saxony from changing sides
in time. As a consequence, Saxony lost over half its lands to Prussia.

Unsurprisingly, these losses rankled and Saxon identity in the early nineteenth century came to be partly defined in conscious opposition to this predatory neighbour. Both Hanover and Württemberg therefore emerged as winners from the Napoleonic era; Saxony as a loser. This was a crucial difference in terms of subsequent state-building and the development of particular identities. The governments of Hanover and Württemberg needed to consolidate their gains and to integrate newly acquired territory; Saxony needed to find a new role in Germany and to come to terms with defeat.

To some extent, the years after 1815 in Germany saw a reversal of many of the changes wrought by Napoleon. Resurrected states like Hanover and Hesse-Kassel set about restoring their traditional social and political structures. Meanwhile, the German great powers, Prussia and Austria, clamped down on the nationalist enthusiasm that they had so readily exploited during the wars of liberation. The new climate of repression was epitomised by the Karlsbad Decrees, a series of measures targeting universities and the press, which were endorsed by all German states in 1819 at the behest of the Austrian chancellor, Metternich. Yet the years after 1815 were also years of political and administrative change. Consequently, recent historians have questioned the traditional distinction between the Napoleonic era, as a time of change and reform in Germany, and the supposedly stagnant 'Restoration era' that followed.[46] Certainly, administrative and constitutional reforms in Hanover, Saxony and Württemberg designed to consolidate state authority through a process of centralisation and standardisation stretched well into the 1820s.

Of the three, Württemberg was the most successful in instigating reforms that were sufficiently radical and wide-ranging to stand the test of time. To some extent the success of these measures reflected the lack of well-established noble interests in Württemberg. Before 1806 powerful nobles in that part of South-West Germany had enjoyed sovereign status; after 1806 they suddenly found themselves outsiders and subordinates in the enlarged neighbouring state. The most important of the Württemberg reforms was without doubt the introduction of a 'modern' constitution in 1819. This was similar to those introduced in neighbouring Baden and Bavaria, but infinitely more progressive than the limited constitutional change experienced in Hanover and Saxony before

---

[46] See the excellent collection of essays based on a recent conference: Hans Peter Ullmann and Clemens Zimmermann (eds.), *Restaurationssystem und Reformpolitik. Süddeutschland und Preußen im Vergleich* (Munich, 1996), which compares South Germany and Prussia.

1830.[47] Besides the constitution, these years also saw the reorganisation and decentralisation of local government and the creation of a new Catholic bishopric whose borders were coterminous with those of the state. This combination of constitutional and administrative change meant that the institutions of the new Kingdom of Württemberg were associated with progressive change from the outset. Moreover, the Württemberg constitution was deliberately introduced a day before the promulgation of the Karlsbad Decrees and significantly reduced their impact in this state, because it explicitly asserted its primacy over Confederal legislation. This had important implications for the relationship between Württemberg and the German Confederation and created a strong association between constitutionalism and independent sovereignty in Württemberg. An unusual pattern developed, whereby the sovereignty of a progressive state protected its people from a more reactionary German order. Even after the revolutions of 1830 the constitution of 1819 continued to act as a buffer against reactionary Confederal legislation.

In the aftermath of the French occupation, the Hanoverian government also attempted to create a more cohesive unitary state. Here, however, the resistance of entrenched noble interests undermined these efforts – a situation strikingly similar to that in neighbouring Prussia.[48] Historically, the nobility had always been strong in Hanover, partly as a consequence of over a century of rule by monarchs based in London, who had placed government in the hands of the nobility and left them to get on with it. The nobility were therefore able to prevent the government from abolishing the seven Provincial Estates in Hanover, despite the creation of a new representative body, the General Estates, which could speak for the whole country. The Provincial Estates ensured the persistence of centrifugal regional forces within Hanover and provided a base from which they could successfully oppose the changes introduced during the revolutions of 1830 and 1848/9. These limitations meant that the administrative reforms introduced in Hanover after 1815 were probably more significant than the constitutional change that took place at this time. Between 1816 and 1825 the Hanoverian government created

---

[47] For more detail on constitutional change at this time, see Franz Mögle-Hofacker, *Zur Entwicklung des Parlamentarismus in Württemberg. Der 'Parlamentarismus. Der Krone' unter König Wilhelm I.* (Stuttgart, 1981), pp. 10–24; also Karl Johannes Grauer, *Wilhelm I., König von Württemberg. Ein Bild seines Lebens und seiner Zeit* (Stuttgart, 1960), pp. 124–74, 199–211, 229–38. For a general account of parliamentary politics under the 1819 constitution see Hardtwig Brandt, *Parlamentarismus in Württemberg 1819–1870. Anatomie eines deutschen Landtags* (Düsseldorf, 1987).

[48] For further details and, indeed, a general history of nineteenth-century Hanover see Reinhard Oberschelp, *Politische Geschichte Niedersachsens 1803–1866* (Hildesheim, 1988), pp. 69–91.

specialist departments at ministerial level, rationalised local government through the creation of standardised administrative units (the *Amt* and the *Landdrostei*) and dismantled internal tariffs.

Attempts to create an integrated unitary state were least successful in Saxony, which was easily the most regressive of the three states in the 1820s. This reflected Saxony's different experience during the aftermath of the Napoleonic era. Substantially weakened by its losses in 1815, the Saxon government was quite simply unable to enforce change against the wishes of entrenched local and noble interests. Thus the Saxon government failed to persuade the Estates of Upper Lausatia, a relatively recent addition to Saxony, to amalgamate with the rest of Saxony.[49] Equally, it proved impossible to rationalise central government in Saxony because the Saxon Estates rejected bureaucratic initiatives to modernise the Privy Council in the years 1816–18. Nevertheless, it is worth noting the success of official propaganda in strengthening support for the Saxon state after 1815.[50]

State-building in Hanover and Württemberg was more far-reaching than in Saxony because of the immediate need to integrate new territory with the traditional heartlands. Yet the integrational imperative also rendered state-building in these states more problematic. Administrative and constitutional change was often counter-productive and frequently encountered resistance from those attached to the old ways. Resistance was aggravated where religious differences or economic interests further differentiated the new lands from the rest of the state. This fostered the growth of regional political traditions and identities, often for the first time. For instance, the mediatised lands in Upper Swabia acquired a common regional identity partly as a result of their incorporation into Württemberg. Indeed, new territories frequently became centres of opposition to the regime. It was no coincidence that many leaders of the Hanoverian opposition came from Osnabrück – men such as Johann Carl Bertram Stüve, Johannes Miquel and, to a lesser extent, Ludwig Windthorst. Similarly, East Friesland never came to terms with Hanoverian rule, largely because the province faced serious economic decline once cut off from its traditional hinterland after 1815.[51]

It is worth emphasising the role religion played in obstructing the integration process in both Hanover and Württemberg. Both states had traditionally been Protestant powers and both acquired substantial

---

[49] For details of reformist efforts during this period see Schmidt, *Reformbestrebungen in Sachsen*.

[50] See Flockerzie, 'State-building and nation-building in the Third Germany: Saxony'.

[51] On particularism in East Friesland under Hanoverian rule, see Helene Borkenhagen, *Ostfriesland unter der hannoverschen Herrschaft, 1815–1866* (Aurich, 1924).

Catholic minorities. In Hanover they were concentrated in Hildesheim and Osnabrück; in Württemberg they were concentrated in Upper Swabia, formerly a stronghold of the imperial nobility and consequently particularly resistant to Württemberg rule. Integrating these minorities into a traditionally Protestant state provoked new kinds of religious and political tension, but it was also vitally important. Indeed, the new religious composition of these states was a major catalyst for state-building measures. Hitherto, Protestantism had been a central element of state identity in both Hanover and Württemberg. Now the governments of these states needed to find a new, secular source of identity which transcended the religious divide. Saxony too had a small Catholic minority, in the Sorb population of Upper Lausatia. Here, however, ethnic and linguistic tensions reinforced the religious divide. More generally, religion was politically contentious in Saxony because, since the conversion of Augustus the Strong in 1697, a Catholic dynasty had ruled this archetypally Protestant state. Indeed, this anomaly acted as a trigger for the outbreak of revolution in Leipzig in 1830, during celebrations held to mark the three hundredth anniversary of the Augsburg Confession.

Of course, the revolutions which broke out in much of Germany in 1830 were about much more than religion. Indeed, to a very great extent these revolutions were about political participation, although they also reflected the need for social and economic change. There were a few isolated outbursts of nationalist feeling. By and large, however, revolutionary activity in 1830 targeted the individual German states. Tellingly, the revolutions of 1830 left Württemberg, with its fairly progressive constitution, unscathed, but prompted the introduction of similar constitutions in both Saxony (1831) and Hanover (1833). In both cases, liberal constitutional change was accompanied by other reforms, notably the emancipation of the peasantry and the empowerment of local communities through self-government.[52] In both cases, the towns played a central role in pressing for change. For instance, unrest in Leipzig

[52] Reforms in Hanover were: the constitution of 1833; division of the Privy Council into five specialist sections with a Cabinet Council in 1831; amalgamation of crown and state income in 1834; a series of new municipal constitutions for towns according to guidelines laid down in the constitution; emancipation of the peasantry. On these reforms in Hanover see Oberschelp, *Politische Geschichte Niedersachsens 1803–1866*, pp. 119–21, 125–31. Reforms in Saxony were: the constitution of 1831; the reorganisation of urban government in 1832 and of rural government in 1838; emancipation of the peasantry and agrarian reforms; creation of specialist ministries and a State Council in 1831; various financial and tax reforms; educational legislation in 1835, which rendered local communities responsible for schools; bourgeois access to the officer corps. For further details of these reforms in Saxony, see Gerhard Schmidt, *Die Staatsreform in Sachsen in der ersten Hälfte des 19. Jahrhunderts, eine Parallele zu den Steinischen Reformen in Preußen* (Weimar, 1966).

reflected anger at the lack of popular representation on the town council, despite the rising level of municipal debt and a municipal tax burden which was commonly perceived as unfair.[53] Subsequent reforms in Hanover and Saxony in the 1830s reflected these pressures, extending and reinforcing urban privilege through measures that standardised municipal self-government and granted more representation to the towns at state level.

Yet there were two important differences between the changes introduced in Hanover and in Saxony. First, discontent in Saxony before 1830 related to the economic difficulties created by territorial losses as well as to the constitutional deficit. Territorial losses had crippled the Saxon economy because protectionist Prussian tariffs cut off important trade routes and left industrial areas without easy access to markets or food. So one consequence of the revolution was that Saxony joined the Prussian-led *Zollverein*, of which Württemberg was already a member – a move which dynamised the Saxon economy. Hanover did not join the *Zollverein* until 1854. Secondly, the lack of change in Saxony before 1830 ensured that institutions reformed after this date were more closely associated with the constitution than was the case in Hanover. Of course, there was also resistance to change in Saxony and reactionary elements remained powerful in the new Saxon Parliament. Crucially, however, Saxon administrative reforms were clearly linked to the new identity of the state as a constitutional monarchy, as was the case in Württemberg. This meant that in the 1850s and 1860s the governments of both states were able to claim long-standing traditions of constitutional statehood and to contrast these traditions with the more reactionary histories of Prussia and Austria.

The Hanoverian government was unable to appeal to such a tradition because the liberal constitution of 1833 proved short-lived. Alongside other changes introduced after the revolution, the 1833 constitution had significantly reduced the power of the monarchy. In 1837 the accession of a woman, Victoria, to the British throne brought an end to personal union. Ernst August, the fourth son of George III, became King of Hanover. He was an arch-conservative with strong military inclinations and a positively diabolical reputation. On his arrival in Hanover Ernst August immediately refused to recognise the 1833 constitution, then revoked it, alienating many of the government's natural supporters in

---

[53] See Robert Beachy, 'Local protest and territorial reform: public debt and constitutionalism in early-nineteenth-century Saxony', *German History* 17:4 (1999), 471–88.

the towns. Indeed, opposition to Ernst August's action was primarily rooted in the defence of urban privilege by urban corporations, which stood to lose most with a reversal of the 1830–3 reforms.[54] The Hanoverian coup of 1837 provoked the famous protest of seven Professors at Göttingen University and became a *cause célèbre* throughout Germany, prompting numerous petitions to the Confederal Diet in Frankfurt. But the Diet failed to uphold the 1833 constitution. In Hanover, the reputation of the German Confederation never recovered from this betrayal. Thenceforth it was regarded as a partisan institution, concerned not with justice but with the preservation of traditional authority. A new Hanoverian constitution was finally agreed in 1840, which significantly increased the power of the monarch at the expense of the General Estates. Constitutional monarchy in Hanover was therefore very different in character from its Saxon and Württemberg counterparts. Nevertheless, the composition of the General Estates remained unchanged after 1833 and other reforms of the 1830s were not reversed, since they did not undermine the power of the crown. Indeed, in the years after 1840 the government adopted a conscious policy of moderation and modernisation, building railways and reforming land-ownership in an attempt to conciliate urban opposition. The potential interface between the conservatism of Ernst August and the entrenched interests in the 'liberal' towns was clearly demonstrated in the new commercial regulations issued in 1847, which pointedly did not abolish guilds.

By 1840 Hanover, Saxony and Württemberg had all acquired constitutions. This was considerably in advance of either Prussia or Austria, even if the Hanoverian constitution of 1840 left much to be desired. In fact, the constitutions of 1819, 1831 and 1840 remained in force in all three states until 1866, except during the revolutionary years 1848–50 in Württemberg and Saxony, and for the longer period 1848–55 in Hanover. However unpopular, these constitutions therefore formed the political framework in which government and opposition operated for most of the time. All three constitutions attempted to establish a balance between the monarch on the one hand and the parliament or general estates on the other. In all three states, these representative bodies consisted of two houses, and delegates in the lower house were elected on the basis of an indirect franchise. The composition of the Saxon

---

[54] This argument is advanced by Karlheinz Kolb and Jürgen Teiwes, *Beiträge zur politischen Sozial- und Rechtsgeschichte der Hannoverschen Ständeversammlung von 1814–1833 und 1838–1849* (Hildesheim, 1977), pp. 160–7.

Parliament was the most innovative, since representatives of the Saxon towns sat alongside noble landowners in the Lower House, and representatives of trade and industry sat alongside representatives of all three estates in the Upper House. Nevertheless, none of these constitutions could really be called modern. All three explicitly endorsed the monarchic principle – in other words, the idea that the monarch was the source of all legitimate power in the state and that, as a gift from the monarch to his people, the constitution acted as a voluntarily imposed means of limiting this power. The extent to which the constitution actually limited monarchic authority nevertheless varied from state to state. Unsurprisingly perhaps, monarchic authority was greatest in Hanover and most circumscribed in Württemberg, whilst the situation in Saxony lay somewhere between the two.

All three constitutions were temporarily overturned by the revolutions of 1848/9. To some extent this simply reflected a wider international phenomenon. Revolution swept across Europe from Sicily to Hungary in the early months of 1848. Indeed, to observers there appeared to be something of a domino effect, as regime after regime fell in the face of the revolutionary onslaught. Fundamentally, however, the simultaneous outbreak of revolution in some forty different European states points to a major structural crisis on the continent, as a result of the painful transition to the modern world.[55] This crisis was prompted by socio-economic upheaval and by the collapse of traditional forms of political legitimacy.

There were, in fact, three distinct strands to the revolution in Germany. On one level, the German revolutions revealed widespread discontent in both towns and the countryside as a result of demographic growth, industrialisation and the emancipation of the peasantry. On another level, the German revolutions were about domestic politics. They expressed dissatisfaction with existing political regimes and the desire of many for constitutional reform and basic liberal freedoms. On yet another level, the revolutions of 1848 were about nationhood and the need for new political institutions, which would guarantee national unity and freedom from repression through a nationally elected parliament on the liberal model. Broadly speaking, these different concerns corresponded to three different arenas of revolutionary activity in Germany: locality, state and nation. At a local level, peasant

---

[55] See for instance Gareth Stedman Jones, 'The mid-century crisis and the 1848 revolutions', *Theory and Society* 12 (1983), 505–20.

unrest in the countryside, riots and machine-breaking in the towns gave vent to the anger and frustrations of urban and rural poor. At state level, liberal opposition leaders suddenly found themselves in government and set about implementing long-awaited political reforms: constitutions were either revised, as in Hanover, or set aside, as in Saxony and Württemberg, where new state assemblies were elected by a wider franchise to draw up new constitutions. Meanwhile, at a national level, the 1848 revolutions were arguably the first concrete political expression of German nationalist aspirations. Liberals from different states came together at a so-called Pre-Parliament in Frankfurt, where they did the necessary groundwork in order to dissolve the German Confederation and its Diet and to replace them with a firmer and more liberal political structure. Nationwide elections followed. The new National Assembly based in Frankfurt then set about drawing up a basic Bill of Rights and a liberal constitution for the whole of Germany. In many ways, developments at these different levels followed distinctive if inter-related trajectories, but the boundaries between the three arenas of revolutionary activity were also fluid. Peasant unrest remained fairly localised, but artisans from different parts of Germany came together at the Congress of German Trades and Craftsmen held in Frankfurt in the summer of 1848, and 15,000 artisans joined societies that later affiliated to a nationwide Union of Workers' Associations. These organisations gave the artisans a voice in national debates. State politics also shaped 'national' developments in Frankfurt. Thus the victory of the reaction in the Habsburg Empire in the autumn of 1848 meant that the Imperial Constitution drafted by the Frankfurt parliament excluded Austria, appointing Friedrich Wilhelm IV of Prussia hereditary ruler of the new *kleindeutsch* Germany by default. Equally, Friedrich Wilhelm IV's successful reassertion of his authority in Berlin gave him the confidence to reject the crown offered him and, subsequently, to propose a less liberal *kleindeutsch* solution to the German question, in the shape of the Erfurt Union. Conversely, the national question was often the most divisive issue for governments and opposition in the German states.

In Hanover, Saxony and Württemberg the challenge posed by the revolutions of 1848/9 inevitably reflected different social, economic and political contexts. Surprisingly given Hanover's experience of constitutional conflict, the revolution here was the quietest in Germany, probably as a result of relatively low levels of social tension. Hanoverian radicals made a poor showing and failed to make their mark either inside or outside parliament. An assembly of Co-Deputies, established by

Hanoverian democrats as a kind of anti-parliament in 1848, fizzled out after only a few months. Subsequently, Lang, leader of the left-wing opposition in the Hanoverian parliament, rejected the opportunity of forming a government in 1849.[56] Yet economic and political backwardness did not prevent either urban-middle-class political dissatisfaction or socially motivated unrest among the urban and rural lower classes from playing their part in the Hanoverian revolution. In practice, rural unrest in Hanover was not necessarily directed against the state, since malcontents often appealed to government authorities to correct local injustices. The towns asserted their interests more effectively than this: rural protest achieved ad-hoc concessions, but comprehensive liberal reforms met most urban demands. These reforms marked a decisive shift of influence from the nobility to the towns, similar to that of 1830–3. The dominance of the former opposition leader and Mayor of Osnabrück, Johann Carl Bertram Stüve, in the March ministry symbolised this shift. Stüve's government introduced a free press, freedom of association, freedom of conscience and an independent judiciary. It emancipated the Jews, abolished noble privilege, made ministers responsible to the new Hanoverian parliament and granted this body far greater legislative and financial influence. But Stüve was basically a conservative home townsman and certainly no revolutionary. He himself remarked, 'it is an extraordinary thing, that I, a conservative to the core . . . should . . . have reached the top at a time of global democratic upheaval'.[57] Tellingly, therefore, although Stüve's government abolished the distinction between Upper and Lower Houses in the Hanoverian Estates, it did not touch the corporate representation of the towns, which was based on a fairly narrow urban electorate. In the event, Stüve's essential traditionalism enabled him to build a good working relationship with Ernst August – somewhat to the astonishment of both parties. Ernst August reputedly declared Stüve to be 'a famous fellow' and Stüve in turn was said to have remarked 'I expected to find a self-willed tyrant and found instead a kindly and understanding old gentleman'.[58]

Unlike Hanover, both Saxony and Württemberg experienced genuine revolutionary upheaval. In May 1849 an uprising in Dresden caused

---

[56] See Heribert Golka and Armin Reese, 'Soziale Strömungen der Märzrevolution von 1848 in der Landdrostei Hannover', *Niedersächsisches Jahrbuch für Landesgeschichte* 45 (1973), 275–301.

[57] Stüve, to Frommann, 30 September and 5 October 1849. Walter Vogel (ed.), *Briefe Johann Carl Bertram Stüves, 1848–1872*, 2 vols. (Göttingen, 1960), Vol. 2, p. 672.

[58] Friedrich Ferdinand, Graf von Beust, *Aus drei Viertel-Jahrhunderten, Erinnerungen und Aufzeichnungen*, 2 vols. (Stuttgart, 1887), Vol. 1, p. 92.

King Friedrich August II to flee the city. Safely ensconced in the fortress of Königstein, he called in Prussian troops to restore order. Weeks later the Württemberg government resorted to force when the extremist rump of the Frankfurt parliament moved to Stuttgart, where it attracted wide support. This radicalisation reflected the deeper-rooted social tensions in Saxony and Württemberg, as well as a higher level of politicisation, which was both organisational and ideological. At first, in both Saxony and Württemberg the opposition formed a state-wide network of local associations, linked to a central committee, in order to fight national and state elections. Then ideological divisions between the left and right (or democrats and liberals) set in. In April 1848, a month after the foundation of the democratic Fatherland Association in Saxony, conservative liberals formed a rival German Association. In June 1848 the Württemberg democrats seceded from the liberal movement to create a democratic central committee. Violent mutual recrimination and animosity on both sides hardened these divisions, as both 'parties' competed for votes and seats. The existence of party organisations during the revolution was the first key step towards developing a genuine parliamentary democracy in Saxony and Württemberg, even though these organisations did not survive into the 'reaction'.

The German question also proved more explosive in Saxony and Württemberg than it did in Hanover. Once again, this reflected the lack of radical alternatives in Hanover, and Stüve's underlying conservatism. For most of the revolution he and Ernst August saw eye to eye over the need to defend Hanoverian sovereignty.[59] Disagreements between monarch and minister over the national reform only emerged later, once Hanover had joined the *Dreikönigsbund*, an alliance with Saxony and Prussia formed in June 1849. Stüve's willingness to go along with Prussia at this point testified to his greater openness to state-led initiatives for reform of the German Confederation. For Ernst August it was, quite simply, a step too far and contributed to his growing inability to work with Stüve. By and large, however, national issues did not determine the outcome of power struggles between Ernst August and his ministers, or between the government and the Hanoverian parliament. This contrasted starkly with the situation in Saxony and Württemberg, where disagreements over the German question persistently caused the fall of ministries and the dissolution of elected assemblies. These disagreements were so important because they reflected equally important differences

---

[59] See Fritz Winzer, *Hannover und die deutsche Frage 1848/9* (Berlin, 1937), passim.

between government and opposition over domestic policy. The opposition defended the bill of rights and the Imperial Constitution drafted by the National Assembly in Frankfurt because they seemed to guarantee domestic freedoms won in 1848, and provided a rare source of unity. Conversely, Beust, the Saxon Foreign Minister, described the restoration of Saxony's pre-revolutionary constitution in 1850 as 'more than the response of an autonomous *Mittelstaat* to threats to its independent sovereignty, also the counter-attack of established authority within the state against new political forces. Domestic and foreign policy interlocked'.[60] Ironically, however, governments in Saxony and Württemberg were actually more open to the prospect of change at a national level than was the case in Hanover. As late as spring 1851 Wilhelm of Württemberg publicly acknowledged the need for a radical and democratic reform of the German Confederation. Equally, Helmut Rumpler's detailed study of Saxon foreign policy during the revolution has shown Beust to be surprisingly open-minded about the German question.[61] Traditionally, historians have dismissed Beust as a petty particularist. Rumpler argues, however, that Beust only adopted this stance after Prussian particularism prevented the *Dreikönigsbund* from providing a solution to the national question that would have been acceptable to the *Mittelstaaten*. This contrast between Hanover's resolute defence of state sovereignty and the greater flexibility of Saxony and Württemberg in handling the German question persisted during the 1850s and 1860s.

Ostensibly, the revolutionary gains of 1848/9 were short-lived. In early 1851 a conference of all the German states held in Dresden failed to reach any kind of agreement about the future state of Germany. Far from reforming the German Confederation, the delegates at Dresden eventually reinstated it as the least offensive solution to the German question. The restoration of the German Confederation brought with it a return to the reactionary priorities of the Metternichian era at national level. The Confederal Diet established a constitutional watch-dog, nicknamed the 'Reactionary Committee', designed to oversee developments within the different states and to ensure that revolutionary reforms left little trace. Meanwhile, the Diet also introduced Confederal legislation

---

[60] Cited after Heinz Georg Holldack, *Untersuchungen zur Geschichte der Reaktion in Sachsen, 1849–1855* (Berlin, 1931), p. 69.

[61] Helmut Rumpler, *Die deutsche Politik des Freiherrn von Beust 1848 bis 1850. Zur Problematik Mittelstaatlicher Reformpolitik im Zeitalter der Paulskirche* (Vienna, 1972). For the traditional interpretation, see Holldack, *Geschichte der Reaktion in Sachsen*, for instance his dismissal of Beust's negative foreign policy goals, p. 24.

that inhibited freedom of assembly, regulated the German press and limited freedom of expression. Tellingly, a forum established to coordinate political policing in the larger German states, the German States' Police Association, became the first national institution to facilitate non-diplomatic contact between different German governments.

These reactionary developments had their counterpart at state level. Just as the German Confederation was reinstated in 1851, so governments in Hanover, Saxony and Württemberg arbitrarily restored pre-revolutionary constitutions in these states. Once again the Hanoverian experience was distinctive. In Saxony and Württemberg this step coincided with the victory of the 'reaction' throughout Germany in 1850. But Ernst August missed the opportunity and his son, Georg V, did not take this step until 1855. Since the coup in Hanover was belated, it appeared isolated and created more fuss. Not that the coups in Saxony and Württemberg had passed unnoticed. Both Leipzig University and, more importantly, the standing committee of the Württemberg parliament questioned the legality of government actions. In this sense, the response in these states was not dissimilar to that in Hanover, where a regional court at Aurich in East Friesland declared the coup of 1855 invalid. Nevertheless, resistance to the old constitution lasted considerably longer in Hanover, in part because it was significantly less liberal than the pre-revolutionary constitutions reimposed elsewhere. Apart from timing, however, there was a further crucial difference between the coups of 1850 in Saxony and Württemberg and the Hanoverian coup of 1855: the former were autonomously implemented; the latter was instigated by the Reactionary Committee of the German Confederation at Georg V's behest. Confederal intervention also distinguished the Hanoverian coup of 1855 from its predecessor in 1837. Indeed, the appeal to the German Confederation in 1855 sat awkwardly with the government's rigid defence of Hanoverian sovereignty throughout this period. This second coup was a decisive turning-point in Hanoverian politics. For Hanoverian liberals, it underlined the impressions of 1837 and permanently alienated them from the status quo. The combination of bad timing and the unique experience of 1837 ensured that this alienation was more deep-rooted than in either Saxony or Württemberg.

In all three states, these constitutional changes foreshadowed further reactionary measures. Besides issuing new restrictions on civil and political freedoms, governments instituted purges of bureaucrats and teachers, revised the oaths of loyalty customarily taken by all state officials and attempted to step up police surveillance of political dissidents. The nature and impact of these measures inevitably varied from state to state. Historians have usually viewed both Saxony and Hanover as hard-line reactionary states, and Württemberg as more liberal. To some extent this view is borne out by what we know of the persecution of dissidents in these states. The Saxon chief of police certainly reported more frequently to the Police Association on the behaviour of dissidents than did the representatives of any state apart from Prussia. Conversely, Württemberg had recourse to the Police Association less regularly than any state except for Baden.[62] At the same time, it is important not to over-estimate the impact of these reactionary measures, since few were really successful. Liberals complained bitterly about both press control and political policing, but their complaints were probably exaggerated. Even in reactionary Hanover, only ten newspapers received official warnings between 1855 and 1863. Equally, the number of policemen in these states was tiny. In Saxony, 173 policemen were responsible for a population of over two million.[63] In the equivalent sized states of Hanover and Württemberg there were 415 and 431 respectively. Of course, the army also played a vital role in policing. Nevertheless, it remains doubtful whether official lists of political dissidents, such as Beust's infamous Black Book in Saxony, were worth much more than the paper on which they were written. However repressive the intentions of 'reactionary' regimes in Hanover, Saxony and Württemberg, enforcement remained problematic.

Under these circumstances, it comes as no surprise that the governments of these states also made positive efforts to attract support. To some extent this entailed wooing that most traditional of pro-government constituencies: the nobility. In all three states, the collapse of the revolution and the renewal of political repression provided opportunities for the nobility to reassert their traditional prominence – with varying success. Legal reforms in Saxony in the 1850s gave the local nobility a new role as Justices of the Peace, which enabled them to retain their traditional responsibility for law enforcement despite the abolition of feudal justice. At the same time, the failure to differentiate between justice and administration at the lowest levels of government bitterly disappointed Saxon liberals. Meanwhile, in 1851 the nobility in both Hanover and Württemberg appealed to the Confederal Diet against the abolition of noble privileges in these states. In Hanover this protest was successful.

---

[62] Wolfram Siemann, *Gesellschaft im Aufbruch*, p. 48.
[63] Holldack, *Geschichte der Reaktion in Sachsen*, p. 130.

Initially, it prompted a constitutional conflict because the rights of the nobility were tied up with those of the Provincial Estates. On his accession to the throne in 1851, King Georg V threw in his lot with the nobility and appointed a series of progressively more reactionary ministries, which refused to compromise with the Hanoverian parliament, and in 1855 finally appealed to the German Confederation to revoke the 1848 constitution. Ultimately, however, the conflict between the interventionism of central government and the provincial interests of the nobility meant this alliance of crown and nobility was too fragile to last. By contrast, the attempt of the Württemberg nobility to preserve their rights failed utterly. When the Württemberg government proposed indemnifying the nobility for their losses to the tune of five million *Gulden*, the parliament united in outrage. The government eventually abandoned the plan in 1861. The contrasting fates of these initiatives in Hanover and Württemberg highlight the different internal dynamics in the two states, as well the greater success of earlier state-building initiatives in Württemberg.

More importantly, however, the 1850s marked the beginning of a second wave of state-building in the larger German states, as governments attempted to formulate a meaningful response to the challenges posed by the 1848/9 revolution. As we shall see, governments in Hanover, Saxony and Württemberg attempted to strengthen support for their 'reactionary' regimes through propaganda and cultural policy, as well as through modernising legislation, like economic liberalisation, railway construction, primary school reforms and the founding of state museums. Moreover, governments in Hanover and Württemberg actively attempted to strengthen the allegiance of the Catholic minorities in these states by redressing long-standing grievances. Thus Georg V of Hanover reinstated the historic Bishopric of Osnabrück in 1856, and the Württemberg government agreed a concordat with the papacy, although parliamentary opposition prevented the government from introducing it.[64] In all three states, propaganda and other kinds of cultural policy aimed to foster a popular awareness of the state as a community. Meanwhile, modernising social and economic policies were intended to demonstrate the continued relevance of conservative regimes in the modern world, and to foster state patriotism by enabling German governments to take the credit for their role in promoting social, cultural

---

[64] For a discussion of conciliatory policy towards the Catholics see Hans-Georg Aschoff, *Das Verhältnis von Staat und katholischer Kirche im Königreich Hannover (1813–1866)* (Hildesheim, 1976).

and economic change. This official concern with placating public opinion acknowledged a fundamental shift in patterns of political activity and governance. Historians have long recognised the extent to which the revolution diverted the attention of German liberals towards social and economic rather than political issues during the 1850s, when they supposedly abandoned naïve idealism in favour of a more pragmatic and materialistic approach to politics.[65] That conservative governments underwent a similar process of re-evaluation and political realignment has, however, been largely ignored. Yet major economic developments, such as the abolition of guilds in Saxony and Württemberg in 1861, cannot be understood without reference to this wider political context.

In the 1860s efforts to reinforce popular loyalty to the status quo in all three states moved beyond cultural and economic initiatives into the political arena. This reflected the renewed vitality of German politics and, in particular, the growing insistence of the national question. In many ways, Italian unification in 1859 acted as a catalyst for this development. On the one hand, outrage at the French seizure of Nice and Savoy provoked a mass outpouring of jingoistic nationalism. On the other hand, some Germans saw Italian unification as a potential role-model for Germany, and looked to Prussia to take the lead in displacing Austria, as Sardinia-Piedmont had done in Italy. The stirring Italian example prompted liberal nationalists in North Germany to found the *Nationalverein* – a proto-political party which sought to hasten national unification, ideally through encouraging the ambitions of a liberal Prussia.[66] Unlike earlier political organisations, the *Nationalverein* was not locally based and, at its zenith in 1862–3, it attracted up to 20–25,000 members from all over Germany. This was clearly in breach of Confederal legislation regulating the membership of political associations, but the German Confederation lacked the political will to clamp down on the new organisation. The failure to do so marked the collapse of the reactionary alliance between Austria and Prussia that had characterised the 1850s. For the Prussian government refused to suppress the *Nationalverein* as it had suppressed other political dissidents. To liberals, this appeared to confirm the dawn of a 'new era' in Prussian politics, now that Wilhelm had succeeded his brother Friedrich Wilhelm IV. To

---

[65] See, for instance, Leonard Krieger, *The German idea of freedom: history of a political tradition* (Chicago, 1957), pp. 341–97.

[66] The two best accounts of the *Nationalverein* are Shlomo Na'aman, *Der Deutsche Nationalverein, die politische Konstituierung des deutschen Bürgertums 1857–1867* (Düsseldorf, 1987), and Andreas Biefang, *Politisches Bürgertum in Deutschland 1857–1868. Nationale Organisationen und Eliten* (Düsseldorf, 1994).

historians, Prussian policy towards the *Nationalverein* also appears to indicate a greater willingness on the part of those in power to exploit liberal nationalism to their own ends. In the event, however, the Prussian new era proved short-lived, as monarch and parliament were soon at loggerheads over plans for military reform. This confrontation propelled Bismarck to power from relative obscurity in the Foreign Ministry. Bismarck promised Wilhelm not to give way in the face of liberal pressure, and he kept his word. When he failed to persuade the opposition to change its mind, he simply governed Prussia in defiance of both parliament and constitution, outraging liberal opinion throughout Germany.

Nevertheless, the much-vaunted liberalisation of Prussian politics in the early 1860s was not without influence elsewhere in Germany. Indeed, the 1860s saw a limited relaxation of the 'reaction' in both Saxony and Württemberg that proved more lasting than in Prussia. Superficially, the transition to a more liberal regime was easiest in Saxony. Here, there were no changes in government, but the new climate prompted a policy of 'gentle practice', whereby repressive legislation remained in place but was no longer actively enforced by the government. This policy shift proved so fruitful that in the mid-1860s Beust was forced to defend his 'popularity-seeking' measures to the Prussian government.[67] By 1866 even the opposition had to admit the regrettable success of Beust's 'pseudo-liberalisation'.[68] The surprising ease of Saxony's transition to a more liberal regime testifies to Beust's flexibility as a politician, and calls in question assumptions that Saxony was especially reactionary during the 1850s. Conversely, the notion of a mild 'reaction' in Württemberg is undermined by the government's failure to adopt more liberal policies before King Wilhelm's death – although a relatively liberal constitution ensured that the 'reaction' was always kept within bounds.. When he came to power in 1864, Wilhelm's son Karl appointed a more liberal government, led by the Foreign Minister von Varnbüler. Karl himself was an insubstantial figure and his ministers rapidly took the initiative in adopting liberal domestic policies. Württemberg's long-standing constitutional traditions enabled the new, more liberal government to regain lost ground fairly swiftly in the 1860s.

In both Saxony and Württemberg, a more liberal domestic policy went hand in hand with greater openness to the possibility of national

---

[67] Friedrich Ferdinand, Graf von Beust, *Aus drei Viertel-Jahrhunderten*, Vol. 1, pp. 406–11.
[68] *Deutsche Allgemeine Zeitung*, 8 November 1866. Cited after Herbert Jordan, *Die öffentliche Meinung in Sachsen 1864–66* (Kamenz, 1918), pp. 23–4.

reform. Of the two states, Saxony was more serious about change. As early as 1861 Beust presented a comprehensive series of proposals for reform of the German Confederation in response to the revival of German nationalism after 1859. Nothing came of the initiative, but Beust continued to woo nationalist opinion. When mass gatherings of the nationalist movements of singers and gymnasts met in Leipzig and Dresden in 1864/5, Beust took the opportunity to address them person-ally, thereby underlining the Saxon government's commitment to the nationalist cause. By contrast, Varnbüler, the Württemberg Foreign Minister, was sceptical about the feasibility of Confederal reform and preferred to play down the issue, rather than raise false expectations.[69] But he too was drawn into a limited alliance with democratic German nationalists in Württemberg, based on their support for a federal Germany on the Swiss model and their vehemently anti-Prussian stance.

Events in Hanover followed a very different pattern. Here, the hard-line government of the 1850s, headed by von Borries, toughened its stance still further after the emergence of the *Nationalverein* in 1859. A less reactionary ministry finally came to power under von Hammerstein and Windthorst in 1862. Yet this change was the result of an internal politi-cal crisis unleashed by the introduction of a more orthodox catechism, not the result of a political change of heart. In any case, the Hammerstein–Windthorst ministry proved short-lived. Its fall in 1865 brought any kind of liberalisation in Hanover to an abrupt halt – at a time when governments in Saxony and Württemberg were intensifying this policy. Moreover, even the Hammerstein–Windthorst ministry could not change the rigidly particularist foreign policy of the Hanoverian government.

When possible, however, even the particularist Hanoverian govern-ment sought to play the nationalist card. As a North German state, Hanover was very close to the duchies of Schleswig and Holstein on the Danish border. The two duchies were indissolubly linked and both were ruled by the King of Denmark, but whereas Holstein was German-speaking and a member of the German Confederation, largely Danish-speaking Schleswig was not. In 1863 Christian IX succeeded to the

---

[69] See Fritz E. Hellwag, *Varnbüler und die deutsche Frage 1864–66* (Stuttgart, 1934), pp. 20–22. Varnbüler was, however, more open to serious *Bund* reform than Wilhelm had been. See Norbert Wehner, *Die deutschen Mittelstaaten auf dem Frankfurter Fürstentag 1863* (Frankfurt, 1993), pp. 216–27, on Wilhelm's defence of Württemberg voting rights when negotiating a new *Bund Direktorium* at the *Frankfurter Fürstentag*.

Danish throne through his mother, but stood to forfeit Schleswig-Holstein, where the title only passed through the male line. He therefore drew up a new constitution, which would effectively have incorporated Schleswig into Denmark. This outraged many Germans, who clamoured to rescue their brothers in the North from the Danes' clutches by bringing Schleswig into the German Confederation. Feeling ran particularly high in parts of North Germany, such as Hanover. The Hanoverian government had nothing against incorporating Schleswig-Holstein into the German Confederation. Indeed, like other *Mittelstaat* governments, it welcomed the prospect of another medium-sized state. Consequently, Hanover took a particularly belligerent line during debates on the matter held at the Confederal Diet in Frankfurt in a rare moment of agreement with liberal nationalists.

This was the not only way in which the Schleswig-Holstein issue turned accepted patterns of German politics on their heads. Popular agitation on behalf of the two duchies created a transient consensus in Germany, which overshadowed traditional divides between *kleindeutsch* and *großdeutsch* parties, between liberal nationalists and conservative *Mittelstaat* governments, and even between Austria and Prussia. A national network of Schleswig-Holstein Associations emerged, endorsed by both the pro-Prussian *Nationalverein* and its less prominent *großdeutsch* counterpart, the *Reformverein*.[70] Furthermore, *Mittelstaat* governments appeared to be more in tune with the aggressive nationalism of the Schleswig-Holstein movement than Prussia and Austria, which initially showed little inclination to go to war with Denmark over the matter. But the smaller German governments could not take action alone. Instead, the line taken by the two great powers determined the timing and outcome of the war with Denmark.

To some extent, the conclusions drawn by liberals after the war with Denmark reflected the domestic politics of the different German states. In Hanover, the government's combination of particularism and repressive conservatism caused the opposition to lose all faith in the possibilities of spontaneous domestic change.[71] Consequently, many Hanoverian liberals

---

[70] On the *Reformverein* see: Willy Real, *Der deutsche Reformverein. Großdeutsche Stimmen und Kräfte zwischen Villafranca und Königgrätz* (Lübeck, 1966), and Hope, *The alternative to German unification*, Chapter 1.

[71] See Michael John on the formation of an anti-government alliance of rural and urban elites in his 'Liberalism and Society in Germany', 581–90. This article provides a very useful analysis of the regional context for Hanoverian liberalism.

reached the conclusion that only a German nation state could guarantee basic constitutional and civil rights. It was therefore no accident that Hanover was the birthplace of the *Nationalverein*, nor that Hanoverian liberals were readier to overlook the Prussian constitutional conflict than liberals elsewhere, since their expectations were lower. Conversely, developments in Prussia were very worrying indeed to Württemberg liberals precisely because they contrasted so markedly with their own state's constitutional traditions and relatively progressive government.[72] Even so, the Schleswig-Holstein affair persuaded Julius Holder and a minority of other Württemberg liberals of the impotence of the Third Germany and the unavoidable need for nationalists to work with Prussia in order to attain their goal. Most Württemberg liberals were more radical and less pragmatic than this. *Großdeutsch* democrats led by Karl Mayer seized control of *Der Beobachter*, the leading opposition newspaper, and formed the Württemberg People's Party.[73] To the Württemberg People's Party, the Schleswig-Holstein affair was definitive proof of the fundamentally selfish motives of the two German great powers. The People's Party therefore hoped to create a truly democratic and federal nation state through reform at state level, and consistently put liberty before unity in their vision of national renewal. Such views provided a potentially rich seam of support for the government, notwithstanding the gulf between it and the People's Party in terms of domestic politics. In some ways, the situation in Saxony was not dissimilar. Here too, pro-Prussian liberals like Karl Biedermann and Heinrich Treitschke appear to have been a high-profile and vocal minority, although the lack of research into Saxon politics in the early 1860s means that it is hard to be sure. Certainly, if membership of the *Nationalverein* can be taken as a barometer of the views of a politically active elite, then particularism in both was unusually strong in both Saxony and Württemberg – the states with the lowest number of members in 1866 (Table 1.5). On the other hand, membership of the *Nationalverein* was stronger in Hanover than in any state apart from Prussia and Hesse-Darmstadt.

In the summer of 1866 Austria and Prussia went to war. The war was fought over Prussia's right to claim the spoils of the Schleswig-Holstein

---

[72] For a discussion of the Württemberg response to the German question in the 1860s see Adolf Rapp, *Die Württemberger und die nationale Frage, 1863–1871* (Stuttgart, 1910).

[73] See Gerlinde Runge, *Die Volkspartei in Württemberg von 1864 bis 1871. Die Erben der 48er Revolution im Kampf gegen die preußischkleindeutsche Lösung der nationalen Frage* (Stuttgart, 1970) on the emergence of the *Volkspartei* and the development of party politics in Württemberg at this time.

Table 1.5. Nationalverein *membership in the major German states 1860–6*[a]

State	Year: 1860	1861	1864	1865	1866
Hanover	194	664	1,157	964	707
Saxony	124	228	454	193	47
Württemberg	45	386	82	38	8
Prussia	3,073	8,421	8,355	4,399	2,358
Bavaria	193	355	264	97	59
Baden	433	1,173	752	583	302
Hesse-Darmstadt	32	1,416	1,383	1,039	184
Hesse-Kassel	0	2	278	243	184
Nassau	109	513	493	256	66

Note:
[a] Figures cited after Biefang, *Politisches Bürgertum in Deutschland*, p. 104.

campaign and dominate North Germany accordingly. Prussia won. The German Confederation was dissolved and partially replaced by a new, Prussian-dominated North German Confederation. Meanwhile, Austria's historic ties with the rest of Germany were finally severed. The settlement of 1866 transformed both the political map of Germany and the internal political situation in all three states. Both Hanover and Saxony fought alongside Austria in the war and were occupied by Prussian forces almost immediately. Prussia then annexed Hanover – along with Nassau, Hesse-Kassel, Frankfurt and part of Hesse-Darmstadt – finally uniting the two halves of the Prussian state. Saxony narrowly escaped the same fate and became instead Prussia's junior partner in the North German Confederation. Württemberg sided with Austria, but did not actively participate in the war and emerged from the confrontation apparently unscathed. Like the other South-West German states, Württemberg did not join together with the rest of Germany until 1871.

These events prompted strong outbursts of particularist feeling in all three states, but particularly in Hanover and Saxony, which experienced the trauma of war first-hand. Prominent liberals in both states initially welcomed the prospect of Prussian annexation. The Saxon Heinrich Treitschke joyfully proclaimed the Welfs and the Wettins to be 'ripe, over-ripe for their well-deserved destruction'.[74] But these views were not

[74] Cited after Siegfried Weichlein, 'Sachsen zwischen Landesbewußtsein und Nationsbildung, 1866–1871', in Simone Lässig and Karl Heinrich Pohl (eds.), *Sachsen im Kaiserreich. Politik, Wirtschaft und Gesellschaft im Umbruch* (Cologne, 1997), pp. 241–70 (pp. 251–2).

widely shared. In July 1866 von Hardenberg, the Prussian commissar in charge of occupied Hanover, warned Bismarck of the strength of Hanoverian particularism, which was, he reported despairingly, based on 'the very firmly rooted conviction that nowhere else is life better than it is in Hanover'.[75] Miquel and his fellow liberals were forced to backtrack in the face of overwhelming popular feeling and, as Heide Barmeyer has shown, soon moderated their pro-Prussian politics and successfully defended Hanoverian institutions against Prussian interference in 1867.[76] In Saxony too, annexationists proved to be very much in the minority and the Prussian occupation aroused widespread antagonism.[77] According to an article in the *Preußische Jahrbücher*, anti-Prussian demonstrations were held in Chemnitz, 'which used to be so well-disposed towards Prussia' and there was no converting the Dresdners: 'they sulk, do what they have to, and wish the Prussians in hell'.[78] As in Hanover, these feelings went together with a desire to defend Saxon institutions. The liberal court archivist, Carl von Weber, was relatively well disposed towards Prussia, but he spoke for many when he told the Prussian commissar, von Wurmb, that Saxons did not wish to become Prussian: 'We are a well-governed people. We have an excellent King... We have a ministry, in which the country has complete confidence... We wish to keep our King, our sovereignty and our constitution.'[79] Indeed, the atmosphere was such that August Bebel and Wilhelm Liebknecht seized the opportunity to found the Saxon People's Party in the summer of 1866.[80] The socialism of the Saxon People's Party marked a new beginning in German politics and reflected the unusual level of industrialisation in Saxony at this time. Even so, the name of this party, its radical anti-Prussian politics and its readiness to ally with conservative particularists for electoral purposes were strongly reminiscent

[75] 29 July 1866. Cited after Heide Barmeyer, *Hannovers Eingliederung in den preußischen Staat. Annexion und administrative Integration, 1866–1868* (Hildesheim, 1983), pp. 15–16.

[76] See ibid., pp. 81–124, and Heide Barmeyer, 'Die hannoverschen Nationalliberalen 1859–1885', *Niedersächsisches Jahrbuch für Landesgeschichte* 53 (1981), 65–85.

[77] On the peculiarly negative impact of the occupation, see James Retallack, '"Why can't a Saxon be more like a Prussian?" Regional identities and the birth of modern political culture in Germany, 1866–7', *Canadian Journal of History* 32:1 (1997), 26–55 (pp. 41–6).

[78] *Preußische Jahrbücher* 18 (1866). Cited after Weichlein, 'Sachsen zwischen Landesbewußtsein und Nationsbildung', p. 251.

[79] Cited after Hellmut Kretzschmar, *Die Zeit König Johanns von Sachsen 1854–1873* (Berlin, 1960), p. 64.

[80] On the role of the Saxon People's Party in unification see Sinclair W. Armstrong, 'The Social-Democrats and the unification of Germany, 1863–1871', *Journal of Modern History* 12:4 (1940), 485–509.

of the democratic Württemberg People's Party founded a few years earlier.

Given the strength of anti-Prussian feelings in both Hanover and Saxony, it was no surprise that the National Liberals did relatively badly here in the 1867 elections for the constituent parliament of the North German Confederation and the elections for the North German *Reichstag* which followed. The outcome was significant because these elections were largely fought over the national issue, and were also the first to introduce direct and near-universal manhood suffrage in Germany. In Hanover pro-Welf particularists won nine seats in the first of these elections – a narrow victory over the National Liberals, who won one less seat but nevertheless obtained an overall majority of the vote. By the time of the *Reichstag* elections some months later, the balance had shifted further in favour of the liberals, who won thirteen seats against the particularists' five. In Saxony, the National Liberals did far worse than this. Fourteen of the twenty-eight Saxon delegates to the constituent parliament of the North German Confederation and eight of those in the new *Reichstag* were old fashioned particularists. By contrast, the National Liberals won only one seat in the former and four in the latter.[81] Moreover, seventeen of the twenty-eight Saxon seats in the new *Reichstag* were in the hands of their opponents – particularists, left-liberals and socialists. The stronger showing of the National Liberals in Hanover reflected widespread alienation from Georg V's regime and the dual role of liberal leaders like Miquel and Bennigsen, who had dominated opposition politics in pre-unification Hanover. Even so, the particularist vote remained a significant factor in Hanoverian politics well beyond 1870/1. The defeat of the Saxon liberals was more comprehensive. Yet the elections were hardly a vote of confidence in the Saxon government. In particular, the *Reichstag* elections of August 1867 revealed a strong increase in the vote for liberal, democratic and socialist parties, all of them opponents of the government. In any case, these exercises in mass democracy made it difficult for the Saxon government to continue with its out-dated constitution and legal system as if nothing had happened. The government rose to the challenge presented by this new situation and introduced a series of constitutional and administrative

---

[81] For a more thorough analysis of these elections see Weichlein, 'Sachsen zwischen Landesbewußtsein und Nationsbildung', pp. 253–9.

reforms, starting with a progressive suffrage law in 1868. In the late 1860s and early 1870s for the first time, nation-building and state-building in Saxony went hand in hand.

Württemberg was a bystander during the dramatic events of 1866. It was not occupied by Prussian troops, nor did it subsequently join the North German Confederation. Yet particularism in Württemberg was even stronger than in Hanover and Saxony – indicating that it was more than a knee-jerk response to military occupation and the threat of annexation. As a result of the war of 1866, Württemberg remained independent of Prussia in theory, if not in practice. Despite being outside the North German Confederation, the Württemberg government was forced to consolidate ties with the *Zollverein* by sending elected delegates to Berlin, where they sat alongside the rest of the North German *Reichstag* in the new *Zollparlament*. Equally, Württemberg's military and diplomatic independence was compromised by an offensive and defensive alliance with the North German Confederation. Both measures were highly controversial. Pro-Prussian candidates famously failed to win a single seat in the *Zollparlament* elections of 1868 – an unparalleled success for those opposed to *kleindeutsch* unification, which indicated that anti-Prussian feeling ran higher here than in any other state.[82] Similarly, the Württemberg parliament nearly rejected the military alliance, and the Württemberg People's Party subsequently mustered 150,000 signatories to a petition opposing the introduction of Prussian-style military reforms, which it successfully portrayed as the thin edge of the *kleindeutsch* wedge. Even so, the Württemberg government could not afford to be complacent. The victory of anti-Prussian candidates in the *Zollparlament* elections was more of a vote against Bismarck than a vote for the government, and the pro-Prussian German Party did surprisingly well in elections to the Württemberg parliament itself, where domestic rather than national politics were the name of the game. As in Saxony, the Württemberg government embarked on a series of progressive reforms designed to bolster the state and its institutions. Once again, a suffrage reform in 1868 was the centrepiece of these changes. As the pro-Prussian *Schwäbische Volkszeitung* noted with bitter accuracy, 'All of a sudden there is a passionate enthusiasm for reform . . . now that it is a question of building up Württemberg opposition to Germany; they need

---

[82] As compared with 6:8 in Baden and 27:21 in Bavaria.

popularity and Württemberg patriotism in order to fight off the terrible threat of unity.'[83] Here, where state-building and nationhood were still at odds, the tensions between particularism and nationalism remained acute.

These tensions were the product of two contradictory processes at work in pre-unification Germany. On the one hand, the Napoleonic era saw the birth of German nationalism, which gradually became a force to be reckoned with. For much of the nineteenth century, political nationalism was the concern of an elite few. Occasionally, however, dramatic events abroad – the Rhine crisis of 1840, Italian unification and the Schleswig-Holstein crisis – prompted more widespread outbursts of nationalist feeling and testified to the existence of a less explicitly politicised nationalist consensus. By the 1860s, a combination of political agitation by the *Nationalverein* and mass demonstrations of cultural nationalism, in the shape of national gatherings of the singing, shooting and gymnastic movements, meant that the perceived pressure for change had become almost irresistible. Even Austria was forced to jump on the bandwagon in 1863, when the Austrian government invited the German princes to the conference known as the *Frankfurter Fürstentag* in an attempt to bounce the Prussians into accepting a *großdeutsch* solution to the German question. As for Prussia, Bismarck's aims were those of a Prussian patriot, but he too felt a need to pander to the nationalism of his liberal opponents in order to resolve the constitutional conflict. In the event, Germany was unified by Bismarck and not by the German people, or even by the liberal nationalists of the *Nationalverein*. Even so, Bismarck probably would not have taken this course without the prompting of the nationalist movement. On the other hand, the Napoleonic reorganisation of Germany strengthened the German states as individual units and the governments of these states successfully consolidated their new position in the decades that followed. In 1866 Hanover, Saxony and Württemberg bore little resemblance to the states that bore the same name in 1800, but by 1866 Hanoverians, Saxons and Württembergers had a strong sense of these states as political units. To some extent this was just a matter of time. Half a century of shared political institutions and administrative structures was long enough for the disparate territories which made up these states to begin to grow together.

---

[83] Cited after Langewiesche, *Liberalismus und Demokratie in Württemberg*, p. 78.

What was the relationship between these two developments? What was the appeal of particularism? How far was it the product of deliberate state-building policies in these three German states? What did these policies actually consist of? How did state-building and the growth of state patriotism reflect and influence the wider process of nation state formation in Germany? What did it mean to be a Hanoverian, a Saxon, a Württemberger, yet also a German?

CHAPTER TWO

Modernising monarchy

Bismarck, writing many years after German unification, saw the Germans as a uniquely monarchic people.[1] He believed that German patriotism could only be awakened through dynastic loyalty, whilst other European nations managed perfectly well without. Yet Bismarck was also aware that this dynastic loyalty was a double-edged sword. On the one hand, he saw the German dynasties as the 'glue' which held a disparate nation together; on the other hand, he recognised that they were the source and focus of centrifugal forces within Germany, 'the point around which the German drive for separatism crystallises'.[2] In many ways, Bismarck's assessment hit the mark – even if he did overlook the strength of civic patriotism in the free cities of Bremen, Frankfurt, Hamburg and Lübeck. In terms of sheer quantity, the Germans simply *were* more monarchic than their European neighbours. The German Confederation was awash with kings and dynasties, numbering thirty-five different monarchies amongst its thirty-nine member states. More importantly perhaps, the existence of most of these thirty-five states was only explicable in terms of monarchy. As late as 1815, the German states were still treated as the personal property of their rulers. It was therefore perfectly acceptable for monarchs to re-draw the map of Germany with scant regard for the loyalties or interests of its inhabitants. Yet many of the states that emerged from this process were simply too small to be viable as independent units, and even large states could be geographically incoherent and awkward to govern. After 1815 Prussia, Bavaria and Hanover all included isolated territories that were not linked to the main body of the state at all. Consequently, the size and shape of most (if not all) states in the German Confederation only made sense in terms of their relationship with a particular monarch. More than political or administrative institutions, it was the monarch who defined

[1] Otto von Bismarck, *Gesammelte Werke*, 15 vols., ed. Gerhard Ritter and Rudolf Stadelmann, Vol. xv, *Erinnerung und Gedanke* (Nendeln-Liechtenstein, 1972, reprint), pp 197–203.
[2] Ibid., p. 203.

and gave meaning to a state; he and his dynasty formed the core of a state's identity.

Yet the relationship between monarch, state and people in early nineteenth-century Germany was considerably more problematic than this implies. The secular rationalism of the Enlightenment and the political upheavals of the French Revolution and Napoleonic hegemony in Europe had shaken the foundations of divine right monarchy and eighteenth-century absolutism. Monarchy could no longer be taken for granted in the 'age of revolution'. Instead, after 1815 monarchs sought to justify their role in terms of dynastic legitimacy and the monarchic principle. Thus conservative thinkers, like Friedrich Julius Stahl, argued that hereditary monarchy provided the state with a crucial source of stability in a time of flux.[3] Legitimacy was the catch phrase of Restoration Europe and the unifying idea behind the Holy Alliance of Austria, Prussia and Russia, which sought to keep the forces of revolution at bay. It was, of course, a fantasy. The legitimist rulers of states like Württemberg had shown no compunction in riding roughshod over the rights of the imperial nobility and ecclesiastical princes when it suited them, and they would happily have done the same again if given half the chance. Indeed, Prussia did precisely this when it annexed Hanover, Hesse-Kassel and Nassau in 1866. Nevertheless, dynastic legitimacy was a convenient and surprisingly convincing fiction. After all, none of the German dynasties were precisely new and their rule did appear to be justified by the hereditary principle. In any case, none of the German monarchs were willing to accept that their position owed anything either to Napoleon or to the forces of revolution. Typically, the first King of Bavaria, Max I, portrayed his new title as the restoration of a medieval kingdom, rather than the innovation that it really was. Similarly, the Kings of Hanover preferred to emphasise their ancient rights to East Friesland, which had been in Welf hands several centuries earlier, rather than to treat the area as an entirely new acquisition. Thus the authority of the crown appeared to be hallowed by ancient tradition, even where, as was often the case, such claims had little basis in reality.

Increasingly, however, this appeal to dynastic legitimacy proved inadequate in the face of pressures for representative government and a modern constitution. Monarchs in the South-West German states of Baden, Bavaria and Württemberg were the first to succumb to these pressures by

---

[3] See for instance Stahl's pamphlet *Das monarchische Princip: eine staatsrechtlich-politische Abhandlung* (Heidelberg, 1845).

issuing new constitutions in the years immediately following the Treaty of
Vienna. It was no coincidence that all three states had grown dramatically
in size during the Napoleonic era. Before 1815 the backing of Napoleon
had enabled the rulers of these states to introduce a range of 'enlightened
absolutist' reforms designed to strengthen the position of the monarch and
his government. The new King Friedrich of Württemberg, for instance,
modernised the Württemberg bureaucracy and sought to rule without
consulting the Württemberg Estates. After 1815 such an approach was no
longer viable. Lacking the support of Napoleon's armies, monarchs
needed to anchor their rule more firmly in the state itself. Consequently,
state-building ceased to be purely administrative and became constitutional as well. Even Friedrich was forced to think again, summoning the
Württemberg Estates and announcing his intention to promulgate a new
constitution. Where Baden, Bavaria and Württemberg led, other states
were forced to follow – sooner or later. The revolutions of 1830 and 1848
prompted successive waves of constitution-granting in the German states;
by 1866 only a very few unimportant states had managed to buck the trend.

To liberal contemporaries these new constitutions appeared to be a
step forward. They limited the arbitrary power of the absolute ruler by
defining the rights of the monarch and his people, strengthening the rule
of law, introducing an elective element in the legislature and clarifying
the role of representative institutions in government. Yet none of these
constitutions in any way undermined the principle of monarchic
authority or reflected an acceptance of the idea of popular sovereignty.
For a start, the new German constitutions were invariably granted by a
monarch to his people. In this sense, they represented a series of voluntary, self-imposed limitations on the monarch's absolute authority, and
as such accepted the existence of this authority in principle. Indeed,
most constitutions spelled out the fact that the monarch remained the
ultimate source of all governmental authority. By implication, therefore,
the constitution could also be revoked, as it was in Hanover in 1837 and
again in 1855. Unsurprisingly, the constitution introduced after both
these coups was particularly explicit in stressing the supreme authority
of the monarch. It stated that '[a]s sovereign, the King unites in Himself
the whole and undivided authority of the state, and will only be bound
by the constitution to collaborate with the Estates in the exercise of *specific* rights'. The constitution elaborated on this point in some detail,
stating that the King was the source of all governmental authority in
Hanover, that state organisations only exercised their authority at his
behest, that no law was valid before the King had promulgated it, that

he exercised sole control of the army and foreign policy, and that he was the sole source of all jurisdiction although he did not have the right to interfere with due legal process.[4] Both the famously progressive Württemberg constitution of 1819 and the Saxon constitution of 1831 made the same claim, albeit somewhat more concisely. In fact, the wording of the two constitutions on this point was identical. They stated: 'The King is sovereign head of state, and unites in himself all the rights of the state authority and exercises them in accordance with regulations laid down in the constitution. His person is holy and inviolable.'[5] Moreover, the Kings of all three states continued to describe themselves in official documents as ruling 'by the grace of God'.

In practice, however, the rights of the Kings of both Saxony and Württemberg were less extensive than those of the King of Hanover. For instance, the King of Württemberg was required to keep his parliament abreast of foreign policy developments and to submit all foreign treaties to it for approval. Tellingly, whereas the King of Hanover retained direct control of his finances, the Kings of Saxony and Württemberg handed most of their income over to the state, in exchange for a civil list. Indeed, the separation of royal and state incomes was arguably the most important difference between the Hanoverian constitution of 1840 and its more liberal predecessor, the short-lived constitution of 1833. For Ernst August, this was a matter of pride. As he wrote to the Grand-Duke of Mecklenburg-Strelitz, 'I would rather eat dry bread with honour than live in the greatest luxury, if my means were not my own, and I had always to beg from them [the Estates] the bread which I ate.'[6] At the same time, Ernst August described his efforts as 'a battle that I have won for *you all* to save the monarchical principle'.[7] He clearly recognised that if a monarch lost control of his purse strings, his room for manoeuvre would be severely limited and the much-vaunted monarchic principle weakened accordingly.

Ernst August was right to be worried. Even where constitutions explicitly endorsed monarchic authority, in practice the habit of constitutionalism significantly reduced the monarch's independence, by reinforcing

---

[4] Landesverfassungs-Gesetz für das Königreich Hannover vom 6. August 1840, ~~ 3–11.
[5] Verfassungsurkunde für das Königreich Württemberg vom 25. September 1819 ~4; Verfassungsurkunde für das Königreich Sachsen vom 4. September 1831, ~4.
[6] Ernst August to the Grand-Duke of Mecklenburg-Strelitz, 4 and 19 April 1839. Cited after Geoffrey Malden Willis, *Ernest Augustus, Duke of Cumberland and King of Hanover* (London, 1954), p. 320.
[7] Ernst August to the Grand-Duke of Mecklenburg-Strelitz, 24 August 1839. Cited after ibid., p. 321.

the rights and status of representative bodies. This had important implications for public perceptions of monarch, constitution and parliament.
Thus Monika Wienfort has traced changes in the language used by the
Bavarian parliament when responding to the King's opening addresses
to parliament between 1815 and 1848.[8] With time, traditional monarchic
attributes like wisdom and justice ceased to be ascribed to the King and
began to be applied to the constitution and the people instead.
Conversely, monarchs acquired characteristics that were more personal
and less clearly related to their office, such as gentleness, graciousness,
benevolence and warmth. More importantly still, parliamentary
addresses began to stress the role of the monarch as guardian of the constitution. These semantic developments testify to a fundamental change
in assumptions about monarchic government, and to a shift in attitudes
towards both monarchy and the constitution among the political classes.
This transformation belied the commitment to the monarchic principle
reflected in the constitutions themselves.

Even so, the power of most German monarchs remained considerable, and this was certainly true of the Kings of Hanover, Saxony and
Württemberg. Crucially, in all three states the monarch retained an
exclusive right to initiate legislation. The Estates or parliament had the
right to be consulted over legislation, but they were unable to set the
political agenda and could only follow where the monarch led. Under
these circumstances, the King remained, as Robert von Mohl wrote of
Wilhelm I of Württemberg, 'really the focal point (*Mittelpunkt*) of the
state'.[9] Consequently, the character and attitudes of the monarch mattered a very great deal, because each King brought a highly personal
touch to his office. Indeed, the personality of the monarch was perhaps
the single most important factor influencing the different paths taken by
Hanover, Saxony and Württemberg before unification. This was true
both in terms of direct political impact and in less tangible ways, since
a monarch's charisma determined his popularity and his ability to act as
a unifying element within the state. The monarch's character dictated
how far he was able to adapt monarchy to the constraints of constitutionalism and to modernise its appeal to the masses. At the same time,
monarchs throughout Germany had similar political interests and faced
the same pressures at both domestic and national level. In fact, the twin

---

[8] Monika Wienfort, *Monarchie in der bürgerlichen Gesellschaft. Deutschland und England von 1640 bis 1848*
(Göttingen, 1993), pp. 175–9.
[9] Robert von Mohl, *Lebens-Erinnerungen von Robert von Mohl 1799–1875* (Stuttgart and Leipzig, 1902),
p. 17.

forces of liberalism and nationalism ensured that both their room for manoeuvre and their ability to affect developments were surprisingly limited. How successfully did the Kings of Hanover, Saxony and Württemberg rise to these challenges, and what did they contribute to the process of state-formation in each state?

Taken as individuals, the constitutional monarchs of Hanover, Saxony and Württemberg had relatively little in common.[10] The eldest were Ernst August of Hanover (1771–1851) and Wilhelm I of Württemberg (1781–1864).[11] Wilhelm was ten years younger than Ernst August, his political views were at odds with those of the older man, and he was brought up in Germany as the eldest son of a relatively unimportant Duke rather than in England as the third son of George III, a major European monarch. Inevitably, therefore, their outlook on life was very different. Nevertheless, the two belonged to the political generation that was forged in the turmoil of the revolutionary wars and the Napoleonic era. Ernst August was an arch-conservative and Wilhelm relatively progressive (at least in his youth), but both understood these terms in the context of the Enlightenment and the French Revolution. Moreover, both fought the French and played their part in the wars of liberation. Having seen active service, they saw themselves as soldiers and were perceived as such by contemporaries. This set them apart from the next generation of German monarchs, represented here by Friedrich August II (1797–1854) of Saxony and his younger brother Johann (1801–73). For these monarchs, the Napoleonic wars were also an important formative experience, although they themselves had been too young to fight.[12] In his posthumously published memoirs, Johann described the war against

[10] For the sake of simplicity, this survey focuses only on constitutional monarchs. I have therefore chosen to omit Friedrich I of Württemberg, Friedrich August the Just of Saxony, and his brother Anton (who was already in his seventies when he became king and ruled for just three years before the 1830 revolution led to the appointment of his nephew Friedrich August II as joint-monarch and effective ruler). The survey will also omit Karl of Württemberg, who ruled for less than two years before the collapse of the German Confederation in 1866.

[11] The fullest biography of Ernst August is Willis, *Ernest Augustus,* but see also Anthony Bird, *The damnable Duke of Cumberland, a character study and vindication of Ernest Augustus, Duke of Cumberland and King of Hanover* (London, 1966). Both Willis and Bird take a very partisan approach to biography. The only biography of Wilhelm I is Grauer, *Wilhelm I.* – uncritical in its treatment both of Wilhelm and of some of the source material. By contrast, Mögle-Hofacker, *Zur Entwicklung des Parlamentarismus in Württemberg,* provides a subtle analysis of Wilhelm's changing political views.

[12] Little or nothing has been written about Friedrich August II, but on Johann see Kretzschmar, *Die Zeit König Johanns von Sachsen;* more generally also Kretzschmar, 'Das sächsische Königtum im 19. Jahrhundert: Ein Beitrag zur Typologie der Monarchie in Deutschland', *Historische Zeitschrift* 170 (1950), 457–93.

Napoleon in 1806 as his first important memory, and recalled how in 1813 the hopes of the German people for liberation from the foreign yoke affected himself and his older brother.[13] Like his friend Friedrich Wilhelm IV of Prussia, Johann was caught up in the wave of romantic nationalism that swept German youth during the wars of liberation and their aftermath.[14] His romanticism also revealed itself in a passion for Italy in general and Dante in particular. In fact, both the Saxon brothers developed marked intellectual inclinations that reflected the concerns of their time. Johann translated Dante's *Inferno* and became a distinguished legal scholar, whilst his brother developed a serious interest in the natural sciences. Finally, Georg V of Hanover (1819–78) belonged to the post-war generation, for whom the Napoleonic wars were not even a distant memory and for whom the revolutions of 1848 were probably the central political experience of their lives.[15] Georg spent much of his childhood in pre-constitutional Prussia and his first encounter with Hanoverian politics, the constitutional conflict of the 1830s, certainly shaped his subsequent attitudes. In this, however, Georg was clearly out of step with the times. Generational analysis of this kind is revealing because it is easy to forget how far monarchs were the product of the age and society in which they grew up, sharing their enthusiasms and beliefs, hopes and fears. This in turn had important implications for their approach to both politics and kingship.

Wilhelm of Württemberg came to the throne first. In his youth, he had been something of a rebel – running away to Paris with his mistress and writing an article that took issue with his father's disregard for the constitutional rights of the Württemberg Estates in the *Hamburger unparteiischer Korrespondent*, the most prominent German newspaper of the day. When he finally succeeded Friedrich in 1816, Wilhelm expressed a clear intention to rule differently. In his first official proclamation, he declared: 'The welfare and happiness of the subjects entrusted to Our care will be the sole aim of Our efforts, and Our first endeavour will be to secure the achievement of these lofty goals through a constitution which is in keeping with the spirit of the times and the needs of Our people.'[16] This proclamation was fairly typical of Wilhelm's early years in government,

---

[13] Johann, King of Saxony, *Lebenserinnerungen des Königs Johann von Sachsen*, ed. Hellmut Kretzschmar (Göttingen, 1958), pp. 41, 44–6.

[14] On Friedrich Wilhelm IV's romantic enthusiasms, see David E. Barclay, *Frederick William IV and the Prussian monarchy 1840–1861* (Oxford, 1995), pp. 29–32.

[15] On Georg V see Dieter Brosius, 'Georg V. von Hannover – der König des "monarchischen Prinzips" ', *Niedersächsisches Jahrbuch für Landesgeschichte* 51 (1979), 253–91.

[16] Cited after Grauer, *Wilhelm I.*, p. 125.

2.1 King Wilhelm of Württemberg, as a young man.
Source: Hauptstaatsarchiv, Stuttgart, J 300 (241), all rights reserved

with its acceptance of constitutional priorities and self-conscious desire
to move with the times. In many ways, however, the constitution of 1819
marked the beginning and end of Wilhelm's readiness to move with the
times. Once he had granted the constitution, Wilhelm saw it as a
bulwark against further change. In 1844 he adjured his son Karl that it
was 'an absolute necessity always to stick firmly to our constitution and
through this, and the continual use of our laws, to keep the parties in
check'.[17] Tellingly, he advised Karl that 'the knowledge of our laws and
our conditions, based upon our history' would help him to keep the state
in good order. This emphasis on the particular historical origins of the
Württemberg constitution is redolent of a conservative mind-set, which
saw laws as the product of their environment and rejected the possibility of deliberate and therefore artificial change. Equally, Wilhelm's
response to the revolution of 1848 showed a commitment to the monarchic principle and a distrust of representative government that was more
conservative than liberal. In an electoral appeal to the people of
Württemberg in 1850, he promised a revision of the constitution that
would 'be of genuine benefit to all classes of Our people, but not . . .
relinquish the inalienable rights of the crown'.[18] Writing in 1850, he
described the theory of popular sovereignty as 'one of the most misguided and damaging', since it inevitably led to universal suffrage and
elective government, which was itself a recipe for 'opposition to the
government, the trading of laws and taxes, in which each party outdoes
the rest in intrigues intended to topple the ministry'.[19] Yet Wilhelm also
recognised the need at least to pay lip service to such ideas: 'Can these
tendencies be . . . wholly suppressed? I do not think so! . . . We have no
choice but to render them as harmless as possible.' By this time, therefore, the 'liberalism' of Wilhelm's early years had given way to a pragmatic conservatism. Nevertheless, there is evidence that his earlier
commitment to a limited form of participatory politics was genuine.[20]
His experiences during 1848–9 were central to his rejection of these
ideas. He himself later declared: 'so-called "public opinion" has less
value in my eyes, since the experiences of . . . 1848 and 1849, when an
unworthy and criminal party of agitators led a goodly portion of my

---

[17] Wilhelm to Karl, 6 September 1844. Cited after Mögle-Hofacker, *Zur Entwicklung des Parlamentarismus in Württemberg*, pp. 1–2.

[18] 'An die Württemberger', *Staats-Anzeiger für Württemberg*, 6 July 1850. Cited after ibid., p. 82.

[19] Wilhelm, 'Bemerkungen über die Stände Versammlungen in deutschland und Vorschläge über die Art ihrer Verbeßerung', 1 January 1850, HSAStu G 268 B24 (47).

[20] On Wilhelm's early commitment to parliamentary politics in practice, see Mögle-Hofacker, *Zur Entwicklung des Parlamentarismus in Württemberg*, pp. 25–43.

loyal subjects astray, so that at the moment of truth they voted against my government'.[21]

On the face of it, Ernst August's approach to monarchy could hardly have been more different from Wilhelm's. Whereas the latter's first act on coming to power was to negotiate and grant a new constitution, Ernst August's first act was to revoke the liberal constitution already in place. Ernst August's attitudes were certainly more old-fashioned than Wilhelm's. When he announced to the Hanoverian Estates that 'Our loyal subjects can be assured that Our feelings for them are those of a father for his children,' he testified to an idealised, paternalistic view of monarchy that harked back to a bygone era and had little in common with Wilhelm's awareness of the need to consult his subjects.[22] Moreover, Ernst August believed in the God-given nature of his office because, although only a third son, he had been called by 'Providence' to the Hanoverian throne.[23] In 1850 he declared to Friedrich Wilhelm IV of Prussia that 'as sovereign I am responsible for the safety and good of my country, and the idea of ministerial responsibility cannot be a greater idea than that of [the responsibility] of the sovereign himself, who has been appointed by God, the King of Kings'.[24] Consequently, Ernst August felt that to betray his principles would be to betray his God as well. This profoundly religious view of his calling contrasted starkly with that of Wilhelm, who was, according to a contemporary, 'absolutely not inclined towards religion . . . by education and upbringing a child of the Enlightenment, a pupil and admirer of Voltaire'.[25] In other ways, however, there are striking similarities between the attitudes of the two monarchs. We have already seen how both expressed a strong commitment to the monarchic principle. Moreover, Ernst August shared Wilhelm's desire to rule in strict accordance with the constitution. In his first speech to the Hanoverian Estates elected in accordance with the 1819 constitution, he stated: 'I have always detested arbitrary rule, I wish only to govern my beloved people according to laws and rights.'[26] In this sense, the official biography of Ernst August by High Court Marshal von Malortie was right to describe his approach to monarchy as benevolent and enlightened absolutism, for

---

[21] Wilhelm, 11 September 1854. Cited after Grauer, *Wilhelm I.*, p. 338.
[22] Cited after Willis, *Ernest Augustus*, p. 288.
[23] On this see also the account of C. E. von Malortie, *König Ernst August* (Hanover, 1861), p. 47.
[24] Ernst August to Friedrich Wilhelm I, 6 August 1850: Ernst August, King of Hanover, 'Briefe Ernst Augusts von Hannover an König Friedrich Wilhelm IV. von Preußen 1849–1851, mitgeteilt von Studienrat Dr. Karl Hänchen', *Niedersächsisches Jahrbuch für Landesgeschichte* 10 (1933), 135–197 (p. 167).   [25] Rümelin on Wilhelm. Cited after Grauer, *Wilhelm I.*, p. 234.
[26] Cited after Willis, *Ernest Augustus*, p. 299.

Ernst August did not believe the King to be above the law.[27] His understanding of what this meant in practice, however, was deeply conservative, anchored in the belief that it was wrong to tamper with existing laws
and practices because these had grown organically out of the society in
which they operated. As he wrote to his friend Viscount Strangford,
'[t]here is nothing more dangerous than meddling with old customs and
habits'.[28] According to this view, the constitution of 1833, and not the constitutional coup of 1837, was arbitrary and illegal. This is where Ernst
August's views differed fundamentally from those of Wilhelm. The latter's
willingness to grant a new constitution reflected an enlightened belief in
the possibility of improving on existing conditions. As a conservative,
Ernst August had no time for the 'false idea' that a monarch could 'put a
check or a stop wherever he likes'.[29] Curiously, however, Ernst August
proved better able to rise to the challenges of 1848 than the more progressive Wilhelm. Like Wilhelm, he stuck to his principles, but unlike Wilhelm
he built a good working relationship with his ministers and showed a surprising readiness to listen to their views. Wilhelm had not a good word to
say about his new government, but Ernst August informed Strangford
that he had

> no reason to complain. I told them in my first conversation that I was fully aware
> that our principles up to now had differed widely, but that I trusted they would
> give me theirs, which I should listen to with the greatest attention, and that they
> must expect – if I differed from them – to listen with equal attention to my
> remarks, upon which they one and all agreed, and thus we have gone on per-
> fectly well.[30]

The fact remains, however, that both Ernst August and Wilhelm were
considerably less open to change than the Saxon brothers, Friedrich
August II and Johann. They too were committed to the monarchic principle and resistant to constitutional change, but in terms of practical politics the Saxon monarchs demonstrated a more flexible conservatism and
more genuine enthusiasm for parliamentary government. Friedrich
August came to power in 1830 on the back of the movement for constitutional reform. His brother Johann later recalled that Friedrich August had
'recognised the need for far-reaching reforms better and sooner than I'.[31]

---

[27] Malortie, *König Ernst August*, p. 4.
[28] Ernst August to Strangford, 23 January 1845: Ernst August, King of Hanover, *Letters of the King
of Hanover to Viscount Strangford, G.C.B. now in the possession of his granddaughter Mrs. Frank Russell*
(London, 1925), p. 72.   [29] Ernst August to Strangford, 7 December 1844, ibid., p. 68.
[30] Ernst August to Strangford, 15 May 1848, ibid., p. 150.
[31] *Lebenserinnerungen des Königs Johann von Sachsen*, ed. Kretzschmar, p. 105.

2.2 King Friedrich August II of Saxony, shortly before he became co-ruler of Saxony in 1830.
Source: Staatliche Kunstsammlungen, Dresden, C2824

Johann had by this stage abandoned his youthful liberalism and moved politically to the right 'perhaps more than was desirable'.[32] Nevertheless, he too bowed to the force of circumstance, and 'increasingly understood the need for reforms and only took the view that as little as possible of the

[32] Ibid., p. 72.

historical-conservative principle should be given up'.[33] Consequently, Johann collaborated in drafting the Saxon constitution of 1831, but remained vigorously opposed to granting a general bill of rights, since 'such *droits de l'homme et du citoyen*' smacked of the French Revolution.[34] His determination to minimise the novelty of the 1831 constitution, and instead 'to improve on that which was already in existence in keeping with the demands of the time', reflected a realistic attempt to adapt his conservative principles to the new context. Johann's reaction to the events of 1848 reflected a similar pragmatism. In March 1848 he urged Friedrich Wilhelm IV of Prussia to give way because 'public opinion is too strong . . . It is no good hitting one's head against a brick wall.'[35] Six months later, he wrote that 'the time of *l'état c'est moi* is over and kings nowadays cannot do everything that they want to do'.[36] The general public tended to see Friedrich August as more open-minded than his brother. Ironically, it was Friedrich August – not Johann – who declared his determination not to give way 'until the monarchic principle in Germany is completely bankrupt' and who eventually supported Beust's decision to reinstate the constitution of 1831.[37] As Crown Prince, Johann was himself a member of the Saxon Upper House and had come to enjoy this activity.[38] He subsequently claimed to have opposed the return to the constitution of 1831: 'For my part, I was unable to suppress my constitutional concerns . . . [These steps] were taken without my agreement and I bowed to the better judgement of others the more readily because I was convinced of the practical necessity of the measure.'[39] Johann's parliamentary experience inevitably gave him a unique insight into representative government, and he was unusual in embracing the parliamentary principle so whole-heartedly.

The different political approaches and reputations of these four monarchs make it easy to overlook how much they had in common. As constitutional rulers, all four were preoccupied with the defence of the monarchic principle and the need to rule constitutionally (however they chose to interpret this). In government, Johann of Saxony appeared to strike a very different balance between monarchy and constitution from that reached by Ernst August. In reality, the two shared many of the

---

[33] Ibid., p. 105. [34] Ibid., p. 111.
[35] Johann to Friedrich Wilhelm IV, mid-March 1848, *Briefwechsel zwischen König Johann von Sachsen und den Königen Friedrich Wilhelm IV. und Wilhelm I. von Preußen*, ed. Johann Georg, Herzog zu Sachsen (Leipzig, 1911), pp. 231–2.
[36] Johann to Friedrich Wilhelm IV, 12 November 1849, ibid., p. 258.
[37] Friedrich August II to von der Pfordten, 1849?. Cited after Rumpler, *Die deutsche Politik des Freiherrn von Beust*, p. 100.
[38] See *Lebenserinnerungen des Königs Johann von Sachsen*, ed. Kretzschmar, p. 233. [39] Ibid., p. 240.

same assumptions about monarchy and about the virtues of what Johann termed the 'historical-conservative principle'. In this context, Georg V of Hanover (1819–78) was very much the exception, because his fanatical belief in the monarchic principle was barely tempered by an acceptance of the constraints of constitutional government. For Georg shared his father's religious view of kingship and believed that only the 'pure monarchic principle' could guarantee the welfare and happiness of his people.[40] Unlike his fellow monarchs, he was quite unwilling to dilute this principle in any way, famously remarking that he wanted either to be 'completely a king, or not at all'.[41] To some extent, these views were simply the product of his upbringing. Yet Georg's belief in the divine mission of the Welf dynasty and his preoccupation with its past glories also reflected a more personal obsession. Equally, the obstinacy with which he clung to these views contrasted strikingly with the flexibility his father showed in 1848/9. Whereas Ernst August came to accept constitutional reform in 1848, Georg never did. He signed the new constitution only with the greatest reluctance – after being assured that he might subsequently revoke it, provided the Ministry and parliament could be brought to agree. Unsurprisingly, the constitution of 1848 did not survive Ernst August for long. Both contemporaries and historians have attributed Georg's rigidity and devotion to the monarchic principle in part to his personal problems. Blinded in early childhood, Georg was in many ways a tragic figure: desperate to overcome his resulting inadequacy as a monarch, excessively touchy about his status and unable to come to terms with political reality. Even Georg's confidant and adviser Oskar Meding, who drew a highly idealised portrait of the king, admitted that 'in government . . . his blindness probably made him more mistrustful and jealous of his authority than he would have been otherwise'.[42] Another contemporary, Otto Borchers, described how intolerable it was for a monarch like Georg, utterly convinced of the sublime nature of his office, to be dependent on others because of his disability.[43] As a result, he treated every opinion that differed from his own as an attempt to diminish his authority, and surrounded himself with a clique of self-seeking yes-men. Certainly, Georg's fantasies about

---

[40] Georg, in a speech made whilst laying the foundation stone of the Ernst August Monument, 5 June 1860. Cited after Brosius, 'Georg V. von Hannover', 265.

[41] As reported in Stüve to Frommann, 25 and 27 April 1854: *Briefe Johann Carl Bertram Stüves, 1848–1872*, ed. Vogel, Vol. II, p. 758.

[42] Oskar Meding, *Memoiren zur Zeitgeschichte*, 2 vols. (Leipzig, 1881), Vol. I, p. 6.

[43] Otto Borchers, *Unter welfischem Szepter, Erinnerungen eines Hannoveraners* (Hof, 1882), pp. 43–4.

the past and future of the Welf dynasty bore the hallmarks of a ruler who had lost touch with reality.

Nowhere was this more apparent than in his assessment of the German question in general and Hanover's position in Germany in particular. Georg and his circle liked to see Hanover as a young power on the make, a state whose importance should be measured 'not by the number of its inhabitants nor by its size, but by its geographical position'.[44] As a sea power, they even believed that Hanover might one day achieve the global stature of Britain. Indeed, Georg preferred to refer to Hanover as a '*Mittelreich*' and not a *Mittelstaat*. Unsurprisingly given these ambitions, Georg was unwilling to contemplate any change to the German Confederation or any dilution of Hanoverian sovereignty. He believed that the Confederation had proved its worth by surviving the revolution of 1848 and would 'with God's help, continue to defy all attacks and other doctrinaire projects. It is my personal conviction that the Confederal Constitution and the Confederal Diet are the only desirable and only possible unifying elements and . . . central institution for Germany.'[45] Here, Georg was very much following in his father's footsteps. Ernst August too had been wholly opposed to the idea of greater German unity, believing the idea of a national constitution to be a chimera, for 'Germany, from its situation and its different habits, manners, customs, and its various parts, cannot nor ever will be enabled to be governed or ruled upon the same one; consequently, however plausible the idea may appear, it is impracticable.'[46] He saw the Imperial Constitution of 1849 as 'reducing ourselves to the mere situation of becoming *Préfets*, or Governors of provinces, to which I for one would never submit'.[47] The uncompromising attitude of Ernst August and Georg to the national question reflected a total lack of sympathy with the strivings of German nationalism, which was itself the product of their English background. Tellingly, Ernst August tended to view the German Confederation primarily from a European standpoint, arguing that its collapse would lead to 'the destruction of the balance of power in Europe'.[48]

Neither Wilhelm of Württemberg nor Johann of Saxony shared this absolute resistance to the idea of Confederal reform. In 1844 Wilhelm

---

[44] Georg writing in an anonymous article, published in the *Kreuzzeitung* and the *Deutsche Nordsee Zeitung*, 1863, reprinted verbatim in Meding, *Memoiren zur Zeitgeschichte*, Vol. 1, p. 323.

[45] Cited after Fredy Köster, *Hannover und die Grundlegung der preußischen Suprematie in Deutschland, 1862–1864* (Hildesheim, 1978), p. 42

[46] Ernst August to Strangford, 8 June 1848, *Letters of the King of Hanover*, p. 156.

[47] Ernst August to Strangford, 15 May 1848, ibid., p. 152.

[48] Ernst August to Strangford, 29 August 1844, ibid., p. 56.

1854

2.3 King Johann of Saxony, on his accession to the throne in 1854.
Source: Staatliche Kunstsammlungen, Dresden, 15057/44657 Dresden Sax.2

wrote of his willingness to make sacrifices in order to maintain the unity of
the German Confederation.[49] In keeping with this policy, he later advised
Schwarzenberg of the need for a constitutional solution at the heart of the
German Confederation, arguing that if there were parliaments in the
German states then there should be a national parliament as well.[50]

---

[49] Cited after Mögle-Hofacker, *Zur Entwicklung des Parlamentarismus in Württemberg*, p. 2.
[50] Wilhelm to Schwarzenberg, 18 January 1851, cited after ibid., p. 134.

Equally, Johann accepted that repressive measures did little to increase the popularity of the German Confederation, and in 1832 declared himself ready to take a less petty approach to the German question.[51] True to his promise, he backed Beust's proposals for Confederal reform in the early 1860s. Ultimately, however, Wilhelm and Johann looked at German politics very differently. Wilhelm's approach was essentially pragmatic and his major concern was with Württemberg, not Germany. He regarded Confederal unity as important because he was aware that Württemberg would depend on Confederal armies in the event of war with France. At the same time, he considered the equal status accorded all members of the Confederation to be a recipe for disaster and wished, ideally, to see the smaller German states swallowed up by Bavaria, Hanover, Saxony and Württemberg.[52] Only the four Kingdoms could be trusted to act in Germany's interests, since they alone reflected public opinion and they alone represented the ancient German stock.[53] These views were almost identical with those of Ernst August, who also considered the status accorded the smaller states to be a great mistake and believed that only the four Kingdoms could bridge the gulf between Austria and Prussia and so foster German unity.[54] Both Wilhelm and Ernst August were principally concerned with power politics in their assessment of the German question. Johann's approach to the same problem was based on fundamentally different assumptions, for he was in some sense a German nationalist. When he wrote to the young Friedrich Wilhelm IV of the need for an effective reorganisation of the Confederation, he wrote also of their 'oft discussed patriotic fantasies'.[55] In his nationalist enthusiasms, as well as in his parliamentary experience, Johann had more in common with the political opposition in Germany than any of his fellow monarchs had.

The ability of a monarch to realise his political vision largely depended on his personality. On a most basic level, a monarch needed to put the necessary hours into his work and to be sufficiently strong-minded to

---

[51] Johann to Friedrich Wilhelm IV, 4 March 1832, *Briefwechsel*, ed. Johann Georg, Herzog zu Sachsen, p. 122.

[52] See Wilhelm, 'Gegenwärtiger Zustand in Deutschland', 31 July 1849; 'Politisches Testament für den künftigen Zustand Deutschlands', 1 January 1848; 'Denkschrift über den wirklichen Zustand in Deutschland', 20 January 1853, HSAStu G268 B24 (3, 37, 57).

[53] Wilhelm, 'Politisches Testament für den künftigen Zustand Deutschlands', 1 January 1848, HSAStu G268 B24 (37).

[54] Ernst August to Friedrich Wilhelm IV, 1 April 1851: 'Briefe Ernst Augusts von Hannover an König Friedrich Wilhelm IV.', pp. 180–1.

[55] Johann to Friedrich Wilhelm IV, 4 March 1832: *Briefwechsel*, ed. Johann Georg, Herzog zu Sachsen, p. 123.

impose his views on his ministers. Ernst August was quite right to describe the 'profession' of a king as 'no sinecure'.[56] He added that 'there is no day in the year that I have not twelve hours' work and very often sixteen'. As King of Hanover, Ernst August was determined to hold the reins of government in his own hands and resolved not to tolerate a 'de facto premier'.[57] According to the British Ambassador, he 'thought it incumbent upon him to attend to the minutest details of the administration of his country', and personally read every request and complaint he received, before writing or dictating a reply.[58] Similarly, Robert von Mohl described the dedication with which Wilhelm of Württemberg took his duties as King: 'The post would be brought to him early every morning and superficial matters decided forthwith. In cabinet he insisted upon carrying out all formal business to the letter . . . Every evening at dinner he signed documents. He met with ministers individually five days a week'.[59] Like Ernst August, Wilhelm was determined to remain in full control of government. He acquired a reputation for double-dealing and for acting 'behind the backs of his ministers and ambassadors'.[60] In fact, most kings were jealous of their authority and unwilling to be seen to play second fiddle to their ministers. Thus Johann of Saxony informed Wilhelm of Prussia in 1866 that his Foreign Minister, Beust, 'does not write a word without my approval, and if he did otherwise he would certainly cease to be my minister'.[61] Similarly, Georg of Hanover informed his Minister of the Interior that 'as monarch in a monarchic state' he had the right to issue special orders to his ministers if he thought it appropriate and, if need be, to ignore their advice.[62] Only Friedrich August II differed from this general pattern, partly as a result of the depression induced by his experiences during 1848/9. Yet it was no easy task for monarchs to remain in control of government in an increasingly parliamentary age. Their ability to do so reflected their personal stature. Both Ernst August and Wilhelm had forceful personalities and were able to impose their will on those around them even in old age. Despite being stone deaf, Wilhelm refused to wear a hearing aid, which must have made things very difficult for his ministers. Equally, Ernst August was so daunting a figure that no one was

---

[56] Ernst August to Strangford, 19 May 1844, *Letters of the King of Hanover*, p. 32.
[57] Ernst August to Friedrich Wilhelm IV, 30 October 1849, 'Briefe Ernst Augusts von Hannover an König Friedrich Wilhelm IV', p. 163.
[58] Bligh, 4 October 1838, cited after Willis, *Ernest Augustus*, p. 310.
[59] Mohl, *Lebens-Erinnerungen*, p. 17.   [60] Ibid., p. 19.
[61] Johann to Wilhelm I of Prussia., 8 May 1866: *Briefwechsel*, ed. Johann Georg, Herzog zu Sachsen, p. 442.   [62] Georg, cited after Brosius, 'Georg V. von Hannover', 275.

willing to cross him even on his death bed, with the result that the court theatre remained open and the last post continued to sound outside his window as he lay dying. Where the monarch did not command respect so instinctively, the situation was more problematic. Whilst the former Hanoverian minister, Stüve, was full of admiration for Ernst August's grasp of affairs, he had nothing but contempt for Georg's efforts to manage everything himself. Stüve reported how 'the poor King torments himself and his ministers with the desire to know everything down to the tiniest detail, sits up every evening until midnight hearing presentations, and becomes irritable and wretched with it all as a result of his physical frailty'.[63] This approach to rule was not in fact particularly unusual. Unfortunately for Georg, however, his blindness made it much harder for others to take either him or his vision of absolute royal authority seriously.

As this indicates, the success or failure of a monarch often had as much to do with style as with substance. Recent work on eighteenth-century absolutism has stressed the importance of representational culture in reinforcing the perception and reality of monarchic authority both at home and abroad. Ostentatious display, in the form of splendid buildings, monuments and celebrations, provided vivid and concrete proof of the power and wealth of a monarch. In particular, grand public ceremonies enabled onlookers to visualise and internalise the position of the monarch at the pinnacle of a complex social and political hierarchy, which he dominated absolutely. More specifically, historians such as Norbert Elias have focused on the role of the court and court festivities in subordinating the nobility – and, by extension, the state – to more effective royal control.[64] The court was an indispensable trapping of monarchy. It helped to set the King apart from his people and testified to the uniqueness of his office. Without a court, the King would have been little more than a glorified bureaucrat. At the same time, for Elias the absolute authority of the King over his household (the court) was essentially the same as that of any father in a patriarchal society.[65] Traditional views of monarchy were similarly paternalistic. A king was often described as *Landesvater*, or father of his country, and old-fashioned

---

[63] Stüve to Frommann, 16, 19 and 21 December 1851: *Briefe Johann Carl Bertram Stüves*, ed. Vogel, Vol. II, p. 714.

[64] See Norbert Elias, *The court society* (Oxford, 1983). Jeroen Duindam, *Myths of power. Norbert Elias and the early modern European court* (Amsterdam, 1995), provides an incisive critique of Elias's work. Duindam argues that the King was as much prisoner as master of court ritual, etiquette and the pressures for conspicuous consumption as a gauge of status.   [65] Elias, *Court society*, p. 41.

monarchs like Ernst August likened their relationship with their subjects to that of a father with his children. In this context, the court acted as a model for the whole state, providing a paradigm of absolute royal authority in action. Indeed, the court was an integral part of society, forming the core of a state's social elite. Exclusive at its centre, the court nevertheless remained open at the periphery to the forces of social change. Indeed, the ability of a court to integrate new elements was an important factor in the survival of monarchy and its continued relevance in the state as a whole.

By 1815 the royal courts of Germany had already undergone a substantial transformation since their eighteenth-century heyday.[66] The Seven Years War had drained many monarchs of resources. Consequently, they were forced to cut back on their lavish spending and to rationalise the new, more modest, courtly life-style in terms of the contemporary cult of simplicity. Court expenditure in a German *Mittelstaat* in the early 1820s averaged about 10% of the annual state budget, compared with up to 20% in eighteenth-century Bavaria and 50–60% in late eighteenth-century Baden.[67] Yet changes in the style of courtly life were not motivated by economic factors alone. Rulers like Friedrich Wilhelm III of Prussia genuinely internalised the values of their bourgeois subjects and came to expect a separation of their public role from the private sphere of home and family. The court of Württemberg provided a striking example of this process in action.[68] As a newly elevated King with absolutist aspirations, Friedrich I had lavished money, time and effort on his court during the Napoleonic era. Friedrich himself loved pomp and circumstance, but he also understood courtly representation as an important way in which Württemberg could claim equality of status with more well-established European monarchies. In 1807 Friedrich's court was already 1130 strong; by 1812 it numbered 1510 and its annual expenditure was 256,000 *Gulden* – significantly higher than the budget allocated.[69] Court ceremonial also provided an effective way of depressing the pretensions of the mediatised nobility, by consistently underlining their subordinate position in the new Kingdom of Württemberg. In this sense, it played an important part in the state-building process. In the years immediately following his elevation,

[66] For a good summary of this tranformation see Ute Daniel, *Hoftheater. Zur Geschichte des Theaters und der Höfe im 18. und 19. Jahrhundert* (Stuttgart, 1995), pp. 115–25.   [67] Ibid., pp. 119–22.
[68] For further detail see Paul Sauer, 'Der württembergische Hof in der ersten Hälfte des 19. Jahrhunderts', in Karl Möckl (ed.), *Hof und Hofgesellschaft in den deutschen Staaten im 19. und beginnenden 20. Jahrhundert* (Boppard am Rhein,1990), pp. 92–127.   [69] Ibid., pp. 97–8.

Friedrich published three different orders of precedence (*Hofrangordnung*) and two guides to court ceremonial and etiquette. Each was more grudging than the last in the status it accorded the mediatised nobility, promoting those with court offices in their stead. All this changed under Friedrich's son Wilhelm. Wilhelm was temperamentally averse to court ceremonial. In 1815 he wrote to his second wife Katharina, 'I shall always loathe large gatherings of people who, most of the time, dislike one another cordially and wish to make us forget this by their false courtesy.'[70] On coming to power, he drastically reduced the cost and size of his court and sought to restrict representational splendour to special occasions. In 1821 Wilhelm issued a new *Hofrangordnung*, which concerned itself exclusively with those in court or state service, and excluded members of the nobility. Indeed, non-mediatised nobles who did not also hold high office lost their automatic entitlement to attend at court. This reflected an important change in the self-image of the courtly social elite, since the latter ceased to be defined in terms of birth and began instead to be defined by its service to the King and his state. Similar changes took place in the Saxon court during the nineteenth century.[71] In 1819 the court employed 1200 functionaries, but by 1900 it employed a mere 619. More importantly, the Saxon constitution of 1831 brought with it a new *Hofrangordnung*. Previously the High Court Marshal had taken precedence over state ministers and the presidents of the upper and lower houses of parliament. After 1831 the situation was reversed, reflecting the changed priorities of a constitutional state. By 1900 the order of precedence had become a mirror of the Saxon administration, including the mayors of Leipzig and Dresden, the manager of the Saxon coal works and so forth. This reflected a conscious effort to integrate new structures into the Saxon court. Consequently, the court acted as a focus for the whole state and a forum in which leading figures could socialise with one another. If the personnel was different, much of the court ritual remained the same and the court therefore provided a source of stability and continuity in a time of change.

It is tempting to equate this decline in grandeur with the domestication of monarchy that has been identified during this period. Historians such as David Cannadine and Simon Schama have attributed the revival of the British monarchy during the course of the nineteenth century to

---

[70] Wilhelm to Katharina, 1815, cited after Mögle-Hofacker, *Zur Entwicklung des Parlamentarismus in Württemberg*, p. 195, n. 1375.

[71] For further detail see Karlheinz Blashke, 'Hof und Hofgesellschaft im Königreich Sachsen während des 19. Jahrhunderts', in Möckl, *Hof und Hofgesellschaft in den deutschen Staaten*, pp. 177–206.

a combination of ceremonial and domesticity, as Queen Victoria successfully came to project both the power of Empire and the middle-class
morality of a happy family life.[72] The strength of the late nineteenth-
century British monarchy, however, lay precisely in its combination of
these two factors. Certainly, it was important for court ritual and court
society to move with the times. Yet it was equally important for the court
to retain its exotic otherness. Bourgeois morals were one thing, a bourgeois life-style was quite another. The British public may have approved
Victoria's happy domesticity, but they were less enthusiastic when her
bereavement led her to retire from public life altogether. The example of
the Hanoverian court before 1866 demonstrates only too clearly the
dangers of excessive embourgeoisement.[73] Under Ernst August, the
Hanoverian court had seen a brief return to its past glories. According to
Malortie, Ernst August and his wife Friederike understood only too well
how to 'secure the prestige of the court . . . to summon forth the aura that
is called for in order to raise the standing of the crown and to set the tone
at court in such a way as to reap the significant political benefits that
render the court itself of such importance'.[74] At the same time, Malortie
stresses that Ernst August's penchant for etiquette and ceremony was
restricted to his public activities. In private, of course, he lived simply and
modestly.[75] Consequently, court life under Ernst August did combine the
'British' virtues of both grandeur and domesticity. Under Georg,
however, the balance shifted too far towards the latter. For despite Georg's
belief in the divine authority of monarchy, he had little liking for court
ritual. His confidant Oskar Meding described how during the summer,
when Georg and his wife Marie holidayed on the Island of Nordeney,
they lived the lives of ordinary citizens as far as possible.[76] The King and
his entourage exchanged their court uniforms for civilian dress, and even
his servants for the most part wore black travelling uniforms. Every
evening Georg would invite some forty of his fellow tourists to dinner,
many of whom were not strictly eligible to attend court at all. For
Meding, this behaviour testified to Georg's charming informality.

---

[72] On the revival of royal ceremonial in Britain, see David Cannadine's seminal article 'The
context, performance and meaning of ritual: the British monarchy and the "invention of tradition", c. 1820–1977' in Eric Hobsbawm and Terence Ranger (eds.), *The invention of tradition*
(Cambridge, 1983), pp. 101–64; on the imagery of the royal family, see Simon Schama, 'The
domestication of majesty: royal family portraiture, 1500–1850', *The Journal of Interdisciplinary
History* 17:1 (1986), 155–84.

[73] For further detail see Heide Barmeyer, 'Hof und Hofgesellschaft in Hannover im 18. und 19.
Jahrhundert', in Möckl, *Hof und Hofgesellschaft in den deutschen Staaten*, pp. 239–73.

[74] Malortie, *König Ernst August*, pp. 51–2.   [75] Ibid., p. 69.

[76] Meding, *Memoiren zur Zeitgeschichte*, Vol. I, pp. 163–5.

2.4 King Georg V of Hanover. Georg is dressed in uniform, as was usual in
monarchic portraits of this kind. In Georg's case, however, his blindness meant that
the military associations of the image were entirely symbolic.
Source: Historisches Museum, Hanover, VM8815

In fact, it was probably a consequence of the blindness that made it
impossible for Georg to appreciate the visual drama of ceremonial occasions. Yet Georg always sought to fulfil his duties impeccably. Julius
Hartmann, a Hanoverian soldier, recalled how Georg 'sought to hide his
blindness. Often he spoke as if he saw, and the person guiding him had
to nudge him imperceptibly so as to let him know in time when and

where the King was to go or whom he was to greet.' Under these circumstances, the demands of elaborate ritual must have been particularly trying.[77] In any event, Georg's contemporaries were scathing about the consequences. Otto Borchers noted the preference accorded 'bourgeois elements' at the Hanoverian court, and described how the nobility, which had been a bulwark of legitimacy under Ernst August, began to avoid the court altogether, so that they became 'remarkable for their absence'.[78] Instead, all kinds of unsuitable individuals were invited to the court balls, which took place in the court theatre. This did nothing to enhance the standing of the monarchy and its court – quite the reverse. Borchers explained that Queen Marie hoped to make herself popular through neglecting the stiff rituals of the court gala and socialising informally with her guests. Instead, she attracted only widespread ridicule. Indeed, Borchers laid the blame for the decline of the Hanoverian court under Georg V squarely at her door.

The fate of the Hanoverian court under Ernst August and his son is certainly a striking case study of the crucial supportive role played by a royal consort. Tellingly, Malortie paid particular tribute to Queen Friederike when describing the panache with which Ernst August brought the Hanoverian court back to life after 1837: 'in this respect the Queen made the greatest contribution; the distinguished lady had the most extensive experience of everything which might add to the court's dignity and standing'.[79] The fame of the Hanoverian court spread far and wide in consequence. Friederike's flair for court life was the product of her early years in Berlin, as the sister of Queen Luise and wife of Friedrich Wilhelm III's brother. Consequently, she knew what was expected of her. The life experience of Marie could hardly have been more different. Brought up at the modest court of her father, the Duke of Saxe-Altenburg, she never became comfortable with the elaborate etiquette of the Hanoverian court under Ernst August, who exacerbated her difficulties by his brusque and unkind behaviour. According to Julius Hartmann, her manner was shy and uncertain and she consequently preferred to socialise in small groups.[80] Whatever the reasons for her conduct, contemporaries were fairly unstinting in their criticisms. Borchers spoke damningly of the 'more than simple, I would even say petty-bourgeois attitude with which the Queen approached her duties'.[81]

[77] Julius Hartmann, *Meine Erlebnisse zu hannoversche Zeit, 1839–1866* (Wiesbaden, 1912), p. 118.
[78] Borchers, *Unter welfischem Szepter*, pp. 56–7.   [79] Malortie, *König Ernst August*, p. 51.
[80] Hartmann, *Meine Erlebnisse zu hannoversche Zeit*, pp. 118–19.
[81] Borchers, *Unter welfischem Szepter*, p. 56.

Georg's blindness rendered these failings all the more disastrous, since her influence (or lack of it) was commensurately greater. Moreover, her attitude had important political ramifications. For Marie's social awkwardness was such that she avoided contact with other German royalty. Whereas Friederike and Ernst August had received a glittering array of royal visitors, under Marie and Georg 'the social pull of the Hanoverian court was reduced to a minimum, excepting only occasional interaction with the Altenburg relatives and the Queen's married sisters'.[82] More seriously still, Marie did nothing to further the connection between Crown Prince Ernst August and the next generation of German monarchs, nor did she make any effort to find him a suitably well-connected wife. Meding recalled how, for instance, she discouraged the young Ernst August from accepting Ludwig II of Bavaria's invitation to visit him in Munich.[83] As a consequence, the Welfs were left isolated during the critical months of 1866. This contrasts strikingly with the position of the Saxon royal family at the same time: Johann nurtured his family ties with the Prussian royal house through his close friendship with Friedrich Wilhelm IV, whose wife was his own wife's sister.

More generally, a popular and active consort was an indispensable adjunct for any ruler and an important aspect of the monarchy's popular appeal. In Württemberg, the memory of Wilhelm's second wife, Queen Katharina, was cherished long after her death to an extent wholly out of keeping with her very brief reign. Official literature invariably stressed Katharina's motherly concern for the people of Württemberg during the famine years 1816/17, and her various far-sighted philanthropic activities.[84] There are strong parallels here with the process of beatification that overtook Queen Luise of Prussia after her similarly untimely death.[85] A neo-classical mausoleum was built for Katharina on top of the Württemberg itself, the site of the royal family's long-vanished ancestral seat. Like Luise's, Katharina's benevolent spirit was believed to be watching over the country. In 1858 when Wilhelm lay seriously ill, the Swabian romantic writer Justinus Kerner wrote a poem entitled 'On January the Ninth' (the day of Katharina's death), and addressed the Queen as follows:

---

[82] Ibid., p. 55.   [83] Meding, *Memoiren zur Zeitgeschichte*, Vol. 1, p. 255.

[84] On Queen Katharina, myth and reality, see Eberhard Fritz, 'König Wilhelm und Königin Katharina von Württemberg. Studien zur höfischen Repräsentation im Spiegel der Hofdiarien', *Zeitschrift für Württembergische Landesgeschichte* 54 (1995), 157–78.

[85] On this see Wulf Wülfing, Karin Bruns and Rolf Parr, *Historische Mythologie der Deutschen, 1798–1918* (Munich, 1991), pp. 58–95.

Angel thou, amongst the stars, float earthbound, close at hand
Thou, whose heart still feels for us, though bath'd in heavenly light.
Disperse from us with a breath of love this dark and fearful night
Oh Katharina! Guardian spirit, watching o'er our land![86]

Unsurprisingly, perhaps, Wilhelm's third wife Pauline found it hard to live up to her predecessor's reputation. Nevertheless, she too received her due in Wilhelm's official obituary, which was read aloud in churches throughout the land the Sunday after his death.[87] The obituary dwelt among other things on Wilhelm's philanthropic activities, adding that in this 'his consort . . . worked faithfully and tirelessly at his side'. Yet the language used to describe Pauline was of a very different order to that which described Katharina. With Katharina's death, the King had lost 'his treasured consort, the people the beloved mother of the country (*Landesmutter*)', but with Wilhelm's remarriage he himself had gained merely a 'noble consort' and the people a 'well-loved princess', whilst only Wilhelm's orphaned children had found a 'loving mother'. Even this was a fairly idealised view of the situation, since the marriage was far from happy. According to Robert von Mohl, the royal couple only kept up appearances and often went for years without exchanging a word, whilst Wilhelm's long liaison with an actress significantly diminished his popularity.[88] Under these circumstances, the emphasis accorded his third marriage in the obituary is striking. It testifies to the important role of the royal family in general and the Queen in particular in the public image of monarchy. The King and Queen were often referred to as one unit, 'the royal couple' (*das Königspaar*), and in many ways the two functioned as different sides of the same coin. As a woman, the Queen mediated the more feminine facets of rule, enabling the King to demonstrate tender, loving care for his subjects alongside the sterner monarchic qualities of wisdom, justice and honour. To simplify, the King commanded fear, respect and obedience as well as loyalty, but the Queen inspired more uncomplicated feelings of love and gratitude for her charity and good deeds.

This well-worn paradigm began to change in the nineteenth century. Gradually, the King ceased to be as distant and awesome a figure as the absolutist rulers of the past. Instead, the King was expected to be close

[86] Justinus Kerner to H. M., 13 January 1858, HSAStu 14 30 [1858] (9).
[87] 'Zur Vorlesung in den Kirchen des Landes am Sonntag den 24/07/1864: Lebensabriß des verewigten Königs Wilhelm von Württemberg', HSAStu E200 508 (ad24).
[88] Mohl, *Lebens-Erinnerungen*, p. 19.

to his people, to be both different from his subjects and at the same time 'one of us'. This was a hard balance to strike, as the Hanoverian example indicates, for a successful monarch needed to be approachable and open without diminishing his own worth. Still, it was possible – as Ernst August of Hanover and Wilhelm of Württemberg demonstrated. Both were redoubtable and intimidating figures, but accounts of their reign also stress the simple warmth with which they interacted with their subjects. Ernst August, for instance, was available to see all his subjects on Wednesday afternoons, and subsequent propaganda made much of this fact. A pocket calendar published by the Welfist German-Hanoverian Party in 1887 described one such encounter between Ernst August and Friederich Schmidt, a toll-gate keeper and tailor from Walsrode, who was encountering difficulties obtaining a medal and small pension for his service during the Napoleonic wars.[89] Schmidt had made himself a replica of the Hussar's uniform from 1813, and on seeing this strange outfit Ernst August cried 'Yes, it's definitely a Hussar, an old Hussar!' and they chatted about his war experiences for a while, before Ernst August promised to see to the matter. This was not good enough for Schmidt, however, who confided to the King that he dare not go back to his wife without the medal. 'A Hussar under the slipper,' Ernst August laughed, 'Well, you need not worry; you shall have it.' In stories like this, Ernst August's majesty was briefly overshadowed by his humanity, since he related to the hen-pecked Schmidt as man to man, and not as King to subject. Of course, this easy relationship between the King and his people was very much a two-way phenomenon, in which each stretched out towards the other. An official account of Wilhelm's silver jubilee celebrations reported that the oldest man in the jubilee procession was a baker called Merz, from Dürrwangen, 'who could not overcome the urge' to take part.[90] Merz was so weak that he had to be supported by two of his fellow bakers, who lifted his hat for him when Wilhelm passed by because Merz lacked the strength to do so himself. On seeing this, the King rode up to him and bowed to the old man. Merz's devotion was quite as important to this story as Wilhelm's touching respect for his years. The same point was made by Napoleon III on his visit to Stuttgart in 1857 during a conversation with Wilhelm's chief adjutant, General Lieutenant von Braur-Breitenfeld.[91] Napoleon remarked on the warmth of his welcome in Stuttgart, to which Braur-Breitenfeld replied 'that the

[89] Cited after Willis, *Ernest Augustus*, pp. 308–9.   [90] Cited after Grauer, *Wilhelm I.*, pp. 260–1.
[91] Cited after ibid., p. 371.

King went into the city almost every day, riding or driving, without any company and without being insulted by anyone'. Napoleon was much struck by this, commenting: 'he is to be envied'. This kind of casual inter-action between monarch and subjects would have been unthinkable in the days of Wilhelm's father Friedrich, who would have regarded it as beneath his dignity. Even if largely apocryphal, such stories reflect a new, more populist approach to monarchy at this time. Ernst August and Wilhelm were not exceptional, they were part of a wider pattern. Thus Heinz Gollwitzer has shown how Max I of Bavaria likewise adopted a more informal image and cultivated direct contact with his subjects.[92] Equally, Friedrich Wilhelm III of Prussia was known as the Citizen-King. Yet not all monarchs were able to make this transition to a more populist monarchy. Georg of Hanover's blindness inevitably placed a barrier between him and his subjects, for all his informal intercourse with musicians and historians. Similarly, the scholarly Johann of Saxony was temperamentally unsuited to such an approach and his fervent Catholicism always set him apart from the staunchly Protestant Saxons.

By contrast, both Ernst August of Hanover and Wilhelm of Württemberg went to great lengths to get to know their subjects. Ernst August was an avid reader of the Hanover police reports, which kept him abreast of what was happening. Indeed, one story recounts that he informed a doctor that his home had been burgled before the man even knew himself. Similarly, the *großdeutsch* journalist Albert Schäffle described how Wilhelm always read the small advertisements in the Württemberg press so that he could understand his people's needs.[93] According to Schäffle, Wilhelm had a wonderful memory for faces and studied how his people lived through contact with 'members of every estate'; he was 'not just King of the Swabians, but a Swabian himself'. Robert von Mohl endorsed this verdict, stating that Wilhelm 'knew the country and its people better than anyone because he travelled widely, without any fuss, and often without any entourage'.[94] Royal travels of this kind played a very important part in popularising the monarchy and making it relevant to those who lived outside the capital. Men like Merz and Schmidt no longer needed to travel so far in order to encoun-ter royalty. Moreover, these trips helped the King to reach out beyond

---

[92] See Heinz Gollwitzer, 'Fürst und Volk, Betrachtungen zur Selbsbehauptung des bayerischen Herrscherhauses im 19. und 20. Jahrhundert', *Zeitschrift für bayerische Landesgeschichte* 50 (1987), 723–47, especially 726–30.
[93] Albert Eberhard Friedrich Schäffle, *Aus meinem Leben* (Berlin, 1905), pp. 125–6.
[94] Mohl, *Lebens-Erinnerungen*, p. 18.

2.5 King Ernst August of Hanover. This portrait of the King at work is a relatively
informal image, which presents Ernst August in a private moment – even though it
depicts him wearing military uniform in grand surroundings. Revealingly, it was the
only portrait of the Ernst August to appear in his official commemorative album,
indicating the fine line between traditional symbolism and more modern images of
monarchy in government propaganda.
Source: By permission of the British Library, J/9930.h.21

the dissatisfied newspaper-reading classes to the supposedly loyal
masses. When Ernst August came to power in 1837 and announced his
intention of revoking the Hanoverian constitution, he promptly set out
on a tour of his realm. He wrote to his wife that he was 'fully convinced
that my tour is *worth millions*', and described to his brother-in-law how
'everywhere that I have been, I have witnessed the greatest proofs of
love, respect and loyalty. Peasants, you know, are not courtiers, or make
pretences, so that if they come eight to twelve miles on foot in rows,
yearning only to see their King and master and to give a cheer for him,
then it is their genuine taste that moves them.'[95] More objective sources

---

[95] Ernst August to Friederike, 20 November 1837 and to the Grand-Duke of Mecklenburg-Strelitz,
24 November 1837. Cited after Willis, *Ernest Augustus*, pp. 290–1.

confirmed the warmth of Ernst August's welcome in his new country. The British ambassador wrote that his reception had been 'everywhere . . . very warm and even enthusiastic'.[96] Certainly, Ernst August's travels enabled him to get his message across to a wide audience. For instance, in 1838 he passed through the town of Winsen, which had benefited from his provision of the necessary funds to replace a burst dyke. Ernst August took advantage of this connection, and reportedly told the inhabitants of Winsen:

> I wish to prove to each of you that . . . I have only your welfare and happiness at heart. I demonstrated this when I came to your aid in your time of need . . . Do not, then, believe all this nonsense from newspapers and evil-minded people. These people do not desire your happiness . . . Just trust your King, who is really sincere with you, and you will be happy.[97]

In a society where the locality remained the primary frame of reference, such an appeal was very likely to succeed.

The arrival of the King in a particular town or area was almost always cause for celebration by its inhabitants. Flags, cheering crowds, triumphal arches and official delegations marked the monarch's progress through his country. During his tour of 1838, Ernst August was met everywhere by 'friendly faces and hearty greetings which one could see came from the heart, all villages decorated with flowers and garlands, the streets packed, the windows full, and the women waving their kerchiefs'.[98] Popular greetings of this kind drew on long-standing traditions of welcoming great men, just as the royal tours of Ernst August and Wilhelm echoed the royal progresses of previous eras. Yet in terms of quantity and scale, the royal tours of the nineteenth century marked a new departure. In part, this simply reflected greater ease of travel in the age of the post road and the railway. On another level, however, popular welcomes of this kind reflected a wider democratisation of royal ceremony that is apparent in other aspects of monarchic practice. In the past, monarchic rituals had primarily taken place behind closed doors. That is to say, their principal audience had been the court nobility, who were also the main participants. Besides this, court festivities had been intended to impress fellow monarchs and the European aristocracy, but they had neither targeted nor involved the general public. In the nineteenth century, however, royal ceremonial began to address a wider audience, and the people themselves acquired a limited role in the proceedings. To some extent this

---

[96] Bligh, 17 July 1838, cited after ibid., p. 305. [97] Cited after ibid., p. 301.
[98] Ernst August to Friderike, 23 June 1838. Cited after ibid., p. 301.

reflected the diminished grandeur of German courts and the more populist tastes of their monarchs. Wilhelm of Württemberg, for one, confided in his wife Katharina: 'I delight above all in *fêtes populaires*, I love to mingle with the crowd, to hear and see that honest gaiety, and to study the national character thereby, I prefer it a thousand times to the fashionable society parties.'[99] Yet the democratisation of ceremony also reflected the conscious deployment of royal pageantry as an attempt to conciliate the masses.

Unlike their British counterparts, the German monarchs rarely went in for coronations. Instead, they found other opportunities for the public celebration of monarchy. Most common were the celebrations that marked the monarch's birthday and the rites of passage of his family – christenings, weddings and funerals. There were more notable occasions, such as Wilhelm of Württemberg's silver jubilee in 1841 or the festivities that marked Ernst August's fifty years of service in the Hanoverian army. Equally, there were commonplace occurrences made extraordinary by their political context, like Johann's return to Dresden after the *Frankfurter Fürstentag* in 1863 or the ageing Wilhelm's return to Stuttgart after a brief holiday shortly before his death.

The celebrations that were held to mark Ernst August's eighty-first birthday provide a typical example of such an occasion. Malortie recounts that the King of Prussia arrived in Hanover the day before the main festivities began, and that night Ernst August received a procession of 412 miners from the Harz mountains. The procession consisted of ironworkers, miners carrying lanterns, musicians, and waggoners dressed in white aprons, all of whom carried flags and emblems. The reception ended with a cheer and a musical salute. This was followed by a Ceremonial Tattoo with fireworks in the city centre, which raised hearty cheers from the assembled crowds. The birthday itself was greeted by a peal of bells rung throughout the city, whilst flowers and flags waved from its towers and trumpets played. The population thronged the streets in their finest clothes. Special church services were held, and Ernst August received deputations from government authorities throughout the land. At noon there was a grand parade, and then the palace gardens were opened to the populace. That night a gala performance was held in the court theatre, followed by a grand court banquet attended by some eight hundred guests. Meanwhile alms were

---

[99] Wilhelm to Katharina, 1815, cited after Mögle-Hofacker, *Zur Entwicklung des Parlamentarismus in Württemberg*, p. 195, n. 1375.

distributed amongst the poor of the city and its suburbs, and bonuses were paid to all employees of the court, as well as those who worked in the royal gardens and palaces. The festivities were orchestrated in such a way as to maximise the combination of grandeur and populism. The arrival of Friedrich Wilhelm IV of Prussia and the 'exclusive' court banquet for eight hundred people testified to Ernst August's standing amongst his fellow monarchs and the Hanoverian nobility, adding a touch of class to the celebrations. The procession from the Harz, the deputations from government authorities and the grand parade demonstrated his popularity amongst ordinary people and the whole country's involvement in the festivities. The fireworks, the opening of the royal gardens and the distribution of alms to the poor all added to the enjoyment of the masses and helped to guarantee their enthusiastic participation in the event. Moreover, the celebrations took place in the immediate aftermath of the 1848/9 revolution. In this context, the presence of Friedrich Wilhelm IV of Prussia and the outpouring of popular loyalty acquired added significance. Taken individually, however, few of the elements of this extravaganza were in any way remarkable. Taken as a whole, these festivities were out of all proportion to the event they celebrated. The increasing frequency of celebrations of this kind reflected the importance attached to public demonstrations of royal popularity. In the past this had been restricted to genuinely significant occasions, now even an eighty-first birthday could unleash a flood of pomp and circumstance. Johann of Saxony himself noted this changing climate, when he recalled the celebrations held to mark Friedrich August the Just's jubilee year in 1818, but noted that 'these were not the effusive celebrations, which are commonly held nowadays even with far less cause'.[100]

By the time of Wilhelm's death in 1864, pageantry had become an indispensable facet of monarchy in the German states. In his will, Wilhelm gave explicit instructions for a simple funeral because, as he said, 'since in my lifetime I found nothing more objectionable than ceremonies or etiquette, so do I desire not to be laid out in state, nor for any pomp to accompany my burial'.[101] Wilhelm's son Karl ignored the request. Some 30,000 Hanoverians had filed past the body of Ernst August when he lay in state in Hanover 1851, and Karl clearly wanted Wilhelm's death to provide a similar demonstration of state unity.[102] His

---

[100] *Lebenserinnerungen des Königs Johann von Sachsen*, ed. Kretzschmar, p. 59.
[101] Cited after Grauer, *Wilhelm I.*, p. 421.   [102] Figure given by Malortie, *König Ernst August*, p. 202.

hopes were not misplaced, since more than 15,000 Württembergers came to pay their last respects to Wilhelm, dressed in their Sunday best.[103] The sheer number of mourners who attended these occasions testifies to the enduring power and popularity of monarchy in mid-nineteenth-century Germany. There can be no doubt that monarchy remained enormously relevant to many people's lives. In this sense, the monarchs of states like Hanover, Saxony and Württemberg appear to have risen triumphantly to the challenges of the post-1815 era, successfully adapting monarchy to the new, nineteenth-century context.

How can we reconcile the popularity of monarchy with the undoubted strength of liberalism in pre-unification Germany? Of course, the two phenomena were not necessarily contradictory. After all, like the kings themselves, most liberals were advocates of constitutional monarchy and only very radical democrats advocated a republic. Nevertheless, it is worth asking whether the personal popularity of an individual monarch bore any relationship to the political situation whatsoever. After all, the popularity of Wilhelm of Württemberg and Ernst August of Hanover did nothing to prevent the outbreak of revolution in 1848 in either of these states. Conversely, the emergence of the Württemberg People's Party and the growing pressure for political reform during the early 1860s was perfectly compatible with the mass outpouring of public grief which greeted Wilhelm's death in 1864. One explanation for this dichotomy is that the Württemberg public who filed past Wilhelm's corpse were not the same people who represented liberal 'public opinion'. In other words, monarchy and liberalism appealed to two very different constituencies. This is certainly how monarchs themselves understood the situation. Ernst August, for one, made a clear distinction between the peasants who flocked to see him on his journey through Hanover in 1837 and '*Messieurs les avocats, les canailleurs et les libéraux*', who made such a fuss about the 1833 constitution.[104] Similarly, Wilhelm of Württemberg blamed a seditious communist minority for the events of 1848, believing that they had led his 'good subjects' astray.[105] There is some evidence to support these views. For instance, official accounts of Wilhelm's funeral stressed the fact that 'large numbers of country folk came from near and far', indicating that the monarchy was particularly popular amongst the

---

[103] Figure given in Grauer, *Wilhelm I.*, p. 422.
[104] Ernst August to Friederike, 20 November 1837 and to the Grand-Duke of Mecklenburg-Strelitz, 24 November 1837. Cited after Willis, *Ernest Augustus*, pp. 290–1.
[105] Wilhelm, 11 November 1854, cited after Grauer, *Wilhelm I.*, p. 338.

peasantry – hardly a major source of membership for the Württemberg People's Party.[106] Nevertheless, this interpretation was essentially misleading. In moments of crisis, the lower classes proved no more reliable than other sectors of the population. Peasants revolted in 1848 just as readily as townspeople. Thus Wilhelm himself was surprised to find that his personal presence was not enough to quell the Stuttgart riots of 1845 peacefully. He wrote that 'I thought that in showing myself and in calming things down I could prevent yet greater misfortune, but the cries and the anger were stronger than reason: I gave the order to shoot'.[107] Such incidents point up the fundamental conflict of interest between King and people, for all their public demonstration of unity on occasions like royal birthdays and state funerals. Equally, the popular support shown for monarchy was clearly not unconditional. Indeed, it was quite possible to combine loyalty to the monarchy and opposition to his government. To some extent, this was merely a variant on the age-old practice of loving the monarch and loathing his advisors. Thus an undercover agent attending an agricultural festival in the Hanoverian town of Celle in the 1860s heard many worthy citizens argue: 'One must have a ruler, and our King is very good. He just needs good advisors'.[108] The same agent encountered one particular farmer who would willingly 'die for His Majesty, but nevertheless set great store by the fact that he had been an elector for the past twenty-seven years and *always* voted for the *opposition*'. The author concluded rightly that this kind of opposition to the government would never become truly revolutionary. In other words, where royalism and opposition coexisted in a single breast, each diluted the other.

Even so, the character of monarchy in nineteenth-century Germany was clearly shaped by the political context. Monarchy may not have affected the growth of liberalism, but liberalism certainly forced monarchy to change. By the end of their reigns, Ernst August, Wilhelm of Württemberg, Friedrich August II and Johann of Saxony had all faced up to the demands for modern constitutional and representative government, recognising the need to cooperate with parliament, to work with not against the will of the people, in short to move with the times. For all their personal and political differences, the fundamental similarity of

[106] Cited after ibid., p. 422.
[107] Wilhelm to Hohenlohe-Kirchberg, 9 May 1847: Mögle Hofacker, *Zur Entwicklung des Parlamentarismus in Württemberg*, p. 42, n. 251.
[108] 'Die Säcularfeier der K. Landwirtschaftsgesellschaft zu Celle am 3. und 4. Juni 1864', 13 June 1864, HSAHan Dep. 103 IX 286.

developments under these four monarchs is hard to ignore. Only Georg V of Hanover did not conform to this pattern. He alone made the disastrous mistake of refusing to follow the liberal constitutional path. Yet even Georg was not averse to modernising the monarchy in other ways, through cultural, journalistic and educational propaganda. This concern with public opinion reflected an awareness that the views of the people mattered and that kings could no longer afford to ignore their subjects. In eighteenth-century politics, the nobility were to all intents and purposes the nation. Consequently, the nobility had been the main focus of royal interest and activity. In the nineteenth century, this was no longer the case. To survive, monarchy needed to become outward looking. Through the greater openness of their courts and the democratisation of monarchic ritual, the Kings of Hanover, Saxony and Württemberg showed their willingness to find a new place in public life.

CHAPTER THREE

Cultures of the Fatherland

In 1822 the *Württembergisches Jahrbuch* neatly summarised the predicament of the Württemberg state in the years after 1815: 'We have Old and New Württembergers, Hohenlohers, Ellwangers, Upper Austrians, Imperial City dwellers, and all the rest, but as yet we have no Württemberg *Volk*.'[1] From the point of view of many German governments, this analysis was alarmingly accurate. States that had expanded during the Napoleonic era were not yet meaningful units for their inhabitants; they were simply a hotchpotch of people and places. Consequently, the need to forge a state out of these disparate entities was probably the most important challenge faced by governments at this time. The constitutional and administrative reforms of the 1810s and 1820s were one approach to this problem and many governments chose to go down this path. Yet measures of this kind only tackled the problem indirectly. Some voices advocated a more direct approach. The *Württembergisches Jahrbuch*, for instance, argued that '[t]here can be no true love of the Fatherland, where there is no knowledge of the Fatherland' and consciously sought to promote both. The *Jahrbuch* provided an outlet for the scholarly study of Württemberg and its people with the explicit intention of fostering patriotism. By adopting Württemberg as the basic unit for the study of history, geography and natural history, contributors to the *Jahrbuch* hoped to establish the state as the natural frame of reference for its inhabitants.

Neither the *Jahrbuch* itself, nor the underlying assumptions behind it, were particularly unusual in states like Württemberg. After 1815 German governments did all they could to encourage popular awareness of the particular Fatherland through state-sponsored cultural

---

[1] *Württembergisches Jahrbuch* (1822). Cited after Friedemann Schmoll, *Verewigte Nation, Studien zur Erinnerungskultur von Reich und Einzelstaat im württembergischen Denkmalkult des 19. Jahrhunderts* (Tübingen, 1995), p. 20.

activities, which were intended to unite the people behind their King
and his dynasty. By 1871 a culture which celebrated the particular
Fatherland had emerged in many of the larger German states. These
new state cultures were both genuine and artificial. On the one hand,
spontaneous cultural activities often focused on the particular
Fatherland because it was closer and more accessible than the wider
Germany. On the other hand, government policy actively promoted
cultural activities in four important areas: history, museums, monuments and festivities. Before 1848, spontaneous cultural activity predominated. After the revolution, cultural policy became an increasingly
important element in particularist state-building and the official character of state culture was more apparent. What was the relationship
between the apparently spontaneous and the more programmatic elements of particularist culture during this period? How far were these
state-based cultures a genuine expression of particularist feeling? How
did state-based cultural activities in these states relate to national cultural developments and, indeed, to national political issues?

Certainly, the emergence of these state cultures went hand in hand
with the growth of a self-consciously German culture at national level.
Indeed, the two developments were closely linked. The cultures of the
particular Fatherland were the building blocks of a German national
culture, just as the states themselves together made up Germany. There
was nothing new about this. In the past, German cultural activity had
been almost exclusively state-based because artists, writers and musicians had depended on the German princes for their livelihoods. Official
sponsorship of the arts remained very important in the nineteenth
century, despite the emergence of other (principally bourgeois) patrons.
Moreover, just as cultural activities at state level played a part in national
culture, so growing interest in a national culture and heritage prompted
these cultural activities in the first place. For contemporaries, the two
levels were inter-connected: interest in the particular Fatherland was an
expression of interest in the greater, national Fatherland.

Cultural activities at both national and state level should also be
understood in the context of the wider transformation of European
politics and culture as a consequence of the French Revolution. In the
past, high culture had always been closely related to the exercise of
political power because only the rich and powerful could afford to pay
for it. Consequently, high culture had served to reinforce the values of
a social and political elite. This changed with the French Revolution,
when successive revolutionary governments consciously attempted to

create a new political culture to fit the new political context. As a result, culture became both more explicitly politicised and more contentious. Revolutionary festivals and celebrations were perhaps the most important expressions of this new political culture, but the revolution permeated all the arts: architecture, painting, theatre, music, monuments and museums. To some extent, this revolutionary political culture created its own symbolic language – revolutionaries sang the *Marseillaise* and wore *tricolore* cockades – but it also drew heavily on older practices. Thus processions of burghers, schoolchildren and virgins clad in white made their way through the streets during revolutionary festivals, just as they always had done in traditional civic celebrations. Equally, the 'liberty trees' planted by revolutionaries in the German Rhineland were strongly reminiscent of the traditional maypole, despite being crowned with the *tricolore* cap. Moreover, official revolutionary festivals usually had strong religious resonance. An altar dedicated not to God but to *la Patrie* was the focal point of the festivities, for the revolutionaries sought to replace the old religion with a secular cult of *la Patrie*. Their museums became temples to their country; their monuments were icons for their nation, heralding the sacralisation of nationhood which took root in nineteenth-century Europe.

Many of these new cultural practices refused to die with the revolution.[2] Indeed, political repression after 1815 meant that cultural activities became a vital weapon in opposition to the status quo in Germany. Opponents of the restoration order were not free to express themselves politically, but they could still sing nationalist songs, build nationalist monuments and participate in nationalist celebrations. On one level, activities of this kind simply reflected the cultural basis of German nationhood. On another level, cultural nationalism had clearly political implications. As a result, German governments responded to these activities in kind, adopting and adapting revolutionary cultural policy in an attempt to tap new sources of legitimacy. Whereas opposition cultural activities expressed aspirations, official cultural activities sought to affirm German political realities. The result was a fusion of the traditional representational culture of monarchy with more democratic elements that placed great emphasis on popular participation. Cultural activities consequently became a key area of conflict for liberal and conservative, nationalist and particularist forces in Germany.

[2] See for instance Jonathan Sperber, 'Festivals of national unity in the German revolution of 1848', *Past and Present* 36 (1992), 114–38, on the use of French revolutionary symbols in the Rhineland in 1848.

This development was closely linked to the wider trend of association formation that swept Germany at this time, radicalising and democratising the cultural sphere.[3] If culture was a major battleground between the forces of change and reaction, then the new craze for societies and associations was the favoured weapon of both sides in this war. Voluntary associations sprang up all over Germany after 1815. Initially, they were mostly social clubs, private libraries and scholarly societies, dedicated to the study of history, geography, statistics and other academic concerns. These associations represented a new kind of collectivity that differed fundamentally from existing social organisations. Indeed, the process of association formation was central to the emergence of civil society in Germany, because societies and associations united individuals who shared common interests in the pursuit of a common goal. Societies proved such an effective form of social mobilisation that by the late nineteenth century the associational model had been adapted for innumerable cultural, philanthropic, educational, economic, confessional, political and economic purposes. In the beginning, however, the social motivation behind association formation was of prime importance. Societies provided a forum for informal, social interaction outside the traditional spaces of the household and the corporation. This kind of sociability had radical implications on many levels. First, societies were socially levelling organisations because members of the same society related to each other as equals, regardless of their background. Secondly, the increasingly wide scope of associational activity paved the way for a more participatory society because many of these activities had previously been the preserve of a narrow aristocratic elite. In this sense, voluntary societies heralded the emancipation and embourgeoisement of culture. Third, as Habermas has so famously argued, association formation contributed to the emergence of public opinion as a political force because societies provided a public sphere, in which members could exchange views and formulate opinions on a range of intellectual, cultural and political issues.[4] Finally, the very

---

[3] The general historiography on association formation is extremely extensive. Thomas Nipperdey's article 'Verein als soziale Struktur in Deutschland im späten 18. und frühen 19. Jahrhundert. Eine Fallstudie zur Modernisierung I.' in Nipperdey (ed.), *Gesellschaft, Kultur, Theorie. Gesammelte Aufsätze zur neueren Geschichte* (Göttingen, 1976), pp. 174–205, provides an excellent introduction, as does Otto Dann (ed.), *Vereinswesen und bürgerliche Gesellschaft in Deutschland, Historische Zeitschrift*, Beiheft NF9 (1984), pp. 55–115. For a comparative international approach see Etienne François (ed.), *Geselligkeit, Vereinswesen und bürgerliche Gesellschaft in Frankreich, Deutschland und der Schweiz 1750–1850* (Paris, 1986). Similarly, Jürgen Kocka (ed.), *Bürgertum im 19. Jahrhundert. Deutschland im europäischen Vergleich*, Vol. III (Munich, 1988).

[4] See Jürgen Habermas, *The structural transformation of the public sphere, an inquiry into a category of bourgeois society* (Oxford, 1992), pp. 72–3.

process of association formation was emancipating because organisation entailed formulating statutes, holding membership assemblies and electing society officers. In this sense, association membership was an inherently political experience, however harmless the goals of a particular society may have been.

Voluntary societies played a central part in both national and liberal politics in Germany in the years preceding the revolutions of 1848/9. At state level, repressive restoration governments placed restrictions on associational activity, with the result that many societies acquired an anti-establishment character by default. At the same time, scholarly or cultural societies often masked real subversion. For instance, the Schiller Society founded in Leipzig in 1840 acted as a front for the political activities of the Saxon democrat Robert Blum. Meanwhile, at national level, the unofficial ties formed by like-minded societies scattered across Germany helped to overcome political fragmentation, to create national networks and to provide a sense of national community. The contribution of the nationwide associations of gymnasts, singers and sharpshooters to the German nationalist movement is a case in point. Ostensibly, these were cultural, not political, organisations; in practice they nurtured strong nationalist sentiments. The gymnasts' concern with physical fitness and the sharp-shooter's concern with marksmanship were both part and parcel of the liberal nationalist's desire to arm the people in defence of the Fatherland, whilst choral societies cultivated a German musical aesthetic, through singing nationalist songs.[5] Gymnastic, singing and sharpshooting societies were essentially local organisations despite their nationalist flavour. With time, however, they coalesced into regional – then national – networks and ultimately formed the basis for a popular nationalist movement in the 1860s.

Crypto-politicisation of this kind was far from unusual, but it was by no means universal. In fact, the relationship between voluntary societies and the political establishment was highly ambivalent, as a result of the elite membership of most such societies. Although societies may have been socially inclusive in theory, they were often exclusive in practice

---

[5] This has been intensively studied by Dieter Düding and others. See for instance Düding, 'Die deutsche Nationalbewegung des 19. Jahrhunderts als Vereinsbewegung. Anmerkungen zu ihrer Struktur und Phänomenologie zwischen Befreiungskriegszeitalter und Reichsgründung', *Geschichte in Wissenschaft und Unterricht* 42:10 (1991), 601–24, and 'Nationale Oppositionsfeste der Turner, Sänger und Schützen im 19. Jahrhundert' in Dieter Düding, Peter Friedemann and Paul Münch (eds.), *Öffentliche Festkultur. Politische Feste in Deutschland von der Aufklärung bis zum Ersten Weltkrieg* (Reinbeck bei Hamburg, 1988), pp. 166–90. Also Klenke, 'Nationalkriegerisches Gemeinschaftsideal'.

because a relatively high level of education was usually a *sine qua non* of membership. A decent education posed no obstacles for the aristocracy and many noblemen were happy to join the voluntary societies, which consequently provided a forum for social interaction between the nobility and the new middle classes, encouraging the fusion of a new elite. Ultimately, however, state officials remained the key constituency for the new societies because they dominated the educated middle classes, particularly in state capitals. Consequently, voluntary societies often enjoyed a very cosy relationship with the state.[6] On the one hand, many officials understood their activities as officials and their activities as members of a particular society to be complementary. After all, both entailed a commitment to the common good and perhaps a degree of social engagement. On the other hand, state bureaucracies fostered voluntary societies as a prop for their own activities and compensated in this way for the limited resources of the state itself. Moreover, just as societies served as a front for the liberal and nationalist politics of the opposition movement, they also provided a veneer of independence for essentially establishment activities. Nowhere was the conservative potential of associational cultural activity more apparent than in the proliferation of local historical societies in Germany after 1815.[7]

In many ways, the German preoccupation with history in the nineteenth century was a product of the Napoleonic era and closely linked to the emergence of German nationalism. During the Napoleonic wars, German nationalists had seen the struggle with the French in historical – and indeed mythological – terms. In this context, Napoleon appeared to be the last in a long line of French aggressors, beginning with the

---

[6] Charlotte Tacke provides an extremely sensitive study of the complex relationship between officialdom and voluntary societies and the role of officials in the case of the Detmold Society for the Hermann Monument. See Tacke, *Denkmal im sozialen Raum. Nationale Symbole in Deutschland und Frankreich im 19. Jahrhundert* (Göttingen, 1995), pp. 80–96.

[7] The work of Hermann Heimpel is an essential starting point for the historiography on historical societies. See Heimpel, 'Über Organisationsformen historischer Forschung in Deutschland' in Theodor Schieder (ed.), *Historische Zeitschrift* 189, *Hundert Jahre Historische Zeitschrift 1859–1959*, *Beiträge zur Geschichte der Historiographie in den deutschsprachigen Ländern* (1959), 139–222, and *Geschichtsvereine einst und jetzt. Vortrag gehalten am Tag der 70. Wiederkehr der Gründung des Geschichtsvereins für Göttingen und Umgebung* (Göttingen, 1963). Also of interest is Rudolf Vierhaus, 'Einrichtungen wissenschaftlicher und populärer Geschichtsforschung im 19. Jahrhundert' in Bernward Denecke and Rainer Kahsnitz (eds.), *Das kunst- und kulturgeschichtliche Museum im 19. Jahrhundert. Vorträge des Symposion im Germanischen Nationalmuseum, Nürnberg* (Munich, 1977), pp. 109–17. On scholarly societies in general see Jürgen Voss, 'Akademien, gelehrte Gesellschaften und wissenschäftiche Vereine in Deutschland, 1750–1850' in François (ed.), *Geselligkeit, Vereinswesen und bürgerliche Gesellschaft*, pp. 149–69. For a study of more locally based historical societies see Erich Maschke, 'Landesgeschichtsschreibung und historische Vereine', *Jahrbuch für württembergisch Franken* 58, *Festschrift für Gerd Wunder* (1974), 17–34.

Romans themselves. Nationalists liked to contrast recent German defeats with the great victory of Hermann and the united German tribes over the Romans more than a thousand years earlier, arguing that the Germans could overcome the French only if they united as one people. Moreover, the rise of political nationalism went hand in hand with a rediscovery of the German nation as a historic and cultural unit, for nationalists liked to stress the unique achievements of the German people. Fichte's rousing 'Speeches to the German Nation', delivered after the Prussian defeat at Jena to the Berlin Academy in 1807–8, were path-breaking in this respect.

Ironically, however, the most widespread expression of historical interest in Germany at this time remained rooted in the particular Fatherland. Local historical societies sprang up throughout Germany during the years after 1815. These societies focused their efforts on the historical study of a specific area (*Landesgeschichte*), published relevant historical source material and collected 'patriotic' (*vaterländisch*) antiquities. The overwhelming majority of these historical societies adopted the state as a framework for their activities. For instance, state-based historical societies were founded in Saxony, Hanover and Württemberg during the 1830s and 1840s: the Royal Saxon Antiquarian Association (1835), the Royal Hanoverian Historical Association for Lower Saxony (1835) and the Royal Württemberg Antiquarian Association (1843).[8] All in all, sixty local historical societies had been founded in Germany by 1850, but there was not as yet a single society dedicated to the study of the greater German Fatherland. Whatever their political beliefs, in practice the Germans remained interested in local not national history.

On one level, state-based historical societies of this kind reflected a genuine interest in the German past. It is telling that nearly a third of the 190 scholarly societies founded in Germany by 1850 were historical

---

[8] For details on the Historical Association for Lower Saxony see Otto Grotefend, '100 Jahre Historischer Verein für Niedersachsen', *Jahrbuch für Niedersächsische Landesgeschichte* 12 (1935), 1–24; Manfred Hamann, 'Die Gründung des Historischen Vereins für Niedersachsen 1835' in Helmut Maurer and Hans Patze (eds.), *Festschrift für Bernd Schwineköper, zu seinem siebzigsten Geburtstag* (Sigmaringen, 1982), pp. 569–582; Angelika Kroker, 'Niedersächsische Geschichtsforschung im 19. Jahrhundert: Zwischen Aufklärung und Historismus', *Westfälische Forschungen* 39 (1989), 83–113; Heinrich Schmidt, 'Landesgeschichte und Gegenwart bei Johann Carl Bertram Stüve' in Hartmut Boockmann *et al.* (eds.), *Geschichtswissenschaft und Vereinswesen im 19. Jahrhundert, Beiträge zur Geschichte historischer Forschung in Deutschland* (Göttingen, 1972), pp. 74–99. For details on the Saxon Antiquarian Association see Hubert Ermisch, 'Zur Geschichte des Königlich Sächsischen Alterthumsvereins 1825–1885', *Neues Archiv für sächsische Geschichte und Alterthumskunde* 6 (1885), 1–50. Apart from very brief jubilee essays, I have found no specialist literature dealing with the Württemberg Antiquarian Association.

societies.[9] Equally, in 1846 a contemporary estimated the combined membership of German historical societies at over 9,000 – a far from inconsiderable figure. Nevertheless, the independence of these societies as cultural initiatives is open to very serious question, since officials and other establishment figures dominated the membership. Prince Johann himself was the first president of the Saxon Antiquarian Association, whilst Presidents of the Historical Association for Lower Saxony included the influential General von der Decken, Interior Minister von Schele, the prominent educationalist and official Kohlrausch, and the court archivist Karl von Grotefend. Similarly, the first president of the Württemberg Antiquarian Association was Count Wilhelm of Württemberg, a relative of the King. Not for nothing were the names of most such societies usually prefixed with the word 'Royal'.

Given the close links between these societies and the state, they inevitably reflected government concerns. Indeed, the emergence of these historical societies was often explicitly linked to the imperative of particularist integration in the different German states – the need to create a Hanoverian, a Saxon, and a Württemberg *Volk*.[10] In both Hanover and Württemberg, historical societies developed out of explicitly political initiatives. In Hanover, the journal *Vaterländisches Archiv*, subtitled 'Contributions to a General Knowledge of the Kingdom of Hanover, as it Was and Is', was founded in 1819. In Württemberg, an Association for Fatherland Studies, which published the *Württembergisches Jahrbuch*, was founded in 1822. Both initiatives acknowledged the identity deficit in these newly enlarged states and set out to foster state patriotism. The editors of the *Vaterländisches Archiv* expressed the hope that readers would 'become more closely acquainted with our Fatherland, as defined by the current borders of the Kingdom of Hanover'.[11] Similarly, the first edition of the *Württembergisches Jahrbuch* lamented the fact that 'each part [of the Württemberg *Volk*] is a stranger to the others'. The *Jahrbuch*'s founders hoped to compensate for this by dwelling on the historic links between dynasty, state and people in Württemberg, 'the early development of civic liberties and the current, so enviable constitution' – in other words, they sought to generate the myth of a common past as a means of fostering patriotic feeling.[12] Neither the *Vaterländisches Archiv*, the

---

[9] Figures from Vierhaus, 'Einrichtungen wissenschaftlicher und populärer Geschichtsforschung', p. 156.
[10] This was certainly true in Baden, Bavaria and Hesse-Darmstadt. See Heimpel, 'Über Organisationsformen historischer Forschung', pp. 195–212.
[11] Cited after Kroker, 'Niedersächsische Geschichtsforschung', 89.
[12] *Württembergisches Jahrbuch* (1822). Cited after Schmoll, *Verewigte Nation*, p. 20.

Württembergisches Jahrbuch nor the Association for Fatherland Studies survived, but the spirit that had motivated them lived on. In both states more specifically historical societies were founded with similar aims, often by those involved in the earlier initiatives.

This explicitly political motivation has led Heinrich Heimpel, the leading authority on historical societies, to dismiss them as the product of 'official influence, government aims, state administration . . . [and] state policy'.[13] Yet this assessment is not entirely fair. In fact, most such societies were not founded exclusively by the establishment for political reasons. Prince Johann may have become president of the Saxon Antiquarian Association, but its forerunner, the Royal Saxon Association for the Research and Preservation of Patriotic History and Artistic Monuments, was founded in 1824 by scholarly enthusiasts, not by government officials. More strikingly still, the first person to propose founding a historical society in Hanover was none other than the future leader of the opposition.[14] Stüve was a Westphalian patriot, a progressive on many of the key political issues of the 1820s, and only ever grudgingly came to terms with Hanoverian rule. He was certainly no government stooge. Nevertheless, in 1827 Stüve proposed the foundation of a Hanoverian historical society and also published an essay on the history of Osnabrück in the *Vaterländisches Archiv*. His decision to promote Hanoverian history and to adopt Hanover as the framework for his own activities was not in itself patriotic, but it testified to Stüve's acceptance of the political realities of his day. However reluctantly, he realised that Hanover was 'after all, the state in which I find myself living'.[15]

Whatever their founders' motivations may have been, in practice most historical societies were heavily dependent on the state – not least for financial reasons. Governments could subsidise historical societies either directly or indirectly, for instance through providing public buildings in which the societies housed their growing collections, as was the case in Saxony. Direct and regular financial backing tended to be forthcoming only after the revolution of 1848/9. Once again, this was usually for political reasons. In 1851, for instance, the Hanoverian Estates granted an annual sum of 1,500 *Thaler* to support various scholarly societies.[16] This rose to 1,600 *Thaler* in 1864. The grant was not directed exclusively at

---

[13] Heimpel, *Geschichtsvereine einst und jetzt*, p. 9.
[14] On Stüve's involvement with the *Historischer Verein für Niedersachsen* see Schmidt, 'Landesgeschichte und Gegenwart', pp. 74–99. [15] Ibid., p. 81.
[16] Gesammtministerium to Allgemeine Ständeversammlung, betr. Geldmittel zur Unterstützung von Vereinen für Wissenschaft u. Kunst, 12 February 1851, HSA Hann 113 K I 34 (1–2).

historical societies; local scientific and artistic societies also benefited.[17] Nevertheless, the government made it clear that it regarded historical societies as particularly worthy of support for political reasons. In the original proposal, the government claimed that 'Historical societies especially whet the appetite for research into particular history, and so lead to a more accurate understanding of events and the quickening of an effective sense of community'.[18] Although the Hanoverian parliament granted the money, it did not appear to share the government's priorities, merely noting the general contribution of scholarly societies to the state's well-being.[19] Similarly, in Württemberg the government granted an annual sum (250 *Gulden*) to the Antiquarian Association in 1860, as a contribution towards the rent of a public venue where the society could exhibit its collection. Once again, this was a politically motivated gesture. 'It is true,' noted the *Kultusminister*, 'that [the Antiquarian Association] is a private organisation, but its ceaseless efforts in researching the art and history of the Fatherland and in preserving its monuments are not without a beneficial effect on the level of education and civilisation of the people and the awakening of a patriotic spirit.'[20]

The political motivation behind institutionalised government support for state history was not, however, always so clear-cut. In the 1860s the Saxon parliament agreed to fund the publication of a collection of Saxon historical documents and, slightly later, a historical periodical, the 'New Archive for Saxon History' (*Neues Archiv*). The *Neues Archiv* was the brainchild of Weber, the court archivist, who petitioned the government in 1862 with the backing of twenty-seven other scholars.[21] In his petition, Weber placed the proposal in the context of developments in Austria and Bavaria, suggesting that Saxony's need for a historical journal of this kind was 'the more glaring, because other countries boast such collections'.

[17] Societies benefiting from this grant included the Hanoverian Historical Society; the Natural History Society; the Society to found a Public Art Collection and the Society to found a Natural History Museum in Hanover; the Society for the Research of Nature and the Society for Fine Art in Emden; the Physical Society in Leer; the Society for Knowledge of Nature and Art in Hildesheim; the Natural Science Society in Lüneburg; the Historical Society for the Principality of Osnabrück; the Historical Society for the Duchies of Bremen and Verden. For full details see HSAHan Hann 113 K I 34.

[18] Gesammtministerium to Allgemeine Ständeversammlung, betr. Geldmittel zur Unterstützung von Vereinen für Wissenschaft u. Kunst, 12 February 1851, HSA Han Hann 113 K I 34 (1–2).

[19] 6 March 1851, HSA Hann 113 K I 34 (3–4).

[20] Ministerium des Kirchen- und Schulwesens to H. M., betr. die Bitte des Ausschußes des württembergischen Alterthums-Vereins dahier um eine Staatsunterstützung, 1 September 1860, HSA Stu E 14 1577.

[21] Weber and others, An Se. Ex den Herrn Staatsminister von Falkenstein 25 March 1862. HSA Dre Ministerium f. Volksbildung 14310 (1–10).

Weber implied that the journal would add to Saxony's prestige and underline her importance as a state, both past and present. 'Saxony may be small in size,' he wrote, 'but her history is great'. His proposal also reflected overtly political priorities, for he argued that the journal would work 'hand in hand with the collection of historical documents, to present old and new material from Saxon history to the public, and so awaken love for the Fatherland and its rulers'. Of course, this was exactly the kind of argument calculated to appeal to Weber's superiors. Nevertheless, Weber took the political aspect of the project sufficiently seriously to wish to underplay it in public. Writing to the government three months later, he suggested that the title of the new periodical should include the word 'Archiv' 'in order to avoid the mistaken impression that it was politically motivated'.[22] Here he reveals the uneasy balance between genuine historical interest and more calculating political concerns that was so common in such enterprises.

Government support for *Landesgeschichte* inevitably coloured the kind of history produced by local historical societies and other state-sponsored historians. Usually, the *quid pro quo* was fairly indirect. For instance, in 1853, 1856 and 1861 the Württemberg government made three one-off grants to a historical society in Franconia, a relatively new territorial acquisition.[23] Although these contributions came from the royal purse, they were prompted by recommendations from the Württemberg Ministry of Culture. Finally, the Historical Association for Württembergish Franconia was granted an annual sum of 50 *Gulden*. This generous gesture was very warmly received. In March 1866, as an expression of thanks, the society produced a pamphlet entitled 'The Ancient Ties of Württemb. Franconia with the Württemberg Royal House'.[24] As its title suggests, the pamphlet was designed to illustrate the heritage Franconia shared with the rest of Württemberg. The closing words of the pamphlet made this point very clearly:

In this way, our own Württemb. Franconia gradually became a part of the County, the Duchy, the Electorate and the Kingdom of Württemberg. The pains which naturally accompany every change of statehood have long since metamorphosed into a feeling of well-being under the rule of King Wilhelm I and the sceptre of our most worthy protector, King Karl.

[22] Weber to Falkenstein. 22 June 1862. HSADre Ministerium f. Volksbildung 14310 (16–21).
[23] Details to be found in HSAStu E 14 1579. For details on the society itself see Maschke, 'Landesgeschichtsschreibung und historische Vereine'.
[24] *Die älteren Verbindungen des württemb. Frankens mit dem Württembergischen Fürstenhause.* A copy to be found in HSAStu E 14 1579. It is worth noting that, as a Catholic area, Franconia may have been particularly loyal to the state in the crisis months of 1866.

The society in question was local rather than state-based, with a membership less dominated by state officials than that of most historical societies. Karl's grant can therefore be seen as a canny response to genuine popular interest, which then helped to colour the form this interest took. Elsewhere, the politicisation of history was rather more deliberate. Nowhere was this clearer than in Hanover, where Georg V personally sponsored historical writing with a Welfist agenda. This was most apparent in his close relationship with the teacher, historian and government publicist Onno Klopp.[25] Klopp was a secondary schoolteacher, who made a name for himself by writing a pro-Welf history of East Friesland that took issue with the Prussophile orthodoxy.[26] The first volume of this work was so controversial that the provincial Estates, which had funded it, initially refused to subsidise the sequel. Instead, Georg made good the shortfall. This was the beginning of a close relationship between the two men, based on delusions of grandeur on both sides. Georg bolstered Klopp's pretensions as a historian. In return, the star-struck Klopp reinforced Georg's faith in the historical mission of the Welf dynasty. For instance, in a letter to his wife in 1865, Klopp describes one conversation he had with Georg as 'historiographer' of the Welf dynasty: 'He gave me several ideas, which I declared to be wonderful . . . The thing is, in fact, that both the origins of Austria and the origins of Prussia are founded in wrongs done to his ancestors (Destruction of the Duchies of Bavaria and Saxony by Frederick Barbarossa). How I admire his insight!'[27]

Klopp rapidly became a mouthpiece for Georg's regime. In the 1860s he published a number of works supporting a *großdeutsch* and anti-Prussian view of German history, notably his biographies of Frederick the Great and Tilly.[28] During this period, Klopp also produced an officially sponsored edition of the collected works of Hanover's greatest son, Leibniz. Like most of Klopp's history, this was a blatantly political undertaking. Both Schaumann, the Hanoverian court archivist, and Kohlrausch, a prominent educationalist, agreed that Klopp was intellectually unequal to

---

[25] On Klopp see Wiard Klopp, 'Der Lebenslauf von Onno Klopp', *Jahrbuch der Gesellschaft für bildende Kunst und vaterländische Altertümer zu Emden* 16/21 (1907), 1–182; Ernst Laslowski, 'Zur Entwicklungsgeschichte Onno Klopps. Ein Beitrag zum Problem Persönlichkeit und Geschichtsauffassung', *Historisches Jahrbuch* 56 (1936), 481–98. Georg V even sent Klopp on diplomatic missions during the final months of his reign.

[26] Onno Klopp, *Geschichte Ostfrieslands bis 1570* (Hanover, 1854); *Geschichte Ostfrieslands von 1570–1715* (Hanover, 1856); *Geschichte Ostfrieslands unter preußischer Regierung bis zur Abtretung an Hannover* (Hanover, 1858).   [27] Cited in W. Klopp, 'Der Lebenslauf von Onno Klopp', 63.

[28] Onno Klopp, *Der König Friedrich II. von Preußen und die deutsche Nation* (Schaffhausen, 1860); *Tilly im dreißigjährigen Kriege* (Stuttgart, 1861).

the task and suggested that Leibniz await a more suitable editor.[29] More-over, Georg Pertz, whose scholarly credentials as editor of the *Monumenta Germanica Historica* were beyond dispute, had been commissioned to produce such a collection in 1842.[30] Indeed, he had already published twelve volumes by 1861. These considerations cut no ice with Georg, who chose to finance the Klopp edition of Leibniz from his own purse.[31] He declared that he would give Klopp the benefit of the doubt, rather than indefinitely delay the enterprise or (worse still) allow a foreigner to take credit for this glorious achievement.

In the 1850s and 1860s German governments became ever readier to exploit the past for their own political ends. Yet official sponsorship of particularist history also had to take into account the growth of nationalism. In 1852 the various German historical societies united to form a national umbrella organisation: the General Association of German Historical and Antiquarian Societies. The name carried clear political overtones: this was a *general* not a *national* association. As such, it reflected the conservative and state-based roots of historical societies in Germany. The General Association paid lip-service to German nationalism, but in essence it was very much in keeping with the particularist bias of existing historical societies. The President of the General Association was Prince Johann of Saxony, testifying to its close links with the German dynasties. Moreover, the General Association explicitly sought to promote that 'genuine national feeling, which draws upon ancient history and therefore rests on a truly conservative basis, which fosters love and loyalty for Prince and Fatherland'.[32] Once again, this underlines the extent to which historical activity in nineteenth-century Germany had consciously political aims, reflecting a widespread belief in the contemporary relevance of historical study. The link between history and politics has long been established for nationalist historians like Droysen, Sybel and Treitschke.[33] For instance, in 1859–62 the Sybel–Ficker controversy over the Italian policy and universal aspirations of the medieval

[29] Bar, Ministerium des K. Hauses to K. Ministerium der geistlichen & Unterrichts Angelegenheiten, 2 July 1861, HSAHan Hann 113 K I 1788 (2); Kohlrausch to Verehrter Herr General-Secretair, 8 August 1861, HSAHan Hann 113 K I 1788 (4).
[30] Malortie, Ministerium des K. Hauses, 19 November 1863, HSAHan Hann 113 K I 1788 (17–19).
[31] Bar, f. d. Minister des K. Hauses to K. Ministerium der geistlichen & Unterrichts Angelegenheiten, 19 November 1863, HSAHan Hann 113 K I 1788 (8–16).
[32] Directorium des Gesammtvereins der deutschen Geschichts- und Alterthumsvereine, 5 November 1852, HSADre Ministerium f. Volksbildung 14261 (123–6).
[33] See Wolfgang Hardtwig, 'Geschichtsinteresse, Geschichtsbilder und politische Symbole in der Reichsgründungsära und im Kaiserreich' in Ekkehard Mai and Stephan Waetzoldt (eds.), *Kunstverwaltung, Bau- und Denkmalpolitik im Kaiserreich*, (Berlin, 1980), pp. 47–75.

German empire can be seen as a response to Prussian and Austrian differences over Italy, reflecting more fundamental divisions between the *kleindeutsch* and *großdeutsch* camps. Similarly, the emergence of a Borussian school in German historiography clearly relates to the rise of *kleindeutsch* nationalism and the creation of the Prussian-led German Empire. It is important to grasp, however, that nationalist history of this kind had its particularist corollary: at federal level in the activities of the General Association and at state level in the local historical societies.

Heinrich Heimpel has argued that the preoccupation of historical societies with the distant (and therefore uncontroversial) past reflected a conservative and particularist agenda. The ancient Germans and the Middle Ages were certainly favourite fields of study. Moreover, many societies engaged in relatively uncontroversial activities, such as publishing historical source material or collecting and cataloguing patriotic antiquities, rather than actually writing history. Once again, however, Heimpel's assessment is too harsh. Admittedly, those like Stüve, who believed that history had contemporary political relevance, often favoured the study of the seventeenth and eighteenth centuries. Equally, the Saxon government was extremely cautious in authorising even the most conservative works of contemporary history. For instance, the Saxon cabinet allowed Hugo Häpe only restricted archival access to write a biography of Friedrich August II in 1856, although as a government publicist and official he was unlikely to publish anything controversial.[34] Similarly, in 1862 the Saxon cabinet blocked an officially commissioned biography of the former minister von Einsiedel, written by Weber, the court archivist.[35] Nevertheless, studies of the ancient Germans and the Middle Ages could also be politically loaded. After all, enthusiasm for the ancient Germans reflected a developing sense of historical continuity with strongly nationalist implications, immediately apparent in the growing popularity of the Hermann myth.[36] Similarly, the high Middle Ages exemplified the great flourishing of German culture, fostered by the unity of the German empire and undermined by subsequent fragmentation and division.[37] In any case, the very process of historical research entailed the opening of state archives to a wider public and a shift away

---

[34] Zschinsky, 24 May 1856, HSADre Gesammtministerium Loc. 44, No. 8 (78–9).

[35] Friesen, 1 January 1862 and Johann, 1 January 1862, HSADre Gesammtministerium Loc. 66, No. 7 (109–13, 120–1).

[36] See Andreas Dörner's 'theory-heavy' *Politischer Mythos und symbolische Politik. Sinnstiftung durch symbolische Formen am Beispiel des Hermannsmythos* (Opladen, 1995), pp. 111–99, for details on the development of the Hermann myth at this time.

[37] See Hardtwig, 'Geschichtsinteresse, Geschichtsbilder und politische Symbole', p. 48.

from history written about the state's rulers for its rulers. This was in itself a significant change, symbolised by Stüve's decision to broaden access to the Hanoverian archives when he came to power in 1848.

Crucially, the role of voluntary historical societies in collecting and preserving patriotic antiquities had a number of radical implications. First, collections of this kind had previously been the preserve of the ruling elite and – most frequently – of the royal house. Through their efforts, the new historical societies appropriated this area of cultural activity for their middle-class members. Moreover, the societies were actively supported by princes and governments. Secondly, these histori-cal collections were more truly public than the royal collections of art and antiquities on display in the great museums of Berlin, Dresden and Munich. At the same time, the wide-scale collaboration between rulers, governments and historical societies in establishing the new collections indicates that it is too simplistic to distinguish crudely between the great royal museums opened before 1848 and the 'bourgeois' museums that followed.[38] Finally, the museums founded by historical societies conveyed a relatively democratic view of history, which moved beyond the state and its dynasty to a celebration of the people and their culture through the display of popular artistic and technical artifacts. Yet like the histor-ical societies themselves, the public museums that emerged in Germany during the nineteenth century testify to the profoundly ambivalent role of culture at this time. If historical societies were an instance of conser-vative cultural politics with surprisingly radical implications, then the development of museums demonstrated the extent to which apparently popular, even democratic, change could serve conservative ends.

In many ways, the place of museums in German public life during the nineteenth century was a further legacy of the French Revolution.[39] The

---

[38] As does Volker Plagemann, *Das deutsche Kunstmuseum 1790–1870. Lage, Baukörper, Raumorganisation, Bildprogramm* (Munich, 1967), pp. 30–5.

[39] There is a wide historiography on the development of the modern museum. A good starting point is Walter Grasskamp, *Museumsgründer und Museumsstürmer. Zur Sozialgeschichte des Kunstmuseums* (Munich, 1981). Karl Hammer, 'Preußische Museumspolitik im 19. Jahrhundert' in Peter Baumgart (ed.), *Bildungspolitik in Preußen zur Zeit des Kaiserreichs* (Stuttgart, 1980), pp. 256–77, pro-vides a basic introduction to the development of museums in Prussia. Various issues in museum history are discussed in the excellent Denecke and Kahsnitz (eds.), *Das kunst- und kulturgeschichtliche Museum*. Hildegard Vieregg, *Vorgeschichte der Museumspädagogik, dargestellt an der Museumsentwicklung in den Städten Berlin, Dresden, München und Hamburg bis zum Beginn der Weimarer Republik* (Münster, 1991), is widely researched, although less helpful than its title suggests and almost exclusively based on published sources and secondary literature. Plagemann, *Das deutsche Kunstmuseum*, charts in detail the construction of numerous German museums, principally from an architectural per-spective. A consideration of the role of national museums is provided in Marie-Louise von Plessen (ed.), *Die Nation und ihre Museen. Für das Deutsche Historische Museum* (Frankfurt, 1992).

opening of the French royal collections to the public and the founding of the *Musée des Monuments Français* had transformed the meaning and role of museums in revolutionary France. Before this time, art collections had reflected the wealth and power of their owners and the art itself affirmed the position of those who commissioned it, for instance through portraiture and religious painting. By appropriating rather than destroying these symbols of authority, revolutionary governments altered their political symbolism. Through opening private collections to the public (particularly in a palace like the Louvre), the revolutionaries demonstrated that the traditional ruling elite had been dispossessed of its treasures and that these were now the property of the people. Under Napoleon, moreover, the new public collections became repositories for the cultural riches of defeated states. Public museums enabled the victorious French nation to admire its booty and became an important symbol of French political hegemony. In keeping with this, museums acquired a new role: the education and improvement of the masses. Such education could take the form of imparting art-historical knowledge and cultural sensitivity. Paintings and sculpture were hung academically, according to their artistic and historical context, so that the whole collection presented the development of art and culture from classical antiquity to the present day. At the same time, museums sought to mediate a new sense of French nationhood. The path-breaking *Musée des Monuments Français* was essentially a collection of confiscated church art, and its catalogue stressed that artifacts had been selected for their artistic qualities.[40] Nevertheless, the museum included the tombs of French monarchs and the surrounding park contained monuments to great Frenchmen, like Descartes and Molière. The museum provided visitors with a particular interpretation of French history and the development of the French nation that contributed to their education as French citizens.

German monarchs learnt from these developments. After 1815 they too began to open their art collections to the public and to construct a series of grandiose 'monumental' museums for this purpose, such as the *Glyptothek* and the *Pinakotheken* in Munich, or the Old and New Museums in Berlin. These new museums differed from the old royal collections in being more accessible. Indeed, public display was their *raison d'être*. On the one hand, they were not truly public museums, since the collections

---

[40] For an analysis of this museum as both museum and monument, see Rainer Kahsnitz, 'Museum und Denkmal. Überlegungen zu Gräbern, historischen Freskenzyklen und Ehrenhalle in Museen' in Denecke and Kahsnitz (eds.), *Das kunst- und kulturgeschichtliche Museum*, pp. 152–75, (pp. 154–5).

did not belong to the public. On the other hand, the collections ceased to be simply the private property of the royal family as they had been in the past. Tellingly, the return of the Prussian art plundered by Napoleon to Berlin was celebrated as a Prussian 'national' triumph. Similarly, the Russian governor general in charge of occupied Saxony in 1813 ordered the return of the royal art collection from Königstein to Dresden, so that it could be made available to the people. In both cases private royal collections were treated as 'national' cultural treasures.

The new museums were a cultural expression of royal power and benevolence. They were designed to bolster the reputation of the rulers behind them – both as patrons of the arts and as benefactors of the people. The legitimising role of such museums in the German states was most explicit in the *Alte Pinakothek* in Munich, where the Founders' Chamber contained portraits of the Wittelsbach princes responsible for assembling the collection on show there. The initial reluctance of state parliaments to fund such projects demonstrates the extent to which they were the products of princely rather than popular enthusiasm. Yet these refusals did not stand the test of time. In 1823, for instance, the Württemberg parliament rejected King Wilhelm's plans for a Chamber of Antiquities like the Munich *Glyptothek*.[41] Twenty years later, the parliament was happy to fund a complex housing the Art School and various royal collections. In practice, representative institutions were now willing to recognise art collections as public property and culture as the responsibility of the state.[42] Events in Saxony demonstrate the complexities of this transition particularly clearly.

In the years after 1815, the Saxon government granted the people increasingly easy access to the great royal art collections assembled by Augustus the Strong and his successors. To some extent, this was a deliberate response to political change. For instance, the Historical Museum – a collection of armour and weaponry – was opened to the public in 1833, three years after the revolution of 1830 and only two years after the promulgation of the Saxon constitution. In 1838 the Saxon gallery commission instructed the architect Gottfried Semper to draw up plans for a new museum to house the dynasty's old master paintings. This was partly a practical measure because the paintings were housed at the time in a cold and damp building, where mildew was a serious problem. Nevertheless, the plans also represented a government response to

[41] See Plagemann, *Das deutsche Kunstmuseum*, p. 65, for details on this.
[42] See Ulrich Scheuner, 'Die Kunst als Staatsaufgabe im 19. Jahrhundert' in Mai and Waetzoldt (eds.), *Kunstverwaltung, Bau- und Denkmalpolitik*, pp. 13–46.

public pressure for greater access. Retrospectively, the museum authorities certainly interpreted the move to the New Museum in these terms.
In 1863 Dr Ludwig Reichenbach, director of the Natural History
Museum, described how 'before [the opening of the New Museum]
these art treasures were only accessible to a relatively small number of
art lovers, now the plan was to expand their use as much as possible'.[43]
The Saxon government demonstrated its commitment to public access
by distributing a number of free tickets to this and other Dresden
museums on a regular basis. Reichenbach claimed that by 1863
60–70,000 people visited the Painting Gallery every year.

Saxon plans for the New Museum reflected an awareness of the need
for greater public access to the royal collections. Yet implementing these
plans was contingent on a related process, whereby the objects themselves became quasi-public property. In the aftermath of the 1830 revolution, responsibility for the royal collections passed from the crown to
the Ministry of the Royal House. Nevertheless, when Semper first presented the Saxon parliament with his ambitious vision of a purpose-
built museum they were unsympathetic.[44] Like the Württemberg
parliament when initially faced with a similar request, the Saxon parliament did not regard the fate of the collections as a matter for public
concern. This decision provoked a heated public debate, in which
Wilhelm Schulz's pamphlet, 'On the need for a new painting gallery for
the royal art collection in Dresden', was particularly influential.[45] Like
its Württemberg counterpart, the Saxon parliament eventually caved
in. In 1847 it authorised a scaled-down version of the plan for a publicly
funded and openly accessible museum, which was finally completed in
1855. By this time the management of these collections had become
fully accountable. After 1853 the Ministry of the Royal House shared
responsibility for running the collections with the Interior Ministry,
which answered to parliament for the money spent.[46] To all intents and
purposes the Saxon royal collections had become public, not private,
institutions.

---

[43] Dr Ludwig Reichenbach, *Die zum Königlichen Hausfideicommiß gehörigen Sammlungen für Kunst und Wissenschaft während der Verwaltungsperiode vom 1. October 1853 bis 1. October 1863* (privately printed, 1863), p. 7. A copy can be found in HSADre Ministerium f. Volksbildung 18792 (13–26).
[44] On Semper's ideas for the museum see Harry Francis Mallgrave, *Gottfried Semper, architect of the nineteenth century* (New Haven and London, 1996), pp. 107–29.
[45] *Über die Nothwendigkeit eines neuen Gemäldegebäudes für die Königliche Gemäldesammlung zu Dresden.*
[46] See Regulativ f. d. Beaufsichtigung und Verwaltung der zum Königlichen Hausfideicommiß gehörigen Sammlungen für Kunst und Wissenschaft, 23 September 1853, HSADre Ministerium f. Volksbildung 18995.

Yet the Dresden New Museum was by no means an exclusively civic or bourgeois (*bürgerlich*) foundation, as historians such as Hildegard Vieregg have argued.[47] Like the royal museums of Berlin and Munich, it remained a vehicle for monarchic cultural policy. For one thing, the New Museum was extremely impressive to look at. The museum acted as the fourth side of a square formed by the famous Dresden *Zwinger*, a baroque pavilion built by Augustus the Strong. Resembling a great triumphal arch, the New Museum towered over the more delicate proportions of the older building. Indeed, architectural historians have stressed the extent to which Semper was influenced by the example of Schinkel's Old Museum in Berlin, a building with obviously monumental and representational intentions.[48] In practice, moreover, the New Museum retained close ties with the Saxon monarchy. Thus significant events were timed to coincide with important moments in the life of the royal family, in order to emphasise the museum's dynastic connection. For instance, the collection of prints and drawings was opened to the public for the first time on the King's birthday. In a very real sense, the collections therefore remained royal collections, testifying to the cultural achievements and former glories of the Saxon dynasty. Yet increasingly these achievements were conflated with (and celebrated as) the cultural achievements of Saxony as a state. In 1857, for instance, the Association of Independent Artists boasted: 'It is Saxony's undying fame to have acquired through art-loving princes – at a time when the other German states were still philistines in artistic matters – art collections which are still counted among the finest in the world and now indeed, have finally been shown . . . to their full advantage.'[49] Once private collections had become public institutions, financed by the public and open to the public, museums came to represent not merely the prestige of monarchs, but also the cultural standing and political power of peoples and states.

In fact, some kind of museum became an essential accessory for every capital city. Where great royal collections along Saxon lines were lacking, the citizens of these cities fell back on their own resources. In

[47] Vieregg, *Vorgeschichte der Museumspädagogik*, pp. 110–12. In general Vieregg perhaps relies too heavily on GDR historiography, which was keen to claim Semper as a revolutionary and to relate cultural stagnation in Saxony to political backwardness. Thus Vieregg describes Dresden as relegated to the status of a 'gloomy *Residenzstadt*', declining in importance culturally as a result of Saxony's political decline (ibid., p. 300). Given the presence of Caspar David Friedrich, Semper and Richard Wagner (to name but a few) in pre-revolutionary Dresden this seems an extraordinary judgement.   [48] Mallgrave, *Gottfried Semper*, pp. 116–17.
[49] Verein selbständiger Künstler to Ministerium des Innern, 1 May 1857, HSADre Ministerium des Innern 17305 (28–31).

1851 a committee of Hanoverian notables, representing three
Hanoverian cultural and scholarly societies, appealed to Georg V for
help with a new project.[50] They wished to build a museum to house
their artistic, historical and scientific collections. The notables themselves were motivated largely by municipal pride. Over a century of
absentee monarchy had left the Hanoverian capital without the great
cultural treasures of comparable German cities. The notables wanted
a museum that would 'adorn and honour Your Majesty's capital city, an
institution the like of which it has lacked until now – so that [Hanover]
may find her place amongst the great capitals of Germany'.[51] Besides
appealing to Georg, the committee of notables also formed a joint stock
company to help raise the necessary funds – a fund-raising technique
subsequently adopted elsewhere. Consequently, the Hanoverian
Museum of Art and Science has been seen as a model for the bourgeois
museums of the post-revolutionary era. This is, of course, an over-
simplification. The Hanoverian Estates gave a generous sum to the new
museum, but Georg's personal contribution of 10,000 *Thaler* nevethe-
less amounted to over half of all the money that had been raised by the
time the foundation stone was laid in 1853. Indeed, the sum was so significant that the museum seemed likely to pass into crown, not state,
hands.[52] Equally, the foundation stone and inauguration ceremonies
placed great emphasis on the King's contribution to the new museum.
Yet the building itself remained a primarily bourgeois institution, since
it also functioned as a headquarters for the various voluntary societies
involved in its foundation. Consequently, the museum is best understood as a product of the collaboration between monarch and citizens;
as such, it was by no means unusual.

What, besides civic vanity, prompted governments and monarchs to
fund museums of this kind, when (as was often the case) the collections
themselves were so undistinguished? The foundation of an official collection of patriotic art and antiquities in Württemberg gives an interesting insight into this question. As early as 1855 the state budget had set
aside 700 *Gulden* to fund a Conservator responsible for the upkeep of

---

[50] The Society for the Foundation of a Public Art Collection, the Hanoverian Historical Society
and the Natural History Society.

[51] Cttee behufs Gründung eines Actienvereins zur Herstellung eines Etablissements in hiesiger
Stadt, bestimmt zu Zwecken der Kunst und Wissenschaft, in sich fassend die Institute und
Vereine, welche in hiesiger Stadt jene hohen Zwecke verfolgen, deren kräftige Förderung und
Hebung sich zur Aufgabe stellend to H.M., 24 December 1851, HSAHan Dep. 103 xxviii 557.

[52] See Malortie, 'Pro Memoria, die Erbauung eines Museums betr.', 1 February 1852, HSAHan
Dep. 103 xxviii 557.

Württemberg's historic monuments. In 1858, 1859 and 1860, the new Conservator, Professor Hassler, repeatedly recommended that the Württemberg government should found a collection of patriotic art and antiquities – to no avail.[53] In fact, Hassler's proposal was not approved until June 1862, when the Finance Minister agreed to allocate a provisional annual budget of 6–8,000 *Gulden* for the purpose.[54] In his report in favour of the proposal, Golther, the Minister of Culture, advanced three different arguments. First, he argued that it was important to preserve antiquities in a time of rapid change, a concern which frequently motivated similar collections founded by historical societies at this time. Secondly, just as the citizens of Hanover were influenced by a sense of competition with other capital cities, so Golther felt a keen sense of cultural competition with other German states. He claimed that a historical collection of this kind was '[a] sort of necessity'. Indeed, the governments of neighbouring states like Bavaria and Baden had already founded similar collections, rightly recognising their scholarly, aesthetic and patriotic value. If the government did not act 'soon and without hesitation', neighbouring states would snap up many of Württemberg's finest treasures. Golther also argued that Württemberg's historic cultural traditions made it all the more important for the government not to 'lag behind the other German states in this respect', and trusted that the new collection would add to Stuttgart's reputation and increase its popularity with tourists. Thirdly, the role of such a collection in fostering love for the particular Fatherland was of crucial importance. For Golther was acutely aware of

how very much such a collection is likely to foster knowledge of patriotic history and, in particular, the cultural history of the Fatherland . . . how very much – and at a time of rival unification tendencies this should certainly not be underestimated – such a collection will serve to promote an awareness of *particular* traits in the development of a single tribe [*Stamm*] keeping alive a remembrance of the past of the *particular* Fatherland among the people, and encouraging a new love and duty for the narrower homeland (*Heimat*).

It seems probable that this final argument was decisive. Certainly, the political motivations behind cultural initiatives of this kind could hardly be more explicit.

Similar concerns motivated the foundation of a Welf Museum in Hanover at roughly the same time. In 1861 Georg V announced his

[53] Reference is made to this and later reports in Golther, Ministerium d. Kirchen- und Schulwesens to H.M. 'betr. die Anlegung einer besonderen Sammlung vaterländischer Kunst- und Alterthumsdenkmale', 16 June 1862, HSAStu E 14 1577 (8).   [54] Ibid.

plans for a museum to celebrate the Welf dynasty, 'out of respect for
the memory of Our house and . . . the conviction that this is generally
shared, due to the proven loyalty of Our faithful subjects and their love
for their old, ancestral ruling house'.[55] Prussian annexation in 1866
meant that plans for the museum were never brought to fruition.
Nevertheless, a skeleton collection was open to the public before this
date. As its name suggests, the museum was principally preoccupied
with Hanover's royal past and formed part of Georg's attempt to re-
establish the monarchy as the core of the Hanoverian state. Yet the
Welf Museum was not purely dynastic: it also included a portrait
display, celebrating the great men born under Welf rule, and a collection of historical objects. In this, as in other ways, the initiative was
inspired by the Bavarian National Museum in Munich, founded in 1852
as one plank of Max II's 'nation'-building strategy.[56] Like the Welf
Museum, the Bavarian National Museum combined a dynastic view of
Bavarian history (typified by the grand first floor dedicated to historical
frescos of the Wittelsbach past) with a display of cultural history, demonstrating the development of the Bavarian people. Such a vision of
history was more democratic than the traditional dynastic interpretation, but more dynastic than the history collected and displayed in
Württemberg's state collection of antiquities. The Bavarian and
Hanoverian museums were intended to demonstrate the historic continuity and community of dynasty and people and to bolster Bavarian
and Hanoverian patriotism accordingly. Both the museums themselves
and the motivation behind them were curiously similar to better-known
'national' initiatives. For instance, the portraits of great men on show
in the Welf Museum can be compared with the busts of great Germans
displayed both in Ludwig of Bavaria's temple to German culture,
Walhalla, and in the Germanic National Museum, a private initiative
based in Nuremberg. On one level, these displays were merely exhibitions of portraiture or sculpture. Collectively, however, they functioned
as a patriotic monument.

   The Welf Museum was a royal museum *par excellence* – founded by the
monarch as a tribute to his dynasty and its ties with the people. It exemplified, in its most extreme form, the primacy of politics over culture in
museum construction. Indeed, it is hard to see the Welf Museum as

[55] A copy of the founding order can be found in HSAHan Hann 113 A 113 (1–4).
[56] See Hubert Glaser, '". . . ein Bayerisch historisches Museum im weitesten Sinne des Wortes . . ."'
       and Peter Volk, 'Das Bayerische Nationalmuseum in München – Konstanz und Wandel' in
       Plessen (ed.), *Die Nation und ihre Museen*, pp. 182–90, 191–9.

anything other than an instrument of cultural policy, although we should not underestimate Georg's keen interest in the Welf past. By and large, however, the distinction between royal and 'civic' museums was not clear-cut. Most museums were a mixture of the two, providing some combination of royal art collections, royal prestige and royal money with a bourgeois public and perhaps civic collections. As such, they were instruments of monarchic or government cultural policy, but also a response to popular interests and concerns. Nevertheless, it is important to realise that political considerations were often crucial in deciding governments to support projects of this kind. This was certainly true in the case of the antiquities collection founded in Württemberg in the 1860s. That such political considerations did not predominate in the case of the New Museum in Dresden can be seen as testimony to the genuine cultural worth of the Saxon collections, which were important in their own right. As a general rule, the less distinguished a collection or museum, the more likely it was to be an instrument of politics first and foremost. On the other hand, the very importance of the Dresden collections gave them added symbolic value. Yet even the most distinguished collections could be managed in part for political ends.

Museums were not the only aspect of cultural policy where aesthetic activities were appropriated for political purposes. In Saxony an art fund, the *Postulat für Kunstzwecke*, was set up in 1858 with ostensibly cultural aims. Since 1843 the Saxon Association of Independent Artists had repeatedly petitioned for an annual state grant of 5,000 *Thaler* to found a gallery for contemporary Saxon art and to subsidise major artistic commissions. The aims of the society itself were self-seeking rather than political. Its members simply hoped that they would find it easier to make a living as a result. The petitions invariably mentioned the need to avoid a talent-drain of young artists, and claimed that the fund would raise the standards of Saxon artists and, by extension, Saxon design. Nevertheless, the Association of Artists recognised that such considerations were unlikely to persuade the government to part with the money. Consequently it made three important claims on behalf of the proposed fund.[57]

First, the society claimed that the state had now replaced other individuals and institutions as the major source of patronage for the arts,

---

[57] See HSADre Ministerium des Innern 17305 (1–27) for these petitions (1843–58) and for the position taken by the Academic Council.

just as it had increasingly taken responsibility for other policy areas, such as industry and agriculture.[58] There was much truth in this, for the idea that culture now formed part of the state's remit had become widespread and was reflected in the shift towards public museums.[59] Secondly, the society claimed that artistic achievement reflected the intellectual and moral status of a civilisation.[60] Sponsorship of the arts was therefore bound to redound to the greater glory of a state and its people. The implications of this claim were three-fold. First, art contributed to the civilisation of a state and its people, encouraging their intellectual, spiritual and moral improvement. Secondly, the artistic achievements of a state increased its standing in the world. Thirdly, the society stressed the role of monumental art in public life. Monumental art was, it argued, a uniquely public art form since it appeared in public places and on public buildings; it was therefore uniquely able to foster 'patriotic ideas'. Consequently, in 1849, at the height of the revolution, the society argued that state sponsorship of monumental art was a matter of 'national' importance.[61] Equally, in 1852 the society lamented the fact that so many churches and public buildings lacked elevating motifs, calculated to encourage virtue, piety and love for the Fatherland. The society argued 'that there was never a more appropriate moment to promote the national feelings of our people than now, and how can this be done more effectively than through art?'[62]

The efforts of the Association of Artists to establish a state fund for monumental art were firmly supported by the Academic Council of the Dresden Art Academy. As an official body, the Academic Council was better placed to make the case for such a fund attractive to the authorities. It did so by stressing the contemporary relevance of the initiative. In 1857 for instance, the Academic Council noted that even a city like Munich had managed to acquire 'greater significance . . . simply

---

[58] The parallel with the economic activities of the state was first drawn in the 1849 petition, Vorstand d. Verein d. selbstständiger Künstler to Gesammtministerium, 1 January 1849, HSADre Ministerium des Innern 17305 (11–14).

[59] See Scheuner, 'Die Kunst als Staatsaufgabe', passim. A similar argument was advanced for Hanover in the anonymous pamphlet *Das Staatsbudget und das Bedürfniß für Kunst u. Wissenschaft im Königreich Hannover* (1866).

[60] Proposition der Verein d. selbstständigen Künstler, 1 January 1843, HSADre Ministerium des Innern 17305 (1–8; 9–10).

[61] Vorstand d. Verein d. selbstständiger Künstler to Gesammtministerium, 1 January 1849, HSADre Ministerium des Innern 17305 (11–14).

[62] Vorstand d. Verein d. selbstständiger Künstler to Gesammtministerium, 1 January 1852, HSADre Ministerium des Innern 17305 (14b-16).

through decorating it with monumental art works'.[63] The art fund promised to raise Dresden's profile in a similar fashion. At the same time, the Academic Council presented the initiative in the context of Saxony's historic commitment to the arts, from which it drew important lessons, urging: 'Surely [Saxony] will continue to lead the way for her larger German neighbours, as she has done so gloriously in the past? Here is the opportunity to achieve supremacy by peaceful means, founded in the highest aspirations of the human spirit and its achievements.' The political context of cultural policy in Germany at this time, and the wider implications of cultural competition between states, could scarcely be more explicit. Equally, the chairman of the Academic Council, Schnorr von Carolsfeld, argued that monumental art fulfilled a special function as 'the deep and fitting expression of the feelings, beliefs and desires of the mood of the people as a whole'. Consequently, he believed that the fund should be used exclusively for monumental purposes and suggested that suitable projects included 'statues of Saxon princes, statesmen, artists, thinkers and other worthy men'. By no means all of his colleagues shared these views. Indeed, some vigorously defended the virtues of other art forms, such as portraiture and landscape painting. In the event, however, Schnorr von Carolsfeld prevailed. When it was finally established, the art fund was intended to promote exclusively monumental art. The decision testifies to its fundamentally political vocation.

This vocation was certainly borne out in practice. In 1859 King Johann approved the first projects put forward by the Academic Council, which administered the fund. He was particularly enthusiastic about a projected art gallery in Dresden that would exhibit the work of Saxon artists.[64] Johann noted with satisfaction that plans to decorate the gallery with frescos and sculptures depicting the beauties of the Saxon countryside and the glories of the Saxon past perfectly reflected the aims of the fund. Like the gallery, the first commissions sponsored by the art fund were located in Dresden. Nevertheless, Johann insisted that the benefits of the fund should not be restricted to the capital. He wanted to ensure 'that the artistic interests of other parts of the country are properly taken into consideration'. Cultural outreach of this kind meant that the whole state benefited from the state's new artistic initiative: the impact of the policy was evenly spread. An advertisement in the *Dresdner Journal*, the

---

[63] Petition des akademischen Raths zur Feststellung einer Summe von jährlich 5,000 Thaler für monumentale Kunst, 20 May 1857, HSADre Ministerium des Innern 17305 (23–27).

[64] Allerhöchste Resolution, 29 August 1859, HSADre Ministerium des Innern 17305 (108–13).

official government newspaper, set this process in motion.[65] Published in January 1860, the advertisement expressed the hope that in the future all public buildings would reflect artistic as well as practical considerations, and announced that the government welcomed proposals from the localities for public sculptures, frescos and oil paintings that related to the activities of the church, the state, local communities or charitable foundations. Moreover, the advertisement explicitly noted the possibility that the new art fund might subsidise statues of great men, but only 'under special circumstances, in particular if [the statues] are intended to recall the memory of great historical events'. This proviso almost certainly reflected the enormous popularity of public statues and monuments at this time, and the fact that these monuments usually reflected a nationalist or liberal agenda.[66]

In the past monuments had been the preserve of the authorities. In the nineteenth century, however, monuments became a matter for the people, which gave them new significance. Monument construction was enormously significant for the growth of nationalism before 1871, and indeed thereafter. Voluntary societies indulged in a positive frenzy of monument building at this time, funded through public subscription. The process of building and funding the monuments encouraged communication at a national level, through the formation of networks that fostered a sense of national community. For instance, in the 1840s the activities of the Detmold Hermann Monument Association prompted the formation of similar societies throughout Germany. Societies promoting monuments to Luther and others launched similar nationwide appeals for funds. Public subscriptions of this kind enabled voluntary societies to realise monumental plans independently of the state – perhaps even in tacit opposition to it. More importantly, such subscriptions helped constitute the nation as a voluntary community: individu-

[65] *Dresdner Journal* (Amtlicher Theil), No. 10, 13 January 1860.
[66] Interest in these monuments in Germany was provoked by Thomas Nipperdey's seminal article, 'Nationalidee und Nationaldenkmal in Deutschland im 19. Jahrhundert', in Nipperdey (ed.), *Gesellschaft, Kultur, Theorie*, pp. 133–73. Since then numerous historians have written on the subject. The following is only a selection: Wilfried Lipp, *Natur – Geschichte – Denkmal. Zur Entstehung des Denkmalbewußtseins der bürgerlichen Gesellschaft* (Frankfurt, 1987) examines the origins of the phenomenon in the late eighteenth and early nineteenth centuries. On Württemberg, Friedemann Schmoll, *Verewigte Nation*, is extremely pertinent to the themes of this study. Tacke, *Denkmal im sozialen Raum*, provides an excellent (if rather functionalist) analysis of the social context surrounding such monuments, based on the Hermann Monument and the monuments to Gergovia in France. On the later period see Wolfgang Hardtwig, 'Bürgertum, Staatssymbolik und Staatsbewußtsein im Deutschen Kaiserreich 1871–1914' in Hardtwig (ed.), *Ausgewählte Aufsätze* (Göttingen, 1994), pp. 191–219.

als demonstrated their identification with the nation through voluntary financial contributions. This voluntary community then achieved permanent expression in the monument it had built.

Many of these monuments were intended to make a clear political point. This was most obviously true of the major 'national' monuments built or planned during this period, of which the most striking was without doubt the Hermann Monument in Lippe-Detmold. This was a colossal statue of the mythical Hermann, dressed in traditional German costume and crushing the Roman eagle under foot. Hermann's sword was drawn and the blade inscribed with the immortal words: 'German unity is my strength, My strength is Germany's might.' The Hermann Monument emphasised the historic continuity of the German nation and represented a call for that nation to unite. Monuments did not have to be as ambitious or imposing as this in order to carry a clear political message. Statues of liberal heroes, like the statue of the father of the German press, Gutenberg, in Mainz, could be just as effective. Moreover, statues to individuals also symbolised and celebrated the collective achievements of the Germans, reinforcing popular awareness of nationhood.

Understandably, the Saxon government did not wish the art fund to be used for such purposes. Instead, in the 1860s the Academic Council set out to subsidise a series of politically desirable monuments with official rather than oppositional connotations. The art fund built three statues in Saxony before 1866: a statue of the Saxon Emperor Heinrich I in Meissen and two statues of Elector Johann Georg I, one in Bautzen and one in Johanngeorgenstadt.[67] These statues in no way reflected the initial proposals sent in by the town councils of Meissen, Bautzen and Johanngeorgenstadt. Instead, in all three cases the town council had envisaged a statue of an allegorical female figure, usually with strong local connotations: Lausatia in Bautzen; Misnia in Meissen; a female genius carrying a water jug in Johanngeorgenstadt. In each case the Academic Council dismissed the original idea as 'meaningless' and difficult to execute, and proposed a monarchic monument in its stead.[68] The monarch in question was always chosen for his strong local associations. Meissen and Johanngeorgenstadt had been founded by the Emperor Heinrich and Johann Georg respectively, whilst Bautzen was the capital of Upper Lausatia, first acquired by Saxony during

[67] For details on the statues in Bautzen and Johanngeorgenstadt see HSADre Ministerium des Innern 17390. For details on the statue in Meissen see HSADre Ministerium des Innern 17403 (a).
[68] Vortrag des K. Commissars beim akademischen Rathe, die Herstellung eines Brunnenstandbildes für Meissen betr., 13 July 1861, HSADre Ministerium des Innern 17403 (a) (18–20).

3.1 The Johann Georg monument in Johanngeorgenstadt. The inscription reads: '*Hilf,
Heiliger Gott!* Who would have thought, that a memorial to our praiseworthy Elector
would be founded in such a barren wilderness?'
Photo: Christian Teller

Johann Georg's reign. The political motivation behind these monuments was particularly glaring in the case of Johanngeorgenstadt, a poor mining town in the Erzgebirge mountains. The town council had applied for funds to build the statue beside a plain stone basin near the church, known as the Schiller Fountain and built in 1859 – presumably as part of the Schiller centenary celebrations, which had been manipulated by liberal nationalists for political ends. In this context, the Academic Council's proposal for a statue of Johann Georg I fundamentally altered the symbolism of the fountain. Unsurprisingly, the Johanngeorgenstadt town council objected very strongly to the new proposal. Indeed – in flagrant opposition to the views of the mayor – the town council initially declared that it would prefer to abandon the plan, ostensibly on the grounds that a bronze statue of Johann Georg was too expensive.[69] Exceptionally, the Academic Council agreed to fund the entire project rather than let it drop. In the long term, however, this proved a pyrrhic victory, for the fountain continued to be referred to as the Schiller Fountain, and never became the Johann Georg Fountain as the Academic Council might have wished. Monuments to former rulers like this one portrayed their subjects as local benefactors. They emphasised the historic ties between individual communities and the Saxon dynasty, in an attempt to render these vivid to contemporaries. Yet despite the dynastically motivated monument policy implemented through the art fund, it is important to realise that this did not reflect a coherent policy at government level.

Today the *Goldener Reiter*, a statue of Augustus the Strong in the *Dresdner Neumarkt*, is brightly gilded and widely recognised as a symbol of the city. In the 1860s (during the early days of the art fund) the statue was in a state of deplorable decay. Neither the Interior Ministry, nor the Ministry of the Royal House, nor the city of Dresden was willing to accept responsibility for its upkeep.[70] By 1864 the situation was so serious that Augustus' sword fell down from the statue. It was rescued by a passing porter, who handed it in to the military authorities.[71] Yet even this failed to persuade the government to take action. In fact, the monument was not repaired until 1883. The activities of the art fund demonstrated that the Saxon government took monuments seriously; the fate of the *Goldener Reiter* indicates that it did not take them that seriously.

[69] Stadtrath, Johanngeorgenstadt to Ministerium des Innern, 4 November 1862, HSADre Ministerium des Innern 17390 (33).   [70] See HSADre Ministerium des Innern 17306 (1–8).
[71] As reported in Ministerium des Innern to Finanzministerium, 21 March 1864, HSADre Ministerium des Innern 17306.

In any case, the *Goldener Reiter* was a very traditional monarchic monument and as such it did not fit easily into in the monumental politics of the nineteenth century. Monarchic monuments were not in themselves a new phenomenon. Indeed, the practice of putting statues of monarchs in public places dated back centuries.[72] Such monuments were intended to assert the authority of the monarch and reinforce the loyalty and obedience of his subjects. Like other areas of cultural politics, monarchic monuments of this kind were adapted to reflect the political culture of the nineteenth century. The growth of a monumental cult at national level inspired particularist parallels. If this was true of publicly funded monuments, like those subsidised by the Saxon art fund, it was even truer of numerous semi-official monarchic monuments built through public subscription at this time.

Between 1841 and 1861 monuments were erected to honour Friedrich August II of Saxony, Ernst August of Hanover and Wilhelm of Württemberg. These monuments were traditional in form, portraying the monarch on a column, on horseback or, as in Württemberg, depicting key scenes from the monarch's life and reign in bronze reliefs around the base of a column.[73] Yet they differed from their eighteenth-century counterparts because they symbolised not the authority of the monarchs in question, but rather the devotion of their subjects and the union of monarch and people. The *Goldener Reiter* had been presented by Augustus the Strong to his people. By contrast, all three royal monuments constructed in Hanover, Saxony and Württemberg at this time were presented by the people to their kings – either by the people's representatives in the Estates or through voluntary subscription, on the model of the Hermann Monument.

The Jubilee Column in Stuttgart was erected during Wilhelm's lifetime to commemorate the massively successful state celebration held to mark his silver jubilee in 1841. The initial proposal for the monument came from the Württemberg parliament.[74] The monuments to Friedrich August of Saxony and Ernst August of Hanover were erected after their deaths. In both cases apparently unofficial committees formed for the purpose. In each case, however, those involved had close ties to the state. In Saxony

---

[72] See for instance Ulrich Keller, *Reitermonumente absolutistischer Fürsten* (Munich, 1971).

[73] The following does not provide any art-historical analysis of the monuments. Rather, it focuses on the social symbolism and realities of the monument construction and inauguration processes.

[74] For details on this see Schmoll, *Verewigte Nation*, pp. 86–101. Schmoll argues that the monument symbolised popular endorsement of and enthusiasm for constitutional monarchy in Württemberg.

3.2 The Jubilee Column in Stuttgart.

the presidents of both Chambers headed the Committee for the Erection
of a National Monument Dedicated to the Memory of His Majesty, King
Friedrich August II. In Hanover the initiative behind the Ernst August
Monument Committee came from High Court Marshal von Malortie;
Rasch, a leading Hanoverian official; Major von Uslar Gleichen; the
court architect, Vogell; and a businessman, Werner.[75] The committees in
both Saxony and Hanover issued state-wide appeals for voluntary contributions to fund the monuments. Each monument could therefore claim
to have been built by the people. This claim was explicit in the inscription
on the Ernst August Monument in Hanover, which read: 'To the Father
of the Country from his faithful people'.[76] The symbolism here was
increased in other ways, for instance through the use of Hanoverian stone
and the expressed preference for a Hanoverian sculptor.

The problems faced by these subscriptions in Saxony and Hanover
demonstrate how far the symbolism of these particularist monuments
failed to reflect reality. Indeed, the particularist union of monarch and
people presented through monarchic monuments of this kind was primarily an aspiration. Yet this did not necessarily undermine their symbolic importance, since the same was also true of national monuments.
After all, the Hermann Monument celebrated the existence of a
German nation long before it had truly come into being, claiming for
that nation an ancient continuity which it clearly lacked. Equally, the
existence of a national community constituted by the Hermann
Monument subscription process was also rather doubtful. Like its particularist counterparts in Hanover and Saxony, the Hermann Monument
appeal failed to meet its subscription target (and was eventually bailed
out by the state). Furthermore, as in Hanover and Saxony, the Hermann
Monument movement relied considerably on state support in Lippe,
where the subscription was most successful. In this sense, the relationship between the Hermann Monument and German nationalism was
similar to that between the monarchic monuments of Hanover and
Saxony and particularism in these states. At the same time, the position
of the state official who belonged to the Hermann Monument
Association was not directly relevant to the activities of the society itself,
for the Hermann Monument represented a community without a state.

---

[75] Details on the establishment of the Ernst August Monument Committee are given in the minutes
of a meeting held in K. Oberhofmarschall Amt, Hanover, 4 February 1855, HSAHan Dep. 103
XXVIII 627.
[76] The precise wording of the inscription was considered with great care. See HSAHan Dep. 103
XXVIII 644.

Conversely, the committees behind the Friedrich August and Ernst August monuments were closely linked to the states that they represented. Moreover, the Hermann Monument asserted the legitimacy of the German nation in terms of a very distant – indeed mythological – past. By contrast, particularist monuments bolstered the legitimacy of territorial states in terms of the immediate present and very recent past. Consequently, the success of the subscription appeals in Saxony and Hanover appeared in some sense to be a measure of the genuine popularity or otherwise of these states.

This was certainly recognised by the committees behind the appeals in question. The symbolism of a public, state-wide subscription was central to the significance of the monuments and could therefore create difficulties. The Saxon committee had only succeeded in raising 9,000 *Thaler* for the Friedrich August Monument by 1857, although the monument planned was likely to cost between 33,000 and 100,000 *Thaler*.[77] Nevertheless, the committee was cautious in recommending that the state make good the short-fall. It feared that the monument would lose

the high value attached to it, because the Saxon people have raised the sum from *their own voluntary* contributions. If too great a sum from the state's coffers were added to this, the monument would appear to have been undertaken by the state or the government, and lose its character as a monument built by the people. Indeed, malcontents could even present it as a monument forced upon the people.

In the event the cabinet solved this tricky problem by deciding the necessary extra funds could fittingly come from the 25,000-*Thaler* surplus left by the Friedrich August the Just Monument Fund. The Ernst August Monument committee in Hanover encountered similar problems in raising the necessary funds. Malortie initially anticipated collecting at least 50,000–60,000 *Thaler*.[78] In fact, the committee had difficulty raising half as much and was forced to scale down its ambitious plans accordingly.

The luke-warm reception accorded to the Ernst August appeal in Hanover proved seriously embarrassing for the committee and, indeed, the whole monumental project. Oppositional voices questioned the validity of the monument as a symbol of state unity, comparing the subscription unfavourably with the 130,000 *Thaler* and 60,000 *Thaler* raised

[77] Friedrich von Schönfels and Dr Carl Heinrich Haase to K. Finanz Ministerium, 3 June 1857, HSADre Gesammtministerium Loc. 22, No. 9 (83–5). I have found very little documentary material relating to this monument. Consequently most of this section is devoted to the Ernst August monument in Hanover.
[78] Malortie to Prof. Rauch, Berlin, 16 April 1855, HSAHan Dep. 103 xxviii 624.

by Cologne and Düsseldorf respectively for monuments to Friedrich Wilhelm III of Prussia.[79] Of course, Hanover was not a particularly wealthy state. Nevertheless, the committee had enjoyed substantial support from the state bureaucracy and municipal authorities, which should have ensured the appeal's success. Letters urging state officials to do their utmost for the subscription were sent to every *Amt*, Magistrate, Town Council, Local and District Authority in the land, not to mention the Provincial Estates and numerous individuals.[80] Furthermore, their role as tax collectors meant that many officials were particularly well placed to collect voluntary subscriptions. Official agitation had its effect: all but a quarter of the money raised between 1855 and 1861 in Hanover was raised from official bodies or officially organised collections.[81] Other kinds of social pressure also made it hard for individuals to resist the Ernst August Monument appeal. For instance, the local newspaper in Nienburg announced that it would print the names of contributors to the monument, and the amount contributed in each case.[82] Despite all this, subscription levels remained regrettably low. Indeed, many officials apologised for this when they sent in their contributions to the central committee. Most claimed hardship and drew attention to the competing appeals of other causes. Repeated mention was made of 'regular collections for the victims of fires and floods', which had exhausted the resources of communities and individuals.[83] Consequently, the committee claimed that the low levels of contributions was due 'to events which could not be predicted, and not to a lack of interest in the patriotic undertaking'.[84]

This was disingenuous. There are indications that the lack of interest had more serious origins in political malaise. From this point of view, the collection could hardly have started at a worse time than mid to late 1855, the high point of the second Hanoverian constitutional crisis. This was probably no accident, given the close ties between the committee and the state. Indeed, the Ernst August Monument was in many ways a flagship for Georg V's new, 'monarchic' regime. Equally, it seems likely that the luke-warm reception accorded the appeal reflected the unpopularity of

---

[79] According to an article in *Hannoverscher Courier*, No. 1712, 11 April 1860.

[80] See HSAHan Dep. 103 xxviii 623. A copy of the appeal is to be found in Dep. 103 xxviii 626.

[81] Uebersicht der zur Errichtung des Ernst-August-Denkmal in Hannover eingegangenen Beiträge pro Februar 1855 bis September 1861, HSAHan Dep. 103 xxviii 623.

[82] *Allgemeiner Anzeiger für den Obergerichtsbezirk Nienburg*, No. 18, 3 March 1855.

[83] Schönian, K. Amt Wittlage to Comité f. d. Ernst August Denkmal zu Hannover, 22 September 1856, HSAHan Dep. 103 xxviii 616/1 ii 420.

[84] *Hannoversche Zeitung*, No. 417, 5 September 1855.

the 1855 coup. Only one local official mentioned this explicitly. Wyneken of Melle, near Grönenburg, reported that he had repeatedly spoken up warmly on behalf of the appeal in various district assemblies and had anticipated being able to send a respectable contribution.[85] This hope was rooted in the belief that the inhabitants of Melle had forgotten the unfortunate occurrences of 1837 and 1848. They had been relieved that the reforms had 'finally put an end to the unhappy constitutional mistakes &c . . . and had trusted in a calmer future and in His Majesty's Government. The Confederal legislation, and all that preceded and followed it, has led to a return of uncertainty, worry and discontent in the communities.' Here, Wyneken may have been voicing his own views as much as those of his community. Other, less explicit references to the political situation bear him out. For instance, the Monument Committee wrote to Landdrost von Bar of Hildesheim, regretting that the authorities in this very oppositionally inclined town had proved so 'uncommitted and uninterested' in the matter.[86] Similarly, Vogt Schulze of Schledhausen noted that respected and influential individuals in the area had spoken out against making any kind of contribution, rendering the appeal very unpopular with inhabitants.[87] Quantitatively, such voices are not significant amongst the mass of subscriptions sent in to the committee. Furthermore, it is worth noting that the Ernst August Monument appeal raised substantially more than its Saxon counterpart, despite the second constitutional conflict in Hanover. Nevertheless, the short-fall in subscriptions was an issue. Most officials may have been reluctant to explain it in politically contentious terms, but this should not necessarily be taken at face value. At least in some areas, opponents of the coup seem to have rejected the symbolic aims of the appeal, and instead used the occasion as a means to express their discontent.

Apparently, the Ernst August Monument embodied the ties of affection that had bound the people of Hanover to their former King. As in Saxony, however, the difficulties faced by the collection indicate that this was only true up to a point, if at all. The construction of such monarchic monuments was an attempt to present the aspirations of the political establishment in these states as a reality. In fact, the process of

---

[85] Wyneken, Melle Amt Grönenberg to Comité f. d. Ernst August Denkmal zu Hannover, 18 August 1855, HSAHan Dep. 103 XXVIII 621 I.

[86] Comité f. d. Ernst August Denkmal zu Hannover to Landdrost v. Bar, Hildesheim, 13 August 1855, HSAHan Dep. 103 XXVIII 623.

[87] Amt Schledehausen to Comité f. d. Ernst August Denkmal zu Hannover, 23 July 1855, HSAHan Dep. 103 XXVIII 620 III.

monument construction only served to highlight the gulf between this idealised union of people and monarch and the situation in most German states. This was more serious than the similar gulf between ideal and reality in the case of the Hermann Monument. The reality of a German nation was inevitably vague; the reality of the German states as political units was very concrete.

The Ernst August Monument was unveiled at a grand public ceremony in Hanover on 5 September 1861. A large group of notables assembled in front of the railway station to greet the royal family: government ministers, the diplomatic corps, the court, generals, and various deputations representing the Hanoverian Estates, the different government departments, the Protestant Consistories, the Cathedral chapters of Hildesheim and Osnabrück, Göttingen University, the judiciary, the different regiments in the army, the municipality of Hanover and the local clergy. The ceremony opened with a military parade. Meanwhile, a great civic procession was making its way from the *Waterlooplatz* to the railway station. Members of the festival committee and those involved in constructing the monument itself led the way. They were followed by representatives of forty-two guilds from the capital and other important Hanoverian towns, then by representatives of the railway workers, printers, merchants, gardeners, artists, architects, the Historical Association for Lower Saxony, and workers in local factories. Marching bands accompanied the procession on its way. The royal couple were the last to arrive. When they reached the square in front of the railway station they were greeted by the assembled crowds with cannon fire, military salutes and the strains of the Hanoverian royal anthem. When all had taken their places, a second cannon shot rang out. The President of the Ernst August Committee then made a speech, before begging Georg V to unveil the monument. As he did so, the city's bells pealed, the assembled crowds burst into song, music and cheers, and the cannons began a hundred-and-one-gun salute. Finally, the choral society sang a number of loyal and uplifting songs. The King then mounted a horse and watched as the assembled regiments marched past him, followed by the entire civic procession.

This kind of celebration was by no means unusual in nineteenth-century Germany. In fact, monuments like the Ernst August Monument were invariably unveiled with large-scale public festivities, which were designed to create a sense of unity and to present a particular image of the community involved – in this case, the Kingdom of Hanover. Such

3.3 The inauguration of the Ernst August Monument in Hanover: a leaf from the
commemorative album published to mark the occasion. Above, we see the monument
itself, below the procession through the streets of Hanover.
Source: By permission of the British Library, J/9930.h.21

festivals were a kind of historical microcosm, illuminating the political and social self-image of organisers and participants.[88] Thus the different occasions for public celebrations and the symbolism deployed reflected the political considerations behind the festivities. Divisions within a festival procession, the degree of popular participation and the social exclusiveness of the celebrations mirrored the society in which the festival took place. Nevertheless, public festivities should not be too crudely equated with genuine political feeling. Rather, the very prevalence of such celebrations often created a set of firmly established customs, observed as much through habit as through commitment or enthusiasm. This is made very clear by a lengthy undercover account of celebrations held in the Hanoverian town of Celle in 1864 to mark the centenary of the Royal Agricultural Association.[89] Although the town was handsomely decorated to honour the King's arrival, the author warned that this could not be taken as a sign of genuine loyalty. Instead, the decorations honoured the town itself as much as the royal visitor, for, as one inhabitant explained: 'We would have been ashamed of ourselves, in view of what takes place in other towns when the King arrives, if we had not received His Majesty just as worthily.'

On one level, there was nothing new about large-scale public celebrations of this kind. Yet these celebrations acquired new significance in the nineteenth century as a consequence of the symbolic legacy of the French Revolution, for the revolutionary rituals came to rival the established symbolism of traditional monarchical festivals. In the years after 1815 popular festivities contributed to the creation of a political public sphere because, in a time of repression, they provided a vehicle for the expression of anti-establishment views. Thus festivals held to mark the anniversary of the Baden constitution expressed support for constitutional government and for liberal political ideas. Equally, the famous Hambach Festival of 1832, and the regional festivals of the singers and

---

[88] The role of public festivals in nineteenth-century life has increasingly attracted the attention of historians. Good starting points are Düding, Friedemann and Münch (eds.), *Öffentliche Festkultur*, Manfred Hettling and Paul Nolte (eds.), *Bürgerliche Feste, symbolische Formen politischen Handelns im 19. Jahrhundert* (Göttingen, 1993). Both are collections of essays describing and analysing different individual festivals. Michael Maurer, 'Feste und Feiern als historischer Forschungsgegenstand', *Historische Zeitschrift* 253:1 (1991), 101–30, provides a useful summary of the (relatively) recent writing in the field. Klaus Tenfelde, 'Adventus. Zur historischen Ikonologie des Festzugs', *Historiche Zeitschrift* 235 (1982), 45–84, and Wolfgang Hartmann, *Der historische Festzug. Seine Entstehung und Entwicklung im 19. und 20. Jahrhundert* (Munich, 1976), study the development of different ritual aspects in public celebrations.

[89] Die Säcularfeier der K. Landwirtschaftsgesellschaft zu Celle am 3. und 4. Juni 1864, 13 June 1864, HSAHan Dep. 103 IX 296 06–08/1864.

gymnasts in the 1840s, gave German nationalists an opportunity to express their political aspirations, wave flags and sing nationalist songs.[90] Occasionally, such festivities snowballed into nationwide protest movements. Plans to celebrate the four hundredth anniversary of Gutenberg's discovery of printing in 1840 were orchestrated by a central society, with members from as far afield as Leipzig, Frankfurt and Stuttgart. The committee hoped to use the festivities to promote demands for a free press and to stimulate the emergence of a national voice in public affairs. These plans sparked panic among government authorities – so much so that Metternich threatened to take action at Confederal level, whilst programmes, speeches, toasts and commemorative albums were censored by state governments. In Hanover, for instance, only members of the book trade were allowed to join the local Gutenberg Society. The Württemberg government, however, took a very different stance. Instead of suppressing the celebrations, it sought to appropriate them for its own ends by organising a single state-wide celebration in Stuttgart, where Württemberg flags predominated rather than the national German tricolore. Of course, the festivals of the opposition had their counterparts in traditional monarchic celebrations, such as those held to mark royal birthdays, weddings, funerals and jubilees. Indeed, they partly explain the increasing importance of dynastic demonstrations of this kind. Moreover, just as the inauguration of monuments to liberal heroes, like Gutenberg, became liberal nationalist festivals, so the inauguration of monarchic monuments celebrated the existence of the state community. In both cases, however, the people acquired an active role as participants in the festivals, which reflected their new place in public life as a source of political legitimacy.

By the 1860s public festivals had acquired a pivotal role in the political conflict between conservative particularists on the one hand, and liberal nationalists on the other. Each group held its own festivals and attempted to reinterpret the festivals of its rivals. The sheer number of both nationalist and monarchic festivals at this time testified to their central importance in the public sphere. Following the example of the

---

[90] For instance: Peter Brandt, 'Das studentische Wartburgfest vom 18./19. Oktober 1817'; Cornelia Foerster, 'Das Hambacher Fest 1832. Volksfest und Nationalfest einer oppositionellen Massenbewegung' and ' "Hoch lebe die Verfassung?" Die pfälzischen Abgeordnetenfeste im Vormärz (1819–1846)'; Dieter Düding, 'Nationale Oppositionsfeste der Turner, Sänger und Schützen im 19. Jahrhundert', in Düding, Friedemann and Münch (eds.), *Öffentliche Festkultur*, pp. 10–24, 67–88, 132–146, 166–190. Also Paul Nolte, 'Die badischen Verfassungsfeste im Vormärz. Liberalismus, Verfassungskultur und soziale Ordnung in den Gemeinden' in Hettling and Nolte (eds.), *Bürgerliche Feste*, pp. 63–94.

3.4 Diffusing political protest: officially sponsored celebrations of the Gutenberg anniversary in Stuttgart, 1840.
Source: By permission of the British Library, 819.k.20

Württemberg government in 1840, German governments sought to repress or subvert nationalist celebrations rather than suppressing them altogether. Thus Georg V attempted to undercut anniversary celebrations of the battle of Leipzig held in Hanover by banning the use of the German colours (black, red and gold) and by instigating a more congenial rival festival, Waterloo Day. In this case, his efforts were misplaced, for the ban proved unenforceable and the Waterloo Day celebrations were a damp squib. Yet government efforts to colour nationalist celebrations were not always such a failure. The Saxon government was fairly successful in its attempt to appropriate the national gatherings of singers and gymnasts held in Saxony in the 1860s. Beust participated as a keynote speaker on these occasions, and used them to project a positive image of Saxon policy over the German question. In 1863, for instance, he told the gymnasts in Leipzig 'that Germany's princes and their governments do more than recognise and appreciate the gradual rise in general German consciousness, they positively welcome it because they see this growth of German feeling as the best support for their own efforts'.[91] Far from banning the German colours, the Saxon government actively displayed them on official buildings and royal palaces for the gymnastic festival of 1863 in Leipzig. According to the *Leipziger Tageblatt* the Berlin gymnasts were amazed at the gesture, asking if this could really be the royal palace.[92] On finding that it was, they cheered: 'How noble, how great-hearted, long live King Johann!' The festivals were extensively reported in the official Saxon press in order to maximise their impact.

Conversely, liberals and nationalists attempted to reinterpret particularist festivities to suit their political views. For instance, the 1860s saw two important royalist festivals in Hanover: the centenary of the Royal Agricultural Association in Celle and the celebration of fifty years of Hanoverian rule in East Friesland in 1865.[93] Both government and opposition accepted the symbolic importance of these celebrations, but disputed their meaning. The East Friesland Jubilee in particular was a highly contentious event, since Hanoverian rule was notoriously unpopular in this province. Even before the celebrations, the *Weser Zeitung* commented that their outcome was the subject of much speculation. Many believed that the East Friesland nobility had proposed the celebration in

---

[91] Speech reported in full in *Dresdner Journal*, No. 178, 5 August 1863.

[92] The *Leipziger Tageblatt* report formed the basis of the account in the *Dresdner Journal*, No. 179, 6 August 1863.

[93] The government documents relating to similar celebrations in Saxony have been destroyed.

order to curry favour with the King. The *Weser Zeitung* argued that 'a correct judgement of the real significance of the celebration will depend upon its resonance among those sectors of the population which, besides the Provincial Estates, represent the material interests of the province'.[94] The Hanoverian press supremo, Oskar Meding, took steps to ensure the celebrations were favourably covered in the Hanoverian and German press, with some success.[95] Yet opposition newspapers in Hanover and elsewhere contrasted Georg's assertion of historic Welf claims to the province with the Prussophile nostalgia and grudging acceptance of the benefits of Hanoverian rule expressed by the Provincial Estates. Such newspapers ridiculed the lack of public enthusiasm for the event.[96] These attacks hit home. An article in the *Weser Zeitung* decried their critique. Seldom, it claimed, had a provincial festival been 'so single-minded and harmonious'.[97] Yet the tone of the article was defensive. 'What more can one ask for?' the *Weser Zeitung* wondered, 'A popular festival in December?' Such disputes testify to the symbolic importance of public festivals and celebrations in political culture, but complicate the efforts of historians to interpret them. The impact of these festivals was determined as much by the relative success of different propaganda efforts as by the popularity of the festivals themselves.

Contemporaries do, however, seem to have agreed that the success of public celebrations was directly related to their popularity and that this, in turn, was reflected in the numbers attending. In these terms, the Munich *Oktoberfest* (better known as the Munich Beer Festival) was probably the most successful particularist festival in Germany at this time, but it was not an isolated phenomenon. Indeed, the *Oktoberfest* served as the model for a similar event held in Württemberg, the *Cannstatter Volksfest* – literally the Cannstatt People's Festival.[98] The *Volksfest* took place in Cannstatt, a small town just outside Stuttgart, and was founded by Wilhelm of Württemberg in 1818. Yet it quickly acquired the status of long-standing custom. By 1848 Duvernoy, the Württemberg Interior Minister, could describe it without a hint of irony as 'this long-

---

[94] *Weser Zeitung*, 13 December 1865. Cited in Tagesberichte der RegR. Meding, December 1865, HSAHan Dep. 103 IX 293 11–12/1865.

[95] For details of arrangements made see for instance Meding to Lex, 12 December 1865, HSAHan Dep. 103 IX 64. It would seem that there was much positive coverage, from the reports to be found in Tagesberichte der Regierungsrat Meding, December 1865, HSAHan Dep. 103 IX 293 11–12/1865.

[96] Notably the *Wochenblatt des Nationalvereins*. See Tagesberichte der RegR. Meding, 01–02/1866, HSAHan Dep. 103 IX 294.   [97] *Weser Zeitung*, No. 6879, 6 January 1866.

[98] On this see the fairly popular: Hans Otto Stroheker and Günther Willmann, *Cannstatter Volksfest. Das schwäbische Landesfest im Wandel der Zeiten* (Stuttgart, 1978).

established and beloved *Volksfest*.[99] Consequently, the *Volksfest* can be seen as an invented tradition – a practice which, through regular repetition, implied continuity with the past and served to encourage a sense of social cohesion and community, often designed to bolster a state or regime.[100] Given the sheer size of the *Volksfest*, it was very important in these terms – particularly for a state as small as Württemberg. Over 30,000 attended the first *Volksfest* in 1818, at a time when there were only 25,000 inhabitants in Stuttgart and a further 3,000 in Cannstatt.[101] By 1867 some 120,000 were travelling between the *Volksfest* and Stuttgart, not to mention those arriving from elsewhere.[102] The festival also grew longer: the official celebration remained restricted to one day but the unofficial *Volksfest* lasted nine days by 1853. In terms of genuine popularity, therefore, the *Volksfest* was at least as successful as the mass nationalist celebrations of this period, although it catered not to a national but to a local Württemberg audience. After all, only 25,000–30,000 attended the much-vaunted Hambach Festival in 1832. Similarly, 8,000–20,000 members of singing, shooting and gymnastic societies attended the national gatherings held in the 1860s, although attendance was bolstered to nearly 100,000 by the populations of the cities in which they were held (all of which were larger than Stuttgart).[103] By these standards the *Volksfest* was, quite simply, huge. The festival was so popular that Swabian emigrants to America even founded a *Cannstatter Volksfest* in Chicago.

The festival combined dynastic and representational elements with more pragmatic aims. In 1818 the motives for founding the *Volksfest* were primarily economic. This was a time of severe agricultural hardship, and the government hoped that the *Volksfest* would stimulate and improve the standards of Württemberg agriculture and, increasingly, industry.[104] Consequently, the main event of the day was the presentation of prizes to the owners of exceptional domestically bred livestock, as well as prizes for other services to agriculture, industry and enterprise. There were horse-races (again designed to encourage higher quality livestock) and a competition drawing attention to the activities of the Neckar fishermen. In each

---

[99] Duvernoy to H.M., 5 August 1848, HSAStu E 10 79 201.

[100] Eric Hobsbawm, 'Introduction: inventing traditions' in Hobsbawm and Ranger (eds.), *The invention of tradition*, pp. 1–15.

[101] According to Stroheker and Willmann, *Cannstatter Volksfest*, pp. 30–1.

[102] Ibid., p. 98. Stroheker and Willmann reach this figure on the basis of railway ticket sales.

[103] See Düding, 'Nationale Oppositionsfeste'.

[104] This reflected the Enlightenment belief that popular festivities could be improving as well as entertaining, and contribute to the spread of practical, primarily agricultural, ideas. For more on these ideas see Peter Münch, 'Fêtes pour le peuple, rien par le peuple. "Öffentliche Feste" im Programm der Aufklärung' in Düding, Friedemann and Münch, *Öffentliche Festkultur*, pp. 25–45.

case, King Wilhelm presented the prizes himself. Yet the *Volksfest* was always more than an agricultural festival. In fact, the famous Cannstatt meadows boasted a wealth of other, less serious attractions. In 1845 the *Illustriertes Volksblatt* described how '[t]asty morsels and excellent beer heighten the joyous mood . . . Merry songs and lively jests add spice to the meal – that is, if they are not drowned out by the continual clamour of ever-changing music'.[105] Yet the festival always retained its economic focus. It provided an opportunity for the government to hold various exhibitions of exemplary livestock, fruit, modern agricultural equipment, handicrafts and industrial machinery. All were designed to educate, inspire and entertain, but also to add to the attractions of the *Volksfest*.

With time, the *Volksfest* became an increasingly important political symbol in Württemberg. Its central role was acknowledged as early as 1841 in the design of the Jubilee Column in Stuttgart, which was closely modelled on the Fruit Column, symbol of the *Volksfest*. This indicated how far the festival had come to be identified with the state and vice versa. The process was actively encouraged by Wilhelm and his government, in an attempt to exploit the festival's popularity. The festival was timed to coincide with Wilhelm's birthday; his involvement in the prize-giving ritual was central to the whole event, and the festival's agricultural focus contributed to Wilhelm's image as 'the Farmer King'. Moreover, the *Volksfest* was frequently incorporated into wider festivities, such as Wilhelm's Jubilee in 1841, the opening of the Bruchsal–Stuttgart railway in 1853 and the meeting of the French and Russian Emperors held in Stuttgart in 1857. After the revolutions of 1848 the government did all it could to render the festival still more popular, a *Volksfest* in every sense of the word. Extra trains were laid on to enable more people to reach Cannstatt, and a range of other measures encouraged participation and increased the 'fun factor'.[106] These ranged from subsidised travel for prize-winning live stock to gymnastic displays, a hot-air balloon ascension and corporate-style entertainment for the representatives of local agricultural societies.[107] In moments of crisis the government consciously

[105] Stroheker and Willmann, *Cannstatter Volksfest*, pp. 136–7.
[106] See Chapter 6 for more details of the role of railways in increasing the festival's popularity.
[107] Details of such measures: in 1848 the cheapest tickets were reduced to half price and gymnastic and singing societies were allowed to participate (as on subsequent occasions); in 1862 subsidies were provided for prize-winning livestock travelling to Cannstatt from far afield and non-comissioned officers were invited to participate in the horse-races; in 1860 a Carrousel was set up on the *Cannstatter Wasen*; in 1861 a hot-air balloon ascension coincided with Wilhelm's arrival and representatives of the local agricultural societies were given a special tribune and invited to a meal at the government's expense.

3.5 Two sides of the *Cannstatter Volksfest*. (*a*) Formal presentation of prize livestock to the King and the general public. The famous *Fruchtsäule* can be made out in the distance. (*b*) Visitors to the *Volksfest* make merry.
Source: By permission of the British Library, J/9930.e.9

attempted to exploit the popularity of the *Volksfest*. For instance, in 1848 Duvernoy, the Interior Minister, recommended holding the festival despite the political situation, because it might help to 'calm the dominant uproar'.[108] This proved overly sanguine. In fact, radicals attempted (and failed) to turn the popular gathering to their own ends – a further instance of political opponents attempting to reinterpret public festivities. Similarly, in 1854 the Interior Minister recommended holding the *Volksfest* despite fear of a cholera outbreak, because it would prevent the public from panicking.[109] The *Volksfest* had come to represent the stability of the polity.

The success of the *Cannstatter Volksfest*, particularly when compared with the particularist festivals held in Hanover during the 1860s, may have been partly a product of its less blatantly political aims. Although the *Cannstatter Volksfest* acquired symbolic importance within Württemberg, it retained the façade of a popular, agricultural festival. As such, it appealed to the daily concerns of many Württembergers. By contrast, the political symbolism of the centenary of the Celle Agricultural Association and the East Friesland Jubilee was apparent to all. These were deferential occasions first and foremost, celebrating the achievements of Welf rule. Moreover, the arrival and participation of the monarch took centre stage. As such, these celebrations were fair game for the opponents of the Hanoverian government. Conversely, despite the involvement of the monarch, the *Cannstatter Volksfest* was not really a deferential occasion in this sense. Attending the festival principally provided an opportunity to have a good time. This made it hard for the opposition to criticise the festival, because its popularity meant that critics appeared grudging and out of step with the mood of the people. The union of monarch and people celebrated in Hanoverian festivals was largely show. In Württemberg it was more genuine. The *Cannstatter Volksfest* contributed to a sense of this union for participants, even though these feelings may not have lasted long outside the confines of the *Volksfest*.

The emergence of particular state cultures in Hanover, Saxony and Württemberg had strong parallels with contemporary developments at national level. The activities that contributed to the growth of these state cultures were often the same kinds of activity that contributed to the

---

[108] Duvernoy to H. M., 5 August 1848, HSAStu E 10 79 201.
[109] Linden, Ministerium des Innern to H.M., 10 August 1854, HSAStu E 10 79.

growth of a national culture in the nineteenth century. Interest in particularist history had its counterpart in German and nationalist historical activity, and the two were intimately connected. Nationalist historical interest inspired particularist historical activity and particularist history contributed to national historical achievement. The founding of state museums for antiquities from the relevant fatherland was mirrored at a national level by the Germanic National Museum. This museum was the product of citizen initiative, not state policy, but its very existence testified to the importance of state museums as cultural institutions and as expressions of state cultural identity. By contrast, the erection of particularist public monuments – in particular the adoption of the subscription approach – echoed the erection of nationalist monuments throughout Germany. If nationalists learned from official initiatives in their plans for a German national museum, then conservative particularists learned from nationalists in their appeals for popularly funded monarchic monuments. Both nationalist and particularist monumental projects experienced similar difficulties in raising the necessary funds for their monuments. Both kinds of monument relied unofficially on the state bureaucracy in their appeals, although this reliance was much more extreme for particularist monuments. Both nationalist and particularist monuments also reflected aspirations rather than reality, but this was probably more glaring in the case of nationalist monuments. Yet it was more problematic for their particularist counterparts, since the development of particular state cultures was rooted in political reality. Finally, both liberal nationalists and conservative particularists exploited public festivals and celebrations for political purposes in extremely similar ways. Frequently, each group attempted to reinterpret the festivities of the other, in an attempt to draw different political lessons from them. This demonstrates the conflict between nationalist and particularist forces in the cultural sphere very clearly.

Despite these similarities between nationalist and particularist cultures, there were also important differences. Crucially, nationalist cultural activity was always spontaneous, in that it depended exclusively on private initiative. This was inevitable, given the political fragmentation of the German 'nation' at this point. It is worth noting, however, that the political establishment often backed such voluntary initiatives. Many German princes contributed to nationalist fund-raising appeals in a personal capacity. Furthermore, the predominance of officials in participating societies enabled these societies to make use of bureaucratic structures in pursuing their ends. There was therefore a certain amount of interaction between nationalist cultural activities and the German states. This interaction was, however, qualitatively different to the interaction between particularist cultural activities and the German states, since particularist cultural activity was primarily driven by the state. It is true to say that some particularist cultural activity appeared to be spontaneously generated by societies and committees. This was most obviously true of state-based historical societies, but also of the Hanoverian Museum of Art and Science and the Friedrich August and Ernst August monuments. Despite this, the interface between such societies and the state proved far more compromising for particularist cultural activities than for their nationalist counterparts. The particularist orientation of such activities encouraged royal and government sponsorship and financial support. This in turn could colour the actual activities of the society, as was the case for the Historical Association for Württembergish Franconia in 1866. Furthermore, in their capacity as members of particularist societies, state officials were more clearly influenced by their professional concerns than was the case for officials who were members of more nationally oriented societies. In this sense, the historical societies of Hanover and Württemberg and the monarchic monument committees in Hanover and Saxony were indirectly instruments of state policy. Other kinds of particularist cultural activity, like the new museum in Dresden, the antiquities collection in Württemberg, the Welf Museum and the *Cannstatter Volksfest,* were directly the product of state or royal initiatives.

What motivated cultural initiatives of this kind? State-building concerns appear to have been fundamental, both for governments and for less official associational activity. Many key elements of cultural policy, particularly in Hanover and Württemberg, date back to the immediate post-Napoleonic period, when the integrational imperative in these states was at its most acute. This was true for the development of historical societies in these states, but also for the *Cannstatter Volksfest.* After 1848, the integrational imperative once again became an important factor in state politics. The desire to bolster a state-wide community through cultural activities was reflected in the appeals for monarchic monuments in all three states, and in official festivals and celebrations. More importantly, the wider German political context proved decisive in the decision to fund a collection of Württemberg antiquities. This context was also clearly very relevant to the Saxon creation of a government art fund and, given the timing, probably at least equally relevant to the foundation of the Welf Museum. Certainly, those involved in such policies appear to have been well aware of their political implications.

Clearly there were other motivations for cultural policy. Democratic pressures and practices obviously influenced the changing nature of the museum in this period and also the new kind of monarchic monument, funded by popular subscription. Genuine scholarly and aesthetic commitment was also an important factor, although there was a political aspect to this too. As we have seen, cultural achievement in the arts was perceived as a bench-mark by which the different states could be judged. Thus arts sponsorship enabled a state to maintain its standing in the world. This idea of cultural competition as a continuation of politics by other means is most clearly expressed by the Saxon Academic Council in connection with the art fund, but it appears to have been generally accepted. In other cases, cultural achievements elsewhere in Germany were used as an argument to support demands for state action. This was true for the Württemberg antiquities collection, the Hanoverian Museum of Art and Science and the Welf Museum.

Notwithstanding this awareness of culture as a means to encourage political integration within the state and as a factor in international relations, it would be wrong to interpret cultural initiatives in these states as a systematic cultural policy with clear state-building objectives. Rather, the approach in these states was very much *ad hoc* – in stark contrast to the situation in Bavaria. In Hanover, Saxony and Württemberg cultural policy did not form part of an over-arching cultural project. This is most apparent in the discrepancy in Saxony between the new statues funded by the art fund and the failure to maintain the *Goldener Reiter*. Equally, it is important not to over-estimate the scale of official cultural policy.

Table 3.1 shows the different levels of government expenditure on culture in the five German kingdoms. From this it is immediately apparent that Hanover spent pitifully little on culture, although this was augmented by Georg V's private expenditure, which could be quite significant. For instance, Georg contributed 10,000 *Thaler* to the Museum of Art and Science between 1861 and 1863. Nevertheless, the size of the Hanoverian cultural budget serves as a useful corrective to the impression that Hanoverian cultural initiatives like the Welf Museum formed part of a wider cultural policy, or that this cultural policy was a crucial plank of the new Welf order. The awareness of the integrative potential of cultural policy apparent in the Welf Museum does not really seem to have translated into substantial cultural expenditure. By contrast, the Saxon cultural budget was indeed relatively large – over a third that of Prussia, although Prussia was roughly eight times the size of Saxony. Indeed, Saxony also spent proportionately more than Bavaria

Table 3.1. *Annual government cultural expenditure in
the five German kingdoms*

(at this time there were roughly 6.8 *Thaler.* to 12 *Gulden*).[a]

Hanover	1,600 *Thaler*
Saxony	90,416 *Thaler*
Württemberg	30,000 *Gulden*
Prussia	250,000 *Thaler*
Bavaria	245,784 *Gulden*

Note:
[a] Figures from Anon., *Das Staatsbudget und das Bedürfniß
für Kunst und Wissenschaft im Königreich Hannover*
(Hanover, 1866). These figures should probably be
treated with some caution, as the author does not cite
his sources or make clear what constituted cultural
expenditure in each state. We cannot therefore be sure
that he was truly comparing like with like.

on cultural projects, although Bavarian cultural policy clearly had a
higher profile. This indicates the important role of culture in the Saxon
polity, reflecting Saxony's historic commitment to the arts and the
genuine distinction of the Saxon royal collections. Württemberg seems
to have fallen between the Hanoverian and Saxon extremes, but expenditure on culture here did not approach that of Saxony or Bavaria.

What was the impact of the various kinds of government cultural
policy analysed here? Of course, this is hard to assess with any certainty.
Despite the evidence of wide-scale involvement, it is impossible to see how
such involvement translated into individual experiences and political
beliefs. Nevertheless, tentative conclusions may be drawn on the basis of
the numbers involved. Some particularist cultural initiatives had a relatively restricted impact. The fostering of historical societies, for instance,
targeted a small elite, although this elite was probably disproportionately
influential in terms of opinion formation. Other kinds of government cultural initiative reached a surprisingly wide audience, at least when at their
most successful. The *Cannstatter Volksfest* attracted perhaps as many as
100,000 visitors by the end of this period, a figure that certainly puts it on
a par with nationalist festivals and celebrations. In terms of numbers
alone, the *Volksfest* was probably more successful than most, if not all, of
these. Equally, the New Museum in Dresden was very successful, attract-
ing some 60,000–70,000 visitors annually by the 1860s. This too is a very

significant figure, although it is hard to judge how many of those visiting the collections were actually Saxons and how many were foreign tourists. Nevertheless, there is evidence that the limited free tickets available for the Dresden museums were very popular, as demand for those regularly allocated at the Historical Museum far exceeded supply. A contemporary described the ticket allocation in 1865: 'As usual, at seven o'clock in the morning thirty-six free tickets were given out there, and it was clear that of the seventy or so individuals who had assembled in front of the museum not many more than half would be able to get tickets'.[110] Even the somewhat problematic state-wide appeals for royal monuments in Hanover and Saxony involved thousands of subscribers in the construction process. These appeals may have been less successful than anticipated or desired, but the sheer numbers involved mean that they must in some way have contributed to a sense of state community. Clearly cultural initiatives of this kind did have a mass impact. Particularist cultural initiatives may have been less spontaneous, in that they were frequently driven by the state, but they were popular nonetheless.

In this sense state-based cultures were an important phenomenon, distinct from but not necessarily conflicting with the nationalist culture emerging in Germany at this time. In fact particularist and nationalist culture was closely related. The similar kinds of cultural activity in question point to the close links between these two manifestations of German culture, and to a high level of cross-fertilisation. Particularists and nationalists, conservatives and liberals, learnt from the activities of their opponents. In any case, German cultural activity had to recognise territorial fragmentation. The Germanic National Museum in Nuremberg was never intended to supplant the museums and collections in the various German states: it was intended to complement them, for instance through providing a central catalogue of their treasures. Similarly, the idea of distinct German peoples within the German nation was a central tenet of the Hermann myth. In keeping with this, monarchs saw no contradiction between sponsoring nationalist projects like the Germanic National Museum and sponsoring state-based projects like the historical societies or monarchic monuments. Equally, the societies behind such initiatives saw no contradiction in appealing to monarchs and states for support. Particularist and nationalist cultures in this period were not mutually exclusive; they were interdependent.

---

[110] H. Sundick to Ministerium des Königlichen Hauses, 19 July 1865, HSADre Ministerium f. Volksbildung 19243:1 (156–7).

CHAPTER FOUR

Propaganda

'The daily press,' a Saxon official lamented in the early 1850s, 'can no longer be prevented from discussing state affairs before a wide public, although the latter is seldom capable of forming a correct judgement in these matters.'[1] For the Saxon government this freedom of expression was a new and rather disturbing state of affairs. Before the revolution of 1848, tight censorship laws had created a mundane and highly localised press, which published little that might frighten the authorities. Most newspapers were printed in small towns and reflected the narrow local interests of their immediate surroundings, consisting primarily of official announcements and private advertisements. Editors rarely if ever published political articles, and usually restricted themselves to humorous pieces, gossip columns and sound practical advice. One or two political newspapers existed in more liberal states, such as the *Beobachter* and the *Schwäbischer Merkur* in Württemberg. Even these trod extremely carefully. As Otto Elben, editor of the *Schwäbischer Merkur*, recalled in his memoirs: 'On a daily basis, the marks of the censor's pen prevented us from developing quick working habits and forced the editors into a kind of self-censorship.'[2] All this changed with the removal of censorship at Confederal level in March 1848, one of the earliest consequences of the German revolutions. This was not the first time that censorship had been relaxed in nineteenth-century Germany: it had happened before at the height of the national struggle against Napoleon (1812–15), and during the first German revolution (1830–1). In 1848, however, the change was permanent and its impact profound. The collapse of direct pre-emptive censorship dealt a death blow to government attempts to stifle the growth of an independent public sphere.

Why did the relaxation of censorship in 1848 prove so much longer lasting than it had been earlier in the nineteenth century? On one level,

---

[1] Geschäftsbericht über die Angelegenheiten der *Leipziger Zeitung* und des *Dresdner Journals*, HSADre Ministerium des Innern 9510 (20–9).

[2] Otto Elben, *Lebenserinnerungen, 1823–1899* (Stuttgart, 1931), p. 125.

this reflects the fact that the revolution of 1848/9 failed less comprehensively than contemporaries realised. On another level, it reveals how the impact of the revolution transformed government policy in the years that followed. For Germany after the revolution differed fundamentally from the Germany of the 1830s and 1840s. At both domestic and national level, the upheavals of 1848/9 were far more serious than anything experienced in 1830/1. Despite the apparent defeat of the revolutions, monarchs and their governments understood that many of the domestic and national challenges they had posed for the German states remained. The persistence of these challenges created a dilemma for the 'reactionary' governments of the 1850s. On the one hand, they were tempted to turn back the clock by depoliticising society. To this end governments restored pre-revolutionary constitutions, reduced the recently enlarged franchise and clamped down on new political freedoms. On the other hand, faith in this kind of solution had been brutally shattered. German governments were now terrified of public opinion and no longer believed that the forces of repression could suppress it. Instead, they gradually adopted a new approach. Rather than attempting to control public opinion, governments now resolved to direct it into healthy channels. As the Saxon government saw the situation in 1855, the task was simple: 'the Government press must take care that public opinion does not alienate itself too much from the true interests of the state, that unrealistic desires do not take root and that the people do not obstruct or oppose the government's well-intentioned efforts'.[3]

The history of the press in nineteenth-century Germany is usually seen in terms of the rise of a free press in the face of government resistance, and the gradual removal of official restrictions.[4] The end of censorship in March 1848 was the decisive turning-point in this transition. Yet there is another side to the story, for in Germany the official press and the so-called free press grew hand in hand.[5] Initially, the collapse of

[3] Geschäftsbericht über die Angelegenheiten der *Leipziger Zeitung* und des *Dresdner Journals*, HSADre Ministerium des Innern 9510 (20–9).
[4] See the classic histories of the German press: Heinz-Dietrich Fischer, *Handbuch der politischen Presse in Deutschland 1480–1980. Synopse rechtlicher, struktureller und wirtschaftlicher Grundlagen der Tendenzpublizistik im Kommunikationsfeld* (Düsseldorf, 1981), especially pp. 47–67; Kurt Koszyk, *Deutsche Presse im 19. Jahrhundert, Geschichte der deutschen Presse*, Vol. II (Berlin, 1966).
[5] Historians have recently become interested in this relationship. See Kohnen, *Pressepolitik des Deutschen Bundes*; Eberhard Naujoks, 'Die offiziöse Presse und die Gesellschaft (1848/1900)' in Elger Blühm (ed.), *Presse und Geschichte. Beiträge zur historischen Kommunikationsforschung. Referate einer internationalen Fachkonferenz der Deutschen Forschungsgemeinschaft und der Deutschen Presseforschung/Universität Bremen 5.-8. Oktober 1976 in Bremen* (Munich, 1977), pp. 157–70; also Wolfgang Piereth, 'Propaganda im 19. Jahrhundert. Die Anfänge aktiver staatlicher Pressepolitik in Deutschland 1800–1871' in Wolfram Siemann and Ute Daniel (eds.), *Propaganda, Meinungskampf, Verführung und politische Sinnstiftung 1789–1989* (Frankfurt, 1994), pp. 21–43.

censorship created a domino effect in the German press. First, the removal of censorship radicalised the existing political press and encouraged links between political groupings and particular newspapers. For instance, the *Beobachter* developed close ties with the Württemberg democrats.[6] Secondly, the removal of censorship led to the politicisation of this local press, which was now entitled to print political articles and did so with abandon. Thirdly, the removal of censorship led to the rapid proliferation of local newspapers, which began to make inroads into the countryside, as writers and publicists seized the chance to express their views in print for the first time. The first two of these developments were inter-related, because the politicisation of the local press often took the form of reprinting articles from high-profile opposition newspapers.

The hundreds of different local newspapers that appeared during and after the revolutions of 1848 were infinitely more important in quantitative terms than high-profile political publications, of which there were a very few in each state: the Bremen-based *Weser Zeitung* and the *Zeitung für Norddeutschland* in Hanover; the *Constitutionelle Zeitung* and the *Deutsche Allgemeine Zeitung* in Saxony; the *Beobachter* and the *Schwäbischer Merkur* in Württemberg. In practice, however, the few truly political (and generally oppositional) newspapers were disproportionately significant, thanks to their influential readership and the regular reprinting of articles in less prestigious newspapers. Understandably, therefore, historians of the period have paid disproportionate attention to more overtly political newspapers.[7] This reflects the links between these newspapers and important political figures and groupings, as well as the absolutely crucial role such papers played in shaping political debate in the public sphere. Yet they should not necessarily be taken as representative of the press between 1850 and 1866. Ultimately, the proliferation of local newspapers was probably the most important element in the transformation of the German press.

The sheer scale of the increase in journalistic activity in 1848 cannot be over-estimated: the number of newspapers published more than doubled during the revolution. This was true throughout Germany, regardless of relative levels of social and economic development. For instance, in absolute terms the number of newspapers published in Saxony was always far greater than in a backward state like Hanover. In both states, however, the relative increase in newspapers published was

---

[6] See Langewiesche, *Liberalismus und Demokratie in Württemberg*, pp. 147–8, on the relationship between political 'parties' and the press in Württemberg.

[7] See, for instance, the approach taken in Koszyk, *Deutsche Presse*, pp. 106–209.

Table 4.1. *Newspapers published in Hanover, Saxony and Württemberg*[a]

State	Number of newspapers		
	Before 1848	Refounded 1848–50	Founded 1848–50
Hanover	37	3	55
Saxony	124	25	179
Württemberg	92	32	56

Note:

[a] Figures taken from Martin Henkel and Rolf Taubert, *Die deutsche Presse 1848–1850, eine Bibliographie* (Munich, 1986), pp. 152–65, 443–502, 536–64. The introductory essay in this volume gives further details on the effects of removing censorship between 1848 and 1850.

not dissimilar during 1848/9. The extent of the increase in newspaper publication throughout Germany is clearly shown by Table 4.1, which compares the numbers of newspapers published in Hanover, Saxony and Württemberg before and after the revolution.

This journalistic explosion was particularly significant in the German context, since Germany was an unusually literate society. In Prussia, for instance, over 80% of the population could read by this time.[8] Moreover, it appears that a surprising number of those who could read newspapers actively chose to do so. Indeed, it may be that as many as half of the adult male population were regular newspaper readers.[9] Anecdotal evidence supports this. In 1868 a survey conducted by the *Innere Mission* in Bremen established that even amongst the very lowest social classes a daily newspaper was regarded as 'absolutely indispensable', and many of the poor took out family newspaper subscriptions.[10] The proliferation of local newspapers in Germany after 1848 was important precisely because it enabled a new public to follow state and national affairs.

These developments were too widespread to be reversed. Arguably the authorities did not even try. Instead, governments throughout Germany turned to positive propaganda in the years 1849–51. These

[8] See the figures given by Ludwig von Friedeburg, *Bildungsreform in Deutschland. Geschichte und gesellschaftlicher Widerspruch* (Frankfurt, 1989), p. 37, or Kenneth Barkin, 'Social control and the *Volksschule* in *Vormärz* Prussia', *Central European History* 16:1 (1983), 31–52 (p. 50).

[9] As suggested by Wehler, *Deutsche Gesellschaftsgeschichte*, Vol. II, p. 522.

[10] Rolf Engelsing, *Massenpublikum und Journalistentum im 19. Jahrhundert in Nordwestdeutschland* (Berlin, 1966), p. 73.

years did not necessarily see the birth of a government-sponsored political press, which often dated back to the Napoleonic era.[11] Nevertheless,
they did mark a definitive shift in government press policy – away from
repression and towards propaganda. Admittedly, monitoring and suppressing the press was one of the major activities of the German States'
Police Association, which coordinated the reaction throughout
Germany during the 1850s. Furthermore, in 1854 the German
Confederation introduced regulatory legislation that placed strict limits
on political expression in the press. Thereafter, every newspaper had to
appoint an editor, who would be legally answerable for its content.
Publishers had to apply for an official concession to print newspapers,
for which they paid a large deposit that was forfeit if the newspaper over-
stepped the mark. A copy of every edition had to be shown to the local
authorities, often shortly before publication, and the police had the
power to seize offending publications before legal action against them
had been initiated. The legislation attempted to regulate and suppress
the press, but it did not reintroduce the pre-publication censorship of the
period before 1848. In practice, the shift from what governments and historians have called a 'negative' (or repressive) press policy to a more 'positive' (or propagandistic) approach continued.

This shift was nearly complete by the mid-1860s, when governments
throughout Germany were finally confronted by their failure to control
the free press. In June 1863, for instance, Bismarck reintroduced hard-
line press controls in Prussia, in the hope that it would weaken the united
stand taken by the liberals in the constitutional conflict. The hope
proved a faint one. The press became slightly more colourless and less
critical of the government, but no sea change in public opinion followed.
Instead, the press decree provoked outrage because, of course, it had
been introduced unconstitutionally and without parliamentary backing.
Bismarck withdrew the decree shortly afterwards. Like the Prussians,
many other German governments concluded that repression was
actively harmful. In 1863 the head of the Hanoverian Press Office,
Oskar Meding, advised that withdrawing the concession from an opposition newspaper would be counter-productive. 'Every time,' he wrote,
'that a newspaper loses its concession, the reputation and circulation of
that newspaper increases, whilst the standing of the government in
public opinion falls.'[12] Similarly, in 1864 Gessler, the new Württemberg

---

[11] See Piereth, 'Propaganda im 19. Jahrhundert', p. 22, and, for Saxony, Flockerzie, 'State-building
and Nation-building in the Third Germany: Saxony', 281–3.
[12] Meding to Hammerstein, 15 March 1863, HSAHan Dep. 103 IX 307.

Interior Minister, argued that the German Confederation should revoke the press legislation of the 1850s, which was excessively repressive but not in the least effective.[13] Lifting the restrictions, he argued, could only have a positive impact. By this time, German governments had come to terms with the existence of a public sphere, in which individuals could debate public issues and form opinions independently of the state itself. Attempts to stifle this public sphere had failed and governments were forced to accept it as an important political factor. Now, attempts to control and influence the new public sphere began: the period 1850–66 saw the birth of the 'spin-doctor' and marked the transition to the kind of systematic and consistent government media manipulation that is only too familiar today.[14]

What did government news-management entail? German governments used official newspapers, semi-official newspapers and indirect press influence in order to put their views across to the public at large. Official newspapers were openly controlled and funded by German governments and acted as their mouthpiece in the press. Semi-official newspapers maintained a pretence of independence, although in practice they too were controlled and funded by the government. Governments also attempted to influence the press indirectly. Most commonly, they pressured the editors and publishers of particular newspapers into taking a pro-government line. Usually, governments also tried to place authorised articles in the provincial press. The practice of reprinting articles from official and semi-official newspapers in the provincial press further increased indirect government influence.

Arguably, indirect press influence was in fact the most effective way for governments to shape the wider political climate. In 1860 a circular from the Württemberg royal office put the matter in a nutshell, when it noted that 'an argument is less important to political news reporting than colouring the presentation of the facts'.[15] This was certainly the view of Professor Bülau, editor of the official Saxon newspaper, the

---

[13] Gessler to Neurath, 12 November 1864 and 2 December 1864, HSAStu E 150 (IV) 1588 (222, 227).

[14] The continuity in propaganda techniques is stressed in recent treatments of the subject, notably in Kohnen, *Pressepolitik des Deutschen Bundes*, pp. 173–86, in a chapter entitled 'Ursprünge moderner Pressepolitik'. As its title suggests, the assumption of such a continuity is also implicit in Jürgen Wilke (ed.), *Pressepolitik und Propaganda. Historische Studien von Vormärz bis zum Kalten Krieg* (Cologne, 1997). Systematic manipulation of the kind which emerged after 1848 was quite different from earlier government press influence.

[15] Undated proposals accompanying K. Circular Note 'an sämmtliche Minister und Depart. Chefs', 15 February 1860, HSAStu E 14 1186 (342–1).

Leipziger Zeitung. In a letter to the Interior Minister in 1851 he posed the question 'How does the Opposition press do it?' For Bülau the answer was simple: 'Fulminating leading articles do not give them [the opposition newspapers] such impact. Most of the public does not read them at all, and is simply interested in the news. But this is where their strength lies – in presenting and reporting every little thing from their point of view.'[16] The dominant figure in Hanoverian press policy, Oskar Meding, would have agreed with him. Like Bülau, Meding emphasised the role of correspondence articles in shaping public opinion. These correspondence articles were regular – mostly political – reports provided by freelance contributors at home and abroad, which usually appeared in several newspapers at the same time. The articles were unsigned, but carried a symbol attributing them to a particular author. Few people knew or cared who had actually written the articles; most readers simply accepted them as fact. Meding believed that '[t]he newspaper reader looks with deferential admiration at the many letters identified by cabalistic signs, which newspaper editors receive from all over the world'.[17]

Considerations like this were particularly important for government newspapers, which operated under added restrictions. Ministers and editors never tired of pointing out how constrained the official press was by its status. Government newspapers could not appear to be partisan publications because the governments of post-revolutionary Germany aspired to be above party politics, and in any case violent polemic or inaccurate reporting could embarrass the government. This created an almost insoluble dilemma. As Gessler, the Württemberg Interior Minister, noted bitterly in 1866:

[A]n official newspaper . . . should use moderate language and discuss all important matters . . . in a moderate fashion, but at the same time the paper should appeal to the broadest possible public, so that it will be suitably widely read. Experience has shown that the risk in fulfilling both these tasks is either that moderation becomes boring through neglecting the popular . . . or that moderation is sacrificed on the altar of popularity.[18]

---

[16] Bülau to Euch Hochwohlgeboren (Interior Minister?), 4 September 1851, HSADre Ministerium des Innern 9491 (181–5).

[17] Meding, *Memoiren*, Vol. 1, pp. 71–2. In many respects Meding's memoirs should be regarded as a highly unreliable source, since Meding himself was a notoriously unreliable character and his memoirs were clearly intended as personal propaganda. His views on the mechanics of government propaganda should, however, probably be taken seriously as here he had no axe to grind.

[18] Gessler, an den König, betr. der Regelung des Verhältnisses des *Staats-Anzeigers*, 3 February 1866, HSAStu E 150 (IV) 1600 (430).

Indirect press influence was one way in which governments attempted to steer a course between the Scylla of boredom and the Charybdis of populism. Indeed, government press policy probably influenced public opinion more effectively through news and correspondence articles than through straightforward political argument.

Throughout Germany, the development of government press policy is best understood in the context of domestic and national politics. Governments were most concerned with influencing the press when they felt least secure in the hearts of the people. The history of press manipulation is therefore very revealing of government priorities. This history is fairly well established for the German great powers, for whom foreign policy considerations were often decisive.[19] In the context of the struggle for mastery in Germany, the Prussians set the propaganda agenda. The first Prussian press office was established as early as 1842, although it did not survive the early days of the revolution. A second press office was created some months later, under the supervision of the Interior Minister, von Manteuffel. When Manteuffel moved to the Foreign Ministry in December 1850, the press office moved with him. At the same time, its funding increased from 26,500 to 35,000 *Thaler.* The director of the press office met daily with the Foreign Minister to report on the state of the German press. The press office was also responsible for producing daily correspondence sheets and innumerable memoranda. The close connection between the press office and Prussian foreign policy led to a significant Prussian press presence in Frankfurt. At the same time, the press office played an important role in Prussian domestic policy during the 1850s. With the onset of the new era in 1858/9, however, funding for the press office fell and its director was replaced. Official support for government press policy revived under Bismarck, who in 1863 launched a successful newspaper that provided pro-government news for the local press, the *Preussische Provinzialkorrespondenz.* Throughout the period, the unofficial

---

[19] Most of the literature on press policy in this period concerns Prussia, although see Kohnen, *Pressepolitik des Deutschen Bundes,* and Piereth, 'Propaganda im 19. Jahrhundert', for a comparison of Prussia, Austria and Bavaria. On Prussia see: Irene Fischer-Frauendienst, *Bismarcks Pressepolitik* (Münster, Westf., 1963); Eberhard Naujoks, *Bismarcks auswärtige Pressepolitik und die Reichsgründung, 1865–71* (Wiesbaden, 1968) and Gertrud Nöth-Greis, 'Das Literarische Büro als Instrument der Pressepolitik', in Wilke (ed.), *Pressepolitik und Propaganda,* pp. 1–79. For Hanoverian press policy during this period see Alfred Hildebrandt, 'Die Pressepolitik der hannoverschen Regierung vom Beginn der Reaktionszeit bis zum Ende des Königreichs Hannover' (unpublished doctoral thesis, Leipzig, 1932). For Württemberg press policy in the 1860s see Eberhard Naujoks, 'Der "Staatsanzeiger" und die württembergische Regierungspresse in der Krise der Reichsgründungszeit (1864–1871)', *Zeitschrift für Württembergische Landesgeschichte* 50 (1991), 271–304. There have been no similar studies of Saxon press policy at this time.

Kreuzzeitung and other conservative newspapers also made a significant contribution to supporting government press policy, although the official *Preussische Zeitung* was rather less influential. Prussia was consistently more interested in influencing public opinion through manipulating the press than Austria, and Prussian press policy was consistently more innovative. Historians have therefore tended to see Austrian press policy as a response to Prussian propaganda within the German Confederation.[20] Certainly, the foundation of the Austrian Central Office (for press matters) in 1848, and the subsequent increase in funding in 1852 can be clearly related to foreign rather than domestic concerns and very much followed in the footsteps of Prussian measures. At the same time, the belated nature of Austrian efforts to influence the press reflects the backwardness of the regime.

The primacy of foreign policy in Prussian and Austrian press policy can scarcely be seen as typical of the rest of Germany. Of course, foreign policy concerns were important here too. At the same time, however, the small size of other German states ensured a limited foreign policy agenda, whilst making the states more vulnerable in other ways. What does the evolution of government press policy in other German states reveal about the priorities of their governments and the nature of these states themselves?

HANOVER

In 1842 a contemporary described the official Hanoverian newspaper, the *Hannoversche Zeitung*, as the very model of a court newspaper.[21] This was probably not intended as a compliment. By all accounts, the *Hannoversche Zeitung* was a terrible publication.[22] Ernst August himself commented scathingly that he knew of nothing as 'pitiful, stupid and uninteresting as the *Hannov. Zeitung* in its current form . . . it really is a waste of money'.[23]

Various efforts were made to improve the paper in the aftermath of 1848, when the government established closer institutional ties with the newspaper.[24] Ministers undertook to support the editor through

---

[20] See Kohnen, *Pressepolitik des Deutschen Bundes*, pp. 140–5, especially p. 144.

[21] Cited in Koszyk, *Deutsche Presse*, p. 90.

[22] The archival material covering Hanoverian press policy in this period is patchy as a result of war damage and post-war flooding of the archive. Hildebrandt, 'Pressepolitik der hannoverschen Regierung', is therefore very useful, since it draws on sources now lost to the historian.

[23] Hildebrandt, 'Pressepolitik der hannoverschen Regierung', p. 7.

[24] See Abschrift f. K. Ministerial Department der geistlichen und Unterrichts- Angelegenheiten, 6 February 1851, HSAHan Hann 113 A 37 (59).

providing important news and official documents. They encouraged officials to contribute articles to the newspaper, and set aside an hour a week in each ministry for a meeting with the editor. In 1854 subscription to the *Hannoversche Zeitung* became obligatory for local authorities (*Ämte*), in order to ensure wider distribution. These efforts to improve the *Hannoversche Zeitung* were neither vigorous nor persistent. Not surprisingly, they failed. In May 1857 Wermuth, the very unpopular chief of police in Hanover, echoed Ernst August's earlier criticisms. He described how the *Hannoversche Zeitung* 'provides . . . nothing decisive on political matters . . . reprints meaningless articles from other newspapers and appears to have been unwittingly influenced by the Prussian Press Office on at least one occasion'.[25] By this stage the *Hannoversche Zeitung* had, in any case, ceased to be the focus of government press activity.

In October 1856 Klindworth, the court printer, announced his intention of founding a 'major, domestic political newspaper with conservative inclinations'.[26] This new paper was the *Hannoversche Nachrichten*. In a circular sent to all six ministers, Georg V declared his support for the new publication as a forum in which conservatives could 'publicise facts which have been distorted or kept from the public . . . and present, defend and disseminate their own principles and views'.[27] As a semi-official newspaper, the *Hannoversche Nachrichten* was free to toe the government line more energetically than its official rival. This, as far as the government was concerned, was the point. The Interior Ministry therefore supported the *Hannoversche Nachrichten* indirectly. The government granted the newspaper similar advertising rights to those of the *Hannoversche Zeitung*, encouraged contributions to the paper from state officials and attempted to increase its circulation by word of mouth.[28] Support in the shape of journalistic contributions came right from the top. Indeed, the name of Interior Minister von Borries himself appears in highly confidential lists of the newspaper's anonymous contributors.[29] Both the time of its founding and the nature of its calling indicate that the *Hannoversche Nachrichten* was a child of the second Hanoverian constitutional conflict. A confidential memorandum written in February 1857 announced that the *Hannoversche Nachrichten* would be a bulwark against

[25] Wermuth, 'Vergleichungen der Einrichtungen in Preußen, Sachsen und Hannover wegen Einflusses auf die Presse', 14 May 1857, HSAHan Dep. 103 IX 299.

[26] Klindworth, 'Gehorsamstes Promemoria', 20 October 1856, HSAHan Hann 80 I Hannover A 1070.

[27] Georg V, Circular to royal, finance, foreign, war, justice and culture ministers, 20 October 1856. HSAHan Dep. 103 IX 299.

[28] Minutes of meeting held in Interior Ministry, 29 October 1856, ibid.   [29] Ibid.

the tide of oppositional newspapers threatening to undermine the monarchic principle.[30] In particular, the memorandum stressed that the newspaper would 'disseminate information about Hanoverian affairs and spread among increasingly wide circles an understanding of the great advantages arising from Hanover's geographical situation and her good, gradually evolving institutions'. This would encourage dynastic loyalty, Hanoverian patriotism and satisfaction with the status quo. With time, the *Hannoversche Nachrichten* might form the kernel of a monarchic-conservative party in Hanover, through providing a forum in which conservative officials could take up the pen in defence of their beliefs.

Despite initial success, the circulation of the *Hannoversche Nachrichten* soon plummeted. Rather than let it die, the government merged the newspaper with the *Hannoversche Zeitung* and a local advertiser (the *Hannoversche Anzeigen*) to form the *Neue Hannoversche Zeitung* in 1858. This was an official newspaper run on traditional lines. Unsurprisingly perhaps, the *Neue Hannoversche Zeitung* was no more successful than its predecessor. According to Oskar Meding, the articles published in the *Neue Hannoversche Zeitung* at this time were aggressively polemic, dull, poorly written and rarely – if ever – reprinted in the local press. 'And so it came to pass,' he wrote subsequently, 'that the articles of the *Neue Hannoversche Zeitung* sounded as lonely as the voice of a preacher in the wilderness, whilst the opposition dominated the press and public opinion . . ., right up to the very smallest little newspapers in the most insignificant provincial towns.'[31]

In October 1859, as nationalist agitation reached a crescendo, the Hanoverian government tried once more to assert its authority over the press. Borries, the Interior Minister, appointed Meding to coordinate and oversee Hanoverian press policy. Meding was a Prussian, who had previously worked in the Prussian Press Office. Inevitably, therefore, he adopted its techniques and concentrated on increasing indirect government influence throughout the German press, rather than on attempting to improve the *Neue Hannoversche Zeitung* itself.[32] Meding began by asserting this influence from outside Hanover, where it could less easily be attributed to the Hanoverian government. In November 1859 he travelled to Berlin, hoping to set up a collaboration with the conservatives of the Prussian *Kreuzzeitung*. This failed, but Meding did appoint two correspondents there to write reports reflecting Hanoverian interests for publication

[30] Höchst Vertraulich, P. M., 5 February 1857, ibid.   [31] Meding, *Memoiren*, Vol. i, pp. 46–8.
[32] Meding to Lex, 8 November 1859, HSAHan Dep. 103 ix 38, does however list raising the standard of the *Neue Hannoversche Zeitung* as the first of his three aims. This was not really borne out in practice.

in a range of German newspapers.[33] On his return, Meding personally approached the editor of the *Weser Zeitung*, and Cotta, publisher of the *Augsburger Allgemeine Zeitung* – arguably the most prestigious German newspaper of the day.[34] Both approaches succeeded in ensuring relatively favourable coverage of Hanoverian politics in these two influential newspapers. Later, Meding even negotiated with Julius Reuter to establish a telegraphic bureau in Hanover, in competition with Wolff's telegraphic bureau in Berlin.[35] This ambitious and far-sighted plan aimed to provide an alternative source of news in Germany, which would be less biased in favour of the Prussians. The project was still in its infancy when Prussia annexed Hanover in 1866. Unsurprisingly, the new government dropped it.

The creation of a press office on the Prussian model in 1862 marked the high point of Hanoverian efforts to influence the press indirectly.[36] Once again, Meding dominated the operation. The Hanoverian Press Office had two aims.[37] First, it monitored public opinion by preparing daily overviews of the press for government ministers. Secondly, it defended government policy in the press. The ability of the Press Office to manipulate the media and to influence the presentation of political events depended primarily on personal contacts. Hanoverian officials intimated to the publishers and editors of local newspapers that it was their loyal duty to publish the views of the government as well as those of the opposition. Despite a few exceptions in the larger towns, most local newspapers welcomed these advances. Indeed, according to Meding, 'most of them had only reprinted articles from opposition newspapers out of a lack of other material, and were very pleased to be able to appear to offer their readers something original and at the same time enter into friendly relations with the authorities'.[38] By the end of 1862, twenty-five Hanoverian newspapers (54.3%) were wholly under the influence of the government, printing all the articles sent to them by the Press Office.[39] A further twelve newspapers (26.1%) were susceptible to occasional government influence. Only nine newspapers (19.6%) were totally outside the government's sphere of influence.

[33] Ibid.   [34] Meding, *Memoiren*, Vol. I, pp. 75–88.   [35] Ibid., pp. 329–33, 348–9.
[36] The Press Office was funded by the government but this funding was not authorised by parliament. The Interior Ministry provided 10,000 *Thaler* for initial expenditure, thereafter a maxiïum of 8,000 *Thaler* p.a. from the *Gesammtministerium*. Notatum, 17 November 1862, HSAHan Hann 26a 555.
[37] Anlage zum Protokolle vom 1 November 1862, HSAHan Hann 26a 555 (25–9).
[38] Meding, *Memoiren*, Vol. I, p. 62.
[39] Figures from Hildebrandt, 'Pressepolitik der hannoverschen Regierung', pp. 29–33.

This was no mean achievement. Still, it failed to satisfy Meding, who had grand plans for a truly national conservative newspaper, based in Hanover but supported by other conservative regimes, like the governments of Austria and Saxony. Georg welcomed the plan, which endorsed his belief that Hanover was the true home of German conservatism. Other governments were less enthusiastic and the project never got off the ground. Instead, in 1864 Meding set up a less ambitious semiofficial newspaper, the *Deutsche Nordsee Zeitung*. The newspaper was funded through government printing contracts. In his memoirs, Meding relates the *Deutsche Nordsee Zeitung* to his earlier project, but it should probably be seen in more local terms – as an attempt to meet the need for a semi-official newspaper left by the demise of the *Hannoversche Nachrichten*.

Meding's success in asserting government influence over the press made life very difficult for his opponents – both within the government and outside it. In 1865 Meding took Augustus Göhmann, editor of a Hanoverian newspaper, the *Hannoversche Tagespost*, to task for the paper's failure to support the government.[40] The complaint came as a shock to Göhmann. He told Meding that the ministers Hammerstein and Windthorst had approached him in 1863, promising him a loan of 6,000 *Thaler* if he would print the articles that they provided on a daily basis (mostly written by Hammerstein). Göhmann declared that he had been proud to think he was working for King and country. In fact, however, either Göhmann was extremely naïve or his presentation of the matter was disingenuous, for factionalism within the government was plain to see. Indeed, Göhmann had first-hand experience of this himself. He told Meding how, during the ministerial crisis of 1865, Hammerstein and Windthorst had commissioned articles presenting their fall as a disaster for the country. The incident demonstrates clearly the limitations of government press policy, even where it seemed to be successful. Factionalism within the government could seriously undermine efforts to create a pro-government press.

SAXONY

Only days after the May uprising in 1849, the Saxon Interior Minister, Richard von Friesen, noted: 'In the current exceptional circumstances the Interior Ministry recognises that one of its most important duties is to influence public opinion, to prepare the way for government measures,

---

[40] Meding, Bericht, 1 December 1865, HSAHan Dep. 103 VII 147.

to support and, where necessary, to defend government policy.'[41] Within a month of this pronouncement, control of the well-established official newspaper, the *Leipziger Zeitung*, had passed to the Interior Ministry from the Finance Ministry, symbolising the new primacy of politics in Saxon press policy.[42] Before the revolution the *Leipziger Zeitung* had been principally viewed as a source of government revenue; now this was a subsidiary consideration. Indeed, the newspaper's profits were to be used to finance other press activities. In the first place, this meant the purchase of a second official newspaper, the *Dresdner Journal*, which – it was hoped – would respond more flexibly to the government's needs than the *Leipziger Zeitung*.[43]

Ironically, Saxon press policy before 1849 was hampered by its own success. The *Leipziger Zeitung* was the oldest newspaper in Germany. As such, it was a huge asset for the Saxon government because it boasted a large and loyal readership. Indeed, the *Leipziger Zeitung* was unique among official newspapers in actually making a profit – of some 25,000 *Thaler* a year.[44] This was a tidy sum: the entire Prussian press organisation cost 35,000 *Thaler* a year to run and Prussia was some nine times the size of Saxony. Understandably, the Saxon government was wary of tampering with a tried and tested formula, since changes to the *Leipziger Zeitung* could result in the loss of readers, profits and influence.

No newspaper in Germany [wrote Friesen] is so widely read in such a small area. Almost all classes of people have grown used to it, like an old friend, and the advertisements it carries ensure that even those who do not wish to do so are forced to buy the political section as well. The loathing with which the radicals attack it demonstrates the importance of this organ more clearly than anything else. But on the other hand, this importance means that the newspaper must be used extremely carefully.[45]

[41] Friesen, 'Communicat des Ministerium des Innern, die Einrichtung der Leipziger Zeitung u. den von der Redaction derselben allein in polit. Hinsicht festzuhaltenden Standpunkt betr.', 22 May 1849, HSADre Gesammtministerium Loc. 13, No. 17 (33–8).

[42] See Gerhard Hense, 'Leipziger Zeitung, Leipzig (1665–1918)' in Heinz-Dietrich Fischer (ed.), *Deutsche Zeitungen des 17. bis 20. Jahrhunderts* (Pullach bei München, 1972), pp. 75–91, for a detailed history of the *Leipziger Zeitung*, especially before 1848.

[43] The *Dresdner Journal* was finally purchased in September 1851. Regulativ für die Leipziger Zeitung und das Dresdner Journal, 1 September 1851, HSADre Ministerium des Innern 9491 (186–209). The new financial arrangmeents were made at a meeting held on 26 July 1849. See minutes of this meeting, HSADre Ministerium des Innern 9490 (194–7).

[44] Figure for Prussia from Kohnen, *Pressepolitik des Deutschen Bundes*, p. 138. Figure for the *Leipziger Zeitung* from Friesen, 'Communicat an dem Gesammtministerium', 9 May 1851, HSADre Gesammtministerium Loc. 7, No. 7 (128–35).

[45] Friesen, 'Communicat des Ministerium des Innern, die Einrichtung der Leipziger Zeitung u. den von der Redaction derselben allein in polit. Hinsicht festzuhaltenden Standpunkt betr.', 22 May 1849, ibid., Loc.13, No. 17 (33–8).

Unfortunately, the *Leipziger Zeitung* suffered from serious shortcomings as far as the government was concerned because it was hard for ministers to develop a close working relationship with a newspaper printed outside the capital. Yet the *Leipziger Zeitung* could hardly move to Dresden without – at the very least – a change of name. In 1849, to set up an additional official newspaper, the *Dresdner Journal*, seemed the best solution to this problem.

For the next four years, the government tried (and failed) to establish a reasonable division of labour between the two newspapers. In September 1851 the government placed an official commissar in charge of each newspaper, although the Interior Minister retained control of editorial appointments and the finances of the two papers were jointly administered.[46] At this stage, the two government papers were intended to serve different purposes. *Leipziger Zeitung* leaders were 'semi-official' and could be printed without prior government approval; *Dresdner Journal* leaders were more closely monitored so that they kept strictly in line with government policy. *Leipziger Zeitung* leaders were broader in focus than those in the *Dresdner Journal*. The former covered current events, trade and industry, but the latter focused on Saxon affairs. News reporting reflected this division of labour. Reports in the *Leipziger Zeitung* were supposed to be more objective than those in the *Dresdner Journal*. These arrangements pointed the way forward in differentiating between a strictly official role for the *Dresdner Journal* and the more semi-detached position of the *Leipziger Zeitung*.

In practice, the unnatural division between foreign and domestic news that was central to this set-up prompted endless bickering between the two publications. In 1853 Witzleben, the Commissar for the *Dresdner Journal*, complained that only his newspaper had kept its side of the bargain. The *Dresdner Journal* reported extensively on 'the affairs of the Fatherland', but the *Leipziger Zeitung* had utterly failed to build up its foreign coverage as promised. As a result, the *Leipziger Zeitung* was losing its regular readership, but former subscribers were not turning to the *Dresdner Journal* instead. Supporters of the *Leipziger Zeitung* responded that the policy was simply unreasonable.[47] The *Leipziger Zeitung* was a Saxon newspaper and its readers could expect it to provide domestic news coverage. Surely the aim of an official newspaper was to attract a Saxon

[46] Regulativ für die Leipziger Zeitung und das Dresdner Journal, 1 September 1851, HSADre Ministerium des Innern 9491 (186–209).
[47] Illegible, 'Vortrag des Herrn v. Witzleben die Leipziger Zeitung betr.', 18 January 1854, HSADre Ministerium des Innern 9492 (108–17).

audience and to elevate the level of Saxon political debate? How was this possible, they wondered, if a newspaper focused exclusively on foreign affairs?

In the event, the awkward division between domestic and foreign coverage did not last. In 1854 the *Leipziger Zeitung* became a semi-official newspaper – broadly in line with government policy, but more independent and objective than before.[48] The *Dresdner Journal* retained full official status. At the same time, the government dropped the rigid distinction between foreign and domestic news coverage, although the original arrangement left its mark. Foreign news and comment in the *Leipziger Zeitung* was consistently fuller than in the *Dresdner Journal*. Indeed, the Saxon government began to see the *Leipziger Zeitung* as a potential source of influence in Thuringia, and therefore as a foreign policy instrument in its own right. The first hint of this appeared in an internal memorandum, written in 1854: 'In the interests of our relations with the Saxon and Thuringian states, it is certainly worth noting that the newspaper should do more than simply maintain its current position there, and should gradually seek to regain lost ground'.[49] Witzleben himself, now Commissar for the *Leipziger Zeitung*, picked up on this suggestion in 1857. He suggested that the *Leipziger Zeitung* could become a voice 'for the particular interests of Saxony's smaller neighbouring states'.[50] He was not slow to implement this plan. By early 1858 von Wustemann, a minister in the Saxe–Anhalt government, had already become one of the *Leipziger Zeitung*'s most regular leader writers.[51] A year later, the paper's network of correspondents covered the whole of Thuringia, in part thanks to the support of smaller Saxon governments, like that of Saxe–Weimar.[52] Beust's close involvement with the newspaper means that this campaign for a Thuringian readership should be seen as a clear indicator of his own priorities within Germany and of the role he envisaged for Saxony, as leader of the Thuringian states.

The changes of 1854 reflected the difficulties of running an official newspaper from outside the capital – difficulties that became painfully clear with the outbreak of the Crimean War. In practice, however, even running an official newspaper inside the capital proved far from easy. In

[48] Ministerium des Innern, Communicat to Gesammtministerium, 22 March 1854, HSADre Gesammtministerium Loc.13, No. 17 (55).

[49] Illegible, 'Vortrag des Herrn v. Witzleben die Leipziger Zeitung betr.', 18 January 1854, HSADre Ministerium des Innern 9492 (108–17).

[50] Witzleben, 'Vortrag', 29 August 1857, HSADre Ministerium des Innern 9493 (171–98).

[51] Witzleben, 'Vortrag', 21 January 1858, HSADre Ministerium des Innern 9493 (225–48).

[52] Witzleben, 'Vortrag', 21 January 1859, HSADre Ministerium des Innern 9494 (1–18).

1857 Beust attempted to improve government liaison with the *Dresdner Journal* through weekly meetings between representatives of the different ministries and the *Journal*'s Commissar. Yet Beust's fellow ministers were unwilling to cooperate, and did so in the end only with the utmost reluctance.[53] In 1858, the Commissar for the *Dresdner Journal* described the unsatisfactory liaison meetings held as a result: 'In response to my asking whether the Commissars had anything to say about the *Journal* from the perspective of the ministries they represented, they usually replied in the negative, and with that the gentlemen were finished, leaving me with the not inconsiderable task of finding matter for discussion.'[54] As in Hanover, lack of government unity undermined Saxon press policy from within.

The change in status of the *Dresdner Journal* and the *Leipziger Zeitung* was not the only innovation in government press policy during the Crimean War. After 1855 the Saxon government began to cultivate indirect press influence at local level, through granting politically compliant local newspapers official status, as authorised *Amtsblätter*.[55] *Amtsblätter* had a monopoly on local government advertising, which provided these newspapers with a steady source of revenue. This gave them a major advantage over their competitors – but there was a catch, for *Amtsblatt* editors were obliged to publish anonymous articles sent them from the *Dresdner Journal* office. Indeed, they risked losing the *Amtsblatt* concession if they failed to toe the government line. These articles spread government views discreetly and enabled propaganda to reach a wider audience than the readership of the *Leipziger Zeitung* and *Dresdner Journal* alone. The government also hoped that the initiative would colour the political climate indirectly. The idea was that the readership of pro-government newspapers would increase because they carried official announcements, whilst opposition newspapers struggled to survive without government advertising revenue. In practice, however, the *Amtsblatt* initiative did not succeed in redirecting circulation patterns at a local level. Readerships proved more loyal than expected and often local authorities simply ignored the requirement to advertise exclusively in the *Amtsblatt*. The initiative may nevertheless have been successful in infiltrating the local papers with pro-government news and views.

[53] Beust, Ministerium des Innern to Gesammtministerium, 2 January 1857, and responses, HSADre Gesammtministerium Loc. 7, No. 7 (155–75).
[54] Jahresbericht des Commissars für die Angelegenheiten des Dresdner Journals auf das Jahr 1857, 16 April 1858, HSADre Ministerium des Innern 9511 (96b–105).
[55] See HSADre Ministerium des Innern 3681–5 for details of this initiative.

Like the Crimean War in the 1850s, the events of the early 1860s forced the government to reassess the line taken by the official press. In 1862 the Interior Minister suggested to Witzleben that the *Leipziger Zeitung* could exploit its editorial independence by paying lip-service to liberal ideas.[56] In words dripping with bureaucratic caution, he indicated that the government would not object – provided that the *Leipziger Zeitung* continued to defend conservative principles, particularly as regards the German question. This broad hint indicates that, in practice, the perceived expectations and opinions of newspaper readers played an important part in shaping government press policy. The implication here was that the *Leipziger Zeitung* should take a less uncompromising line on liberalism, in order to retain its hard-line stance on the national issue. This underlines just how far the Saxon government was willing to adopt a more liberal and populist approach in response to the *kleindeutsch* nationalist threat in the 1860s.

WÜRTTEMBERG

Four months before the revolution of 1848, Heinrich Elsner wrote to King Wilhelm of Württemberg proposing a comprehensive reorganisation of the Württemberg press.[57] Elsner was a journalist who had renounced his radical views in favour of hard-line conservatism. He suggested four alterations to Württemberg press policy: an Information Bureau, to keep the conservative press abreast of interesting developments; a regularly appearing *Korrespondenz* newspaper, to publish news from the localities; the systematic dissemination of leading articles, authorised by the government, in the local press; the creation of two district newspapers (*Kreisblätter*) in Catholic Oberschwaben and the liberal Tübingen area, to be funded by government advertising, which would be withdrawn from the popular *Schwäbischer Merkur*. Elsner added that he himself was well placed to take over 'central control of the whole operation'; and ended the letter by requesting an urgent loan of 5000 *Gulden* to finance his conservative newspaper, the *Ulmer Kronik*.

Unsurprisingly, the Württemberg government rejected Elsner's plan, but the Interior Minister did write a lengthy consideration of his

---

[56] An Regierungsrath von Witzleben, 13 March 1862, HSADre Ministerium des Innern 9494 (235–42).
[57] Elsner to H. M., 10 November 1847, HSAStu E9 94 I (200–5). For details on Heinrich Elsner see Eckhard Trox, 'Heinrich Elsner: Vom Jakobinismus zum Konservatismus. Ein Beitrag zur Entstehungsgeschichte der konservativen Partei in Württemberg', *Zeitschrift für Württembergische Landesgeschichte* 52 (1993), 303–36.

proposals.[58] The minister disputed Elsner's view that a monopoly of government advertising would provide a solid financial basis for the proposed *Kreisblätter*, because many such advertisements were carried free of charge. In fact, he argued that government advertising would not attract a large enough readership because subscribers to the *Schwäbischer Merkur* were primarily interested in private rather than official advertisements. Moreover, Elsner himself was too disreputable a character to be allowed so prominent a role. Crucially, the minister argued that introducing polemical articles of any kind would mean the end of the local press in its currently harmless form. Such articles would introduce politics to people who had previously shown no interest in them whatsoever – an extremely undesirable development.

These considerations fell by the wayside during the revolution of 1848/9. In January 1851 the Württemberg government bowed to events and founded an official newspaper along the lines Elsner had suggested: the *Staats-Anzeiger für Württemberg*. On one level, the *Staats-Anzeiger* was an attempt to rationalise existing press resources. It followed a review of the government press, which consisted at the time of Elsner's *Ulmer Kronik* and another semi-official newspaper, the *Laterne*.[59] Yet the initiative was clearly influenced by Elsner's earlier proposals and demonstrates the extent to which governments rethought press policy in the light of the revolution. Tellingly, the impetus for the new newspaper came right from the top, from none other than Wilhelm himself.

The new newspaper was funded by a government advertising monopoly and by the obligatory subscriptions of local authorities. The *Staats-Anzeiger* aimed both to defend the government against attacks in the opposition press and to undermine the finances of politically unreliable local newspapers. In other words, the new newspaper targeted the very local communities which the Interior Minister had sought to keep out of politics only two years earlier. Moreover, Elsner himself was to play a central part in the initiative, since he was supposed to publish the new

[58] Bericht des Ministers des Innern an den König, betr. die Vorschläge des Redacteurs der Ulmer Kronik, Dr. H. Elsner, zu Gründung von sogenannten Kreisblätter, 22 November 1847, HSAStu E 9 94 I.

[59] Trox, 'Heinrich Elsner', 327, portrays the *Laterne* and the *Ulmer Kronik* as related publications, principally on the basis of similar design and politics. This is not borne out by documents in the Stuttgart archives which detail the failure of the two newspapers to merge in late 1849 and the tensions between Elsner and Schraishorn, the editors of the two papers (HSAStu E 9 94 I).

4.1 The first edition of the *Staats-Anzeiger für Württemberg*. 1 January 1850.
Source: Württembergische Landesbibliothek

paper.[60] Nevertheless, both Elsner and the cabinet agreed that he was too controversial a figure actually to edit the *Staats-Anzeiger* and that he should be kept behind the scenes. Unfortunately, they disagreed as to who should be appointed in Elsner's stead. Elsner denounced the government's attempt to appropriate his initiative to Wilhelm in no uncertain terms, but the cabinet stood its ground and, crucially, undertook to finance the new newspaper with public money, rather than from Wilhelm's private purse.[61] Control of the *Staats-Anzeiger* thus shifted decisively from the monarch to his ministers.

These initial struggles for control of the government newspaper reflected different understandings of the role it was to play. Wilhelm clearly intended the *Staats-Anzeiger* to be a platform for hard-line conservative polemic. Both the editor, Dr Pressel, and the government envisaged a more subtle approach. In February 1850 Wilhelm complained to the cabinet that Pressel had refused to publish articles sent in to the newspaper from the royal office.[62] He demanded that Pressel be replaced. Pressel rejoined that both the tone and content of the articles in question were calculated to alienate the most well-meaning citizens from the 'ministerial' newspaper.[63] The cabinet sided with Pressel, stressing in particular its own opposition to the aggressive foreign policy line taken in the 'anonymous' articles.[64] Indeed, the cabinet questioned the advisability of addressing such high-political issues at all in a newspaper destined principally for rural communities. As in Hanover and Saxony, factionalism within the government obstructed the smooth workings of government press policy.

Wilhelm then turned his attention elsewhere, having failed for a second time to assert his authority over the *Staats-Anzeiger*. During his dispute with Pressel, he had threatened 'to make use of other newspapers to publicise His Majesty's opinions, even those newspapers that

---

[60] See HSAStu E 14 1186 (200–29) for details of initial negotiations with Elsner over the *Staats-Anzeiger*.

[61] Bericht des Gesammtministeriums betreffend die Herausgabe einer Regierungszeitung, 26 December 1849, HSAStu E 14 1186 (235–6). The cabinet simply requested extra royal subsidy for the first two years. Naujoks, 'Der "Staatsanzeiger"', 276–7, describes the financing of the *Staats-Anzeiger*. 1851/2 2,722 *Gulden* p.a. granted by the parliament (hitherto the provision for the *Regierungsblatt* or government newspaper) for the publication of official announcements, and a further 4,780 *Gulden* for delivery to the *Gemeinde* (community) – a total of 7,502 *Gulden* – rising in 1855–8 to a total of 9,422 *Gulden*, due to increasing subscription costs paid by the *Gemeinde*.

[62] K. Note to Gesammtministerium, 7 February 1850, HSAStu E 14 1186.

[63] Ansichten des Dr. Pressels, 2 February 1850, HSAStu E 14 1186 (258–61).

[64] K. Gesammtministerium to King's personal office, 9 February 1850, HSAStu E 14 1186.

oppose the line taken in the *Staats-Anzeiger*.[65] He made good this threat a month later, when the royal office founded a new semi-official newspaper, the *Deutsche Kronik*.[66] Tellingly, Elsner was responsible for the paper's coverage of Württemberg affairs.[67] Moreover, the newspaper's official editor was August Lewald, a disgruntled former contributor to the *Staats-Anzeiger*. In 1852 Elsner claimed, with some justification, that '[i]n Württemberg the *Deutsche Kronik* stands alone in defending the power of the Throne'.[68] This did not prevent the *Deutsche Kronik* from folding shortly afterwards.[69] Its collapse was due both to declining circulation and to decreasing support from the royal office in the shape of informative tit-bits and leading articles.

This lack of royal interest in the *Deutsche Kronik* was a result of the *Staats-Anzeiger*'s successful relaunch in 1851, following the restoration in Württemberg of the 1819 constitution. In May, the cabinet appointed a new editor and proposed a number of further changes to make the *Staats-Anzeiger* more acceptable to Wilhelm.[70] Henceforth, the Interior Minister, or (where relevant) the Foreign Minister, would approve leaders and the more substantive news stories before their publication. The Interior Minister was also responsible for the general management of the newspaper. A special official coordinated government liaison with the paper, ensuring that different government departments took a consistent line. The monopoly of official advertising was enforced more rigidly and officials were urged to contribute to the newspaper and to pass on interesting information. '[A]s a necessary consequence . . . of Württemberg's external political relations,' the new-look *Staats-Anzeiger* focused almost exclusively on domestic affairs. In principle, the newspaper would cover external affairs only in so far as these were directly relevant to domestic and economic concerns, and it would address wider political issues only if absolutely necessary. These stipulations reflected

---

[65] K. Note to Gesammtministerium, 7 February 1850, ibid.

[66] Subsidy of the *Deutsche Kronik* was 6,500 *Gulden* p.a. in 1850 according to an annual accounting sheet, dated 13 March 1850, HSAStu E 9 94 (378).

[67] Contract between K. Kabinetsdirektor Freiherr v. Maucler and Dr Heinrich Elsner, 13 March 1850, HSAStu E 9 94 I (380). [68] Elsner to H.M., 2 November 1852, HSAStu E 9 94 I (281–3).

[69] See August Lewald, 'Bericht', 1 January 1852, HSAStu E 9 94 I (290).

[70] Bericht des Gesammtministeriums an den König betr. den Staats-Anzeiger für Württemberg, 10 January 1851, HSAStu E 14 1186 (280–1). The proposals were eagerly greeted by Wilhelm, who later admonished the ministry for dragging its feet in the matter. K. Note an das K. Gesammtministerium, 8 September 1851, HSAStu E 14 1186 (292). For details of the changes see Anbringen des Gesammtministeriums an den König, 11 October 1851, HSAStu E 14 1186 (296–305).

an awareness of widespread dissatisfaction with recent political developments in Germany.

Rising nationalist pressures caused the government to reconsider this
policy in 1860, as part of a wider reorganisation of the newspaper.
Ostensibly, the reorganisation was the result of escalating interministe-
rial tensions over the financing of the *Staats-Anzeiger,* which reflected a
lack of commitment to the newspaper outside the Interior Ministry.[71]
The tensions came to a head when the Finance Minister unilaterally dis-
continued 432 government subscriptions to the paper, on the grounds
that it cost too much. Linden, the Interior Minister, appealed in outrage
to the King. As a result, the government as a whole renewed its commitment to the newspaper. The upshot was that every government department designated an official, who reported daily to the editor and kept
him informed of developments worthy of coverage. This, it was hoped,
would render the *Staats-Anzeiger* more popular and enable it to influence
public opinion more effectively. Officials were also to be paid for their
articles and forbidden to write for rival publications, in an attempt to
encourage them to contribute to the newspaper. Most significant,
however, was the new role assigned the Foreign Minister, von Hügel. The
Interior Minister remained responsible for day-to-day management of
the newspaper and for the line it took on domestic affairs, but the Foreign
Minister now directed the *Staats-Anzeiger*'s treatment of foreign policy.
The government considered the increased involvement of the Foreign
Ministry particularly desirable 'given the great influence exercised by
external political relations on Württemberg's affairs'.

The 1860 reorganisation did not, however, prevent tensions between
Wilhelm and his ministry over the content of the *Staats-Anzeiger.* The
years 1860 and 1861 saw at least two important differences of opinion
over the nature of the *Staats-Anzeiger*'s approach to the German question.
In May 1860 Hügel and Linden explained their decision not to print an
article sent by the royal office to the *Staats-Anzeiger.* 'We are,' they wrote,
'far from opposing in any way the underlying ideas behind the article . . .
but it is our firm belief that the approach adopted in the draft (diverg-
ing so widely from journalistic convention) would lay the editor of the

---

[71] This lack of commitment was apparent at a local level in the repeated infringements of the
Staats-Anzeiger's advertising monopoly. See HSAStu E 150 IV 1599. At ministerial level the Justice
Minister repeatedly complained at the extent of direct and indirect government subsidy for the
Staats-Anzeiger; the Interior Minister responded defensively by complaining that other ministers
failed to support its good work.

Staats-Anzeiger open to a libel charge, which of course would be neither the intention of Your Majesty's government nor in the interest of the newspaper.'[72] Wilhelm had little patience with this pussyfooting approach, as he indicated to Linden with regard to a different article in February 1861. How, he asked, could revolutionary agitation be successfully opposed so half-heartedly?[73]

Ironically, the hard-hitting approach advocated by Wilhelm was only implemented after his death, as part of a further reorganisation of the newspaper. In February 1866 the cabinet took joint control of the *Staats-Anzeiger*.[74] This ensured that the *Staats-Anzeiger* represented the views of the government as a whole and that all ministers felt equally committed to its success. Dr Faber, a conservative with extensive journalistic experience, was then appointed as editor, in an attempt to breathe new life into the paper.[75] In late April the government also hired the well-known *großdeutsch* agitator, Julius Froebel, as an official journalist – at the very high rate of 5,000 *Gulden* a year.[76] Thereafter the pages of the *Staats-Anzeiger* were devoted to an increasingly hysterical campaign against the forces of *kleindeutsch* nationalism, marking a shift from biased reportage to polemic that was highly unusual for an official newspaper.[77] The outcome of the Austro-Prussian war in 1866 revealed this tactic to have been somewhat misguided, for the hard-line attitude of its official press had done little to endear Württemberg to the Prussians. In August 1866 Gessler, the Interior Minister, concluded that '[u]nder these circumstances and given the current political situation, it is urgently necessary to introduce editorial changes at the newspaper in the immediate future'.[78] Dr Faber was dismissed shortly

---

[72] Hügel and Linden to H.M., 10 May 1860, HSAStu E14 1186 (360/77).

[73] K. Schreiben an den Minister des Innern Frhr. v. Linden, 9 February 1861, HSAStu E 14 1186 (376/82).

[74] An den König betr. der Regelung des Verhältnisses des Staats-Anzeigers, 3 February 1866, HSAStu E 150 IV 1600 (430).

[75] Faber, a priest from Gschwend, had argued in *Konfessionen eines Großdeutschen* (1863) that South Germany was the true home of German intellectual life, explaining how he had become a *großdeutsch* supporter despite being brought up to revere Prussia as the defender of Protestantism. The Prussians had succumbed to French and Jewish influence; Berlin could not therefore be the intellectual epicentre of Germany. See Rapp, *Die Württemberger und die nationale Frage*, pp. 51–3.

[76] Contract between Foreign Ministry and Interior Ministry on behalf of Württemberg Government and Dr Julius Froebel, 30 April 1866, HSAStu E 14 1186 (158–9/ad2). A more usual salary would be 1,000–1,500 *Gulden*.

[77] Piereth, 'Propaganda im 19. Jahrhundert', p. 38, notes that the *Staats-Anzeiger* in Prussia, Austria, and Bavaria were not polemical.

[78] Gessler to H.M., 3 August 1866, HSAStu E 14 1186 (390–2/91).

afterwards. The close relationship between politics and press policy in Württemberg could hardly be more explicit.

In Hanover, Saxony and Württemberg the revolutions of 1848/9 prompted governments to consider their approach to the press as a means of positively influencing public opinion. This direct causal relationship between the revolution and government press policy was particularly clear both in Saxony, where the Dresden uprising led to a reassessment of government press policy, and in Württemberg, where an official newspaper was founded for the first time in January 1850. Yet the revolutions were not alone in influencing the development of press policy and the interface between the authorities and the public sphere. After 1850 changes in government press policy continued to reflect political concerns. The contrast between Hanover and Württemberg is particularly revealing of the relationship between press policy, political pressures and the nature of the states themselves.

Foreign and domestic considerations were probably equally important in determining government press policy in Hanover. The *Hannoversche Nachrichten* was founded in 1856 in response to the Hanoverian constitutional conflict of 1855, and the domestic focus of the newspaper reflected this context. Conversely, the appointment of Meding in 1859 was clearly a response to the first wave of *Nationalverein* agitation in Germany. The establishment of the Hanoverian Press Office in 1862 was once again a response to domestic pressures, since it followed widespread resistance to the introduction of a more orthodox catechism. The Hanoverian authorities interpreted the catechism conflict above all as a failure of the government press. A key policy meeting resolved that 'above all, consideration should be given to exercising suitable influence in the *Press*; this should have been used more energetically to make the case for the catechism beforehand, and the key now is to regain this lost ground if possible'.[79] As a result, the government set up a working party under Meding to monitor and influence the press, and the press office was founded shortly afterwards. Yet the new press office also reflected wider political concerns. The initial proposal noted that '[t]he current political situation in Germany makes it urgently necessary to defend and promote our own interests through the press'.[80] This combination of internal and external

---

[79] Notatum, Herrenhausen, 6 August 1862, HSAHan Hann 113 K 1127 (2–5).
[80] Anlage zum Protokolle vom 1 November 1862, HSAHan Hann 26a 555 (25–9).

motives is hardly surprising in view of the isolation of the Hanoverian government at home and abroad. The dual motivation behind Hanoverian press policy reflected the extent to which the domestic and liberal agenda interacted with the national agenda here. In Hanover, the regime was unpopular on all fronts.

This was in stark contrast to the situation in Württemberg, where domestic issues were less explosive and government press policy was primarily a response to national pressures. This is clear both from the timing of press policy changes (1851, 1860, 1866) and from the nature of the changes made. Each major overhaul of the *Staats-Anzeiger* entailed a reassessment of its approach to the German question. Interestingly, the decision to concentrate on domestic rather than foreign affairs in 1851 marked a reversal of pre-revolutionary press policy – traditionally, governments had tolerated newspaper coverage of foreign but *not* domestic news precisely because the latter was *more* controversial.[81] The new approach to news management reflected the growing importance of German politics in Württemberg affairs. Ironically, the attempt to reinforce the importance of the state itself as the primary frame of reference for its inhabitants merely underlined the extent to which this was being undermined by events. In 1860 the approach was reassessed because rising nationalism meant that it had ceased to be viable. The re-evaluation encouraged a gradual return to polemic in the *Staats-Anzeiger* during the 1860s, which culminated in the final overhaul of the *Staats-Anzeiger* early in 1866. The transformation of German politics that took place shortly afterwards then prompted a quick reversal of these changes. The extent to which foreign policy issues determined government press policy in Württemberg may reflect the fact that, as a more liberal regime, the government faced fewer domestic pressures. Government press policy in Württemberg focused exclusively on the domestic market, since it consisted solely of the *Staats-Anzeiger*. In terms of the domestic market, however, foreign policy issues were less of a concern. In fact, centralising *kleindeutsch* nationalism was extremely unpopular among many Württemberg liberals and democrats. Nationalism did not really pose a serious internal threat to the government, despite the popularity of the pro-Prussian *Schwäbischer Merkur*. The rabidly anti-Prussian tone of the *Staats-Anzeiger* in 1866 can therefore be

---

[81] See Gert Hagelweide, ' "Inländische Zustände". Zu den Anfängen des Leitartikels in der Presse des deutschen Vormärz' in Elger Blühm and Hartwig Gebhardt (eds.), *Presse und Geschichte II. Neue Beiträge zur historischen Kommunikationsforschung* (Munich, 1987), 329–348 (p. 330).

seen both as playing to the prejudices of the market and as an attempt actively to shape public opinion.

How did the content of official and semi-official newspapers reflect the evolving priorities of governments in these states? This issue is best approached through content analysis of the newspapers themselves.[82] The analysis will focus on two key questions: what kind of news did these newspapers cover, and how? In answering these questions, attention will be paid to the format of the newspaper and to the kinds of topic dealt with by explicitly political leading articles (usually at the head of the newspaper). This is more feasible than analysis of less overtly biased news coverage. Moreover, leaders are particularly revealing because their content can be directly related to the political concerns of government. This analysis reveals a crucial reorientation in government propaganda in Hanover, Saxony and Württemberg. The focus of propaganda shifted away from the states themselves and towards the rest of Germany.

In 1851 the *Hannoversche Zeitung* published a mission statement, outlining its role in the press.[83] 'Of course,' it declared, 'a Hanoverian newspaper will pay particular attention to Hanover.' This was seldom borne out in practice. In fact, the *Hannoversche Zeitung* rarely if ever reflected a supposedly natural bias in favour of Hanoverian news or comment. As early as 1853 the emphasis of leading articles slipped towards German and international events. Of the 141 leaders published in the *Hannoversche Zeitung* between April and December in 1853, only forty-nine (under half) dealt with Hanoverian affairs. Moreover, the bulk of these leaders appeared earlier rather than later in the year. This change of focus was

---

[82] The *Deutsche Nordsee Zeitung, Dresdner Journal, Hannoversche Nachrichten, Hannoversche Zeitung/Neue Hannoversche Zeitung, Leipziger Zeitung* and *Staats-Anzeiger für Württemberg*. Obviously this is a mammoth task, since these were daily newspapers – in fact the *Hannoversche Zeitung/Neue Hannoversche Zeitung* appeared twice daily. The papers listed above have been covered for the entire period from January 1850 to June 1866 in order to provide an analysis of the topics dealt with in leading articles. Where it has not been possible to cover the entire period, the analysis is based on a study of alternate years in the 1850s, but of all years in the 1860s. Care has been taken to cover those years of special importance in the country concerned. Besides this, certain kinds of news coverage (like local news) have been analysed for sample months, and this analysis has been repeated where the nature of the sections in question appears to change. Analysis of local news reveals the image of the state itself as projected in the official newspaper. The format of the newspapers and changes to this format have also been analysed. The approach outlined here obviously combines the systematic with the impressionistic, but is clearly justifiable since the general impression provided by the newspapers is precisely the issue at stake. The general approach taken by the newspapers is of interest here, not a blow-by-blow investigation of their coverage of particular issues. A detailed analysis of news coverage for the whole period is quite clearly beyond the scope of this project and indeed the powers of a single individual.

[83] *Hannoversche Zeitung*, No. 34, 8 February 1851.

reflected in the evolving format of the newspaper: in 1851 the paper opened with Hanoverian news; by 1855 Hanoverian news appeared at the end of the German news section. The reorientation away from domestic politics was briefly reversed at the height of the Hanoverian constitutional conflict, with a series of twenty articles defending the government position. These were in fact almost the only leaders to appear in 1855, except for an article in November concerning the Prussian elections. Indeed, there were few leaders of any kind between 1855 and 1859. In 1859 the balance shifted decisively towards European and German events. Of the seventy leaders that appeared at the height of the *Nationalverein* agitation in the second half of 1859, just under a third addressed the issue of German reform but only two concerned Hanoverian politics. The pattern continued until the leading article virtually disappeared in 1863/4. This may have reflected the deteriorating political situation on all fronts. In the first half of 1866 there were only three leaders in the *Neue Hannoversche Zeitung* at all, covering Romania, the Protestant synod in Amsterdam and police administration.[84] Needless to say, they hardly reflected pressing contemporary concerns. By this stage the *Neue Hannoversche Zeitung* had become an official newspaper run on very traditional lines and avoiding all mention of controversial issues. This is apparent in the paper's treatment of two major political crises: the catechism conflict of 1862 and the ministerial crisis of 1865. In 1862 the government initially operated a blanket ban on coverage of the catechism conflict. Once this was lifted, the *Neue Hannoversche Zeitung* published several leaders defending the new catechism, but failed to report on the continuing turmoil it caused. In 1865 the paper made no attempt whatsoever to cover the ministerial crisis and only three news items referred to the event at all. For want of political coverage in the *Neue Hannoversche Zeitung*, the most consistent element in domestic news was the royal family: popular celebrations of royal birthdays, the warm welcome they received throughout Hanover, their many good works. These reports invariably took pride of place in the newspaper, regardless of its usual format. The dynastic element was somewhat less apparent in government newspapers in Württemberg and Saxony, which invariably reported on the King's birthday celebrations but never gave serious coverage to the birthdays of the Queen, the Crown Prince or Princesses as well.

The total lack of serious domestic or indeed political news in the *Neue Hannoversche Zeitung* at this time may have reflected the pressures for

---

[84] *Neue Hannoversche Zeitung*, Nos. 103, 161, 244, 2 March 1866, 1 April 1866, 29 May 1866.

objectivity in a government newspaper. This was not true of the two
semi-official newspapers backed by the Hanoverian government: the
Hannoversche Nachrichten and the *Deutsche Nordsee Zeitung*. In terms of
content, the *Hannoversche Nachrichten* fulfilled its commitment to concentrate on domestic politics.[85] Only two of forty-seven leaders published in
the last quarter of 1856 covered non-Hanoverian issues. This was not
true of the *Deutsche Nordsee Zeitung*, which was predominantly concerned
with German politics. Only five leaders in the first quarter of 1865
covered Hanover, of which four related to German policy. By contrast,
sixteen leaders were concerned with German politics and a further two
covered non-German issues. This important difference between the
Hannoversche Nachrichten and the *Deutsche Nordsee Zeitung* indicates that
domestic considerations were not the only explanation for the shift away
from domestic coverage in the *Neue Hannoversche Zeitung*. Declining
domestic coverage certainly reflects tensions on the home front.
Nevertheless, more extensive coverage of German politics in both the
Neue Hannoversche Zeitung and the *Deutsche Nordsee Zeitung* also reflected a
reorientation of politics within a wider German context and the increasingly national concerns of German governments at this time.

In Saxony before 1854 the government press acknowledged the existence of distinctively Saxon and distinctively German concerns. The distinction was reflected in the division of labour between the
Saxon-oriented *Dresdner Journal* and a less insular *Leipziger Zeitung*. This line
was not easy to draw. Both papers had the same order of content: perhaps
a leader, followed by daily news from Saxony, Austria, Prussia and so on.
Both papers also trod carefully. Leaders in the *Dresdner Journal* dealt not
merely with domestic politics, but with uncontroversial domestic politics
at that. They were also fairly rare. In the first quarter of 1852 there were
only thirty-two leaders, of which perhaps three were politically significant, and two of these merely corrected reports appearing in the liberal
Constitutionelle Zeitung. As for the *Leipziger Zeitung*, it had very few leaders at
all after 1851. The collapse of this division of labour between the two official newspapers indicates that foreign and domestic politics were less distinct than the government had hoped. In 1854 the *Leipziger Zeitung* was
granted greater editorial independence. Thereafter, leaders mostly consisted of partisan 'Overviews' of the international political situation,
which certainly did not restrict their scope to Saxony, or even to Germany.
In the *Dresdner Journal*, by contrast, leaders became less frequent but rather

[85] Full run of the *Hannoversche Nachrichten* not available.

more interesting. In 1854, for instance, there were just twenty-five leaders, but many of these did cover the German question and other contentious issues, such as the 'Misleading rumours in the press as to the alleged efforts of the *Mittelstaaten*'.[86] In fact, only nine of these twenty-five leaders dealt with Saxony, a pattern that developed in later years. The non-Saxon focus of comment in the *Dresdner Journal* was particularly apparent in the *Zeitungsschau* articles, which reflected regularly on the views of other newspapers after 1859. In the first quarter of 1859 fifty of these dealt with the German question and only one with Saxon politics. This was absolutely typical of what was to come. Saxon news, if covered at all, tended to relate events at court, as well as fires, deaths and other misfortunes in the localities. Initially, therefore, the *Leipziger Zeitung* did not make use of its new freedom to cover domestic affairs, but the *Dresdner Journal* did concern itself increasingly with German and European affairs. The failure of the *Leipziger Zeitung* to address internal affairs was a response to the lack of government editorial control over a newspaper located some distance from the seat of government. In 1861 Witzleben himself suggested that the leaders might occasionally address internal affairs, but dismissed the proposal out of hand, lacking confidence in his ability to overcome the difficulties he anticipated this would cause the *Leipziger Zeitung* as a government newspaper.[87] The predominance of German and international concerns in the *Dresdner Journal* during the 1860s demonstrates clearly the extent to which internal Saxon politics had been subsumed into German affairs.

In Württemberg the *Staats-Anzeiger* was initially founded as a polemical political paper and continued as such for some time. For the first few months it opened almost invariably with hard-hitting political leaders. Topics included, Austrian proposals for a trade and customs union, the elections and the revolution in Baden.[88] In April and May – just after the *Deutsche Kronik* was founded – there was a lull in these articles, when parliamentary reports vied with such compelling issues as the new Hail Insurance Institution.[89] Political polemic revived in June 1850 and persisted, if less consistently, until perhaps March 1851. By this time the leaders were no longer precisely regular – only sixteen for the whole month – and did not cover such controversial issues. Only four of these

---

[86] For instance *Dresdner Journal*, No. 42, 19 February 1854.

[87] Witzleben, Vortrag to Ministerium des Innern, 21 January 1858, HSADre Ministerium des Innern 9493 (225–48).

[88] *Staats-Anzeiger für Württemberg*, Nos. 32, 40, 69–70, 5 February 1850, 15 February 1850, 21–22 March 1850.   [89] Ibid., No. 109, 8 May 1850.

sixteen addressed the German question, despite the fact that the future shape of Germany was being determined in Dresden at the time.[90] A further six could be described as broadly political – of which five were an extended consideration of the role of the peasant.[91] The remainder dealt with issues such as emigration and secondary education. By June 1851 the leader had virtually disappeared from the *Staats-Anzeiger*. Now the newspaper opened with local news. Reports detailed the profits made by state railways, recounted Wilhelm's trips abroad and included important documents relating to internal affairs. In fact, the decision to concentrate on domestic affairs, finalised in late 1851, merely institution-alised existing practice.

The result of this policy was a rather dull paper. The *Staats-Anzeiger* did carry reports from the major German cities and states in the 1850s, but they were listed in order of proximity to Württemberg rather than importance. As for domestic news reporting, when the parliament was in session this included lengthy and partisan extracts from the day's debates. More commonly, however, domestic news consisted of the usual diet of theft, death and disaster – combined with relentlessly up-beat coverage of agricultural progress, local industrial exhibitions, apolitical associational activity, state-sponsored art exhibitions and theatrical per-formances (mostly in the capital). The *Staats-Anzeiger* invariably covered the celebrations to mark the King's birthday and his travels around Württemberg. These reports helped reinforce government cultural policy and projected a fairly consistent image of Württemberg as a model monarchy, the *Musterländle*, a loyal, prosperous, culturally active and contented community.

In the early 1860s the format of the *Staats-Anzeiger* changed.[92] From April 1861, it opened with German news, then foreign news and finally reports from Württemberg. The change represented a major shift of focus for the *Staats-Anzeiger*, indicating a recognition that Germany rather than Württemberg now formed its prime field of interest. The change was followed a year later by another of equal symbolic importance: the incorporation of important news from Stuttgart at the beginning of the German news section. This indicated a definitive recognition by the government that Württemberg did not exist simply as an independent state, but rather as part of a larger German entity. These changes of format were reflected in the gradual return to polemical journalism.

---

[90] Ibid., Nos. 62, 64–6, 13 March 1851, 15–18 March 1851.
[91] Ibid., Nos. 56–9, 61, 6–9 March 1851, 12 March 1851.   [92] Ibid., No. 99, 27 April 1861.

This can be dated back to the summer of 1860, although polemic really returned with a vengeance in the spring of 1866 under the editorship of Dr Faber. The titles of leaders at this time made it quite clear where the newspaper's priorities now lay: 'The mission of the *Mittelstaaten*', 'On Confederal reform', 'A new era, Prussia and Austria in 1866', 'The feudal party in Prussia', 'The popular interest in the Prusso-Austrian conflict', 'German cultural interests in political disputes', 'Theory of the German question'.[93] In the 1850s the importance of the German question had only been apparent in Württemberg in its absence from the government newspaper. The polemical treatment of the German question adopted in 1866 therefore marked a final reversal of the *Staats-Anzeiger*'s earlier policy.

These changes in the content of official newspapers reflect a refocusing of interest on German issues in all three states. They do not imply that the states themselves were sidelined. In the 1860s governments became increasingly aware that the states were not isolated units and needed to be more firmly rooted in their German context if they were to survive. After all, the reorientation of these newspapers took different forms in the different states: all of them continued to reflect their domestic context, whilst the nature and extent of domestic coverage was distinctive in each state. Up to a point, the governments of these states tolerated a reorientation of their official newspapers precisely because they had confidence in the validity of their states as political units: they believed the national issue was an issue on which they could win.

The content of official newspapers, like the development of government press policy, reflected a crucial transition from a culture of official secrecy to a limited kind of open government. Pre-revolutionary governments were not used to sharing political information with the press – in fact this went against their every instinct. The traditional attitude was typified by Wilhelm of Württemberg in 1849, when the royal office rejected a request to pass on news and other information to the semi-official *Laterne*, even though the newspaper itself was funded by the royal purse.[94] Changes in government press policy from 1850 to 1866 can be seen as a gradual learning process, whereby the governments abandoned traditional habits of secrecy in an attempt to render their propaganda more

[93] Ibid., Nos. 63–5, 67–8, 77, 79, 109–12, 92–3, 15–17 March 1866, 21 March 1866, 1–2 April 1866, 9–13 May 1866, 19–20 April 1866.
[94] K. Kabinettsdirektor to Schraishorn, 5 July 1849, HSAStu E 14 1185 (123).

effective. In the three case studies examined here, organisational changes in government press policy represented repeated attempts to improve liaison between the government and the official press. The repetitive character of these efforts testifies to persistent resistance in many government ministries. Reluctance to cooperate was precisely the problem faced by Beust, when he attempted to improve links with the *Dresdner Journal* in 1857. In 1857 the Hanoverian Foreign Minister, von Platen, was similarly unwilling to leak information to the official press. 'As a rule,' he wrote to Georg V, 'the most urgent considerations prevent us from passing on material (usually received from a confidential source) as political news for the public.'[95]

Regimes needed to overcome their instinctive resistance to open government if they were to operate a successful press policy. Coverage of domestic news in the *Neue Hannoversche Zeitung* during the 1860s demonstrates that this was a lesson that the Hanoverian government failed to learn. For instance, the newspaper simply failed to cover the ministerial crisis of 1865. Press policy in Württemberg and Saxony ceased to be so crude. Thus the *Staats-Anzeiger* blanket ban on foreign policy comment, operative in the 1850s, was relaxed in the 1860s. Similarly, although the Saxon government was tempted to adopt such a policy in 1866, wiser counsel prevailed. The editor of the *Dresdner Journal* took issue with a requirement forbidding all reporting of military matters. Such an omission, he argued, would have dire consequences for the newspaper's circulation: 'it is my firm conviction that it would be tantamount to removing the *Dresdner Journal* from among the ranks of political newspapers at a stroke'.[96] The increasing openness of government press policy demonstrates the complex interplay between government newspapers and the reading public. The latter were not passive recipients of propaganda, since if this propaganda was to be effective and to reach a wide audience it had to reflect their tastes. Ultimately, almost all changes in the management of the government press in this period were prompted by a desire to retain and extend popular appeal, in other words to respond to the perceived demands of the readership.

Assessing the actual effectiveness of government press policy is fraught with difficulty. Although the development of official and semi-official newspapers can be studied with relative ease, it is almost impossible to

---

[95] Platen-Hallermund to H.M., 3 February 1857, HSAHan Dep. 103 IX 299.
[96] Hartmann to Häpe (Commissar for the *Dresdner Journal*), 25 May 1866, HSADre Ministerium des Innern 9514 (110a–b).

quantify the extent of indirect government press influence. Both the government and the newspapers they influenced had an interest in downplaying the role of the authorities in shaping the press. Governments hoped to increase the effectiveness of propaganda by concealing its source. Conversely, editors and newspaper owners were embarrassed to acknowledge the degree of government influence over their newspapers. Secrecy was an integral part of the process and is a key factor in explaining the limited interest historians have shown in the official press hitherto. Indirect government influence of this kind complicates any attempt to determine the success of government press policy, since a press that was susceptible to such influence cannot simply be identified with public opinion. More generally, newspapers can be analysed to deduce an intention on the part of the writer, but not as an indicator of the reception of the newspaper by the reader. In this sense, the relationship between newspapers and the actual opinions of the public will inevitably remain obscure.

At the very least, however, newspaper circulation figures do give some idea of how effectively government press policy shaped the climate of the press. How widely were official and semi-official newspapers read? How did this compare with the readership of other kinds of newspaper? It is important to realise that all nineteenth-century newspapers had low circulation figures. According to Eberhard Naujoks, a circulation of 10,000 made for a big paper in the period 1850–1900 in Germany.[97] In fact, very few papers had a print run of over 30,000 and in medium to large towns in the mid-nineteenth century a print run of 2–5,000 was certainly significant. Yet low circulation figures do not imply equally low readership levels, since newspapers were read in public places and passed from hand to hand. Pastor Franz Köhler of Johnsbach described this process in a letter to the Interior Ministry regarding his difficulties in obtaining a copy of the *Leipziger Zeitung*. Köhler complained that '[t]he few copies of the *Leipziger Zeitung* that are read in the little towns around here are already committed to readers for a period of several weeks'.[98] Under these circumstances, it is reasonable to propose a multiplier of ten for newspaper circulation figures at this time.[99] These considerations apply particularly to the 1850s and 1860s, since before 1870 production costs were higher and subscription was more expensive.

[97] See Naujoks, 'Die offiziöse Presse und die Gesellschaft', p. 158.
[98] Köhler to Ministerium des Innern, 28 February 1854, HSADre 9492 (138–9).
[99] See Wehler, *Deutsche Gesellschaftsgeschichte*, Vol. ii, p. 521.

Table 4.2. *Newspaper circulation in the five German Kingdoms*

State	Newspaper	Status	Circulation	Date of figure
Bavaria	*Neue Münchner Ztg.*	Official	2,450	1849
Prussia	*Preuss. Staats-Anzeiger*	Official	4,300	1852
	Kreuzzeitung	Semi-official	4,600–7,610	1852–61
	Kölnische Ztg.	Oppositional	10,200–15,700	1852–61
Hanover	*Neue Hannoversche Ztg.*	Semi-official	2,425–2,500	1865–6
	Deutsche Nordsee Ztg.	Semi-official	2,140–2,500	1865–6
	Ztg. für Norddeutschland	Oppositional	2,425–3,000	1865–6
	Hannoversches Tageblatt	Neutral	7,375–9,200	1865–6
Saxony	*Dresdner Journal*	Official	801–1,188	1858–62
	Leipziger Ztg.	Semi-official	4,964–1,188	1858–62
	Constitutionelle Ztg.	Oppositional	996–1,208	1858–62
	Deutsche Allgemeine Ztg.	Oppositional	917–1,292	1858–62
Württemberg	*Staats-Anzeiger*	Official	4,000	1851
	Schwäbischer Merkur	Oppositional	9,000	1858
	Beobachter	Oppositional	2,000	1858

Table 4.2 provides circulation figures for various newspapers during the period 1850–66.[100] Previous studies of the government press have found it to be relatively lacking in influence.[101] This conclusion is based in part on the low circulation figures of government newspapers in Bavaria and Prussia. For instance, the Bavarian official newspaper the *Neue Münchner Zeitung* achieved a maximum circulation of 2,450 at its zenith in 1849.[102] This is seen as typical for such newspapers. The conclusion does not, however, seem to hold true for the smaller states studied here. Table 4.2 demonstrates that government newspapers in Hanover, Saxony and Württemberg were significantly more successful than their

[100] In comparing newspaper circulations for Bavaria, Prussia and the three states studied here it is important to remember that whilst Hanover, Saxony and Württemberg were similar in size, Bavaria was over twice as large and Prussia was roughly eight times the size. Strictly comparable circulation figures do not exist for all the newspapers included in this table, as figures are not necessarily available for the same years. Obviously the use of different sources for different figures further complicates the picture. Where figures are available for more than one year, the first and last figure available for the period indicated have been given. Figures for Prussian newspapers and other important newspapers are given in Fischer, *Handbuch der politischen Presse*, p. 400. Figures for the Hanoverian newspapers 1865–6 are to be found in HSAHan Dep. 103 IX 311. Figures for the *Staats-Anzeiger* come from Gutachten des Geheime Raths an den König, 21 November 1851, HSAStu E 150 (IV) 1599 (186). Figures for other newspapers come from Saxon records to be found in Verzeichnisse in HSADre Ministerium des Innern 9511–14. The later Saxon figures are based on postal records.
[101] See Kohnen, *Pressepolitik des Deutschen Bundes*, pp. 151–6.   [102] Ibid., p. 152.

counterparts in Prussia and Bavaria. This is true both in terms of official newspaper circulation relative to the size of the population and, for
Saxony and Hanover, in terms of official newspaper circulation in comparison with oppositional competitors. How can we account for the
dichotomy between the situation in Prussia and Bavaria on the one
hand, and in Saxony, Hanover and Württemberg on the other? One
explanation may be size, given the highly fragmented nature of the
German newspaper market. The state was a more immediately relevant
and comprehensible unit to the inhabitants of smaller states. In larger
states like Prussia it was simply too large and the capital too remote.
Thus government newspapers in smaller states were better able to meet
the needs of a reading public concerned primarily with local advertising, issues and concerns.

According to these figures, the least successful official newspaper
studied here was the *Dresdner Journal*, which had a circulation of around
1,000. Nevertheless, the semi-official newspaper in Saxony, the *Leipziger
Zeitung*, had a circulation roughly five times this size. Furthermore, the
Dresdner Journal was not noticeably less successful than either of the
major liberal newspapers in Saxony at that time, although none of these
three high-profile papers had circulations which Naujoks would term
significant. If, however, we can believe Herbert Jordan's figures (which
seem slightly exaggerated), the *Dresdner Journal* boomed in the decisive
year 1866. Circulation rose from 2,925 in the first quarter to 4,500 in the
middle of June and 5,675 in August.[103] This indicates that Saxons turned
to the official newspaper in droves when the existence of their state was
seriously threatened. Similarly, in Hanover the *Neue Hannoversche Zeitung*
was slightly less successful than its liberal competitor, the *Zeitung für
Norddeutschland*. Here too, however, government influence was in fact
greater than this implies. Circulation of the semi-official *Deutsche Nordsee
Zeitung* was not much below that of the *Neue Hannoversche Zeitung*.
Furthermore, in Hanover the *Hannoversches Tageblatt* was the most widely
circulated newspaper. This was not a partisan paper, and it was therefore susceptible to Press Office influence. Indeed, Meding went to some
effort to ensure that it did not pass into democratic hands in 1861.[104] It
seems clear, therefore, that oppositional and specifically *kleindeutsch*

---

[103] Herbert Jordan, *Die öffentliche Meinung in Sachsen*, pp. 48–9. These figures are fairly credible, since
the figures given in the earlier table are probably significant underestimates for the Saxon newspapers. Certainly the figures for the *Dresdner Journal* are roughly half of print-run figures available for the *Dresdner Journal* 1852–64, which are given as 1,000–3,650 in HSADre Ministerium
des Innern 9513 (245).   [104] Meding to Lex, 18 June 1861, HSAHan Dep. 103 IX 38.

liberal newspapers were far from being more influential than government newspapers in either Saxony or Hanover – in stark contrast to the
situation in Prussia. Circulation figures show that the reading public in
both Saxony and Hanover was relatively uninterested in the *kleindeutsch*
liberal press. Yet these states have traditionally been seen as particularly
inclined towards *kleindeutsch* liberalism.

Only in Württemberg is the pattern significantly different – although
ironically Württemberg has traditionally been seen as an area resistant
to *kleindeutsch* nationalism. True, the *Staats-Anzeiger* was twice as successful as the democratic *Beobachter*. The *Staats-Anzeiger* figures are particularly hard to interpret as most of the copies were distributed to officials
at public expense. Consequently, the circulation level of the *Staats-
Anzeiger* cannot be taken as testifying to the actual popularity of the newspaper. On the other hand, this official distribution meant that copies
were relatively evenly spread across the state. Equally, although there
were only 1,200 private subscriptions to the *Staats-Anzeiger* in 1855, this
was in one sense no mean achievement. As the editor noted, much of the
newspaper-reading public had free access to the newspaper.[105] In fact,
however, neither the *Staats-Anzeiger* nor the *Beobachter* approached the circulation levels of the pro-Prussian *Schwäbischer Merkur*, which had a circulation of about 9,000. The *Schwäbischer Merkur* had been established as
the leading newspaper in Württemberg for half a century by 1850. In
this sense the situation in Württemberg was anomalous, since the
Schwäbischer Merkur was, like the *Leipziger Zeitung*, a well-established newspaper with a loyal readership and advertising base. The failure to redi-
rect circulation patterns through the *Amtsblatt* initiative in Saxony is a
further indicator that newspaper readers and advertisers were reluctant
to change their habits in this period. Arguably, therefore, the *Staats-
Anzeiger* could never have hoped to compete with the *Schwäbischer Merkur*.

Although the climate of the press in Württemberg was very different
from that in Hanover and Saxony, it is not clear that this also applies to
the climate of public opinion in general. The pro-Prussian politics of the
Schwäbischer Merkur appear to have had surprisingly little impact on political views in Württemberg. *Kleindeutsch* liberal candidates failed to win a
single seat in the *Zollparlament* elections of 1868, notwithstanding the
large circulation of the *Schwäbischer Merkur*. This difference between the
politics of the *Schwäbischer Merkur* and the politics of its readers is not,
however, entirely surprising. The dominance of the *Schwäbischer Merkur*

---

[105] Bericht der Redaktion des *Staats-Anzeigers*, 14 February 1855, HSAStu E 150 (IV) 1599 (233–8).

was most likely rooted not in politics but in habit. In fact the *Schwäbischer Merkur* had been regarded almost as a government paper before 1848 and only developed a *kleindeutsch* liberal stance after the revolution. Habitual readers of the newspaper may not have sympathised with this change. Probably, therefore, politics were relatively unimportant to the reading public in determining choice of newspaper at this time, both in Württemberg and elsewhere. Yet the lack of a clear link between newspaper content and public opinion does not mean that government press policy was doomed to failure in its attempts to influence public opinion through the press. In Hanover and Saxony official and semi-official newspapers were fairly successful. Furthermore, the dominance of government news in these two states was enormously increased by indirect press management techniques.

Government press policy in all three states was particularly concerned with reaching the population of the countryside and small towns, which supposedly formed a passive conservative majority. Thus the Württemberg ministry described the *Staats-Anzeiger* in 1850 as primarily destined for rural communities. Similarly, Elsner's letters to the royal office repeatedly stressed the need to capitalise on 'the good intentions of the country folk'.[106] Ensuring that local officials took government newspapers, as was the case in Württemberg, was widely regarded as a key step in influencing local opinion. Klindworth noted with regard to distributing the *Deutsche Nordsee Zeitung* that 'many complaints are made about the views of subaltern officials, but in many such cases they do not have easy access to a good newspaper in the local authority'.[107] Similarly, in 1855 Hugo Häpe, the Commissar for the *Dresdner Journal*, lamented the bad impression made when government officials were ignorant of government views, or even opposed them.[108] The private views of officials were, he wrote, surprisingly important due to their social status in small towns and in the countryside, where 'the official usually sets the tone in society and in most cases his judgement is decisive for the common man'. Beust later stressed the importance of targeting the educated classes (*Gebildeten*), who played a decisive role in opinion formation.[109]

---

[106] Elsner to H. M., 25 July 1848, HSAStu E 9 94 1 (145–8).
[107] Klindworth, 'Unterthänigstes Promemoria', 31 October 1865, HSAHan Hann 26a 559 (20–7).
[108] Hugo Häpe, Vortrag to Ministerium des Innern, 1 November 1855, HSADre Ministerium des Innern 9510 (39–44).
[109] Beust to Gesammtministerium, 4 May 1857, HSADre Gesammtministerium Loc. 7, No. 7 (176–83).

In Hanover and Saxony, the governments also attempted to reach beyond this educated and official readership. The *Leipziger Zeitung* was in a position to do this from the first. As the editor, Bülau, wrote in 1851: 'The *Leipziger Zeitung* is so important precisely because a great many of its readers never see any other newspaper.'[110] More important than the *Leipziger Zeitung*, however, were the myriad local newspapers that dominated local communities after 1848. Individually, these newspapers were insignificant. Collectively, their readership was vastly greater than that of apparently more important opposition or government newspapers. The governments of Hanover and Saxony attempted to influence these local newspapers through the Press Office and the *Amtsblätter* respectively. Inevitably, it is hard to assess the success of these initiatives, but they were certainly taken seriously by contemporary opponents of the governments. Thus liberal newspapers repeatedly discussed the surprising lack of opposition in the Hanoverian press.[111] For instance, the *Deutsche Reichszeitung* complained in May 1864 that the Hanoverian people had sunk into apathy after the constitutional conflict of 1837, demonstrating clearly the damage caused by '*coups d'état* and breaches of the law'.[112] It added: 'The position taken by almost all of the Hanoverian Press is no less to blame, although admittedly most of it [the Hanoverian Press] is in the hands of the government or otherwise influenced. But even the liberal press does not do its duty there.' This indicates that the general climate of the Hanoverian press was hardly anti-establishment, although no link is made between this climate and the government press. Commenting on the speedy recovery after the ministerial crisis of 1865 in Hanover, the *Weser Zeitung* indicated more clearly how the line taken by official newspapers was reflected at local level: 'the public newspapers scarcely give an inkling that a change has taken place which has not been warmly welcomed by the country and brings with it serious concerns for the future'.[113] We have seen that this was precisely the approach taken in the *Neue Hannoversche Zeitung* in this instance. Equally, the extent of Hanoverian government press influence in 1862 demonstrates that Meding was very successful in winning over the local press. The picture that emerges in Saxony is fairly similar. Beust indicated the extent of

[110] Bülau to Ew. Hochwohlgeboren, 4 September 1851, HSADre Ministerium des Innern 9491 (181–5).   [111] As cited by the Press Office Tagesberichte in HSAHan Dep. 103 ix 281–96.
[112] Tagesbericht, 11 May 1864, HSAHan Dep. 103 ix 285 (125–6).
[113] Tagesbericht, 8 November 1865, HSAHan Dep. 103 ix 293.

indirect government influence over the press in a communication to his ministerial colleagues in 1857.[114] He claimed that the larger Saxon newspapers, in particular those based in Dresden, reprinted unattributed articles from the *Dresdner Journal* on a daily basis, and that the provincial press also took most of its daily news from the *Dresdner Journal*. Complaints from the opposition indicate that there was substance to Beust's claims. In 1865 the liberal *Deutsche Allgemeine Zeitung* railed against his skill in exerting a positive influence over the Saxon press 'through a finely spun web of threads leading in all directions . . . such that it is extremely difficult for independent public opinion to maintain itself at the same time'.[115]

It seems, therefore, that the governments of Saxony and Hanover were fairly successful in their efforts to influence the press indirectly. The impact of this policy has been under-estimated by historians not merely because of the difficulties in analysing it, but also because government press policy explicitly targeted the provinces and the mass of smaller newspapers. These are harder to study and less obviously important than more prestigious papers. Yet it is clearly wrong to assume that the provincial press was simply an echo of the latter. Collectively, as the governments realised, local newspapers were not unimportant. Meding argued that prominent, politically partisan newspapers were mostly read by those already inclined to agree with their views.[116] Instead, Meding believed that 'the small and very smallest newspapers, which make their way among the people who have yet to form their own opinion and are very inclined to take the printed word as truth, form public opinion in a real and important sense'. These newspapers and this readership were the real targets of government press policy in Hanover and Saxony. The evidence is that this policy had a significant impact on the newspapers themselves. The implications of this for newspaper readers are far less certain. Government press policy could not actively direct public opinion in any meaningful sense, but it could help define the parameters of information within which public opinion was formed. Knowledge of events was refracted through the prism of government news management.

Government strategy in news management did change in the 1860s as a response to the new political climate. Nevertheless, basic government

[114] Beust to Gesammtministerium, 2 January 1857, HSADre Gesammtministerium Loc. 7, No. 7 (116–55).   [115] Cited in Jordan, *Die öffentliche Meinung in Sachsen*, p. 24.
[116] Meding, *Memoiren*, Vol. 1, p. 66–7.

principles remained the same, particularly with regard to the German question. These principles in turn informed government news reporting throughout the period. Pro-government news was, in Hanover and Saxony at least, fairly pervasive. In these states government principles clearly did shape public knowledge of events. It is unlikely that public perceptions remained unaffected.

CHAPTER FIVE

Educating patriots

In the 1850s German conservatives found two explanations for the horrors of revolution in 1848 and the persistence of political dissent thereafter. On the one hand, they blamed the free press for corrupting the traditional loyalties of the masses. On the other hand, they blamed the German education system – and more specifically the teachers themselves – for failing to inculcate into the young the virtues of loyalty, obedience and humility. If anything, the latter was regarded as the greater of the two evils.[1] For instance, Julius Thimmig, a Saxon conservative writing in June 1849, declared that bad teachers were even worse than the free press and the new freedoms of political assembly 'because they poison the minds of the young'.[2] Equally, the Hanoverian Interior Minister, Borries, maintained that if Hanoverian clergy, teachers and officials had 'only done their duty' in the first place, then the 'bad press . . . would never have succeeded in establishing this degree of influence'.[3] Such views were widely shared in government circles. Indeed, in 1849 Friedrich Wilhelm IV of Prussia famously took a conference of teaching seminary staff to task for corrupting his subjects with their rotten doctrines, declaring roundly: 'all the misery that has descended upon Prussia in the past year is your fault, and yours alone'.[4] Likewise, von Wächter-Spittler, the minister responsible for education in Württemberg, interpreted the revolution as an indictment of the moral education of the young and laid the responsibility for this squarely at the door of 'the intellectual and

---

[1] For a more modern comparison of the relative importance of education and newspapers in mentality formation, see Blessing, *Staat und Kirche in der Gesellschaft*, pp. 18–19.

[2] Julius Thimmig, Zwickau, an das K. Ministerium des Innern, 11 June 1849, HSADre Ministerium für Volksbildung 12775 (1–2).

[3] Borries, 'Promemoria . . . über die politischen Gesinnungen der Grundbesitzer und Bauern den Einfluss der Presse, der Geistlichkeit, Lehrer und Beamten; Vorschlage einer Auszeichnung für Verdienste um die Landwirtschaft', 7 September 1854, HSAHan Dep. 103 IX 41.

[4] Cited after Hans-Georg Herrlitz, Wulf Hopf and Hartmut Titze, *Deutsche Schulgeschichte von 1800 bis zur Gegenwart. Eine Einführung* (Weinheim, 1993), p. 60.

moral qualities of the class entrusted with that education'.[5] Small
wonder, then, that in the aftermath of the revolution German governments believed the reform of state education to be every bit as urgent as
the need to raise the tone of the press through government propaganda.

Of course, the two phenomena were intimately linked because the
power of the press depended largely on the size of its readership, which
in turn was dictated by the number of people who knew how to read in
the first place.[6] In fact, rising literacy levels prompted an explosion of
reading in nineteenth-century Germany – a process closely related to the
transformation of the basic education system at the same time.[7] Basic
education in Germany traced its origins back to state endorsement of
catechism schools in Reformation times. In the nineteenth century,
however, most German governments took steps to improve and standardise state education and to enforce compulsory school attendance in
practice as well as in principle – so much so, that the Prussian education
system was widely regarded as a model for other European states to
follow. In fact, however, educational reform in Prussia before 1871 was a
top-down process, which stopped short of comprehensive legislation and
never reached the level of basic primary schooling, except indirectly
through teacher training seminaries and changes to the existing secondary school system. By contrast, comprehensive legislation regulating
primary education was passed even before 1848 in Saxony (1835),
Württemberg (1836) and Hanover (1845).[8] Indeed, historians have

---

[5] Wächter-Spittler to Wilhelm, 'Anbringen des Ministeriums des Kirchen- und Schulwesens an
den König in betr. der Mittel zur Heilung der Mängel des Volksschullehrerwesens, insbesondere
zur Beseitigung der in einem bedeutende Theile des Lehrerstandes eingerissenen verderblichen
politischen Richtung', 28 June 1850, HSAStu E 11 37 II (1).

[6] On the explosion of reading in the nineteenth century see Rolf Engelsing, *Analphabetentum und
Lektüre. Zur Sozialgeschichte des Lesens in Deutschland zwischen feudaler und industrieller Gesellschaft*
(Stuttgart, 1973).

[7] There are numerous general histories of German education, most of which address the issue
from a social-history perspective. An excellent starting point for this period is the comprehensive
Karl-Ernst Jeismann and Peter Lundgreen (eds.), *Handbuch der deutschen Bildungsgeschichte*, Vol. III,
1800–1870. Von der Neuordnung Deutschlands bis zur Gründung des deutschen Reiches (Munich, 1987). A
basic overview, based primarily on the Prussian experience, is Peter Lundgreen, *Sozialgeschichte
der deutschen Schule im Überblick. Teil I: 1770–1918* (Göttingen, 1980). A more state-centred account
is von Friedeburg, *Bildungsreform in Deutschland*. Herrlitz, Hopf and Titze, *Deutsche Schulgeschichte*,
is particularly informed by modernisation theory. This is also true of the best account of the
Prussian *Volksschulen* at this time: Frank-Michael Kuhlemann, *Modernisierung und Disziplinierung.
Sozialgeschichte des preußischen Volksschulwesens 1794–1872* (Göttingen, 1992).

[8] For a study of Hanoverian education at this time, see (on East Friesland) Rudolf Vandré, *Schule,
Lehrer und Unterricht im 19. Jahrhundert. Zur Geschichte des Religionsunterrichts* (Göttingen, 1973). This is
more general than its title implies and certainly does not deal exclusively with religious education. For a general history of Saxon education see Julius Richter, *Geschichte der sächsischen Volksschule*
(Berlin, 1930) – long on detail and short on analysis. For a history of education in Württemberg,

described both Saxony and Württemberg as models of educational reform.[9] This new educational legislation established state-wide standards for schools and their teachers, set out basic attendance requirements, and standardised the seminary training, appointment, pay and supervision of teachers. State regulation of this kind was least effective in Hanover, where a quarter of teaching posts remained in the gift of local authorities until 1866, reflecting the persistence of decentralised structures in this state. Equally, the seminary teacher training system was least well developed here – indeed a provincial seminary was not established in East Friesland until after the revolution of 1848.

Historians have related educational reform in nineteenth-century Germany to three different facets of modernisation.[10] First, the state's successful assumption of responsibility for education was a further step towards centralisation.[11] Alongside tax and the army, education was a key area of interaction between state and people. Education provided a means for the state to mobilise its human resources, both economically (through skills training) and politically (through ideological integration). The emergence of a state education system gradually displaced the

see the very useful Gerd Friederich, *Die Volksschule in Württemberg im 19. Jahrhundert* (Weinheim, 1978).

[9] Nipperdey cites Saxony (and Baden) as examples of states with relatively liberal school policies: 'Mass education and modernisation: the case of Germany 1780–1850', *Transactions of the Royal Historical Society*, 5th Series, 27 (1977), 155–172 (p. 170). Douglas R. Skopp, 'Auf der untersten Sprosse: Der Volksschullehrer als "Semi-Professional" im Deutschland des 19. Jahrhunderts', *Geschichte und Gesellschaft* 6:3 (1980), 382–402 (p. 387), describes Württemberg as the German state which was most consequent in reforming the *Volksschulen* in the nineteenth century.

[10] Modernisation theory views the transition from a traditional to a modern society in terms of a complex web of inter-related processes. These processes are demographic (falling birth and death rates); economic (industrialisation, commercialisation, decline of agriculture, steady growth etc.); social (urbanisation, rising incomes); cultural (literacy, secularisation); institutional (state centralisation; development of a bureaucracy; universal conscription, taxation and education); political (democratisation); general (a shift away from the particular to the general, from the stable to the mobile society, from the simple to the complex). Crises of identity and legitimacy are an integral part of this process. Kuhlemann, *Modernisierung und Disziplinierung*, pp. 42–4, details how modernisation applied to education. In a traditional society: low literacy; no obligatory school attendance; no concept of childhood; undifferentiated educational groups; no differentiation between teacher functions; predominance in education of religion and a religion-centred understanding of the world; dominant church influence; education according to social estate not ability; relative lack of opportunities; no written culture and a dominance of aural communication. In a modern society: high literacy; introduction and implementation of obligatory school attendance; permanent establishment of an artificial educational world between familial and professional socialisation; grouping according to age; permanent attempts to improve teaching process and methods; professionalisation of teaching as multi-functional work; universal norms; state administration and little church influence; equal opportunities; internal differentiation of the system; elementary education as the key to a participatory society, empathy development.

[11] See especially Friedeburg, *Bildungsreform in Deutschland*, pp. 29–37, 60–132, and Lundgreen, *Sozialgeschichte der deutschen Schule*, pp. 26–30.

autonomous authorities traditionally responsible for education. At the same time, state education encouraged the development of a specially trained bureaucracy that could oversee the further expansion of state authority. Secondly, educational reform was intimately linked to wider processes of socio-economic change taking place at this time because it contributed to the emergence of an educational meritocracy, which overlay the traditional society of estates. Nevertheless, the extent to which relatively modern education dictated the pace of industrialisation in Germany remains unproven because reading and writing were hardly essential skills for factory workers.[12] Even so, some historians have argued that universal basic education helped to discipline the industrial workforce through teaching habits of obedience acquired after sitting still on a school bench for hours on end, despite often crushing boredom.[13] Thirdly, the development of a state education system provided the state with a crucial instrument of social control, since schooling could be used to foster conservative values and to contain the forces of social and political change.[14] The response of German conservatives to the revolution of 1848/9 demonstrates that they were acutely aware of this particular function of education. It was here, they felt, that the education system had really slipped up. How far did this insight inform educational policy in Hanover, Saxony and Württemberg after the defeat of the revolution? What values did governments in these states seek to foster? How did educational policy in the three states relate to national political developments and to the changing nature of internal and external political threats?

   For most Germans in the nineteenth century, education did not go beyond the level of the basic state primary school, or *Volksschule*.[15] Indeed, fewer than 10% of those living in the German Confederation had access to secondary or higher education.[16] Nevertheless, *Volksschule*

[12] See Peter Lundgreen, 'Industrialisation and the educational formation of manpower in Germany', *Journal of Social History* 9:1 (1975), 64–80, on the lack of clear links between educational and industrial development.

[13] See Harvey J. Graff, *The legacies of literacy: continuities and contradictions in Western culture and society* (Bloomington, 1987), pp. 262–5.

[14] As is clear from the titles, this is the central thrust of Folkert Meyer, *Schule der Untertanen, Lehrer und Politik in Preußen* (Hamburg, 1976) and of Werner K. Blessing, 'Allgemeine Volksbildung und politische Indoktrination im bayerischen Vormärz. Das Leitbild des Volksschullehrers als mentales Herrschaftsinstrument', *Zeitschrift für bayerische Landesgeschichte* 37:2 (1974), 479–568.

[15] Definitions of the *Volksschule* vary considerably. Here the term will be used to describe all state schools below the level of *Gelehrte Schulen* and *Realschulen*. This definition allows for considerable variation in the *Volksschule*, notably between basic single-class village schools and more sophisticated town schools, providing a far higher standard of education.

[16] See Gerd Friederich, 'Das niedere Schulwesen', in Jeismann and Lundgreen (eds.), *Handbuch der deutschen Bildungsgeschichte*, vol. III, 123–152 (p. 123).

education touched the overwhelming majority of children in any given state because attendance was compulsory for children of school age. Potentially, therefore, the role of the *Volksschule* in shaping the views of the next generation of Germans was, as conservatives realised, crucial. How far educational propaganda in the *Volksschule* actually succeeded in so doing is another matter, for the gulf between education policy and educational practice in nineteenth-century Germany was considerable.

By 1848 most German governments had established a central ministry of religion and education, usually known as the *Kultusministerium*.[17] Nevertheless, *Volksschule* education continued to be funded locally, rather than from the centre. Consequently, governments relied on local priests, officials and communities to implement educational reforms – hardly a recipe for success. On the one hand, the priests and officials in question may have been totally uninterested in education. On the other, they may have had their own axes to grind: rationalist priests unwilling to preside over a return to religious orthodoxy; officials operating according to fundamentally liberal assumptions; reactionary landowners and struggling peasants begrudging every last *Pfennig*; representatives of trade and business facing up to the challenges of industrial capitalism. Under these circumstances, educational reform was likely to be inconsistent at best, chaotic and woefully inadequate at worst. In any case, the lofty educational aims of *Kultusministerium* officials sitting in their offices in the capital bore little relationship to the grim reality in the provinces. This frequently consisted of over-stretched teachers, cold, damp and over-crowded schoolrooms, poor furniture, inadequate teaching aids, reluctant pupils and single-class teaching. Unsurprisingly, therefore, education was subject to enormous regional and local variation within each state. Differing educational standards were most clearly apparent across the town–country divide. Indeed, schools in the country were known to be so much worse than schools in the towns that governments usually endorsed different levels of attainment for their pupils and paid teachers in the towns far better accordingly.

Above all, however, the impact of educational propaganda depended on the teachers themselves, on their willingness to spread a given message in class and on the pupils' reception of this message when (and if) they did so. This too must have varied enormously from school to

---

[17] In Württemberg the *Ministerium des Kirchen- und Schulwesens*; in Saxony the *Ministerium des Cultus und öffentlichen Unterrichts*; in Hanover the *Ministerium der geistlichen und Unterrichts Angelegenheiten*, renamed the *Kultusministerium* in 1862. For the sake of simplicity all three will be referred to as *Kultusministerien* here.

school. Moreover, education policies that were conservative in theory may have been far from conservative in practice. Indeed, historians have increasingly stressed the dichotomy between conservative educational aims and the inherently revolutionary potential of education itself, questioning the viability of introducing sectional modernisation without endangering the conservative social structure.[18] These problems have led historians to reach very different conclusions over the impact of the *Volksschule* on mentality formation. Some, like Ludwig von Friedeburg and Folkert Meyer, have argued that the discipline inculcated into the masses through Prussian *Volksschule* education made a crucial contribution to the military victories of Königgrätz and Sedan.[19] Others, like Frank Michael Kuhlemann, have noted that the *Volksschule* did nothing to prevent the growth of socialism after unification.[20] The figure of the seminary-trained *Volksschule* teacher as agent of change in the rural community is central to this debate – just as it was in the aftermath of 1848.[21]

Why did government circles come to see *Volksschule* teachers as scapegoats for the revolution? To some extent this reflected the relatively high profile of teaching associations during the revolution, as they lobbied for higher status and further educational reform. More importantly, many people believed that teacher activism went beyond professional concerns, and that teachers themselves were disproportionately involved in political protest. Thus in 1849 Wilhelm of Württemberg rejected a proposal to raise teachers' pay because of the dangerous and reprehensible tendencies he believed they manifested.[22] The Württemberg *Kultusminister*, Wächter-Spittler, clearly agreed with Wilhelm, for he claimed in 1850 that teachers had been at the forefront of radical activism during the recent elections. These perceptions had some basis in fact. In Saxony, for

---

[18] The revolutionary potential of educational reform was first stressed by Nipperdey, 'Volksschule und Revolution im Vormärz. Eine Fallstudie zur Modernisierung II' in Nipperdey (ed.), *Gesellschaft, Kultur, Theorie*, pp. 206–27, and 'Mass education and modernisation'. The discrepancy between policy and practice in this context is stressed by Kenneth Barkin, 'Social control and the *Volksschule* in *Vormärz* Prussia'.

[19] Meyer, *Schule der Untertanen*, pp. 11–18; Friedeburg, *Bildungsreform in Deutschland*, p. 79.

[20] Kuhlemann, *Modernisierung und Disziplinierung*, p. 251.

[21] This is stressed by Nipperdey, 'Volksschule und Revolution im Vormärz'. For studies dealing particularly with *Volksschule* teachers see Blessing, 'Allgemeine Volksbildung und politische Indoktrination im bayerischen Vormärz'; Anthony J. La Vopa, *Prussian school teachers: profession and office, 1763–1848* (Chapel Hill, 1980) and 'Status and ideology: rural schoolteachers in pre-March and revolutionary Prussia', *Journal of Social History* 12:3 (1979), 430–50; Meyer, *Schule der Untertanen*; Michael Sauer, *Volksschullehrerbildung in Preußen. Die Seminare und Präparandenanstalten vom 18. Jahrhundert bis zur Weimarer Republik* (Cologne, 1987); Skopp, 'Auf der untersten Sprosse'; Heinz-Elmor Tenorth, 'Lehrerberuf und Lehrerbildung' in Jeismann and Lundgreen (eds.), *Handbuch der deutschen Bildungsgeschichte*, Vol. III, pp. 250–69.

[22] H. M. to Schmidlin, 27 June 1849, HSAStu E II 34 I (45).

instance, 70% of teachers were politically active in 1848/9.[23] As Julius Thimmig complained in a letter to the Saxon *Kultusministerium* from Zwickau in 1849, in almost every town teachers were among the most active members of the democratic Fatherland Association, whilst in the countryside they were 'the most unbridled agitators'.[24] Conservatives like Thimmig were particularly distressed by this situation because they believed that the teachers themselves wielded significant political influence. This belief was based on two assumptions about the importance of education. The first assumption was that many people – particularly peasants – were swayed by the political views of teachers, because teachers were more educated than they were. The second assumption was that, as educators, teachers exercised a decisive influence over the young.

Were the *Volksschule* teachers really as politically influential as German conservatives liked to think? In 1850 Wächter-Spittler called for measures to correct the attitudes of the Württemberg *Volksschule* teacher, because of the latter's heinous influence 'not just over the young people whose education is entrusted to him, but also over the adult population, particularly in the countryside'.[25] *Volksschule* teachers themselves certainly liked to give the impression that such views were justified. In 1849, for instance, Rinker, a schoolmaster from Langoldshausen, wrote to Wilhelm of Württemberg urging him to improve the condition of *Volksschule* teachers because they were so influential in the countryside.[26] Rinker described how he had personally foiled the efforts of a democratic doctor in Langoldshausen to corrupt the local citizens' association. He added that during the recent elections many people had asked him how he intended to vote, and the whole community had followed his lead in electing 'a moderate, insightful and level-headed man'. Rinker attributed this influence to his anomalous position as an educated individual living in the bosom of the rural community. Ten years later, a teacher at the Hanoverian seminary in Osnabrück made the same point when he claimed that 'schoolteachers easily become opinion leaders in their communities'.[27] In practice, however, the evidence for such political influence is slim. These views probably tell us more about the fantasies of *Volksschule* teachers and their own

---

[23] Figure from Tenorth, 'Lehrerberuf und Lehrerbildung', p. 262.

[24] Julius Thimmig, Zwickau to K. Ministerium des Innern, 11 June 1849, HSADre Ministerium f. Volksbildung 12775 (1–2).

[25] Wächter-Spittler to H. M., Anbringen an den König in betr. der Mittel zur Heilung der Mängel des Volksschullehrerwesens, insbesondere zur Beseitigung der in einem bedeutende Theile des Lehrerstandes eingerissenen verderblichen politischen Richtung, 28 June 1850, HSAStu E 11 37 11 (1). [26] Schulmeister Rinker to H.M., 10 August 1849, HSAStu E 11 135 11 (10).

[27] H. H. Schüren, 'Seminarbericht über die Zeit vom 19 October 1857 bis zum 19. September 1859', Osnabrück, 19 September 1859, HSAHan Hann 113 K 1 389 (379).

sense of self-importance than they do about the realities of day-to-day life. For most teachers, this reality was characterised by poverty and the low social status that came with it. Indeed, the teachers' claims of political influence sit uneasily with their frequent petitions for higher pay, which invariably painted a grim picture of the teachers' daily lot. In the words of a Saxon teachers' petition from the Voigtland in 1857: 'How many members of the community already have a very low opinion of a man who lives in want!'[28]

In fact, *Volksschule* teachers traditionally exercised little influence in the countryside, owing to the lack of importance usually attached to education. In the past teachers had been untrained and under-paid, mostly teaching just as a sideline during the winter months. In any case, teachers had to move repeatedly if they wanted to better their salary and get on in the world. Consequently, few teachers remained anywhere long enough to acquire significant influence in the community. True, nineteenth-century regulation and legislation ensured that schools were more regular, better kept and more fully a part of daily life. True, training seminaries and slightly better rates of pay gradually brought *Volksschule* teachers higher status, although they continued to be recruited from the poorest classes.[29] This probably increased the influence of teachers in the long run, since it is reasonable to assume that where education was valued teachers were valued too. In the short term, however, this was not necessarily the case. In fact, the transformation of teachers' status was a slow and complex process. Initially, local communities resented the greater demands on their purse and time made by schools and teachers, and this cannot have improved the position of teachers in the community. Indeed, many teachers probably became more rather than less isolated during the early stages of educational reform. Both the teachers' isolation and their lack of political influence in the countryside became clear during the catechism conflict in Hanover. Initially, the Hanoverian government had hoped that teachers would be able to win over the masses to the new, more orthodox catechism it wished to introduce. In fact, however, although many teachers personally welcomed the new catechism, their efforts to persuade others of its benefits failed spectacularly and the government

---

[28] Petition from 55 Voigtland teachers, 29 October 1857, HSADre Ministerium f. Volksbildung 13107.

[29] Skopp, 'Auf der untersten Sprosse', 390–1, makes this point with regard to trainee teachers at the Esslingen seminary in Württemberg. Similarly, Pabst described would-be teachers in Hanover as coming 'mostly from the lower estates': in Pabst, 'Das Volksschulwesen im Königreich Hannover', 1 June 1860, HSAHan Hann 113 κ 1 98 (80–125).

was eventually forced to back down. This demonstrated the fallacy in official assumptions that a new generation of loyal teachers would spread peace and harmony in the countryside. Instead, they simply created new conflicts. As an 1862 petition complained, '[the Osnabrück Consistory] breeds a generation of teachers in the seminaries, who absorb its rigid principles and introduce them into the school communities, bringing discord and discontent with them'.[30] The catechism conflict demonstrated that in Hanover local notables – inspired in this case by a campaign in the liberal *Zeitung für Norddeutschland* and by a network of opposition activists – retained decisive influence in the countryside. This may have been less clearly true in Saxony and Württemberg, which had better developed education systems and were more advanced in socioeconomic terms.

The belief that teachers influenced the young was probably more justified than the belief that they exercised undue influence over adults in the local community. Educational officials tended to assume, in the words of the Württemberg Interior Minister Schlayer, that 'the schoolmaster influences the young not just through what he teaches but also through his own example'.[31] This belief was fairly universal. Indeed, a circular from the Saxon *Kultusministerium* used almost identical language when it insisted that 'Teachers must influence the young not just through their teaching but also through their own example'.[32] Consequently, governments wanted to ensure both that teachers set a good example to their pupils and that the education they provided was appropriately conservative. Educational officials tackled this problem in three different ways: through disciplinary measures that discouraged political involvement; through pay rises intended to foster loyalty in the teaching classes; and through a back-to-basics approach to teaching in school and seminary that concentrated on the four Rs – religion, reading, writing and arithmetic.

The immediate official response to subversive teachers was punitive. Governments disciplined those teachers who were most severely compromised by their behaviour during 1848/9. Yet these measures were surprisingly restrained in practice. In Saxony, for instance, action was taken against fifty teachers out of a total of three thousand – although a great many more had been politically active during the revolution.[33] More

---

[30] Petition to H. M., Osnabrück, 3 September 1862, HSAHan Hann 113 K I 1132 (9–17).
[31] Schlayer, Minister des Innern, to Frh. v. Maucler, 24 March 1850, HSAStu E 6 245.
[32] Kultusministerium an d. 4 Kreisdirectionen und d. Gesammtconsistorium zu Glauchau, 3 May 1851, HSADre Ministerium f. Volksbildung 13091 (241–3).
[33] Figures from Tenorth, 'Lehrerberuf und Lehrerbildung', p. 264.

importantly, perhaps, governments in both Saxony and Württemberg took steps to prevent such lapses in the future. In Württemberg, a decree of 1851 warned teachers against political involvement and threatened to dismiss teachers who joined political associations.[34] In Saxony, legislation passed in 1851 banned *Volksschule* teachers from taking part in any kind of political activity and extended the grounds on which they might be dismissed to include political subversion, religious dissent and moral depravity. Yet disciplinary measures alone were clearly inadequate. Typically, the Saxon legislation of 1851 offered *Volksschule* teachers a carrot as well as a stick, introducing significant pay rises in the expectation that this would prompt greater loyalty. As the *Kultusministerium* informed regional educational authorities in Saxony:

> The ministry expects . . . that the teachers will see this benevolent concern for their well-being as an urgent inducement . . . to fulfil the demands that the Fatherland makes of them . . . to educate the young in piety and virtue, to shape not just the minds, but also the hearts of their pupils, to plant in their young minds . . . true fear of God, loyalty to the King, love for the Fatherland.[35]

The pay rises indicated that the Saxon government was only too well aware of the role deprivation played in teacher radicalism. The same was also true in Württemberg, where the future Interior Minister, Linden, had declared poor pay to be the major cause of teacher unrest as early as April 1848.[36] In the aftermath of the revolution, the Württemberg government attempted to redress this situation by introducing a system of age-related bonuses (*Alterszulagen*), whereby teachers received an annual bonus for every ten years of teaching service.[37] These bonuses were designed both to alleviate teachers' poverty (and related discontent) and to provide financial incentives for good behaviour, since bonuses were only accorded to those teachers who met with the approval of local authorities. The Württemberg *Volksschule* law of 1858 significantly expanded this system.[38]

---

34 Erlaß an sämmtliche gemeinschaftliche Oberämter, 10 October 1850 and 10 November 1850, enclosed with HSAStu E 200 118 (67).

35 Kultusministerium an d. 4 Kreisdirectionen und d. Gesammtconsistorium zu Glauchau, 3 May 1851, HSADre Ministerium f. Volksbildung 13091 (241–3). There were further improvements to teachers' pay in Saxony in 1858.

36 Linden, 'Bericht des K. Katholische Kirchenraths an das K. Ministerium des Kirchen- und Schulwesens. Eine einfachere Bildung der Volksschullehrer betreffend', 11 April 1848, HSAStu E 200 118 (21).

37 Wächter-Spittler to H. M., Anbringen des Ministeriums des Kirchen- und Schulwesens an den König betr. die Einführung von Alterszulagen für Schulmeister, 17 May 1851, HSAStu E 11 34 1 (54).

38 Skopp notes the unusual commitment of the Württemberg government to improving teachers' pay and status in 'Auf der untersten Sprosse', 387.

Indeed, in Württemberg the attempt to placate *Volksschule* teachers actually led to plans for wide-ranging educational reform in the 1860s. These plans reflected teachers' pay demands but also took account of other complaints, more closely connected with status. For instance, the *Kultusministerium* envisaged giving teachers a greater say in school administration and management and expanding the limited *Volksschule* curriculum.

Developments in Hanover were rather different from those in Saxony and Württemberg. Here too, the 1850s brought harsher discipline and higher pay for *Volksschule* teachers. For once, however, these measures were the product not of revolution but rather of the constitutional crisis of 1855. In December of that year, Georg V wrote to the Hanoverian *Kultusminister* stressing the need to spread religiosity and true monarchist spirit, without which 'all My government's measures to raise the moral tone of the people and to reclaim monarchic principles in the constitution will be in vain'.[39] Decent education must, he wrote, lay the foundations for these values – and decent education depended upon decent and reliable teachers. The role of education in Georg's wider monarchic project could hardly be plainer. Georg therefore instructed the *Kultusministerium* 'that unreasonable and . . . systematic opposition from the teachers is not to be tolerated, and that, in the most important instances, decisive action is to be taken against it'. In keeping with this aim, after 1857 teachers began to swear the oath of loyalty to King and country, customarily taken by state servants, as part of their local investiture ceremony. As in Saxony and Württemberg, tougher discipline for teachers brought higher rates of pay, which were finally introduced in Hanover in 1856, although the initiative dated back to the early 1850s. Once again, the different context for these measures in Hanover indicates a different motivation. In Saxony and Württemberg education policy in the 1850s was clearly a response to the perceived moral crisis of the revolution and the threats this posed. In Hanover, however, educational reform was programmatic, not reactive. Georg's desire to mobilise Hanoverian teachers on behalf of the monarchic principle was one aspect of his grander project for political and moral renewal.

How successful were these measures in creating a loyal teaching class? Disciplinary measures certainly appear to have discouraged teachers from political activity after 1848, although this may have been a natural response to the reactionary climate of the 1850s. Thus Diesterweg, a key

---

[39] Georg V to Kultusminister, 4 December 1855, HSAHan Dep. 103 XI 86.

figure among progressive Prussian educationalists, lamented the readiness with which teacher activists had capitulated to reaction. One consequence of this was that even those teachers dismissed after 1848/9 as dangerous revolutionaries were frequently reinstated a few years later. Typically, a *Lycealrektor* from Reutlingen, Dr Schnitzer, was dismissed for belonging to the central committee of Württemberg democrats during the revolution, but reinstated in 1859. The Württemberg educational authorities opined that there was 'surely no need to worry any longer that he will be exercising an undesirable influence over his pupils through the inappropriate discussion of political matters'.[40] Measures designed to discourage teachers from political activism also appear to have been fairly successful. For instance, one teacher from Leipzig refused to join a commission to reform the Saxon church in 1866 precisely because of the 1851 law prohibiting political activity.[41] Admittedly, the 1860s saw a revival of associational activity amongst teachers, but this activity was primarily a means of voicing their professional interests and did not amount to a political threat.

Even so, pay increases were clearly more likely than disciplinary measures to create genuinely loyal teachers. Throughout the 1850s and 1860s, *Volksschule* teachers continued to complain that they were chronically under-paid – although this was not, strictly speaking, the case. In fact, research into teacher pay levels in Prussia has concluded that teachers were actually better paid than the average worker and that their economic situation was gradually improving – although teachers were significantly less well paid than subaltern officials (with whom they liked to compare themselves).[42] According to this analysis, the contrast between pay and perceived status was the nub of the problem, not destitution. *Volksschule* teacher salaries in Prussia averaged an annual minimum of 150 *Thaler*, the rate introduced in Hanover in 1856 and in Saxony in 1858.[43] Given broadly similar living costs in all three states, similar conclusions can probably be drawn about teachers' pay demands in Hanover and Saxony. In practice, however, conditions in Hanover were far worse than in Saxony. The minimum annual salary in Saxony was

---

[40] Bericht des K. Studienraths an das K. Ministerium des Kirchen- und Schulwesens betr. den vormaligen Lycealrektor Dr. Schnitzer von Reutlingen, 27 August 1859, HSAStu E 200 313 (129).

[41] See Jordan, *Die öffentliche Meinung in Sachsen*, p. 20. Jordan argues the effectiveness of these measures.

[42] See Herrlitz, Hopf and Titze, *Deutsche Schulgeschichte*, pp. 55–6. Kuhlemann discusses the realities of Prussian teacher pay at length: see *Modernisierung und Disziplinierung*, pp. 277–92.

[43] Figures from ibid., p. 282. Maximum salaries in both Hanover and Saxony were 400 *Thaler* p.a. for teachers in large towns.

140 *Thaler* as of 1851. Consequently, the 1858 law simply represented a modest improvement here. In Hanover, the minimum teaching salary was as low as eighty *Thaler* before 1856 and the complaints of Hanoverian teachers were therefore more than justified. Furthermore, greater decentralisation in the Hanoverian education system meant that the new minimum pay rate of 150 *Thaler* was only introduced gradually over the next ten years. The persistence of very low pay in Hanover testified to the continued backwardness of education in this state. As for Württemberg, a strict comparison is difficult since teachers were paid in *Gulden*. Nevertheless, it would seem that teachers' pay rose more swiftly than inflation in the 1850s and 1860s, although teachers continued to be paid less than skilled workers.[44] Yet the teachers themselves do not seem to have appreciated the gradual improvement in their economic situation. Indeed, they barely noticed it, and continued to petition the government for higher pay as if nothing had changed. These petitions consistently painted a very bleak picture of the teachers' lot, although they also paid lip-service to recent improvements. Nevertheless, it is hard to conclude from this that teachers felt particularly grateful to the government for its efforts, or that their gratitude engendered a new sense of loyalty.

Besides disciplinary measures and pay rises, German governments also intervened more directly in the education process by reforming the school curriculum along conservative lines. In practice, this meant returning religion to its former place at the heart of the curriculum, in both teacher training seminaries and the *Volksschulen* themselves. The new focus on religion was designed to foster traditional civic virtues as a bulwark against revolution. Curriculum reform began in the teacher training seminaries, since these fairly new institutions were widely seen as the source of all the rot in the educational system. Friedrich Wilhelm IV of Prussia, for instance, accused seminary directors of spreading *Afterbildung* and impiety disguised as true wisdom amongst the teaching classes.[45] Such views were understandable in Prussia, where teaching seminaries represented the most tangible educational reform of the pre-revolutionary era. They were less understandable in Württemberg and Saxony, where educational reform had been more comprehensive. Nevertheless, similar criticisms of the seminaries in these states led both governments to revise the curriculum along more restrictive lines, in

---

[44] See the figures given in Friederich, *Die Volksschule in Württemberg*, p. 122.
[45] Cited in Herrlitz, Hopf and Titze, *Deutsche Schulgeschichte*, p. 60.

1855 and 1857 respectively.[46] There were no such measures in Hanover, where the standard of education was lower, seminaries developed later and the experience of revolution proved less alarming. Indeed, the catechism conflict indicates that Hanoverian seminaries successfully produced a steady stream of religiously and politically orthodox teachers.

As late as April 1848, Linden, the future Württemberg Interior Minister, had dismissed the idea that the curriculum in teaching seminaries was too ambitious, or that it encouraged teachers to develop unrealistic expectations and so fostered discontent.[47] Two years later, however, the government that Linden headed took a very different view, demonstrating quite how far the experience of revolution led conservatives to rethink education policy after 1848. In 1850 the Württemberg *Kultusminister*, Wächter-Spittler, wrote to Wilhelm describing how the seminary curriculum encouraged 'over-education' and dilettantism amongst teachers, leaving them with an exaggerated sense of their own importance and corrupting their relations with ordinary people.[48] Such sentiments, claimed Wächter-Spittler, engendered aspirations that the state could never hope to fulfil and consequently spread discontent among the teaching class. Wächter-Spittler was determined to put an end to this situation. In 1854 the Württemberg *Kultusministerium* decreed that the seminary curriculum should thenceforth focus on religious education and practical teaching skills.[49] The decree was followed by a new examination regulation in 1855, which amalgamated History, Geography and Nature Studies into a single subject, to be taught mainly through the primary school reader (*Volksschullesebuch*).[50] Those who wished to teach in towns could sit an additional exam that required a deeper knowledge of these subjects, as well as Geometry and Technical Drawing.

---

[46] These changes are in keeping with the spirit of the Prussian Stiel Regulation of 1854, although in both cases the initiatives pre-date this. Interestingly, seminary reforms in both Saxony and Württemberg applied only to Protestant seminaries. In Württemberg both Catholic seminaries and Catholic schools were found to be more satisfactory than their Protestant equivalents. In Saxony there were very few Catholics.

[47] Linden, 'Bericht des K. Katholischen Kirchenraths an das K. Ministerium des Kirchen- und Schulwesens. Eine einfachere Bildung der Volksschullehrer betreffend', 11 April 1848, HSAStu E 200 118 (21).

[48] Wächter-Spittler to H.M., 'Anbringen . . . an den König in betr. der Mittel zur Heilung der Mängel des Volksschullehrerwesens, insbesondere zur Beseitigung der in einem bedeutende Theile des Lehrerstandes eingerissenen verderblichen politischen Richtung', 28 June 1850, HSAStu E 11 37 II (1).

[49] See the account given in Friederich, *Die Volksschule in Württemberg*, p. 93.

[50] Wächter-Spittler to H. M., 'Anbringen des Ministeriums des Kirchen- und Schulwesens an den König betr. eine neue Verfügung über die Prüfungen für den Dienst an evangelischen Volksschullehrern', 27 January 1855, HSAStu E 11 37 II (5).

Developments in Saxony followed a similar pattern. Here, Meußner, a *Kultusministerium* official, concluded that Saxon teaching seminaries had failed to achieve the proper balance between education (*Erziehung*) and instruction (*Unterricht*).[51] 'Our seminarists,' he wrote, 'learn an amazing amount, but they certainly do not undergo any real character building in the seminaries.' In line with Meußner's recommendations, the 1857 Regulation for Protestant Teaching Seminaries in Saxony simplified the curriculum considerably by including History, Geography and Nature Studies only as secondary subjects. The changes indicated the government was no longer so interested in promoting learning first and foremost. Instead, the new Seminary Regulation sought to produce 'a knowledgeable, moral, devoutly Christian and religiously minded . . . teaching class'.[52] In keeping with this mission, the Seminary Regulation repeatedly stressed the role of religion both in the curriculum and in day-to-day seminary life because, as the Regulation put it, religion was the 'living soul' of all popular education.[53]

Changes to the curriculum in teaching seminaries paved the way for similar changes in the *Volksschulen* themselves. Indeed, government officials were only too well aware of the link between the two. In Württemberg, for instance, Wächter-Spittler attributed the demands of the seminary curriculum to the excessive ambitions of the *Volksschulen*.[54] He complained that the *Volksschule* curriculum was now too all-inclusive and divorced from the practical needs of country folk. Ultimately, therefore, changes in seminary training were intended to have a knock-on effect in the classroom. Certainly, educational authorities repeatedly stressed the central role of religion at *Volksschule* level. The Württemberg Privy Council was by no means unusual when it declared in 1857 that the task of *Volksschulen* was religious education first and foremost, then elementary literacy skills.[55] Similarly, a decree issued by the Hanoverian Consistory in early 1855 emphasised that the principal task of the *Volksschulen* was to provide a Christian education.[56] Tellingly, the Hanoverian Consistory drew a clear connection between this Christian

[51] Meußner, Bericht, 23 February 1849, HSADre Ministerium f. Volksbildung 12775 (3–5).
[52] Article 1, *Ordnung der evangelischen Schullehrerseminare im Königreiche Sachsen vom Jahre 1857* (Leipzig, 1857). [53] Article 34, *Ordnung der evangelischen Schullehrerseminare.*
[54] Wächter-Spittler to H.M., 'Anbringen . . . an den König in betr. der Mittel zur Heilung der Mängel des Volksschullehrerwesens, insbesondere zur Beseitigung der in einem bedeutende Theile des Lehrerstandes eingerissenen verderblichen politischen Richtung', 28 June 1850, HSAStu E 11 37 II (1).
[55] Geheimer Rath to H. M., 26 January 1857, HSAStu E 33 902 (79).
[56] Bericht des Consistorii zu Hannover, Regelung des Volksschulewesens betr., 13 January 1855, HSAHan Hann 113 K I 113 (6–10).

education and more immediate political concerns, arguing that religious education would bring 'a wealth of blessed consequences, pleasing to God', for if schoolchildren were taught to be God-fearing Christians, they would also learn to be 'loyal subjects . . ., well-behaved children . . . goodly fathers and mothers, worthy members [of the community]'.

Indeed, the extent to which religious education was explicitly political cannot be over-emphasised. Precisely because of this, subversive teachers found it only too easy to distort religious education for their own ends. One example of this was the case of a teaching assistant in Dresden called Stein. In December 1849 a self-professed Saxon 'patriot' denounced Stein for questioning the very precepts he was supposed to teach.[57] Allegedly, after reading to the class the text 'for the throne is secured through righteousness', Stein added 'but not with bayonets and soldiers'; after reading 'citizens and subjects shall love their Fatherland and their prince', he added 'if he deserves it!'; after reading 'Fear the Lord and the King!', he added, 'if he earns it!' Stein himself readily admitted as much, but claimed to have told the children that the King of Saxony was worthy of love, honour and respect. Similarly, the Württemberg educational authorities paid special attention to the impact of political dissidence on religious education when disciplining teachers. Professor Kapff of Reutlingen, for instance, was accused of neglecting his teaching for political activity in 1849. The verdict of school inspectors that the hymns and bible verses recited in Kapff's class were 'wretchedly learnt and reeled off in a sulky and indifferent tone of voice' was particularly damning.[58]

Nowhere were the links between religious education and politics more apparent than in the Hanoverian catechism conflict. The idea of replacing the rationalist state catechism currently in use with a more orthodox version initially originated with the Hanoverian Consistory, which in 1856 pronounced the state catechism to be unacceptable in its current form, and announced its intention of revising it.[59] Needless to say, the *Kultusministerium* seized upon an initiative so wholly in keeping with Georg V's avowed intention to restore religious morality to the people and monarchic principles to the constitution. With Georg's express

[57] Ein Patriot, Dresden an das Ministerium des Cultus u. öffentlichen Unterrichts, 8 December 1849, HSADre Ministerium f. Volksbildung 11937 (200).
[58] Bericht des K. Studienraths, betr. den Professor Kapff am Lyceum in Reutlingen, 23 October 1849, HSAStu E 200 312 (7).
[59] Bericht des Consistorii zu Hannover, den Hannoverschen Katechismus betr., 3 March 1856, HSAHan Hann 113 K I 1125 I (35–6).

approval, the review of the catechism became a state-wide process, which eventually resulted in a revision of the Walther catechism, a very orthodox version widely used in Hanover in the eighteenth century.[60] Typically, the new catechism included an extended version of the 'genealogy' section, which provided religious justification for the traditional social order. From the start, the Hanoverian Consistory made clear that the catechism reform was fundamentally an educational issue, maintaining that the existing rationalist version made it impossible for confirmation classes to correct the short-comings of elementary schooling.[61] The political implications of this return to catechistic orthodoxy were equally explicit. In 1860 the Hanoverian Consistory claimed: 'We believe that in restoring to the people that true doctrine that is . . . repeatedly obscured in the current state catechism, we will be giving the people the only sure defence against all political upheavals, for these draw on principles that are intimately linked to the religious principles underlying the state catechism'.

Critics complained that the new catechism was so archaic that most children were incapable of understanding it. They also disliked its Catholic tone, which, they argued, encouraged superstition and outmoded religious practices, as well as undermining basic human dignities and freedoms. Such critics were many and vociferous. Indeed, the new catechism provided liberal opponents of the Hanoverian regime with a heaven-sent opportunity to mobilise wide sections of the population against the government. Reports from the provinces repeatedly stressed that the masses mobilised in this way had little understanding of the issues at stake.[62] They were primarily motivated by a sentimental attachment to the catechism *they* had learnt at school and, more particularly, to the hymns they had grown to love. Either way, the new catechism prompted a wave of petitions, public meetings and, finally, riots in the capital. In the face of such hostility, Georg's determination to stand firm crumbled, the Borries ministry fell, and use of the catechism became optional in schools and churches. The catechism conflict demonstrated clearly the politically explosive implications of 'back-to-basics' education policy at both local and state level. Whilst liberals objected to the

---

[60] K. Ministerium der geistlichen u. Unterrichts Angelegenheiten an Consistorii zu Hannover, Stade, Aurich, Osnabrück, 13 March 1856, HSAHan Hann 113 K I 1125 I (38–40).

[61] Bericht des K. hannoverschen Consistoriums zu Hannover betr. den Entwurf eines Katechismus f. Kirche, Schule und Haus, 8 February 1860, HSAHan Hann 113 K I 1125 II (318–420).

[62] For instance, Vertraulich, Bericht des Amts Marienburg, Hildesheim betr. Agitation gegen den neuen Katechismus, 17 August 1862, HSAHan Dep. 103 XI 28.

conservative aims of the new catechism, local notables jumped at the chance to rid themselves of unpopular and orthodox teachers and priests. Attempts to manipulate the educational system to the regime's advantage had certainly made themselves felt. They had also proved extraordinarily unwelcome.

How far did the dissemination of such basic religious and political values through the *Volksschule* encourage the growth of more specific allegiances? On the one hand, belief in the monarchic principle as taught in the *Volksschulen* was always closely tied to dynastic loyalty. On the other hand, a return to more exclusively religious education meant reducing teaching of the 'Realien' – in other words, History, Geography and Nature Studies, the very subjects necessary if the *Volksschulen* were to turn schoolchildren into patriots. In this sense, the impact of back-to-basics education was essentially contradictory.

In each state, the monarchic principle was embodied by a particular monarch. In practice, therefore, the purpose of fostering belief in the monarchic principle through education was really to ensure loyalty to a specific ruler. Thus monarchic education in Bavaria meant that every school boasted a portrait of the current Bavarian King, although this does not appear to have been so consistently the case in Hanover, Saxony and Württemberg.[63] The need to forge a link between the general and the specific in this way was clearly acknowledged by Hanoverian Consistorial Advisor Niemann in 1854, when he advocated revising the traditional prayers for the royal family so that the King and his wife were mentioned by name.[64] Niemann hoped that this would mean the worshipper no longer prayed coldly for an idea but instead entered into a warm, personal relationship with the representatives of that idea – in this case King Georg and Queen Marie. Annual celebrations of the King's birthday provided an ideal opportunity to emphasise for schoolchildren

[63] A reference to portraits of Karl being made available for public places and schools indicates that portraits of the monarch were usual but not universal in Württemberg *Volksschulen*. See Egloffstein to Ministerium des Kirchen- und Schulwesens, 10 September 1865, HSAStu E 200 498 (2). The Hanoverian archives contain a proposal that portraits of the King be lent to Hanoverian schools for the celebration of his birthday, indicating that they were not normally there. See Allerunterthänigste Bitte von Seiten des Hauptlehrers R. Sonnemann, undated, HSAHan Dep. 103 XI 86. In Saxony the teaching seminary in Leipzig did not acquire a portrait of the king (or a Wettin family tree) until 1852, indicating again that such portraits were not commonplace. See Vortrag der Kreisdirection zu Leipzig an das K. Ministerium des Cultus u. öffentlichen Unterrichts, die Geburtsfeier des Königs betr., 27 May 1852, HSADre Ministerium f. Volksbildung 10290 (59).

[64] Consistorialrath Dr. Niemann, to K. Ministerium der geistlichen and Unterrichts Angelegenheiten 'betr. Entwurf eines allgemeinen Kirchengebets', 13 October 1854, HSAHan Hann 113 A 219.

the link between the monarchic principle in abstract, the King in person, and the particular dynasty and state that he represented. These celebrations were customary in most schools, but they were not formally introduced in Hanover, Saxony or Württemberg until after 1848.

In 1851, for instance, celebrations of the King's birthday became obligatory in all Saxon secondary schools and teaching seminaries.[65] The innovation was originally the brainchild of two teachers at the *Landesschule* in Grimma, who had written to the *Kultusministerium* suggesting that the proposed festivities could combine a formal ceremony in the morning (designed to highlight the importance of the day through prayers for King and country) and a holiday activity in the afternoon.[66] The official birthday celebrations were intended both to promote dynastic loyalty and to discourage political radicalism. Consequently, teachers used the opportunity provided by the formal part of the day's proceedings to lecture the children on the benefits of the divinely instituted monarchic order and the happiness of a people living peacefully under the protection of its 'ancestral ruling house'. A speaker to the *Landesschule* in Meißen made the point neatly when he declared: 'We Saxons are held to be lucky, not just because we live in a monarchy, but most particularly because it is our good fortune to have a prince who is distinguished . . . by every royal and civic virtue'.[67] Besides praising the monarch himself, speakers liked to give a specifically Saxon flavour to their speeches. One speaker addressing the teaching seminary in Grimma dwelt on the political, economic, cultural and religious contributions of the Wettins to Saxon development.[68] Another speaker addressing the *Nicolaischule* in Leipzig drew heavily on the achievements of the (Saxon) Ottonian emperors and the Wettins themselves.[69] Once again, the timing of this initiative in Saxony indicates that it was a direct response to the experiences of 1848. Once again, similar measures were not taken in Hanover

[65] Generalverordnung an die Schulinspectionen zu Meißen, Grimma, Gymnas. Commission zu Zwickau, Freiberg, Plauen, Bautzen, Zittau, der Kreuzschule, Thomas und Nikolaischule, Geschlechtsgymnasium und Kreisdirection zu Dresden, Leipzig, Zwickau, Bautzen, Gesammt Consistorium zu Glauchau, 13 October 1851, HSADre Ministerium f. Volksbildung 10290 (10–12).

[66] D. Conrad Benjamin Meißner an K. sächs. Ministerium des Cultus u. öffentlichen Unterrichts, 23 October 1851, HSADre Ministerium f. Volksbildung 10290 (9).

[67] Friedrich Franke, 'Die Inspection der Landesschule Meißen berichtet über dem Feier des Geburtstages Sr. Majestät des Königs an das K. Ministerium des Cultus u. öffentlichen Unterrichts, 21 May 1852, HSADre Ministerium f. Volksbildung 10290 (43–5).

[68] F. A. Köhler, 'Grimma, Gehorsammste Berichterstattung', 19 May 1852, HSADre Ministerium f. Volksbildung 10290 (60–2).

[69] Director and Rector der Nicolaischule, Leipzig, Bericht, 19 February 1852, HSADre Ministerium f. Volksbildung 10290 (41).

until April 1855, at the height of the constitutional crisis. Thus the Hanoverian *Kultusministerium* liked to think that the new festivities would remind the people that they formed one great family, and that they all honoured the same divinely appointed ruler.[70] The form taken by the Hanoverian celebrations was similar to the Saxon model. Moreover, as in Saxony, those involved clearly understood the political motivations behind the marking of the King's birthday in this way. Tellingly, a speaker addressing a teacher training institution in Neuenhaus expressed the hope that God would protect and preserve the King and ensure 'that His wise measures for the good of the people will never be misjudged'.[71] Equally, as in Saxony, speakers repeatedly stressed the particular (here Hanoverian) context. For instance, a speaker to the seminary in Alfeld dwelt upon the good fortune of Hanoverians, who lived 'in a country which is famed on account of its King and Queen among other German-speaking lands'.[72] In 1859, however, Georg put an end to formal celebrations in the schools themselves, when he announced his desire to see schools close on his birthday and that of the queen, so that these joyful occasions could become holidays indeed.[73] Special church services were held instead, but they proved unpopular and the measure itself was generally accounted a failure. Hanoverian newspapers reported that, like other weekday services, the birthday services were poorly attended – the more so since they fell in a busy agricultural period.[74] Unlike those of Saxony and Hanover, the Württemberg government did not institute formal royal birthday celebrations in schools during the 1850s, perhaps because Wilhelm's birthday was already marked by the annual *Cannstatter Volksfest*.[75] This changed with Karl's accession in 1864. Thereafter, Württemberg adopted the Hanoverian practice of closing all schools for the King's birthday and, for the first time, the Queen's birthday was accorded equal status.

[70] K. Ministerium der geistlichen u. Unterrichts Angelegenheiten an d. Consistorien zu Hannover, Stade, Aurich, Oberkirchenrath Nordhorn, 23 April 1855, HSAHan Hann 113 K I 1521 (164–6).
[71] Bericht des Oberschulinspectors Fokke zu Neuenhaus betr. Feier des Geburtstages Sr. Majestät des Königs, 29 May 1856, HSAHan Hann 113 K I 1521.
[72] Bericht des provisorischen Seminarinspectors Dr. Michelsen, Alfeld betr. die von K. Consistorio dem Seminar und den seminarischen Schulen gestattete Feier des Geburtstages Seiner Majestät unseres Allergnädigsten Königs, 25 May 1855, HSAHan Dep. 103 XI 87.
[73] Georg V an Mein Minister der Cultus, 12 April 1859, HSAHan Hann 113 K I 1521 (182).
[74] For instance the *Hannoversche Landeszeitung* No. 142, 24 June 1864; No. 126, 1 June 1865. Similarly *Buxtehude Wochenblatt* as reported in Tagesbericht des Presse Bureaus, 20 April 1864, HSA Han Dep. 103 IX 284.
[75] There are, however, references to such celebrations taking place unofficially in HSAStu E 200 500.

Religion and the monarchic principle could (and did) work hand in hand in such celebrations, through special prayers for the King and his family. An educational alliance between religion and patriotism was harder to forge, because the return to more exclusively religious education in Saxony and Württemberg during the 1850s inevitably limited the curriculum in other ways. In practice, this meant demoting the *Realien*, as the changes to teaching practice in the Württemberg seminaries make particularly clear. How far did governments in Hanover, Saxony and Württemberg actively promote the growth of patriotism through schools?

The renewed focus on religious education in Württemberg was to some extent counteracted by the publication and dissemination of two official readers for use in the *Volksschulen* – one drafted by the Protestant Consistory and one drafted by the Catholic Church Council.[76] These were anthologies of passages for reading practice, which were also used to aid instruction in the *Realien*. The Württemberg *Volksschule* reader initiative itself pre-dated the revolution, but the religious commissions entrusted with the project were purged after 1848/9 and the two readers did not appear until 1854 and 1861 respectively. Both the Consistory and the Church Council understood that these books would primarily be used for reading practice. Yet they were also aware that the new readers formed the basis of most *Realien* teaching in the *Volksschulen*, and that the subject matter itself could be used to influence the attitudes of pupils. For instance, a Church Council report on the newly drafted Catholic reader explained that the religious section was calculated to promote 'piety, faith in the Lord and fear of the Lord, devoted and self-sacrificing love for others, peaceful and amiable behaviour in daily life, cheerfulness and steadfastness in fulfilling professional and social responsibilities, love for and gratitude to parents, respect and obedience etc. in the children'.[77] Equally, the Church Council believed that the historical and geographical sections in particular would awaken love and loyalty for the Fatherland in the hearts of the young. In keeping with this goal, both Catholic and Protestant readers included passages dealing specifically

[76] *Lesebuch für die evangelischen Volksschulen Württembergs* (Stuttgart, 1854); *Lesebuch für die katholischen Volksschulen Württembergs* (Stuttgart, 1862). On the origins of state supervision of schoolbooks in general see Michael Sauer, 'Zwischen Negativkontrolle und staatlichem Monopol. Zur Geschichte von Schulbuchzulassung und -einführung', *Geschichte in Wissenschaft und Unterricht* 49:3 (1998), 144–56.
[77] Bericht des K. katholischen Kirchenraths an das K. Ministerium des Kirchen- und Schulwesens betr. den Entwurf des Lesebuchs f. die katholischen Volksschulen Württembergs, 20 March 1860, HSAStu E 200 107 (73).

with the history and geography of the Württemberg Fatherland, such as Ludwig Uhland's epic poems of Württemberg's heroic past.[78] Some of this patriotic material related to Germany, but most of it dealt with Württemberg – its landscape, its people, its dynasty. This Württemberg bias was most noticeable in the Protestant reader, although the Catholic version was also affected. For instance, seven geographical reading passages in the Protestant reader were devoted to a detailed description of Württemberg and its component parts, but only three dealt with Germany. Similarly, seventeen readings covered the history of Württemberg and the Swabians, compared with nine on the history of Germany.[79] A further eleven provided a general history of the French Revolution and the Napoleonic era. In the Catholic reader the geographical balance was very similar, with five readings about Württemberg and two dealing with the rest of Germany. The historical section, however, principally consisted of a single but fairly lengthy account of Württemberg history, bolstered by Uhland's cycle of historical poems, three passages about the Swabian Frederick Barbarossa, two passages on German history in general, and a further three readings dealing with the execution of Louis XIV and the Napoleonic era. The less particularist flavour of this reader reflected the more problematic relationship between the new Catholic parts of Württemberg and the rest of the state. After all, as the Catholic commission drafting the reader noted in 1857, many of the stories associated with figures from the more distant past, notably the Reformation Dukes Ulrich and Christoph, were ill suited to a Catholic *Volksschule* audience.[80] Tellingly, most of the reading passages in the Catholic reader were taken from other books and only those dealing with Württemberg had to be specially written for the purpose. By including substantial amounts of material about Württemberg, the two official readers were breaking new ground.

It is not too much to say that the new readers transformed *Volksschule* education in Württemberg. First, the introduction of these readers in schools was a crucial step towards standardising *Volksschule* education throughout the state. Most other German governments tended to restrict themselves to standardising the curriculum in general – as was the case in Prussia with the Stiehl Regulation of 1854 – but they did not

[78] Recently reprinted in Ludwig Uhland, *Gedichte, Dramen and Prosa* (Tübingen, 1996), pp. 230–9.

[79] This does not include passages dealing with Luther, included primarily for religious reasons.

[80] Bericht des K. katholischen Kirchenraths an das K. Ministerium des Kirchen- und Schulwesens betr. (i) die Bearbeitung des Lesebuchs für die vaterländischen katholischen Volksschulen, 22 March 1857, HSAStu E 200 107 (67).

concern themselves with the nitty gritty of what schoolchildren actually learned. In Württemberg, however, the new readers ensured that children really did learn the same things, notwithstanding the confessional divide. Secondly, the new readers revolutionised education at *Volksschule* level by introducing formal study of the *Realien* for the first time. In 1863, for instance, Seminary Rector Stockmayer noted that *Realien* teaching had been virtually non-existent in Württemberg before the publication of the *Volksschule* reader and concluded that 'it was with the introduction of the *Volksschule* reader that instruction in the *Realien* really began in our Protestant *Volksschulen*'.[81] The impact of the new readers on *Volksschule* education reflected their popularity, for both readers were widely used from the first. By 1862 the Protestant Consistory reported that only 146 Protestant schools did not use the new reader.[82] By 1864 – only three years after its publication – some 30,000 copies of the Catholic reader were already in circulation.[83] In 1864 the Württemberg government finally made the new readers compulsory in all *Volksschulen*.

This official endorsement of the Württemberg *Volksschule* readers was part of a wider drive to increase study of the *Realien* at *Volksschule* level. In June of the same year, the Württemberg government established a weekly minimum for *Realien* teaching in senior *Volksschule* classes of two hours in the winter and one and a half hours in the summer.[84] The *Kultusministerium* also advised *Volksschule* teachers to prepare the children for studying the *Realien* even in the junior classes. In practice, the *Realien* consisted primarily of History, Geography and Nature Studies, but usually failed to include more practical skills like Geometry and Technical Drawing. Consequently, the links between *Realien* teaching and the acquisition of useful skills were tendentious, to say the least. There can be little doubt, therefore, that the Württemberg government was primarily concerned with fostering patriotism. The official habit of

---

[81] Seminar-Rektor Stockmayer, Referat über die Frage: 'ob nicht gewisse allgemeine Anordnungen zu treffen seien, um dem realistischen Unterrichtsstoffe eine etwas größere Ausdehnung in der Volksschule zu geben und welche?', 15 August 1863, HSAStu E 200 143 (1).

[82] Bericht des evangelischen Consistoriums an das K. Ministerium des Kirchen- und Schulwesens betr. die Einführung des Lesebuchs in den evangelischen Volksschulen, 2 January 1862, HSAStu E 200 107 (79). Resistance to the new reader was restricted to fiercely religious communities who believed education should be limited to the bible. In this sense the new reader was a liberal and modernising reform.

[83] Bericht des K. katholischen Kirchenraths an das K. Ministerium des Kirchen- und Schulwesens betr. die zwangsweise Einführung des katholischen Volksschullesebuchs in der katholischen Schulen des Landes, 19 January 1864, HSAStu E 200 107 (88).

[84] Verfügung des Ministeriums des Kirchen- und Schulwesens betr. die Pflege des realistischen Unterrichts in den Volksschulen, 18 June 1864, HSAStu E 200 143 (3b).

listing History and Geography before the other *Realien* indicates where
the government's priorities really lay. The pietist community of
Affalterbach realised as much when they complained that nowadays
school inspectors were uninterested in the bible or the catechism, and
turned their attentions instead to 'geography, anthropology, patriotic
history' as taught in the new *Volksschule* reader. In fact, however, the
government was aware that study of the *Realien* might bring economic
benefits, not least as a consequence of wide-scale lobbying by teaching
associations for educational reform. Official endorsement of the *Realien*
therefore reflected both concerns. For instance, a report by the
Protestant Consistory into the benefits of *Realien* teaching cited the
examples of France and Belgium, noting that in some areas of France
every schoolchild had a map of his country.[85] The author of this report
added, however, that Württemberg's geographical position and political
circumstances rendered the *Realien* particularly important for both political *and* economic reasons.

These developments in Württemberg were less marked elsewhere.
Officials in both Saxony and Hanover felt the lack of an authorised
Volksschule reader, but little was done in either state to remedy the
problem.[86] In 1854 the regional authorities in Bautzen complained to
the Saxon *Kultusministerium* about the plethora of readers in current use
in the area, noting in particular their role in teaching the 'indispensable *Realien*'.[87] The Bautzen authorities were painfully aware that even
the most admirable foreign *Volksschule* reader was hardly suitable for
use in Saxon schools, where pupils needed exposure to specifically
Saxon material. What, after all, could Saxon schoolchildren find to
interest them in the official Württemberg readers, which were apparently circulated in the area? The government did little in response to
this complaint, partly because it had already taken steps to foster patri-

[85] Seminar-Rektor Stockmayer, 'Referat über die Frage: 'ob nicht gewisse allgemeine
Anordnungen zu treffen seien, um dem realistischen Unterrichtsstoffe eine etwas größere
Ausdehnung in der Volksschule zu geben und welche?', 15 August 1863, HSAStu E 200 143 (1).
[86] See Richter, *Geschichte der sächsischen Volksschule*, pp. 234–40, for details of the *Volksschule* readers in
use in Saxon schools. Die in den hannoverschen Volkschulen am meisten gebrauchten von
Inländern und Ausländern verfaßten Lesebücher, HSAHan Hann 113 K I 308 (16), gives a list of
readers used in Hanoverian *Volksschulen*. Interestingly, the unofficial school readers circulating in
Saxony were far more specifically 'national' in content than the equivalents circulating in
Hanover. In fact of the readers listed for Hanover, only E. Quietmeyer, *Schul- und Hausfreund,
deutsches Lesebuch für Volksschulen* (Hanover, 1850) had specifically Hanoverian content, although
this referred to the geography of Hanover rather than its history. This was not true for Saxony.
[87] Vortrag der Kreisdirection zu Budissin, die Abschaffung der Lesebücher von Hempel und
Körnig betr. an das K. Ministerium des Cultus u. öffentlichen Unterrichts, 14 January 1854,
HSADre Ministerium f. Volksbildung 10802 (56–68).

otic education in the Saxon *Volksschulen*. In 1851 the government offered a prize of 100 *Thaler* for a history of Saxony suitable for general *Volksschule* use, and advertised to this effect in the official Saxon press.[88] The advertisements themselves presented the need to promote popular awareness of Saxon history in the light of the experiences of 1848/9, and claimed that only knowledge of the past could enable the people to judge 'the situation in the Fatherland' in its true light. The book was primarily intended as a teaching aid, but the government also hoped it 'could be taken out of the schoolroom and into everyday life'. Pastor Stichart of Reinhardsgrimma won the competition with 'The Kingdom of Saxony and its Princes', which was published in 1854.[89] The book was illustrated in order to make it more accessible, for this was to be 'a book of the people (*Volksbuch*) to last a lifetime . . . with a place in the domestic library of every town and country dweller'.[90] The *Kultusministerium* took steps to ensure that Stichart's history was available as a teaching aid in all *Volksschulen*.[91] Official interest in promoting history in schools grew during the 1860s, just as it had in Württemberg. In Saxony as well, this interest formed part of wider debates in 1865 over the role of the *Realien* in particular and proposals for the comprehensive reform of the Saxon teaching seminaries in general. Tellingly, the Saxon *Kultusminister* von Falkenstein advocated the promotion of history in the seminaries 'because of its role in character building'.[92]

The Hanoverian approach to teaching patriotic history was not dissimilar to that of Saxony. Here too, local officials drew the government's attention to the lack of available patriotic teaching materials. In 1856 a Hanoverian Superintendent alerted Queen Marie to the urgent need for a properly Hanoverian *Volksschule* reader, and wrote touchingly of his desire 'to give the children of the people a book that they stand in need of, in which they can read of their country and the name of their

[88] Bekanntmachung die Aussetzung eines Preises für die Ausarbeitung eines Lehrbuchs der Geschichte Sachsens zunächst für die Volksschule betr., 22 October 1851, HSADre Ministerium f. Volksbildung 13195 (1). Published in the *Dresdner Journal*, the *Leipziger Zeitung* and the *Kirchen- und Schulblatt*.

[89] Franz Otto Stichart, *Das Königreich Sachsen und seine Fürsten. Ein geschichtlicher Abriß für Schule und Haus* (Leipzig, 1854).

[90] Proposed by Dr Kunath, Dresden an d. Ministerium des Cultus u. öffentlichen Unterrichts, 16 August 1852, HSADre Ministerium f. Volksbildung 13195 (24–7).

[91] Ministerium des Cultus u. öffentlichen Unterrichts an die Kreisdirection zu Dresden, Leipzig, Zwickau; Gesammtconsistorium zu Glauchau, 6 April 1854, HSADre Ministerium f. Volksbildung 13195 (127–8).

[92] Protokol, 1 November 1865, HSADre Ministerium f. Volksbildung 12603 (406–25).

King'.[93] The matter was subsequently investigated by Pabst, a *Kultusministerium* official, who found the school reader situation in Hanover to be every bit as unsatisfactory as it was in Saxony, for despite the diversity of readers in use, none was really suitable.[94] Pabst reported that some readers were written by foreigners and insufficiently patriotic; some were written by humanists and unsuited to Protestant needs and others were too ambitious or too doctrinaire or too abstract or too sentimental or too mannered or too tendentious; all posed problems of one kind or another. Consequently, Pabst suggested following the Saxon example and offering a prize of 100 *Thaler* for a truly Hanoverian school reader, which could become the 'secular bible of the *Volksschule*'. Pabst emphasised, however, that such a reader was hardly an educational priority, and in the end nothing was done about it.[95] In any case, regional educational authorities proved reluctant to over-regulate schoolbooks, arguing that different schools in different areas had different needs. Nevertheless, they did start publishing guidelines listing both obligatory and optional books for *Volksschule* use. For instance, the Aurich Consistory listed the following books as mandatory for *Volksschulen* in East Friesland: the bible, the state catechism, the 'kleine Luther' catechism, the East Friesland hymn book, a further (confessionally specific) hymn book and a German primer.[96] The Consistory also provided a list of recommended *Volksschule* readers and religious histories, but only as optional extras.

The failure to standardise school reading materials in Hanover resulted in part from relatively low educational standards in many parts of the state. Reports from particularly rural areas, like Bentheim, emphasised that many pupils could barely read and write.[97] Indeed, in 1866 only eighteen out of twenty-seven candidates for the teaching seminary in East Friesland had adequate literacy skills – a shocking statistic, since these candidates presumably formed something of an elite.[98] Under these circumstances, instruction in the *Realien* was hardly a priority. For instance, when

[93] O. Aichel, Superintendent, to H. M., forwarded to the *Kultusministerium*, 14 January 1856, HSAHan Hann 113 κ 1 308 (2–7).
[94] A. Pabst, 'Promemoria', 19 February 1856, HSAHan Hann 113 κ 1 308 (14–15).
[95] A. Pabst, 'Gehorsamstes Promemoria', undated, 1856, HSAHan Hann 113 κ 1 308 (12–13).
[96] Bericht des K. Consistoriums zu Aurich, Abth. für Volksschulsachen, betr. Schulbücher in Volksschulen, 19 October 1856, HSAHan Hann 113 κ 1 120 (75–7).
[97] Bericht der Landdrostei zu Osnabrück betr. das Volksschulwesen in der Niedergrafschaft Bentheim an K. Ministerium der geistlichen and Unterrichts Angelegenheiten, 8 January 1850, HSAHan Hann 113 κ 1 100 (92–9); Officieller Bericht des Oberschul Inspectors Cammann zu Stade, dessen Schulsinpectionsreisen vom 1 Juli 1853 bis Juni 1854 betr., 15 July 1854, HSAHan Hann 113 κ 1 294 (12–15).   [98] Vandré, *Schule, Lehrer und Unterricht*, p. 235.

asked to comment on proposals for an official Hanoverian *Volksschule* reader in 1856, the Stade Consistory wondered whether many schools needed such a reader at all – or could even make use of one.[99] Furthermore, as the *Kultusministerium* itself acknowledged in 1857, the *Realien* could hardly become compulsory in *Volksschulen* when not all teachers were competent to teach them.[100] Even where the *Realien* were taught, the relative weakness of central government control in the provinces meant that they did not necessarily include Hanoverian history. Thus a representative sample of school timetables from East Friesland analysed by Rudolf Vandré indicates that in this part of Hanover 'history of the Fatherland' was often interpreted as the history of East Friesland – not Hanover, let alone Germany.[101] All this inevitably undermined official attempts to nurture knowledge of the Hanoverian Fatherland in the *Volksschule*. In 1852, for instance, the *Kultusministerium* informed the Hanoverian Consistory that its guidelines for seminary students were inadequate.[102] The ministry insisted that candidates should also demonstrate a reasonable knowledge of Hanoverian history and geography, such as might be acquired in a good *Volksschule*. The Consistory dismissed these requirements as hopelessly ambitious, since most candidates came from the countryside and could only be expected to know what the average school was likely to teach them. The Consistory maintained that this did not include the *Realien* because 'the teaching of general knowledge or other secular studies in the *Volksschulen* remains undeveloped in our diocese'. Well might Georg V complain in 1864 'that the knowledge of their own history is very little disseminated amongst my subjects, indeed hardly at all'.[103]

Under these circumstances, it comes as no surprise to find that the Hanoverian government did not promote *Realien* teaching in the *Volksschulen* during the 1860s, unlike its Saxon and Württemberg counterparts. Instead, efforts to improve the situation concentrated on the elite minority of pupils in higher schools and seminaries. It was for these pupils that Georg V commissioned the court archivist, Schaumann, to write a history of the Welf lands for secondary school use. Schaumann

[99] Bericht des Consistoriums zu Stade an K. Ministerium der geistlichen and Unterrichts Angelegenheiten zu Hannover, die Preisaussetzung des Superintendents Aichel auf ein Lesebuch für Volksschulen betr., 7 February 1856, HSAHan Hann 113 κ 1 308 (9–11).

[100] K. Ministerium der geistlichen and Unterrichts Angelegenheiten an Oberkirchenrath Nordhorn, 1 July 1857, HSAHan Hann 113 κ 1 123 (58–68).

[101] Vandré, *Schule, Lehrer und Unterricht* pp. 206–12. Under a quarter of the eighteen schools listed by Vandré failed to provide any *Realien* teaching.

[102] Bericht des Consistorii zu Hannover, Abth. für Volksschulsachen, Aufnahmeprüfung für die Bezirksseminaristen betr., 24 April 1852, HSAHan Hann 113 κ 1 411 (44–5a).

[103] Georg V an Mein Ministerium des Cultus, 18 June 1864, HSAHan Dep. 103 XI 92 (20–1).

finally completed his 'Handbook of the Lands of Hanover and Braunschweig, for use in teaching the senior classes of higher teaching establishments in the Fatherland' in 1864.[104] Schaumann sent a copy of the book to the Council for Higher Schools, along with proposals that two hours a week should be devoted to teaching Hanoverian history – a subject currently not taught at all.[105] Georg V endorsed these suggestions enthusiastically, but they do not seem to have been implemented, perhaps because the influential educationalist Kohlrausch opposed the idea.[106] Kohlrausch found Schaumann's book to be far too scholarly and wholly unsuited for teaching purposes, although he suggested it could be made available in school libraries. In any case, Kohlrausch argued that there was no space in the secondary school timetable for Hanoverian history lessons, which were of only limited interest 'because [the material] deals so sparingly with the march of world history, or even German history, and indeed contains very little material suitable . . . for the young'. Consequently, Kohlrausch decided simply to recommend the work as a 'teaching aid' for the use of teachers and particularly keen students. Despite Georg's efforts, the knowledge of Hanoverian history amongst his subjects was unlikely to spread far.

This analysis of education policy in Hanover, Saxony and Württemberg demonstrates that governments clearly understood the potential of education as an instrument of social control, particularly at *Volksschule* level. How successful were their efforts?

As usual, most research into German *Volksschule* education has centred on Prussia.[107] Curiously, however, historians have tended to compare the

---

[104] Adolf Friedrich Heinrich Schaumann, *Handbuch der Geschichte der Lande Hannover und Braunschweig, zum Gebrauch beim Unterricht in den oberen Classen der höheren vaterländischen Lehranstalten* (Hanover, 1864). [105] Schaumann, 'Promemoria', 9 January 1864, HSAHan Hann 113 K 1 647 (1–3).

[106] Georg V an Mein Ministerium des Cultus, 18 June 1864, HSAHan Dep. 103 XI 92 (20–1), endorses Schaumann's proposals. Rundschreiben den Unterricht in der Landesgeschichte auf den Gymnasien und Progymnasien des Königreiches betr., 9 July 1864, HSAHan Hann 113 K 1 647 (22–3), is substantially different in content. I have found no later document relating to the introduction of Schaumann's book or of Hanoverian history in higher schools.

[107] For instance, both Lundgreen, *Sozialgeschichte der deutschen Schule*, and Herrlitz, Hopf and Titze, *Deutsche Schulgeschichte*, deal almost exclusively with Prussia, despite claiming to provide general histories of German education. Friedeburg, *Bildungsreform in Deutschland*, admirably avoids this trap. Contributors to Jeismann and Lundgreen (eds.), *Handbuch der deutschen Bildungsgeschichte*, vol. III, also draw on the experience of other states where possible. Besides the essential Kuhlemann, *Modernisierung und Disziplinierung*, the following histories of Prussian education may be of interest: Franzjörg Baumgart, *Zwischen Reform und Reaktion, preußische Schulpolitik 1806–1859* (Darmstadt, 1990); La Vopa, *Prussian school teachers*; Meyer, *Schule der Untertanen*; from a more strictly educational perspective, Michael Sauer, *Volksschullehrerbildung in Preußen*. A comparison of Prussian and Bavarian education is provided by the fairly weak Karl A. Schleunes, *Schooling and society. The politics of education in Prussia and Bavaria 1750–1900* (Oxford, 1989).

Prussian experience with developments in France, England and Russia, rather than with other parts of Germany.[108] Even studies stressing regional variations in literacy and school attendance rates in Germany are based on Prussian statistics.[109] Indeed, basic statistics of this kind are barely available for other German states, so that it is hard to assess the impact of education policy beyond Prussia.[110] Nevertheless, available figures indicate that basic education in Saxony and Württemberg could be favourably compared with basic education in Prussia, although this was not true for Hanover. Educational achievement is normally measured in terms of rising school attendance rates and broadly corresponding rises in literacy.[111] It is noticeable that school attendance rates of over 80% in the Prussian province of Saxony were the highest in Prussia in 1816, and significantly above the Prussian average of 54.1%.[112] For want of better figures, this may be taken as an indicator of very high levels of educational achievement in the rest of Saxony at this time, since the Prussian province of Saxony formed some three-fifths of the original Saxon state. Similarly, evidence of illiteracy in the Württemberg military recruitment lists dies out as early as the 1840s.[113] By contrast, literacy levels in Prussia are usually estimated at no more than 80%.[114] Conversely, literacy figures for Hanover after Prussian annexation indicate relatively low educational standards. Hanover came sixth out of the twelve Prussian provinces in terms of literacy in 1871.[115] Indeed, we have seen that even the verdict of government officials on the standard of education provided in Hanover was fairly damning. Surprisingly, however, school provision in both Hanover and Württemberg was better than in Prussia. In 1854 the teacher–pupil ratio in Prussian *Volksschulen*

---

[108] See for instance Friedeburg, *Bildungsreform in Deutschland*, p. 37; Barkin, 'Social control and the *Volksschule*', 50.

[109] Notably Etienne François, 'Regionale Unterschiede der Lese- und Schreibfähigkeit in Deutschland im 18. und 19. Jh.', *Jahrbuch für Regionalgeschichte* 17:1 (1990), 154–72. This deals almost exclusively with Prussia, despite its promising title.

[110] Such figures are not even provided by studies dealing with education in other German states such as Blessing, *Staat und Kirche in der Gesellschaft* or 'Allgemeine Volksbildung und politische Indoktrination im bayerischen Vormärz'; Vandré, *Schule, Lehrer und Unterricht*; Julius Richter, *Geschichte der sächsischen Volksschule*; Friederich, *Die Volksschule in Württemberg*. None of these works gives a detailed statistical analysis of education in the state concerned.

[111] The relationship between school attendance and literacy is discussed by Kuhlemann, *Modernisierung und Disziplinierung*, pp. 107–34.

[112] Figure from Gerd Friederich, 'Das niedere Schulwesen', p. 127.

[113] According to ibid., p. 126.

[114] See Friedeburg, *Bildungsreform in Deutschland*, p. 37; Barkin, 'Social control and the *Volksschule*', 50.

[115] See François, 'Regionale Unterschiede der Lese- und Schreibfähigkeit in Deutschland', 166, and ibid. more generally for details of Hanoverian literacy in 1871.

was 1:84 as compared with 1:50 in Württemberg and 1:73 in Hanover.[116] At the very least, therefore, educational provision in both Hanover and Württemberg was substantially better than in Prussia and may well have promoted higher literacy rates in these two states. After all, even in Hanover, basic educational standards were about the Prussian average. Under these circumstances, it is frankly astonishing that Prussia has so readily been accepted as a model of educational development by contemporaries and historians alike.

What did all this mean for the relative success of educational propaganda in Hanover, Saxony and Württemberg? On the one hand, better and more uniform state education is likely to have been more successful in promoting social and ideological integration by transmitting conservative attitudes and values. In practice, therefore, states like Saxony and Württemberg were probably better placed than Prussia to encourage state patriotism through the *Volksschulen*. On the other hand, the inherently revolutionary potential of education could have undermined these effects, since education promoted social mobility and – perhaps – independent thought. Kuhlemann has resolved this dichotomy in his study of Prussian education by differentiating between educational modernisation in towns, designed to meet new economic challenges, and educational backwardness in the countryside, designed to perpetuate the conservative social order. In other words, Kuhlemann links the more rigid social-control aspects of Prussian education with the more backward elements in the educational system. Certainly, it seems plausible to link high educational standards in both Saxony and Württemberg with relatively high rates of urbanisation and population density in both states. Conversely, educational standards in Hanover, which remained a very rural society, were lower than in Saxony and Württemberg and had more in common with Prussia. How far was this reflected in the impact of education in these three states? Was education primarily a conservative force in Hanover but a modernising – even revolutionary – force in Saxony and Württemberg? The 1848/9 revolution in both Saxony and Württemberg was certainly more far-reaching than in Hanover, although it is not possible to relate this specifically to educational differences. More tellingly, it is striking that teaching associations in relatively industrialised Saxony were at the forefront of teacher agitation during 1848/9. In many ways, these differences were simply symptomatic of rel-

---

[116] Figures for Prussia and Württemberg given in Skopp, 'Auf der untersten Sprosse', 390. Figures for Hanover established on the basis of General Zusammenfassung. Das evangelische und katholische Volksschulewesen, Ende des Jahres 1865, HSA Han Hann 113 K 1 288 (214).

ative Hanoverian backwardness. Nevertheless, superficially it does appear that some of the social-control effects of education were less effective in these two states.

Even so, the implications for the formation of state patriotism remain unclear. Conservative education sought to foster a range of values in order to promote social and political conservatism. These values consisted both of civic virtues and of more specifically political orientations: piety, morality, humility, obedience, temperance, economy and industry on the one hand; conservatism, monarchism, dynastic loyalty and patriotism on the other. Governments in Hanover, Saxony and Württemberg clearly saw civic virtues and political conservatism as two sides of the same coin, and understood the former to be the necessary basis for the later. Historians have tended to adopt this assumption unthinkingly.[117] In fact, however, the connection between the fostering of civic values and political conservatism was far from straightforward. To all intents and purposes, conservative education policy meant a restricted curriculum that concentrated on the four Rs but excluded the *Realien*. It is obvious that such a curriculum might foster religious and civic virtues – perhaps even loyalty to the monarch as representative of the divine order. It is less clear how such a curriculum might foster specific dynastic loyalty or patriotic love of the particular Fatherland. After all, patriotic education meant studying the history and geography of the Fatherland – in other words, the very subjects excluded from a primarily religious curriculum. Consequently, higher educational standards in Saxony and Württemberg did not necessarily undermine the particular state, for all that they may have undermined the traditional social order. Indeed, more widespread teaching of the *Realien* in these states at *Volksschule* level probably encouraged stronger identification with the particular Fatherland.

More specifically, conservative education relied upon two key factors: first, the loyalty and commitment of teachers; secondly, the government's ability to determine what was taught in schools. As we have seen, policies designed to ensure teacher loyalty met with qualified success. Such policies may have contributed to the decline in teacher radicalism, but they can only have created a very passive loyalty in the teaching classes at best. Teachers continued to resent the low pay and low status of the teaching profession and to feel under-valued by the authorities at both local and state level. In this sense repression, rather than more positive action, was probably most effective in restraining teacher unrest.

[117] See Kuhlemann, *Modernisierung und Disziplinierung*, pp. 237–47.

Teachers may have refrained from setting a bad example to their communities after 1848/9, but it is far from clear that their teaching was imbued with truly patriotic passion.

State intervention in the teaching process itself could conceivably have compensated for the lack of an actively loyal teaching class. How successful was this? Hanoverian attempts to intervene in the teaching process through the introduction of a more orthodox catechism failed. Furthermore, Hanoverian schools were too backward to allow for a more modern approach through the encouragement of the *Realien* at *Volksschule* level. This was not true for Saxony and Württemberg, where governments took steps to ensure that patriotic teaching material was available in all *Volksschulen* and that studying the Fatherland had an important place in the curriculum. At the very least, this must have significantly increased awareness of the state as Fatherland, and understanding of what that state was, amongst schoolchildren. Lessons based around the Württemberg *Volksschule* readers or the Saxon *Volksschule* history book assumed a larger frame of reference than the immediate community, and the state itself was the defining element in this new framework. Basic general knowledge of Germany and Europe merely provided a context for studying the particular Fatherland. High educational standards in Saxony and Württemberg were a prerequisite for these developments and therefore promoted patriotism at *Volksschule* level.

In all three states governments amended education policy in accordance with the changing political imperatives of the 1850s and 1860s. In Saxony and Württemberg these changing imperatives reflected wider German political developments. In Hanover they reflected the more immediate domestic context. In the 1850s education policy in Saxony and Württemberg was a response to the challenges posed by the revolutions of 1848/9; in the 1860s this policy changed to take account of the nationalist threat. In the 1850s education policy in both states combined discipline, higher pay and 'back-to-basics' teaching; in the 1860s greater recognition for the *Realien* entailed a definitive move away from exclusively religious education. This pattern was most pronounced in Württemberg. In Saxony, education policy responded to the revolutionary challenge on two levels. First, changes in government policy towards teachers and a return to primarily religious education were a response to the moral and social crisis of revolution. Secondly, formal school celebrations of the King's birthday and the acknowledged role of state history in *Volksschule* education demonstrated the government's awareness of the need to reinforce dynastic and patriotic loyalties as early as 1851. Finally, renewed official preoccupation with *Realien* teaching in the 1860s testified to growing awareness of the importance of patriotic education in pre-unification Saxony. In Württemberg the new *Volksschule* readers increased the study of the Fatherland in schools, but this was not in itself a response to the revolution. Nevertheless, the content of the readers reflected contemporary and therefore post-revolutionary concerns. The need to reinforce state-based loyalties through education was not prioritised in Württemberg until the 1860s, when it was clearly a response to contemporary political issues. The growth of German nationalism after 1859 was the most important of these. The nationalist challenge also encouraged the government to conciliate an increasingly dissatisfied teaching lobby, and to promote prosperity through an effective response to the economic challenges of industrialisation.

In Hanover there was no such reorientation of education policy in the 1860s. Rather, Hanoverian education policy should be understood in terms of the coup of 1855. On one level, this was a belated response to the revolution in Hanover, in that it revoked the 1848 constitution. Fundamentally, however, the events of 1855 had a wider significance. They signalled the opening shot in Georg V's campaign for Hanoverian renewal, which aimed to create an ultra-conservative, ultra-monarchic Welf state. Hanoverian education policy was one aspect of this campaign. Georg's obsession with the Welf dynasty, and his belief in Hanover's conservative mission in Germany, ensured that particularism was an essential element of his vision from the first. Consequently, government efforts to foster patriotism did not noticeably increase in the 1860s. In any case, the backwardness of education in Hanover prevented the shift towards *Realien* teaching apparent in Saxony and Württemberg at this time. Unsurprisingly, a traditional, principally religious approach to education as a means of social control persisted in Hanover. In this sense, Hanoverian education policy differed crucially from that of Saxony or Württemberg. This revealed more fundamental political differences, since the Hanoverian approach reflected Georg V's belief in the divine authority of monarchy. Consequently religious education in Hanover was a more political issue than in Saxony and Württemberg, as the catechism conflict clearly demonstrates. Opponents of the regime resented the return to orthodoxy in religious education precisely because of its political implications at both local and state level. Conversely, *Realien* teaching was an essentially progressive enterprise. Opponents of the Saxon and Württemberg governments did not therefore oppose the efforts of these governments to inculcate *Volksschule* pupils with patriotic feeling through the *Realien*.

The period 1850–66 was crucially important for the development of education in Saxony and Württemberg. It marked the beginning of a shift away from the traditional catechism school towards a more comprehensive *Volksschule* education, which aimed to provide more than a basic knowledge of the four Rs. The shift may have been incremental at first, but it was fundamental to the emergence of a more modern educational system. The gradual secularisation of the *Volksschule* through the introduction of the *Realien* increased the educational opportunities of *Volksschule* pupils. It also enhanced the potential of the *Volksschule* as an integrative factor within the state. Restricting education inevitably entailed limiting the basis of the state's appeal to its subjects through education. The persistent religious focus of Hanoverian education meant that education here continued to foster conservative values in traditional ways. The attempt to introduce a more orthodox catechism simply intensified the existing approach to education. Conversely, recognition of the importance of *Realien* teaching in Saxony and Württemberg in fostering patriotism and dynastic loyalty entailed a reformulation of the state's approach to education as a source of popular legitimacy. Study of the history and geography of the Fatherland meant that the state's appeal to its people became more specifically rooted in time and space. The latter was the wiser path, as is clearly demonstrated by a comparison of the disastrous introduction of the new catechism in Hanover with the growth of *Realien* teaching and standardisation of patriotic history and geography in Saxony and Württemberg. The emergence of explicitly patriotic education promised more than continued reliance on religion as a legitimising force.

At first, the growth of patriotic education in the 1850s and 1860s can have had only limited political impact. Many of those affected were still children in 1866, and the proportion of the adult population educated along these lines at that time was low. How far this education penetrated into the homes of schoolchildren is also far from certain. Nevertheless, the long-term impact of these patriotic educational initiatives should not be under-estimated. Schools in Saxony and Württemberg bred a generation of children with a new-found awareness of their immediate Fatherland – past and present – and imbued with a sense of particular as well as national identity.

CHAPTER SIX

Communications

Friedrich List, widely regarded as the father both of the German railway network and of the *Zollverein*, famously described the two as Siamese twins: 'born in the same hour, growing together in spirit and intention, they mutually reinforced each other, striving each towards the same great goal, the unification of the German tribes in a great and educated Nation'.[1] List was certainly right to recognise the crucial importance of railways, which transformed mid-nineteenth-century Germany, just as they revolutionised most of Europe during this period.[2] Railway construction required unheard-of levels of capital investment; consumed vast amounts of coal and iron; demanded modern machinery, innovation, technical and engineering expertise. Railways linked hitherto distant towns, regions and countries; facilitated the mobility of goods, people and ideas; encouraged the development of regional, national and international markets; transformed popular perceptions of time and space. More specifically, railway construction played a crucial role in what Hans-Ulrich Wehler has termed the 'dual revolution' – the twin processes of industrialisation and national unification that changed the face of Germany during the 1850s and 1860s.[3] In this sense, Friedrich List was quite right to emphasise the symbiotic relationship between railway construction and the *Zollverein* on the one hand, economic development and political change on the other. For the impact of railways on both industrialisation and unification was closely related to the process of German economic integration set in motion by the creation of the *Zollverein* in 1834 (see Map 2).

The *Zollverein* was first and foremost an economic institution, intended to facilitate trade within and between its members by removing the

---

[1] Cited after Ulrich Westerdick, 'Aufbruch in das Industriezeitalter: Die Eisenbahn im 19. Jahrhundert', in *Zug der Zeit – Zeit der Züge*, (see note 2), Vol. I, pp. 103–12 (p. 103).

[2] For a general introduction on the impact of railways in Germany see *Zug der Zeit – Zeit der Züge, deutsche Eisenbahn 1835–1985. Das offizielle Werk zur gleichnahmigen Ausstellung* (Berlin, 1985).

[3] Wehler, *Deutsche Gesellschaftsgeschichte*, Vol. III, p. 3.

Map 2 German economic integration before 1888

inner-German tariff barriers that resulted from territorial fragmenta-tion. It started out as a customs union incorporating Prussia and most of the states in Central and Southern Germany into a single tariff zone. The *Zollverein* was not the first customs union to be founded in Germany after 1815 but, unlike its predecessors, the *Zollverein* proved durable. Initially it excluded Austria and much of North Germany, notably Hanover. By 1854, however, most of these states had joined the *Zollverein*, leaving Austria increasingly economically isolated. Both Austrian and Prussian statesmen appreciated the political implications of this situa-tion. In 1851 Schwarzenberg, the Austrian chancellor, warned Emperor Franz Joseph that if Austria remained excluded from German economic policy, she would find it hard to maintain her political leadership of Germany. This prompted several attempts by the Austrian government either to redraw the economic map of Germany by creating a central European customs union incorporating all of Germany and the Habsburg Empire, or, at the very least, to join the Prussian-led *Zollverein*. Yet nothing came of any of these plans and ten years later Austria remained as economically isolated as before. Now, however, the political implications of this isolation were more immediately apparent. Ominously, Bismarck informed the Prussian parliament in the early 1860s that the *Zollverein* provided 'the most suitable basis for the joint handling by . . . German states of . . . political interests'.[4] Subsequent developments seemed to many contemporaries to vindicate this view, since between 1866 and 1871 the *Zollverein* provided the only institutional link between the North German Confederation and the independent South German states. Moreover, almost all the territories in the new German Empire were also members of the *Zollverein*, which now appeared to be the precursor of the *kleindeutsch* nation state.

Later generations of historians have tended to agree with Friedrich List that German unification was as much about iron and coal as it was about blood and iron. This view was first voiced by the Borussian historians of the German Empire, who saw the *Zollverein* as a brilliantly deployed instru-ment of Prussian power politics, which undermined the position of Austria in Germany and paved the way for *kleindeutsch* unification. According to this view, the *Zollverein* fostered the development of eco-nomic interdependencies in the future nation state. This encouraged a convergence of economic interests among member states, exacerbating

---

[4] Helmut Böhme, *Deutschlands Weg zur Großmacht. Studien zum Verhältnis von Wirtschaft und Staat während der Reichsgründungszeit 1848–1881* (Cologne/Berlin, 1966), p. 131.

the socio-economic differences between these and the more backward Habsburg lands. Bismarck then brought the process to a successful conclusion by forcing the economically liberal Franco-German trade treaty on a largely reluctant *Zollverein* in the early 1860s. Austrian economic backwardness and the strength of the protectionist lobby here rendered it unthinkable for Austria to abide by the terms of this treaty. Helmut Böhme, the most recent proponent of this school, has therefore termed the Franco-German trade treaty an 'economic Königgrätz', which excluded Austria from German economic policy for good and made Austria's political exclusion from Germany inevitable.[5] Even historians like Hans-Werner Hahn, who have taken issue with Böhme's overly triumphalist view of the *Zollverein*, continue to stress its importance as a catalyst for German economic growth, through the creation of a national economic market and a more stable trading environment.[6] This interpretation echoes the views of contemporaries, who frequently attributed growing German prosperity to the beneficial effects of the *Zollverein*. Nevertheless, the key period of economic growth is now generally held to have occurred almost twenty years after the creation of the *Zollverein*, in the 1850s and 1860s – incidentally, at the height of the railway construction boom. Once again, therefore, it is best to avoid simplistic assumptions about the causal connections between the foundation of the *Zollverein* and the rapid take-off of German industrialisation.

Instead, historians nowadays understand the progression from *Zollverein* to nation state as a complex and open-ended process, with institutional, fiscal, economic and political components. Institutionally, the *Zollverein* created an environment very favourable to further integration.[7] The *Zollverein* was administered by a national cadre of customs officials – some of whom even swore an oath of loyalty to it. Control mechanisms, such as the exchange of customs officials between states, meant that these officials worked closely together. They often came away with a very positive impression of Prussian bureaucracy and the Prussian state, since *Zollverein* administration and tariff policy were organised on Prussian lines.

---

[5] Böhme, *Deutschlands Weg zur Großmacht*. Böhme's argument is neatly summarised in the introduction, pp. 13–7.   [6] See Hahn, *Geschichte des Deutschen Zollvereins*, pp. 92–4.

[7] From this point of view the *Zollverein* presents particularly interesting parallels with the EU. Interest in this aspect of the *Zollverein* was revived by Wolfram Fischer: see 'Der deutsche Zollverein. Fallstudie einer Zollunion' in Wolfram Fischer (ed.), *Wirtschaft und Gesellschaft im Zeitalter der Industrialisierung. Aufsätze – Studien – Vorträge* (Göttingen, 1972), pp. 110–28. Hahn has explored this more fully for the Hessian states in *Wirtschaftliche Integration im 19. Jahrhundert*, pp. 225–39.

Fiscally, the *Zollverein* became very important to German governments because it made such a massive contribution to state budgets – a point stressed in particular by the historian R. H. Dumke.[8] By and large, persistently low levels of direct taxation meant that government income in Germany failed to keep pace with the growth of the centralised state. To the delight of many governments, however, indirect tax revenues rocketed as a result of *Zollverein* membership – partly because the early Prussian-imposed tariffs were quite high, and partly because the new customs union enabled economies of scale in tariff administration. In Württemberg, for instance, tariffs and tolls made up only 7.4% of the pre-*Zollverein* 1831 budget, but 14.6% of the post-*Zollverein* 1839–42 budget.[9] Member states consequently became financially dependent on *Zollverein* revenue and this proved a powerful incentive for continued membership. Indeed, the financial incentive became an increasingly important consideration as state expenditure grew, most obviously as a consequence of railway construction. Moreover, high indirect taxation was a useful weapon in any government's armoury, for budgetary powers were inevitably the most important source of leverage for the liberal opposition in representative institutions, like the state parliaments and Estates. Leaving the *Zollverein* would therefore have significantly undermined the government's position on the home front. In this sense, the *Zollverein* helped in the short term to stabilise conservative regimes in the German states, particularly before 1848.

Economically, the impact of the *Zollverein* was less straightforward than this. On the one hand, it is not clear that the *Zollverein* directly stimulated economic growth, by creating rather than diverting trade. Indeed, the direct economic gains of *Zollverein* membership may have been as little as 1.06% in South Germany which, since it was originally composed of small markets, was the area most likely to benefit from membership.[10] Nevertheless, the indirect economic effects were almost certainly greater than this because the *Zollverein* was quite clearly a supportive factor in German industrialisation. For one thing, the *Zollverein* contributed to a climate of economic optimism that encouraged investment. At the same time, the bias towards indirect taxation within the *Zollverein* reduced the

---

[8] For a summary of Dumke's arguments see his, 'Tariffs and market structure: the German Zollverein as a model for economic integration' in W. R. Lee (ed.), *German industry and German industrialisation: essays in German economic and business history in the nineteenth and twentieth centuries* (London, 1991), pp. 77–115.

[9] For this, and further, examples see Hahn, *Geschichte des deutschen Zollvereins*, p. 100.

[10] Ibid., p. 89.

tax burden on businesses. To some extent, therefore, the prosperity of member states was indeed the product of *Zollverein* membership. Equally importantly, the *Zollverein* promoted intra-German trade, fostering economic integration and generating a high level of regional interdependence.[11] For instance, relatively industrial and urbanised Saxony was critically dependent on imports of Prussian grain. Similarly, Baden and Württemberg depended almost exclusively on Prussia for imports of coal and iron.[12] Conversely, 50% of wine and 40% of leather and tobacco produced in Hesse-Darmstadt were exported to Prussia.[13] Leaving the *Zollverein* ceased to be a viable option for German governments, as the entanglement of member state economies continued apace.

Politically, the *Zollverein* had always been an important symbol for German liberal nationalists, who, like Friedrich List, saw it as paving the way towards unification. Yet the *Zollverein* also had a direct political impact in member states because it created a favourable impression of Prussia among liberal opponents of the more reactionary German regimes. Close contact with Prussia encouraged the opposition in these states to contrast supposedly pro-active and liberal Prussian economic policies favourably with the conservative approach of their own governments. Indeed, Hans-Werner Hahn argues persuasively that liberal enthusiasm for Prussian economic policy probably contributed to the ready acceptance of Prussian annexation in Hesse-Kassel and Nassau after 1866, although interestingly this was less true in Hanover or Hesse-Darmstadt.[14] Even so, by and large the leap from economic integration to political unification (or *Zollverein* to *kleindeutsch* nation state) remained far from certain. The *Zollverein* was certainly a supportive factor in German unification, but probably no more than this. The wars of 1866 and 1870/1 were the catalysts for unification, not the Franco-German trade treaty or the *Zollparlament* of 1868.

---

[11] Economic interdependencies within the *Zollverein* have been extensively explored by Wolfgang Zorn. See his 'Die wirtschaftliche Integration Kleindeutschlands in den 1860er Jahren und die Reichsgründung', *Historische Zeitschrift* 216:2 (April 1973), 304–34. The implications of this for the *Mittelstaaten* are discussed in Klaus Megerle, 'Ökonomische Integration und politische Orientierung deutscher Mittel- und Kleinstaaten im Vorfeld der Reichsgründung' in Helmut Berding (ed.), *Wirtschaftliche und politische Integration in Europa im 19. und 20. Jahrhundert, Geschichte und Gesellschaft* Sonderheft 10 (Göttingen, 1984), pp. 102–27. According to Megerle, Prussia's trade-balance with the *Mittelstaaten* was passive at best – that is, the *Mittelstaaten* were more dependent on *Zollverein* exports than on *Zollverein* imports (see ibid., pp. 106–8). Of all the *Zollverein* states, Bavaria was most dependent on inner-German exports. Hahn, *Wirtschaftliche Integration im 19. Jahrhundert*, pp. 154–70, provides a more detailed analysis for the Hessian states.

[12] Megerle, 'Ökonomische Integration und politische Orientierung', p. 108.

[13] Hahn, *Zollverein*, p. 154.   [14] Hahn, *Wirtschaftliche Integration im 19. Jahrhundert*, pp. 277–306.

Ultimately, however, railway construction may have played a more important role in dictating the pace of the 'dual revolution' in Germany than its more famous 'twin', the *Zollverein*. Hubert Kiesewetter, for instance, has argued that the economic interdependencies resulting from railway construction were more important in promoting political unity than any other fiscal or economic measure.[15] Certainly, railways are widely acknowledged to have been the leading sector in German industrialisation.[16] They accounted for between 14% and 20% of German economic investment from 1850 to 1871, the years now seen as the break-through period for industrialisation.[17] Railway development exploded across Germany during these years, as the German rail network nearly tripled to a total of 18,810 km by 1870 (see Map 3).[18] By 1873 railways accounted for 55% of German industrial capital and 10% of all German economic capital.[19] Meanwhile, the railway work-force had mushroomed from a mere 26,000 in 1850 to some 204,900 by 1866. Railway construction further stimulated the German economy through a process of import substitution, because railways acted as a catalyst for the crucial machine construction, iron and coal industries. In 1839 not a single Prussian railway engine was German in origin; by 1853 almost all (94.3%) were. Similarly, in 1843 only 10.17% of the rails used in Prussian railway construction were German; by 1863 German-produced rails accounted for 85.39% of the total.[20] This response to domestic demand later translated into international sales. Exports of German-made rails increased from 23,600 tons in 1860–5 to 149,900 tons in 1866–71.[21] Machine construction of this kind entailed an explosion in the German iron industry. In the 1840s rail production had been dependent on imported pig iron, but *Zollverein* pig iron production grew rapidly in the following decades: from 214,560 tons in 1850 to 988,200 tons in 1865 and 1,390,490 tons

---

[15] See Hubert Kiesewetter, 'Economic preconditions for Germany's nation-building in the nineteenth century' in Hagen Schulze (ed.), *Nation-building in Central Europe* (Leamington Spa, 1987), pp. 81–106 (pp. 99–102). Kiesewetter argues that the economic integration resulting from railway construction was more important in promoting political unity than any other economic or fiscal measure. A more nuanced view of the role of railways in German unification is provided by Markus Völkel, 'Einigkeit und Freiheit. Die Eisenbahn ein Mittel nationaler Politik?' in *Zug der Zeit – Zeit der Züge*, vol. I, pp. 219–27.

[16] This was persuasively argued by Rainer Fremdling. A summary of his argument appears in Fremdling, 'Railroads and German economic growth: a leading sector analysis with a comparison in the United States and Great Britain', *Journal of Economic History* 37:3 (1977), 583–604. Fremdling's argument has been generally accepted by historians of German industrialisation: see for instance Wehler, *Deutsche Gesellschaftsgeschichte*, Vol. III, pp. 68–81.   [17] Ibid., p. 43.

[18] Ibid., p. 68.   [19] Ibid., p. 71

[20] Fremdling, 'Railroads and German economic growth', 591.   [21] Ibid.

in 1870.[22] Steel production made similarly rapid progress: from 196,950 tons in 1850 to 707,930 tons in 1865 and 1,044,700 tons in 1870. Meanwhile, German coal production, crucial to the iron and railway sectors, increased by 570% between 1848 and 1871 and the production of brown coal by 498.7% in the same period.[23]

The sheer scale of German industrial growth generated further demand for railways, which became the principal means of transporting bulky goods like coal, iron and grain. Heavy industry was not the only sector to benefit from cheap and rapid transport: railways transformed trading habits and opened new markets for all kinds of agricultural and manufactured products. Between 1850 and 1870 rail freight increased by 16.3% annually.[24] This increase was nearly double the maximum annual growth rate achieved by the dynamic Ruhr coal industry during the same period. The annual increase in passenger traffic of 8.9% was significant, though less dramatic.[25] Railway construction therefore played an important part in German economic integration, facilitating the movement of goods and people. This fostered inter-regional competition and encouraged the emergence of integrated goods markets at a national and international level. The need to finance railway construction was also a crucial factor in the development of more sophisticated financial structures and credit institutions in Germany.

In practice, however, integrated goods and financial markets had a very varied impact at local level. German industrialisation was a highly regionalised phenomenon, proceeding in different ways and at different paces in different states and regions.[26] Railway construction reflected and exacerbated this process. Inevitably, railways tended to be built at first in relatively developed areas because these were likely to generate more traffic and make higher profits. It was certainly no accident that Saxony was the first German state to support railway construction, in the shape of the Leipzig–Dresden railway. The symbiotic relationship between industrialisation and railway building emerges clearly through

---

[22] Wehler, *Deutsche Gesellschaftsgeschichte*, Vol. III, p. 75.

[23] Kiesewetter, *Industrialisierung und Landwirtschaft*, p. 568.

[24] Wehler, *Deutsche Gesellschaftsgeschichte*, Vol. III, p. 68.

[25] Ibid. The more modest growth rate for passenger transport was still roughly equivalent to the maximum annual growth of the Ruhr coal industry (9%) and more than the maximum annual growth achieved by the raw iron industry (8.4%).

[26] The point is neatly made by comparing the proportion of those involved in manufacturing or industry in each state between 1846 and 1871. Although the proportion rose in all German states, it nevertheless varied dramatically from state to state. See Megerle, 'Ökonomische Integration und politische Orientierung', p. 104.

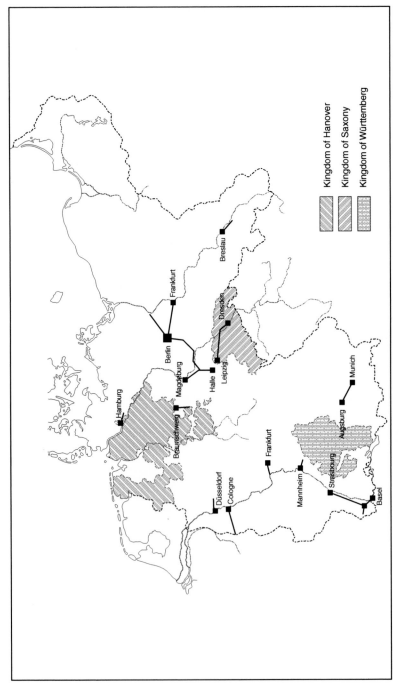

Map 3 (*a–d*) The pace of railway construction in Hanover, Saxony and Württemberg
(*a*) The German railway network, 1842

Kingdom of Hanover

Kingdom of Saxony

Kingdom of Württemberg

Breslau

Frankfurt

Dresden

Berlin

Leipzig

Halle

Magdeburg

Hamburg

Braunschweig

Munich

Augsburg

Frankfurt

Düsseldorf

Cologne

Mannheim

Strasbourg

Basel

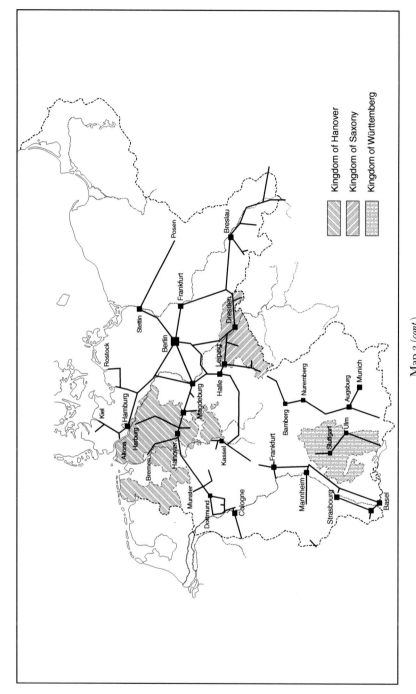

Kingdom of Hanover

Kingdom of Saxony

Kingdom of Württemberg

Map 3 (*cont.*)

(*b*) The German railway network, 1850

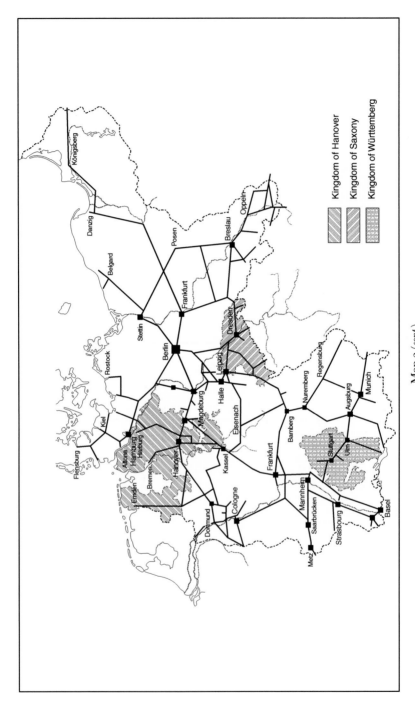

Map 3 (*cont.*)

(*c*) The German railway network, 1860

Kingdom of Hanover

Kingdom of Saxony

Kingdom of Württemberg

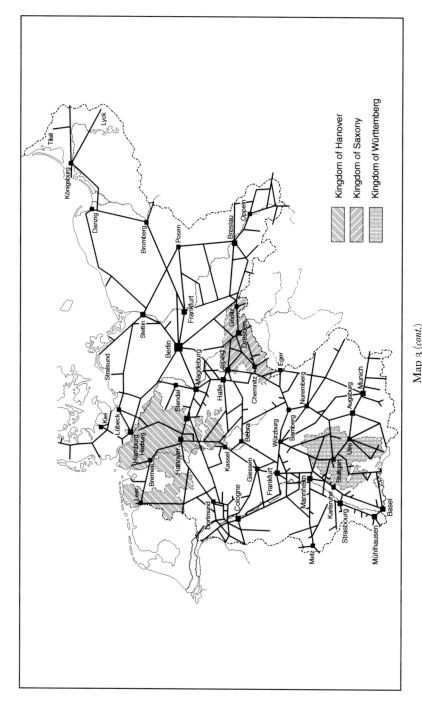

Kingdom of Hanover

Kingdom of Saxony

Kingdom of Württemberg

Map 3 (*cont.*)

(*d*) The German railway network, 1870

Table 6.1. *Kilometrage of railway network in the five German Kingdoms, and the territory of the future German Empire*[a]

	1850	1855	1860	1865	1871
Hanover	359.6	538.7	716.9	811.5	1002.9
Saxony	436.1	529.6	689.3	807.6	1070.7
Württemberg	250	283.9	318.1	551.7	1028.2
Prussia	2649.6	3482.1	5200.2	6197.2	9391.3
Bavaria	610.2	1151.7	1769.2	2420.8	3031.1
German Empire	5856.4	7826.4	11089.1	13899.9	20980

Note:
[a] Kiesewetter, *Industrialisierung und Landwirtschaft*, p. 610.

Table 6.2. *Density of rail network in the five German Kingdoms and the German Empire in 1871*[a]

	Rail km/1000 km^2	Rail km/100,000 inhabitants
Hanover	26	51.1
Saxony	71.4	41.9
Württemberg	52.7	56.5
Prussia	34.2	46.5
Bavaria	40	62.3
German Empire	38.8	51.1

Note:
[a] Kiessewetter, *Industrialisierung und Landwirtschaft*, p. 610.

a comparative analysis of the rate of railway construction in the largest German states. Table 6.1 traces the development of the German railway network in the five German Kingdoms and Table 6.2 shows the relative density of the railway network in each. Unsurprisingly, given their socio-economic profile, the density of the railway network in industrialised Saxony was almost triple that of backward Hanover, with Württemberg roughly half-way between the two by 1871. Indeed, the Saxon railway network was already significantly larger than that of Hanover or Württemberg by 1850, although Saxony did not retain this advantage over Hanover for long. The Württemberg railway network, however, remained significantly smaller than that of Hanover or Saxony until 1865. The slower pace of railway construction in Württemberg probably reflected the state's mountainous terrain and weak geographical position, which enabled it to be bypassed by transit traffic and international trade. By contrast, Hanover was flat and controlled access to important North Sea ports, as well as links between East and West Prussia.

Railway construction did not merely reflect differing regional levels of industrialisation. Instead, railways actively encouraged the polarisation between relatively industrialised areas (like much of Saxony), traditional agricultural areas (like much of Hanover), and more artisanal areas (like much of Württemberg). The polarisation was mirrored on a smaller scale within the various German states, where regional differences remained very significant. This was most obviously true for Prussia, which included highly developed areas (Ruhr, Rhineland, Upper Silesia) as well as the traditional agricultural lands east of the Elbe. Even a small state like Württemberg, with a largely agricultural and artisanal economy, contained pockets of industrialisation, such as the town of Esslingen. Railways encouraged this polarisation process in two ways. Initially, railway construction was concentrated in economically developed and relatively industrialised areas, like Saxony. Railways linked these areas with each other and with smaller industrial enclaves, like Esslingen, rendering them yet more economically vibrant. This encouraged a drain of resources from less developed areas. Consequently, railways exacerbated the gulf between such areas and the more developed parts of Germany. Early access to rail transport exposed developed areas to national and international competition at an earlier stage, but they were relatively well able to cope with this. Later, railways opened up hitherto protected local markets, as all parts of Germany were integrated into the railway network. Whilst integrated goods markets benefited both export-oriented agricultural areas and modernising manufacturing and industrial areas, their impact on backward sectors and regions was devastating. Regions like the traditional textile centres of Saxony and the iron-working areas of Nassau faced serious economic hardship and often terminal decline. Here the advent of rail was a far from unmixed blessing.

The role of railways in creating integrated national markets is often seen as an important contribution to the process of German unification. This development was intimately related to the process of economic integration fostered by the *Zollverein* during the same period. Indeed, without the *Zollverein* the impact of railways on the German economy would have been very different and probably much more limited. By removing the obstacles to national economic integration created by inner-German borders and tariffs, the *Zollverein* created an economic framework in which integrated goods markets might begin to form. Nevertheless, it is important not to exaggerate the extent to which German railway construction and the *Zollverein* worked in tandem. In practice, the borders of the *Zollverein* proved relatively unimportant for the development of the German rail network. Before 1848, cross-border railways were negotiated and built more quickly in North Germany than in the South, although the North was still divided into two tariff zones and the South was not. To some extent, this simply reflected the flatter geography of North Germany, but it was probably also a result of the territorial imperatives dictating railway construction within the divided Prussian state, which made building a link to join East and West Prussia a priority. Certainly, it is important not to over-estimate the relationship between the German railway network and the *Zollverein*. Water transport was probably far more significant than rail in orienting *Zollverein* states towards Prussia. Except for the Danube, all Germany's major rivers flowed north into the North Sea and the Baltic. Thus in 1852 the Württemberg Board of Trade and Industry argued that leaving the *Zollverein* would be very disruptive for Württemberg's primarily north-bound trade flows, because Prussia controlled long stretches of the Rhine.[27] The impact of rail transport was more ambiguous than this. Unlike water transport, railways were not constrained by geographical considerations. Neither were they really constrained by economic or national boundaries. Besides improving communications within the *Zollverein*, railways also improved communications between the *Zollverein* and Austria, as well as other states like France, Belgium and Switzerland. Railways therefore promoted processes of both international and national economic integration. Indeed, *Zollverein* members did not necessarily see railway connections with other *Zollverein* states as particularly important or desirable. In 1858 Bismarck lamented Baden's decision to prioritise a railway link with France, via the bridge at Kehl, over one with Bavaria and a permanent bridge in Mannheim 'where both banks are German'.[28] Bismarck complained that the Baden government had failed to take 'general German interests' into account, neglecting negotiations with Bavaria and subordinating its own interests to those of a major foreign power, which was only too pleased to interfere in German affairs.

Certainly, political considerations often proved quite as important as economic factors in shaping the German railway network, and they did

---

[27] Megerle, 'Ökonomische Integration und politische Orientierung', p. 100.
[28] Cited after Alfred von der Leyen, *Die Eisenbahnpolitik des Fürsten Bismarck* (Berlin, 1914), p. 9.

influence cross-border railway negotiations. In 1866, for example, there was only one railway border crossing between Prussia and the Habsburg Empire, but there were numerous such links between Austria and her allies Saxony and Bavaria. Indeed, the most important factor in shaping the German railway network was territorial fragmentation. In terms of railway policy the state, not the German Confederation or the *Zollverein*, was the decisive political and economic unit.[29]

The state provided the legal and territorial framework for railway construction, and often a high level of financial backing. Railways relied upon state legislation for expropriation, the concessioning of joint-stock companies and so on.[30] This gave state governments important leverage in determining the choice of route. Territorial fragmentation in Germany meant that most German railways crossed state borders. These inter-state railways required complex negotiations between the governments concerned, each of which was concerned to defend its own economic and political interests. Finally, the capital market in Germany was not sufficiently well developed to finance railway construction privately, as was the case in Britain. The first German railways were private enterprises. The state became increasingly involved, however, as these companies struggled to survive, or failed to raise the necessary finance to build the railways in question at all. By 1848 the railway networks in most German states included both state railways and private companies,

---

[29] For an excellent general study of railway policy in the German states see Dieter Ziegler, *Eisenbahnen und Staat im Zeitalter der Industrialisierung. Die Eisenbahnpolitik der deutschen Staaten im Vergleich* (Stuttgart, 1996). Also Bernt Mester, 'Partikularismus der Schiene. Die Entwicklung einzelstaatlicher Eisenbahnsysteme bis 1870' in *Zug der Zeit – Zeit der Züge*, vol. I, pp. 197–205. There are also numerous monographs dealing with individual states. On Prussia see James M. Brophy, *Capitalism, politics and railroads in Prussia, 1830–1870* (Columbus, Ohio, 1998), which is exceptionally well written, thought-provoking and wide-ranging in its implications; also Wolfgang Klee, *Preußische Eisenbahngeschichte* (Stuttgart, 1982). The most useful studies of railway building in the *Mittelstaaten* are Ludwig Brake, *Die ersten Eisenbahnen in Hessen. Eisenbahnpolitik und Eisenbahnbau in Frankfurt, Hessen-Darmstadt, Kurhessen und Nassau bis 1866* (Wiesbaden, 1991); Hildegard Ditt and Peter Schöller, 'Die Entwicklung des Eisenbahnnetzes in Nordwestdeutschland', *Westfälische Forschungen* 8 (1955), 150–80; Hans-Friedrich Gisevius, *Zur Vorgeschichte des preußisch-sächsischen Eisenbahnkrieges. Verkehrspolitische Differenzen zwischen Preußen und Sachsen im Deutschen Bund* (Berlin, 1971); Karl Heinrich Kaufhold, 'Die Anfänge des Eisenbahnbaus in Niedersachsen' in Dieter Brosius and Martin Last (eds.), *Beiträge zur niedersächsischen Landesgeschichte, zum 65. Geburtstag von Hans Patze* (Hildesheim, 1984), pp. 364–87. Numerous local studies of railways exist, usually with more of a social-history perspective. Probably the best of these is Emma Mages, *Eisenbahnbau. Siedlung, Wirtschaft und Gesellschaft in der südlichen Oberpfalz (1850–1920)* (Kallmünz, 1984). Of particular relevance to Saxony is Peter Beyer, *Leipzig und die Anfänge des deutschen Eisenbahnbaus. Die Strecke nach Magdeburg als zweitälteste deutsche Fernbindung und das Ringen der Kaufleute um ihr Entstehen 1829–1840* (Weimar, 1978), which adopts a traditional Marxist line.

[30] For a general discussion of the legal aspects of railway construction, see Anton J. Liebl, 'Anstoß zur Modernisierung. Der Eisenbahnbau als Rechts- und Verwaltungsproblem' in *Zug der Zeit – Zeit der Züge*, Vol. I, pp. 95–100.

as well as private companies in which the state had a significant stake. This mixture of public and private railway ownership survived into the early twentieth century.

The changing pattern of railway ownership and management in Germany reflected evolving government attitudes to railways during the period. Initially, governments were chary of authorising, let alone investing in, this untried and expensive form of transport. Leading conservatives were also dubious about its democratic implications. Ernst August of Hanover famously remarked: 'I am not having any railways in my country, I will not have every locksmith and tailor travelling as fast as I can.'[31] Government reluctance to undertake the large financial commitments entailed in railway construction also reflected an unwillingness to increase government dependence on tax-granting representative bodies. The success of the first German railways forced governments to change their approach for fear of being left out in the cold. Governments faced two options. Either they could create a more favourable environment for railway investment, usually by guaranteeing the interest on railway shares, or they could build the railways themselves. Governments had to opt for the latter option when – as was often the case – private finance failed to raise the necessary sum. Tiny states like those in Thuringia could not hope to finance state railways and depended upon private enterprise if they were to be integrated into the German rail network – and, by extension, for integration in the emergent national economy. Larger states, however, tended to opt for state railways. Hanover was alone in opting consistently for a state railway system, but the railways in most medium-sized German states were overwhelmingly state-run. For instance, this was the case in Baden, Bavaria (apart from the Palatinate), Braunschweig and Württemberg. Saxony was highly unusual in operating a genuinely mixed system. This was a consequence of early Saxon support for railway construction. The private Leipzig–Dresden railway was the major East–West artery in Saxony but, as the first long-distance railway in Germany, it enjoyed peculiarly advantageous concession conditions. The position in Prussia was equally exceptional. Here financial constraints imposed on the government by its failure to grant a constitution prevented the construction of state railways before 1848, although a Railway Fund did provide some state financial assistance to railway companies. The granting of a constitution removed this obstacle, although financial considerations made it impossible for the state to buy up private

---

[31] Cited after ibid., p. 95.

railway companies *en bloc*. In the 1850s, however, the Trade Minister, von der Heydt, operated a policy of creeping 'nationalisation'. He refused to grant railway concessions to new private companies and took over the direction of some existing companies, occasionally in the face of fierce resistance from stockholders and directors. This policy was abandoned during the 1860s, as a consequence both of the rise of economic liberalism in Germany and of the Prussian constitutional conflict. In his brilliant study of the politics of Prussian railway construction, James Brophy has argued that this return to private railways testified to a new spirit of cooperation between businessmen and the Prussian government that was itself the product of the New Era and its aftermath.[32]

In all the German states the decision to opt for state or private railways was primarily pragmatic, varying on a case-by-case basis according to changing financial circumstances. Nevertheless, many governments became convinced of the desirability of state railways in theory, if not in practice. This was certainly true for Hanover, Saxony and Württemberg, despite the continued importance of private railways in the latter. The preference for state railways reflected both political and economic considerations. The experiences of 1848 had demonstrated very clearly the potential role of railways in transporting troops.[33] In Prussia in particular, military considerations proved as important as economic interests in state railway construction on occasion. The state-funded Prussian Eastern Railway, for instance, was primarily built to satisfy military needs. Heydt also took steps in 1852 to purge Prussian railway administrations of democrats, because he felt the 'great political importance' of railways made it an urgent necessity 'that only politically reliable individuals join the administration'.[34] Beust showed a similar awareness of the military and political importance of railways in 1857, when he voiced his concern about the vulnerability of the private Leipzig–Dresden railway line, which linked the two halves of the Saxon railway network: 'in moments of crisis . . . the entire connection depends on covering the crossing of the Elbe . . . Even the state railways can only communicate with each other via the Leipzig–Dresden railway.'[35] Similarly, political considerations were an important factor in the lengthy and impassioned Württemberg debate over the route of the Upper Neckar Valley railway.

[32] Brophy, *Capitalism, politics and railroads in Prussia*, chapter 7, pp. 135–64.
[33] Railway concessions to private companies always included clauses regarding the use of these railways for military purposes.   [34] Cited after Klee, *Preußische Eisenbahngeschichte*, p. 119.
[35] Beust, 'Vortrag des Ministerium des Innern', 14 September 1857, HSADre Ministerium des Innern 141, Dresden–Chemnitzer Eisenbahn (378–445).

Many Württembergers favoured the longer and more expensive route that bypassed the Prussian Hohenzollern principalities, because it would be independent of foreign influence.

Over and above such political concerns, German governments became increasingly aware of the importance of rail as an instrument in economic policy. In 1857, for instance, Beust argued that the advantages for the state in railway construction were primarily macroeconomic, in other words, the fostering of agriculture, industry and trade.[36] Consequently, he believed that whilst private railways were motivated by profit alone, state railways should be influenced by broader considerations, since 'a railway can afford the state advantages of a different kind to those which can only be expressed through dividends on capital'. Indeed, Beust argued that it was crucially important for the state to make good the distortions of competition introduced in Saxony by the new railways. In 1863 the General Directorate of the Hanoverian railways voiced similar views, when he declared that the Hanoverian government would never abandon its commitment to publicly funded railways. Like Beust, Hartmann believed that a state railway system, managed according to macroeconomic rather than financial criteria, could serve the common good most effectively.[37] This was easier said than done, however, as most governments were only too well aware. In reality, the balance between macroeconomic and financial considerations was usually rather different. As Gessler, the Württemberg Interior Minister, remarked in 1864, economic considerations were all very well, but state railways needed to be financially viable if they were to be financed by public debt, 'otherwise the state is in danger of becoming an economic rogue'.[38]

Territorial fragmentation and the importance of state railways in Germany created not so much a single German railway network as a conglomeration of state networks. What did this mean in practice for the pace of railway construction in Germany and for the pattern of the railway network that emerged? Given the importance of territorial states in railway construction, what was the impact of railways on the states themselves? Is it correct to see railway construction as a one-way process leading to national economic integration, or did railways also reinforce existing state structures both economically and culturally? In many

[36] Ibid.
[37] Bericht des Generaldirection der Eisenbahnen und Telegraphen betr. Concessionsgesuch des L.L. Mouton zu einer Eisenbahnanlage zwischen Venloo–Wesel–Osnabrück–Hamburg (Vertraulich), 10 April 1863, HSAHan Dep. 103 IX 413.
[38] Gessler, 'Zu den Protokollen vom 7 u 13 April 1864', 24 February 1864, HSAStu E 33 559 (444).

ways, railway construction appears to be the most glaring manifestation of economic state-building in the *Mittelstaaten* during this period. How did railway construction reinforce other policies designed to foster particularism in these states? In particular, how far did railway construction amplify the impact of particularist cultural activities?

Territorial fragmentation encouraged the various German states to compete with each other over railway policy. As the economic impact of railways became apparent, towns, communities and economic interest groups throughout Germany formed railway committees and associations, which began to lobby for railway connections. Petitions and applications for railway concessions addressed the various state governments because decisions over railway policy were taken at this level. Local communities looked to state governments to meet their railway needs, reflecting the habitual tendency of German businessmen to look to the state for support. Railway construction was therefore an important test of the viability of the German states and of their ability to meet the challenges of government in the industrial era. Hanover, Saxony and Württemberg all attempted to rise to this challenge, borrowing large amounts of money through railway loans in order to do so.

The need for German states to prove themselves through railway policy dictated both the pace of railway construction and the pattern of the railway network that emerged: railways were built more quickly than in neighbouring European states, and the German rail network was polycentric – reflecting Germany's federal structure – not centralised on the French model (see Map 3). Both characteristics of railway construction in Germany resulted from the fear of smaller German states that they would lose traditional trade flows to their neighbours – and perhaps be bypassed by railways altogether. The small size of many German states meant that this was a very real threat. Indeed, Oldenburg met with precisely this fate: its failure to encourage railway investment at a sufficiently early stage left it without a railway connection until 1867. Railway construction in the various German states was therefore usually prompted by developments elsewhere. This was most obviously true in Baden, where French plans for a Strasbourg–Basel railway prompted the construction of the Mannheim–Basel line. The threat of inadequate integration into the German railway network was taken particularly seriously in Saxony, where international trade was so important to the state's second city, Leipzig.[39] Moreover, the

---

[39] On this see Beyer, *Leipzig und die Anfänge des deutschen Eisenbahnbaus*, and Gisevius, *Vorgeschichte des Preußisch-sächsischen Eisenbahnkrieges*, pp. 63–93.

Saxons had already been caught off guard by Prussian road-building policy, which had deliberately bypassed Saxony. They were determined not to make the same mistake again.

Inter-state competition over railway construction had two key components. First, governments aimed to maximise railway profits and the benefits of transit traffic. Second, railway policy reflected important economic interests in the states concerned. Governments needed to guard against economic isolation and competition from elsewhere. They did so by ensuring railway connections both for trading centres, like Leipzig, and for smaller towns and historically more isolated areas, like the Württemberg Black Forest. Narrow financial considerations and broader economic concerns created a conflict of interest between neighbouring German states. This was crucially important in inter-state railway negotiations. Governments tried to maximise the flow of railway traffic passing through their state by ensuring that the stretch of railway on their land was as long as possible, by building railways to compete directly with those of neighbouring states and by blocking the efforts of their neighbours to do the same. For instance, Baden chose to build an expensive and technically difficult thirty-nine-tunnel railway in the Black Forest from Offenburg to Singen, rather than allow the railway to cross the border into Württemberg. Likewise, Bavaria built a railway to Lake Constance in order to divert traffic from the main Württemberg railway line to Friedrichshafen. Conversely, Württemberg was concerned that the cheaper Upper Neckar Valley railway route, which passed through the Hohenzollern principalities, would enable Prussia to build a branch line that competed directly with Württemberg railways for long-distance north–south traffic. Equally, the fear that an Oldenburg railway would divert coast-bound traffic from Hanoverian railway lines was a factor behind Hanover's steadfast refusal to allow Oldenburg a railway connection. For similar reasons, Saxony successfully exerted diplomatic pressure on both Bavaria and Austria to prevent railway links with Prussia, which threatened to divert traffic from existing Saxon railways. State railway administrations also attempted to maximise benefits in other ways. The Hanoverian railway administration banned night trains and express trains in order to increase the profits made through overnight freight storage and to force passengers to spend the night in Hanover. In practice, therefore, railways emphasised the competing interests of neighbouring German states – reinforcing difference within Germany as well as furthering the process of economic integration. Indeed, the extent to which German governments defended their own interests in railway policy has laid them open to charges of 'railway particularism'. The implication behind this charge is that such particularism was influenced by the desire of German states to defend their sovereignty, as well as by economic considerations.

There is some truth in this charge, since there is little doubt that political considerations persistently dictated the railway policy of many German governments. Thus mistrust of Prussia was a key factor in Bavaria's decision to build the Leipzig–Hof railway line, rather than a Prussian alternative. Similar considerations enabled Saxony to exert diplomatic pressure on Bavaria and Austria over the Weissenfels–Gera and Reichenberg–Görlitz connections. Military and political considerations also proved decisive in determining Hanover's refusal to allow Prussia to build a railway through Oldenburg to her naval base on the Jahde.[40] Furthermore, on occasion the particularism of the Hanoverian government actually obstructed the development of a rationally planned railway network. For instance, the Hanoverian government attempted to use railways to promote the port of Gerstemünde at the expense of the Hanseatic ports. Moreover, in the 1860s the Hanoverian government's dogmatic (and principally political) opposition to private railway concessions on Hanoverian territory put paid to plans for a Paris–Hamburg railway – much to the dismay of the citizens of Osnabrück and other areas likely to benefit. Besides railway particularism of this kind, railway policy often reflected official perceptions of a state's role in German politics. In 1857 Beust stressed the importance of Saxon railway links with the Thuringian states, given the gratifying resumption of Saxony's traditionally close ties with the Ernestine lands.[41] This demonstrated the Saxon government's concern with Saxony's leadership role in Thuringia – a concern we have already seen reflected in the editorial policy of the *Leipziger Zeitung*. Meanwhile, Hanoverian railway policy was profoundly influenced by Georg V's geopolitical vision. Official assessments of Hanoverian railway construction reflected Georg's belief that Hanover was destined to wield disproportionate political influence in Germany because it controlled access to the crucial North Sea ports of Hamburg and Bremen. In 1855, for instance, Hartmann, the General Director of the Hanoverian Railways, declared optimistically that 'Hanover's geographical position is so fortunate, at least with regard to its coastline, that

[40] On this see Klaus Lampe, *Oldenburg und Preußen 1815–1871* (Hildesheim, 1972), pp. 227–47.
[41] Beust, 'Vortrag des Ministerium des Innern', 14 September 1857, HSADre Ministerium des Innern 141, Dresden–Chemnitzer Eisenbahn (378–445).

every German state must seek to form transport connections in this direction.'[42]

Besides such diplomatic considerations, governments were aware of the potential role railways could play in bringing different parts of a state together. Prussia provided the most prominent example of territorial railway policy of this kind, since linking the east and western halves of the state was an early priority in Prussian railway construction. The Hanoverian Southern Railway provided a similar link between the main body of the state and the isolated lands around Göttingen. Meanwhile, the Hanoverian Western Railway linked East Friesland and Osnabrück with the main body of the state. Such links were a less pressing concern in Saxony and Württemberg, which were both relatively geographically compact states. Nevertheless, governments in all three states appreciated the benefits of linking outlying provinces with the capital. Typically, when Georg V of Hanover listed the benefits which the Hanoverian Western Railway had brought to East Friesland, he noted that the province now enjoyed links with the capital, with other parts of Hanover and with the rest of Germany – in that order.[43] Similarly, Beust stressed the importance of the Tharandt–Freiberg railway for Saxony in domestic terms first and foremost, arguing that 'as far as *domestic* policy is concerned, *everything* is in favour of filling in the existing gaps in our railway system and linking the capital with the mountain heartlands, and furthermore this railway is very important for our foreign [railway] connections'.[44] In Württemberg, too, railway policy encouraged a process of centralisation focusing on Stuttgart. Not all were convinced of the advisability of such a policy. In 1864 the Württemberg Interior Minister, Gessler, decried earlier attempts to make Stuttgart the 'focus and centre' of the Württemberg railway network.[45] He took particular issue with the decision to make the Stuttgart station a terminus, arguing that Württemberg's railways should follow existing trade patterns, rather than creating an artificial role for Stuttgart at the heart of the state's transport network. Nevertheless, the political implications of links to the capital were obvious to members of the government and railway users alike. The Tübingen town council put it nicely when it promised King

---

[42] Hartmann, 'Bericht btr. die wegen verschiedener Anschlüsse mit Preußen in Aussicht stehenden Verhandlungen', 29 December 1855, HSAHan Dep. 103 IX 397.

[43] Georg V to Kaufmännische Deputation, Emden, 29 August 1855, HSAHan Dep. 103 IX 394.

[44] Beust, 'Vortrag des Ministerium des Innern', 14 September 1857, HSADre Ministerium des Innern 141, Dresden–Chemnitzer Eisenbahn (378–445).

[45] Gessler, 'Zu den Protokollen vom 7. u. 13. April', 24 February 1864, HSAStu E 33 559 (444).

Wilhelm of Württemberg that 'certainly, in bringing us physically closer to the capital, the railway [to Stuttgart] will fill our hearts with yet closer ties of loyalty to our royal family'.[46]

Such considerations were particularly important for railway links with border areas. Without such links, there was a risk that the inhabitants of these areas would turn away from their own state, as they became dependent on its neighbours for their transport needs. Thus the General Director of the Hanoverian railways, Hartmann, urged the government to build an independent Hanoverian railway in the Harz mountains, rather than simply a branch line from the Braunschweig–Harzburg route, which would render the Hanoverian Harz too dependent on the Braunschweig railway administration.[47] Authorities in Württemberg were particularly concerned by the threat railways posed to the allegiance of border areas, perhaps because Württemberg found it so difficult to ensure international connections. In 1857, for instance, the Württemberg Board of Trade and Industry came out in favour of a projected railway to Würzburg, even though strictly speaking the railway was not economically necessary.[48] Nevertheless the Board of Trade and Industry felt that 'it cannot be a matter for indifference to the country if individual districts are diverted from their habitual traffic with its heartlands, and if their economic interests become increasingly entangled with those of a neighbouring state'. In 1861 the Württemberg Privy Council showed similar concerns regarding the projected Upper Neckar Valley railway.[49] Continued prevarication, it argued, would divert increasing amounts of traffic from the Württemberg Black Forest on to Baden railways, encouraging the locals to see themselves 'as depending on the Baden railways'.

Local petitioners for railway links to border areas played upon these concerns by contrasting the failures of their own governments with the achievements of neighbouring states. These petitions encouraged governments to compete with each other over their readiness and ability to respond to local economic needs. In 1860, for instance, the tradesmen of Ebingen complained that the Württemberg government had failed in

[46] Tübinger Bürgerliche Collegien to H.M., 24 November 1858, HSAStu E 146/1 UF 3 (40).
[47] Hartmann, 'Bericht betr. die Anlage einer Eisenbahn von Hildesheim über Schladen nach Goslar in Verbindung mit einer Bahn von Schladen nach Halberstadt' (Vertraulich), 31 July 1861, HSAHan Hann 33c 822.
[48] Bericht der Centralstelle für Gewerbe und Handel betr. den Bau neuer Eisenbahnen, 14 January 1857, HSAStu E 146/1 5930 UF 3 (19).
[49] Geheimer Rat to H.M., Bericht betr. den Bau weiterer Eisenbahnen in der Etatsperiode 1861/4, 29 July 1961, HSAStu E 33 557 (343).

its duty by granting Prussia a telegraph link for the economically backward areas between Hechingen and Sigmaringen, without making sure
that Ebingen was properly provided for.[50] They feared that the government would be similarly out-manoeuvred by Prussia in railway negotiations with the Hohenzollern principalities. Petitioning on behalf of the
Hanoverian town of Duderstadt in 1863, Wernick voiced similar concerns. He feared that Prussian construction of a railway from Halle to
Kassel would divert trade from Duderstadt to the neighbouring Prussian
town of Worbis, which already benefited from the extensive efforts of
the Prussian government on its behalf.[51] Wernick had no compunction
about underlining the political implications of this for the inhabitants of
Duderstadt, noting that 'through the material interests which stand in
our way, the beautiful ties that link the country with its ruling house . . .
might perhaps loosen little by little, as the independent transport links
in this part of the country are to some extent subordinated to Prussia'.
Similar warnings were issued in Württemberg, after the government
failed to assure a railway connection with Baden via the Württemberg
town of Tuttlingen, rather than via the Baden town of Villingen. In 1862
Oberamtmann Holland of Spichingen wrote to King Wilhelm stressing the
need for a railway connection to Tuttlingen.[52] Besides the usual economic arguments, he described how the government's neglect of local
economic interests had encouraged the growth of political radicalism in
the area. Holland urged the government to take action, so as to correct
the view of malcontents that they 'would be better off as Badensers than
as Württembergers!' These arguments proved extremely persuasive.
Indeed, Wilhelm was initially tempted to break off diplomatic relations
with Baden over the issue, in order to demonstrate his devotion to the
Tuttlingen interest. This horrified both Hügel, the Foreign Minister, and
the Tuttlingers themselves – all of whom were aware that such a step
would merely obstruct the projected connections with Baden at
Neckarelz and Villingen, whilst bringing the Tuttlingen railway no
closer to fruition. In the event, the Württemberg government decided to
build unilaterally to Tuttlingen. This decision reflected an earlier suggestion that, given the difficulties encountered in railway negotiations
with neighbouring states, Württemberg should carry on with her

---

[50] Die Handels u. Gewerbetreibende zu Ebingen reichen eine allerunterthänigste Vorstellung u.
    Bitte in einer die hiesige Stadt u. Umgegend betreffende Eisenbahn-Angelegenheit, 1 August
    1860, HSAStu E 46 220 (47).
[51] Wernick to H. M., 22 January 1863, HSAHan Dep. 103 IX 416.
[52] Holland to E.E., 24 June 62, HSAStu E 14 870 [1862] (64).

railway construction plans alone.[53] The resulting railway network would, however, be constructed in such a way as to facilitate cross-border links when these became available.

There can be no doubt that railway construction was an intensely political and politicised issue. Nevertheless, the charge of railway particularism levelled at the German states is unfair, because particularism was the only rational policy, given the territorial divisions in Germany at the time. Railways helped to reinforce the separate identities of German states precisely because the territorial state was so fundamental for railway construction. On occasion, even political opponents of the government accepted this view. An 1859 supplement to the *Schwäbischer Merkur* argued that Württemberg could not be expected to make unilateral concessions for the greater German good in matters of railway policy. 'Some people,' observed the *Merkur*, 'will be inclined to call this narrow-mindedness and petty politics; our answer to them is that prioritising particular interests will remain necessary as long as the behaviour of some states in Germany demonstrates so clearly that they maintain these same priorities.'[54] Indeed, the *Merkur* blamed the Württemberg government for not defending its interests in railway negotiations with Baden more successfully. This was rich, coming from a newspaper which tended to castigate the government for its petty particularism. In the end, however, this kind of support for railway particularism reflected an understanding that the issue at stake was not the doctrinaire defence of state sovereignty, but rather the defence of very real economic concerns.

In fact, inter-state competition over railway construction was as much of an issue for those petitioning for railways as it was for governments. Local communities, which stood to gain most from a new railway connection, were also directly affected by the potential diversion of traditional trade flows. Consequently, railway petitions persistently spoke of the need to compete with neighbouring states in precisely these terms. In 1849 for instance, the Hanoverian inhabitants of Sarstedt and Rathe stressed the dangers of Prussian railway plans for Hanover, and wondered: 'What will be the end of it, if all these interlocking railways are completed, bypassing our country and enabling uninterrupted travel that even costs less in terms of time and money? We do not even want to think about it. Then the rot in our southern provinces will really set in.'[55]

[53] Zum Protokoll vom 13. April 1858, 13 April 1858, HSAStu E 33 557 (285).
[54] Beilage zum *Schwäbischen Merkur* No. 13, 16 January 1859.
[55] An das Ministerium des Innern, Vorstellung von Seiten mehrerer Einwohner von Sarstedt und Rathe, die Erbauung der Südbahn betr., 1 May 1849, HSAHan Hann 108 F 5.

Similarly, a railway petition from the Stuttgart Chamber of Trade and
Industry in 1856 stressed the implications of railway construction in
Switzerland, Baden and Bavaria for Württemberg.[56] The petition noted
particularly the threat these rival railways posed to Württemberg's international trade and asked: 'Can Württemberg hang back any longer . . .
in the face of this lively activity? Certainly not!' In the same year the
Saxon committee for a projected railway from Zittau to Rumburg placed
this request in the context of new threats to Saxony's traditional role in
international trade: 'our fatherland is threatened from all sides with the
loss of international trade through the construction of directly competing railways'.[57] Such railway petitions assumed that it was right and
proper for state governments to defend the economic interests of their
subjects. In this sense, railway construction encouraged popular awareness of the German states as separate economic units, despite the ways
in which railways contributed to German economic integration.

Of course, railway lobbying was deeply rooted in local concerns.
Railway construction invariably aroused strong local interest and tended
to provoke violent controversy over the proposed route. Every local community wanted to make sure that the railway passed through its own
immediate surroundings. Rival localities lobbied for railway connections
through pamphlets, newspaper articles, petitions and assemblies.[58] These
disputes could have serious political implications. In Hanover the route
of the Southern Railway added to tensions between the capital and
Hildesheim, a centre of opposition to the government in the 1850s and
1860s.[59] Hildesheimers hoped that the Southern Railway would enable
the town to regain the international trade traffic it had lost through the
construction of an earlier railway. This would only have been possible
had the railway passed through Hildesheim, not Hanover. As state
capital, Hanover was clearly better placed to assert its interests with the
government, thanks both to its symbolic importance and to closer ties
between municipal and government officials. The government decision
to build the railway equidistant from (and linked to) both cities appeared

---

[56] Handels- und Gewerbe Kammer zu Stuttgart to K. Centralstelle für Gewerbe, Anträge der
Handels- u. Gewerbe Kammer zu Stuttgart in Absicht auf die projektierten Eisenbahnlinien von
Lonsee nach Nordlingen, von Plochingen nach Reutlingen und von Mühlacker nach Pforzheim,
25 November 1856, HSAStu E 146/1 5930 UF 3.

[57] Ausschuß der provisorischen Gesellschaft zur Begründung einer Zittauer–Rumburg Elbebahn
durch seine sächsischen Mitglieder to Ministerium des Innern, 28 February 1856, HSADre
Ministerium des Innern 136. (5–22).

[58] To name but a few: between Crailsheim and Gailsdorf in Württemberg; between Hainichen and
Oederan in Saxony; and those examples given in the main body of the text.

[59] On this see Kaufhold, 'Die Anfänge des Eisenbahnbaus in Niedersachsen'.

to be a compromise. In practice, the solution ensured that the Hildesheim railway remained a branch line and that Hildesheim itself continued to be bypassed by international trade. The issue added to a general sense of grievance in Hildesheim, which had only become part of Hanover in 1815. As the state's second city, Hildesheim felt its interests had been ignored once too often. A petition with 1,790 signatories, caustically entitled 'To be or not to be, that is the question', complained that decades of what it termed 'step-motherly treatment' had caused Hildesheim to lose much of its former prosperity.[60] Discontent of this kind proved a potential source of support for opposition politicians. Württemberg politics in the 1860s was beset by a series of small-scale 'railway wars'. The dispute between Böblingen and Leonberg over the Stuttgart–Calw connection had a particularly high profile, probably because Otto Elben, editor of the *Schwäbischer Merkur*, was a passionate advocate of the Böblingen route. When Elben stood as a candidate in the *Zollparlament* elections of 1868, he naturally chose to stand in the constituency that included Böblingen.[61] Elben lost the election, but his support for the Böblingen railway may well have affected the outcome, for he won a majority in Böblingen itself, whilst Nagold, Calw and Leonberg – all situated on the rival railway route – supported his opponent.

Despite the virulence of such domestic railway disputes, the satisfaction of local railway needs depended in practice on the success of the state railway network as a whole. In 1857 Beust argued that profits from state railways should be reinvested in the railway network, enabling profitable lines to subsidise less directly profitable routes. 'The state,' he wrote, 'can and must see its state railways as a *whole*.'[62] In this sense, competition between German states for railway traffic was of crucial importance for local communities: if state railways were profitable, there would be more money available to meet local railway needs. Railway legislation in Württemberg attempted to encourage this sense of a common railway interest through draft legislation to build a comprehensive state railway network, rather than a series of individual railway lines. This was a deliberate ploy. Knapp, the Württemberg Finance Minister, was only too well aware of the difficulties faced by previous railway legislation in parliament

[60] An die allgemeine Stände-Versammlung des Königreichs Hannover: Ehrerbietigste Vorstehung von Seiten der Einwohnerschaft der Stadt Hildesheim, die Weiterführung der s.g. Süd Eisenbahn betr. 'Sein oder Nichtsein, das ist die Frage', 1,790 signatories, undated, HSAHan Hann 108 F 5.   [61] See Otto Elben, *Lebenserinnerungen*, pp. 144–50.
[62] Beust, 'Vortrag des Ministerium des Innern', 14 September 1857, HSADre Ministerium des Innern 141, Dresden–Chemnitzer Eisenbahn (378–445).

as a result of conflicting local interests. He argued that if the various districts were all assured a railway connection eventually, 'it will be easier to achieve a majority in favour of railway legislation, through which [the different parts of the country] can expect to see the fulfilment of their hopes and dreams sooner or later'.[63] In any case, railway petitions took the existence of a common state railway interest for granted. Petitions inevitably stressed both the immediate local benefits of a proposed railway and its contribution to the general well-being of the particular Fatherland. In Saxony, petitions from the poverty-stricken Erzgebirge for a Chemnitz–Annaberg railway line expressed clearly the identity of interest between local and state-wide concerns. The town council of Annaberg did not mince matters when it explained: 'The mountain districts cannot secede from the state, as the constitution prevents it; but the mountain districts must not be allowed to decay, since the whole country would participate in their decline; the mountain districts must therefore be helped to improve their lot.'[64] Such a community of interest was not present when towns and regions in different states competed for a railway connection.

In fact, the existence of a 'Fatherland' (*vaterländisch*) railway network was generally accepted and proved the basis for many railway petitions. These petitions reflected the assumption that all provinces were equally entitled to railways and that the government should therefore ensure the even distribution of railtrack within the state. Typically, a petition from the Saxon Erzgebirge spoke of the need to extend the network to '*all parts of the country* . . . so that every one of them has the possibility of increasing its prosperity as a result'.[65] Indeed, this belief was so strong that local communities even asserted a right to rail. Typically, a further petition from the Eastern Erzgebirge in 1856 spoke of the area's 'just right' to the next railway because it was the only part of Saxony not yet integrated in the rail network. The basis for such a claim was primarily financial: all areas paid the taxes, which enabled the state to build railways in the first place; consequently, all areas were entitled to benefit. Once again, the importance of the state as administrative unit is crucial here. An 1850 petition from Aurich concerning the Hanoverian Western Railway

---

[63] Knapp to H.M., betr. die weitere Ausdehnung des Eisenbahnnetzes, 6 March 1855, HSAStu E 33 557 (279).

[64] Stadtrath Annaberg to Ministerium des Innern/Finanz Ministerium, die obererzgebirgische Eisenbahn betr., 10 July 1856, HSADre Ministerium des Innern 133, Annaberg–Chemnitz (48–59).

[65] Petition to Ministerium des Innern/Finanz Ministerium, die Untersuchung einer Eisenbahnlinie betr. 16 November 1855, HSADre Ministerium des Innern 133, Annaberg–Chemnitz (32–40).

made this point clearly. The petition argued that East Frieslanders could reasonably expect to benefit from the taxes they had been paying for the past thirty-four years to build roads and railways in other parts of the state.[66] Beside this, local communities claimed the right to a railway connection as a fair means of compensating them for losses induced by railways constructed elsewhere. In 1849, for instance, the Hanoverian town of Elze claimed such losses amounted to 60–100,000 *Thaler* annually in terms of lost transit and postal traffic.[67] Elze demanded compensation in the shape of a railway connection of its own. The municipal authorities of Mantel in Württemberg combined both these arguments when petitioning for a railway from Plochingen to Tübingen in 1853. They described the catastrophic impact on the local economy of railways built elsewhere and asserted their own claim to a railway because 'we have to make good the annual loss made by the existing railways, just like those areas that enjoy the benefits they bring'.[68]

Railway petitions also demonstrated an awareness of the need for greater territorial integrity in the particular Fatherland. When describing the advantages of a particular route, petitioners tended to place the route in a domestic, national and international context. All three were important. Petitions for the Hanoverian Southern and Western Railways in the late 1840s and early 1850s repeatedly stressed the need for links between peripheral provinces and the rest of Hanover. In 1849 the Göttingen Industrial Association petitioned the Hanoverian General Estates, bemoaning the economic decline of the state's southern provinces.[69] The Industrial Association argued that this decline could best be halted by a railway link with the rest of Hanover, with the North Sea and finally with other German states. In the same year, 133 identical petitions from East Friesland regarding the projected Western Railway asserted the need for a railway link 'with the other parts of our kingdom . . . with its long-standing provinces and with the hinterland'.[70] The peculiar shape of the Hanoverian state meant that in both cases the need for such

---

[66] Vorstellung des Magistrats und Stadtverordneten Colegii zu Aurich, die Westeisenbahn betr., 7 May 1850, HSAHan Hann 108 F 6 (Südbahn) II.

[67] Bitte der Bürgervorsteher und Wahlmänner der Stadt Elze, die Südeisenbahn betr. an die Stände, 18 December 1849, HSAHan Hann 108 F 5 (Südbahn).

[68] Allerunterthänigste Bitte des Gemeinderaths und Bürgerausschüsses in Mannweil um möglichst baldige Errichtung einer Eisenbahn von Plochingen, über Nurtingen, Metzingen, Reutlingen nach Tübingen, 22 March 1853, HSAStu E 146/1 5930 UF 3 (22).

[69] An die Stände, unterzeichnete Vereine bitten um schleunige Erbauung der Südeisenbahn, 10 December 1849, HSAHan Hann 108 F 5 (Südbahn).

[70] 133 gleichlautend Petitionen aus der Provinz Ostfriesland, die Westbahn betr., 4 December 1849, HSAHan Hann 108 F 6 I (Westbahn).

ties was very great, since the southern provinces were actually separated
from the rest of Hanover and East Friesland was linked with it only by
a narrow and awkward corridor of land. Links between outlying areas
and the core of the Hanoverian state were a particular issue before
Hanover joined the *Zollverein*. The need for such links was raised less
often in later railway petitions. Conversely, in Württemberg railway petitions became increasingly concerned with domestic rail connections. In
1859 the *Schwäbischer Merkur* argued that the projected Nagold Valley
railway would reinforce links with the capital, which had gradually
become the 'centre of transport in the Fatherland'. 'It is our belief,'
opined the *Merkur*, 'that one should improve communications at home
at least as much as . . . with foreign countries.'[71] Similarly, in 1864 communities in the Württemberg Black Forest lobbied for a branch line from
Stuttgart, linking the area both with the capital and with key export
markets in neighbouring states.[72] Such demands testified in part to the
growing importance of Stuttgart, which was itself partly a consequence
of the capital's central position in the Württemberg railway network.
They also reflected the problems faced by Württemberg in acquiring
railway connections with its neighbours, despite membership of the
Zollverein. In 1862, for instance, *Stadtschuldtheiß* Schuldt of Calw described
the economic problems caused in Calw as a result of the difficulties
encountered by a projected railway link with Baden. He wrote that he
himself and many others would be quite happy with a domestic railway
from Calw to Stuttgart, but some kind of railway they must have.[73] Here
the railway particularism of neighbouring states had reinforced a sense
of Württemberg identity by default.

The importance of the territorial state as the central unit in German
railway construction was primarily reflected in political and economic
terms. Nevertheless, railways also enabled the territorial state to function
more effectively as a cultural community – an aspect of railway development that has been largely ignored by historians. As we have seen,
linking the capital with its provinces was an important goal in railway
construction. Consequently, the capital became a more important focus
for the state and its inhabitants, culturally as well as economically. These

---

[71] Beilage zum *Schwäbischen Merkur* zu No. 13, 16 January 1859.
[72] Ehrfurchtsvollste Bitte von einer Versammlung von Angehörigen des württembergischen Schwarzwaldkreises gewählten Kreises bei dem Bau weiterer Eisenbahnen, 12 December 1864, HSAStu E 14 871 [1864] (75)
[73] Stadtschultheiß Schuldt, Calw, 1 November 1862, HSAStu E 14 870 [1862] (104).

Table 6.3. *Railway passenger traffic 1851–71*[a]

	1851	1855	1860	1865	1871
Hanover					
1st Class	11,622	12,096	21,975	88,829	59,208
2nd Class	203,229	286,049	373,008	652,238	782,529
3rd Class	800,754	1,239,622	1,581,919	1,702,235	2,135,538
4th Class	7,503	38,187	n/a	n/a	1,158,321
Saxony					
1st Class	15,846	17,402	22,001	32,859	50,017
2nd Class	183,233	228,435	227,824	598,073	1,682,262
3rd Class	753,855	749,025	1,101,007	2,489,756	7,058,827
Inter-state[b]					
1st Class	4,807	6,250	8,704	244	251
2nd Class	154,761	226,980	337,970	18,849	26,638
3rd Class	748,677	823,607	1,421,716	129,491	204,015
Württemberg					
1st Class	3,159	8,570	14,894	68,634	161,435
2nd Class	233,143	450,401	617,853	1,065,697	1,459,862
3rd Class	1,516,165	1,479,712	2,409,940	3,289,969	4,613,170

Notes:

[a] Compiled from tables A.30.4, A.302.4, A.305.4, A.307.4, A.31.4; A.44.4; A.60.4 in Rainer Fremdling, Ruth Federspiel and Andreas Kunz (eds.), *Statistik der Eisenbahnen in Deutschland 1835–1989* (St. Katharinen, 1995).

[b] Passenger traffic on inter-state railways included traffic outside Saxony. These figures are for the Saxon–Bavarian, Saxon–Schlesian and Zittau–Reichenberg Railways before 1863 and for the Zittau–Reichenberg alone thereafter.

railway connections to the capital enormously increased the impact of officially sponsored cultural activities there. Railway construction therefore crucially reinforced other aspects of particularist state-building.

Table 6.3 shows the annual railway passenger figures for Hanover, Saxony and Württemberg from 1851 to 1871. It is reasonable to assume that the extent to which railways amplified the impact of state-based cultural activities reflected the relative popularity of railways in the different states. In fact, these figures demonstrate that railway use varied considerably from state to state. The size of the railway network in Hanover and Saxony was fairly similar throughout the period, yet the numbers travelling on Saxon railways were far greater than in Hanover. Indeed, Hanoverian railway use seems to have been surprisingly low. Conversely, railway use was particularly high in Württemberg before

1865, although the Württemberg railway network was relatively under-developed. By 1871, however, railway use in Saxony had rocketed and passenger frequency on the Saxon railways was far higher than in Württemberg or Hanover. Once again, this seems to reflect the socio-economic differences between the three states and, in particular, the con-trast between backward Hanover and fairly industrialised Saxony.

Equally, the figures highlight the crucial importance of third-class pas-sengers on German railways. First-class passengers formed a tiny minor-ity and the overwhelming majority of passengers were third-class in all three states. For instance, third-class ticket sales accounted for roughly four-fifths of the vast increase in Saxon railway passengers from 1865 to 1871. This is where the revolution in travelling habits really took place. Railways were not merely faster and more efficient than traditional forms of transport, they were also cheaper. Consequently, travel became a real possibility for the less well-to-do, to an extent that would have been unimaginable before the railway age. It is likely that cheaper tickets tended to be purchased for shorter journeys, and that many of those travelling third-class were making local journeys. The impact of the railway revolu-tion on passenger travel may therefore have been very different from the impact on freight transport. Rail freight enabled goods to be transported over long distances at cheap rates. This transformed trade patterns and contributed to the growth of integrated goods markets at supra-regional level. Of course, rail travel also enabled passengers to go further more cheaply, but it may not have revolutionised travelling habits in quite the same way. Certainly, more people travelled more often as a result of the railways. Probably, they also travelled further than in the past. How much further they travelled is another matter. In the initial stages of the railway era these journeys were probably more often relatively local, rather than national or international. After all, traditionally most people seldom left their immediate locality at all. In this context, even travel within the con-fines of a relatively small state betokened a significant change in travelling habits. Railways probably served first to familiarise the new travelling public with their immediate surroundings (the state), before they learnt to travel further afield. Cheap rail travel enabled the inhabitants of these states to travel more widely within them and so to know them better.

There is clear evidence that rail travel amplified the impact of state-based cultural activities in Hanover, Saxony and Württemberg. Railways rendered state museums, monuments and festivities accessible to a wider public, which was no longer restricted to inhabitants of the capital and of its immediate surroundings. For instance, the Inspector of the Historical

6.1 The Ernst August Monument in front of the main railway station in Hanover.
Note the fountains playing in the background.
Source: By permission of the British Library, J/9930.h.21

Museum in Dresden described how 'Recently, as a result of the railways and the frequent special offers for journeys at a reduced price, the museum has been much visited in particular by the relatively poorly off, who, until the advent of this means of transport, would never have been able to enjoy Dresden and its world-famous art collections'.[74] He noted that many such visitors were unable to afford the high entry prices, and recommended that the government introduce hourly guided tours at a cheaper rate, so that all could enjoy the collection.

Governments were certainly aware that railways created a larger audience for cultural activities and representational displays. Tellingly, the Ernst August Monument Committee decided to place the monument in the centre of the *Bahnhofplatz*, a square in front of the central station in Hanover. The new monument would at once highlight

---

[74] Bütten to E.E., 15 December 1862, HSADre Ministerium f. Volksbildung 19243:1 (Historisches Museum) (121–2).

Ernst August's role in bringing the railway to Hanover and beautify the area around the railway station itself, so as to render it all the more impressive to new arrivals. The decision prompted a series of other suggestions for improving the aspect of the square itself, notably by installing ornamental fountains. This plan proved both expensive and impractical. Instead, a compromise was suggested, whereby the fountains would only flow for between one and four hours daily – in the afternoon between one and four o'clock, when the most important trains arrived in Hanover.[75]

Nowhere did the government exploit railways more effectively for such ends than in Württemberg. The role of railways in making the *Cannstatter Volksfest* a genuinely state-wide celebration has already been touched upon. During the 1850 festival train tickets were sold in advance, with special booths set up in Cannstatt to sell them. Stuttgart–Cannstatt services ran every ten minutes during the festival, with night trains from more distant parts of Württemberg. In 1852, 23,000 train tickets were sold over four days in Cannstatt; in 1864 the figure was 34,000 over two days.[76] In 1867, 308 extra trains ran between Stuttgart and Cannstatt, over and above the usual fifty-two. Besides transporting visitors to Cannstatt, the railways also enabled the population to participate more fully in the agricultural side of the festival. In 1862 the Württemberg government launched a scheme whereby prize-winning livestock could be transported free of charge on the state railways. The scheme encouraged farmers from more distant parts of Württemberg to compete, which in turn enhanced the character of the *Volksfest* as 'a general state festival'.[77] One contemporary, Heinrich Ebner, described the role of rail in bringing the Württembergers to their *Volksfest* thus: 'you might say that with every newly opened railway line in the country the incredible popularity of the festival grows still further . . . The achievements of the railway administration are huge. Every train spews out hundreds upon hundreds of people.'[78]

It is worth noting that railways could also increase the impact of government propaganda. Hugo Häpe, the official responsible for the *Dresdner Journal*, suggested in 1858 that the newspaper should be distributed in popular public places and that restaurants in state railway stations

[75] Minutes, 18 March 1860, HSAHan Dep. 103 XXVIII 626.
[76] See Stroheker and Willmann, *Cannstatter Volksfest*, p. 98.
[77] Linden to H.M., Anbr. betr. die Erhöhung des Etatssatzes des landwirtschaftlichen Festes in Cannstatt (genehmigt), 24 December 1857, HSAStu E 10 79.
[78] Cited after Stroheker and Willmann, *Cannstatter Volksfest*, p. 99.

should be obliged to subscribe.[79] Such restaurants were particularly important, Häpe argued, because they were frequented by a public drawn from all walks of life and from the entire surrounding area. Furthermore, newspapers were likely to receive closer attention here than in other public places. Those waiting for trains had nothing better to do than read the newspapers lying about the station, which then provided something for passengers to discuss en route.

Finally, governments also attempted to exploit the symbolic capital of railways more directly. Railways were portrayed as a gift from the King to his people for posterity. Thus in 1852 the Director of the *Nicolaischule* in Leipzig described the Saxon monarch as 'Friedrich August, who will be known to posterity as the builder of railways'.[80] As we have seen, the Ernst August Monument in the Hanoverian *Bahnhofplatz* was intended to make precisely the same point.[81] More commonly, the ceremonial opening of different sections of a railway line emphasised the role of the monarch in bringing the railway to his people. Thus in 1853 the opening of the Stuttgart–Bruchsal railway coincided with Wilhelm's birthday and the *Cannstatter Volksfest*; indeed, attending the latter formed an integral part of the celebrations. Local communities understood this point very well. In 1862 the Württemberg finance ministry reported to Wilhelm that the towns along the Heilbronn–Hall railway were keen to express their thanks for the new railway by celebrating what was 'for their region the important and beneficial event of their entry into the Fatherland's railway network'.[82] Various dignitaries were invited to attend the occasion and special trains ran in order to maximise the impact of the event, enabling a wider public to enjoy a free ride. Linden later reported that the event was a great success, and that 'high and low made haste to express their gratitude to His Majesty the King'.[83] The association of monarch and railway was perpetuated by the role of railway stations in public festivities. As the railway network expanded, monarchs increasingly travelled by train when visiting different parts of

---

[79] H. Häpe to Ministerium des Innern, 20 November 1858, HSADre Ministerium des Innern 9511 (173–5).

[80] Director and Rector der Nicolaischule, Leipzig to Ministerium des Cultus u. öffentlichen Unterrichts, 19 May 1852, HSADre Ministerium f. Volksbildung 10290 (41).

[81] See Ernst August Monument Committee to H.M., 21 January 1858, HSAHan Dep. 103 xxvIII 626. Blessing notes a similar process of association between King and railway in Bavaria, with the construction of royal monuments outside train stations, as in Lindau. See Blessing, *Staat und Kirche in der Gesellschaft*, p. 129.

[82] Finanz Ministerium to H.M., die Eröffnung der Eisenbahn zwischen Heilbronn und Hall (genehmigt), 29 July 1862, HSAStu E 14 870 [1862] (72).

[83] Linden to H.M., 4 August 1862, HSAStu E 14 (870) [1862] (76).

6.2 Celebrating the opening of the Dresden–Prague railway, April, 1851. This print formed part of a commemorative collection, published to mark the occasion. Other prints depicted beauty spots in the Elbe valley, through which the railway passed.

Source: Sächsisches Hauptstaatsarchiv, Loc. 37481, No. 144, s.64

their kingdoms. The railway station became central to the festivities that attended such a visit because the monarch usually arrived there. The station was invariably suitably decorated, and welcoming ceremonies tended to take place in the railway station and in the public space in front of it. Indeed, the ceremonial role of railway stations was such that the phrase 'ein großer Bahnhof' (a big railway station) came to refer to this kind of red-carpet treatment.

Besides underlining the association between railways and the ruling monarch, railway opening ceremonies occasionally acquired more specifically political connotations – either as expressions of solidarity with neighbouring states or simply as expressions of loyalty to the regime. Probably the most striking example of the former was the opening of the Dresden–Prague railway in April 1851. This was a moment of acute political tension in Germany, not least because of Austria's proposals for a central European customs union. Moreover, a conference of German governments debating the shape of post-revolutionary Germany was actually taking place in Dresden at the time. Consequently, the governments of Saxony and Austria seized the opportunity provided by the opening of the Saxon-Bohemian railway in order to demonstrate the brotherhood between Austria and the rest of Germany. The opening of the railway became an unusually grand occasion, and all the Confederal delegates present in Dresden were invited to attend. The festivities lasted two days. A ceremonial train left the Dresden station early on Sunday morning for Prague, passing through a long succession of festively decorated Bohemian villages and triumphal arches attended by the usual musical bands (playing the Saxon and Austrian anthems), members of the National Guard, schoolchildren and white-clad maidens, before stopping for breakfast on the other side of the border. Here the guests visited an exhibition of Bohemian industry and attended a short Catholic service, followed by a military salute. On arriving in Prague, guests attended a ceremonial dinner followed by a play at the city theatre, specially written for the occasion. The next day saw a similar succession of events in reverse: festive welcomes for the train in Saxony, a warm welcome from the Dresden crowds, visits to the Saxon royal collections and a gala performance in the Royal Opera House. The participation of high-ranking royals from both states in these festivities indicates their political importance for both Saxony and Austria, and contrasts starkly with the opening of the Cologne–Antwerp railway in Prussia some years earlier, which Prussian royals had declined to attend.[84] Moreover, the festivities themselves stressed at every turn the symbolism of the railway as a bond between the two German states. For instance, the play presented in Prague portrayed the wedding of a Bohemian peasant lad to a Saxon girl. The Genius of Progress attended the wedding and explained to the assembled guests the symbolic significance of the railway.[85] A Prologue specially written for the Gala performance at the Dresden Opera House (and recited by Saxonia herself) made the same point more succinctly:

> Two peoples springing from the same tree,
> We share a source of life and security.
> Thanks to this new tie, once more we're as one,
> Separation and distance are now overcome.[86]

The Saxons and Austrians wished these festivities to demonstrate the union of Austria with the rest of Germany and the potential of economic ties, like railways, as the basis for *Großdeutschland*. The point was made by the *Illustrierte Zeitung*, which noted how the railway assured further ties between the German peoples: 'The material and mutually beneficial interests of the [German] states and tribes [*Stämme*] will be the basis of a new German Empire, which is not artificially constructed but instead grows strong and free on its own terms.'[87]

Emphasising the role of the monarch in railway construction acquired different political connotations in the 1860s, when the German question became increasingly pressing. Thus the Württemberg Interior Minister, Linden, was much gratified by the loyal toasts to King and country made during a feast attended by 4–500 guests, which was held to celebrate the opening of the Heilbronn–Hall railway in 1862. Linden reported to King Wilhelm that the toast proposed by *Stadtschultheiß* Klett of Heilbronn in particular had shown the gathering to be wholly free from any trace of '*Kleindeutsch*-ism'. In their different ways, both Klett and Linden recognised the role of railways in reinforcing local loyalties to the state. This was still more explicitly acknowledged by the Württemberg Foreign Minister, Varnbüler, in 1866. Varnbüler's interest in railways was long-standing, and he had made responsibility for

---

[84] For details on the oppositional nature of these celebrations see Gerhard Stahr, 'Kommerzielle Interessen und provinzielles Selbstbewußtsein. Die Eröffnungsfeiern der Rheinischen Eisenbahn 1841 und 1843' in Hettling and Nolte (eds.), *Bürgerliche Feste*, 37–62.

[85] J. C. Hickel, *Festspiel zur Feier der Eröffnung der Prag–Dresdner Eisenbahn am 6. April 1851. Aufgeführt auf dem Königl. ständ. Theater zu Prag* (Prague, 1851).

[86] Prolog: Saxonia auf den Wappenschlag gestützt, 8 April 1851, HSADre Finanzarchiv, Rep. LVII Sect. 1, No. 144, Loc. 37,481 (61).   [87] *Illustrierte Zeitung*, No. 408, 26 April 1851.

railway policy a condition of taking office. In 1866 Varnbüler made it plain that he drew a clear connection between railway construction in Württemberg and the government's foreign policy worries. Public opinion in Württemberg was, he wrote, at such a pitch that he had but to raise the state flag for the whole population to rally round the government: 'and when the time comes, I will fly the flag. In the meantime I shall keep building railways and wait and see what happens.'[88]

Historians have always accepted the role of particularism in German railway construction before unification.[89] Nevertheless, railway particularism is usually studied in the context of inter-governmental railway negotiations, as a reflection of government concerns over state sovereignty during this period and perhaps as an instrument of economic policy. Consequently, railway particularism is seen to have contributed to diplomatic friction within Germany during this period, but not really to have undermined the process of national unification, fostered by economic integration, the *Zollverein* and railway construction. This analysis presents four problems.

First, railway construction did not encourage economic integration within the *Zollverein* alone. Railways also improved communications with Austria and with non-German states such as Belgium, France and Switzerland, encouraging processes of international as well as national economic integration. These international railways were symbolically important too. The opening ceremonies of railways such as the Dresden–Prague link in 1851 frequently stressed ties of brotherhood between the nations involved. More surprisingly, a similar theme emerged during the ceremonial opening of the Cologne–Antwerp railway in 1843, which stressed the similarities between Belgium and the Rhineland, now linked by the railway.

Secondly, railway particularism was not restricted to state governments. Territorial fragmentation and the predominance of state railways amongst the *Mittelstaaten* meant that local communities looked to their governments to cater for their railway needs. In fact, the particularism of state governments in railway negotiations was rooted in the state's economic interests. These interests reflected the concerns of local communities, who stood to gain most from the coming of rail and to lose most if traffic was diverted elsewhere. Railway petitions demonstrate

---

[88] 14 January 1866. Cited in Hellwag, *Varnbüler und die deutsche Frage*, p. 76.
[89] See Mester, 'Partikularismus der Schiene'; Völkel, 'Einigkeit und Freiheit'; Ziegler, *Eisenbahnen und Staat*, pp. 26–36.

clearly that local communities were fully aware of the extent to which they depended on the state government to defend their interests. Indeed, they expected the government to do just this. Furthermore, local communities were deeply affected by the outcome of railway negotiations, even where they were not directly implicated. The role of the state in financing German railways created a knock-on effect, whereby profitable state railways funded further construction. If competition from railways in other states led to declining profits, the expansion of the state railway network was delayed and local communities had to wait longer for railway connections. This encouraged an identity of interest between local and state railway concerns. The knock-on effect was more important in Hanover and Württemberg than it was in Saxony, since state railways were infinitely more important in these two states. Thus inter-governmental railway negotiations did not merely contribute to diplomatic friction, they also highlighted the opposing interests of different state communities. Railway construction did not merely reinforce the importance of territorial borders during this period. It also reinforced popular awareness of the state as a meaningful unit in economic policy.

Thirdly, territorial fragmentation and railway particularism partly determined the shape of the German railway network. The polycentric nature of the German network at national level reflected the construction of relatively centralised networks at state level. Similarly, railway connections between the provinces and state capitals encouraged integration processes at state level, although connections between the various German states and cities also encouraged integration at national level. In Württemberg in particular this contributed to a reorientation of state provinces towards the capital. The links between the capital and its provinces were partly an expression of governmental state-building concerns, but also reflected the desires of many local communities. Furthermore, in all three states these developments reinforced the impact of state-based cultural activities, making the state a more viable cultural community. In Württemberg, for example, railways contributed to the enormous popularity of the *Cannstatter Volksfest*. In this sense, railway construction was an indispensable adjunct to particularist cultural policy.

Fourthly, despite the radical social, economic and financial aspects of railway construction, railways acted as a politically stabilising factor in many German states, at least in the short term. The popularity of railways contributed to the popularity of state governments, as Varnbüler

Table 6.4. *Railway stock holdings* (Anlagekapital) *in state railway companies 1851–71 (in 1000 Marks)*[a]

	1851	1855	1860	1865	1871
Hanover	50.835	78.065	135.249	165.749	174.297
Saxony State railways	16.32	16.034	16.796	53.825	223.438
Saxon-Bavarian	41.976	43.474	43.861	n/a	n/a
Saxon-Silesian	19.164	20.569	21.184	n/a	n/a
Württemberg	43.500	544.858	68.972	128.512	266.747

Note:

[a] Taken from tables A.44.1; A:30.1, A:302.1, A:305.1; A.60.1 in Fremdling, Federspiel and Kunz (eds.), *Statistik der Eisenbahnen in Deutschland*. The Saxon state had subscribed ¼ of the Saxon-Bavarian railway company stock and ⅓ of the Saxon-Silesian stock. Statistics for these two companies were recorded separately until 1863.

was only too well aware. Local communities were desperate for railway connections, and recognised that their governments were responsible for bringing this blessing to the people. In Saxony and Württemberg governments gained credit for their active railway policy. The situation was more complicated in Hanover. Here the government appeared to be motivated by unrealistic and narrowly particularist concerns in railway policy, such as the desire to promote the Hanoverian port of Geerstemünde over Hamburg and Bremen. Railway policy was yet one more area where the conservative Hanoverian regime failed to meet the needs of its people. In Hanover, therefore, railways were a fruitful source of opposition propaganda, and opposition newspapers made much of the government's shortcomings in blocking the Paris–Hamburg railway project. Despite the anomalous situation in Hanover, governments in all three states attempted to exploit the symbolic capital of railways. Railway opening ceremonies stressed the role of the monarch in railway construction. The location of the Ernst August Monument in front of the railway station in Hanover was a similar attempt to capitalise on the popularity of railways.

State railway finance also had an important impact on the political climate in each state. Railway construction led governments to take out large state loans. Table 6.4 shows the capital invested in state railway companies from 1851 to 1871. This gives some idea of the sums involved – which were huge. In all three states such loans had to be approved by representative institutions. Railway construction therefore strengthened the hand of the opposition against the governments. At the same time, however, the general support for railway construction promoted collaboration between government and opposition over the issue, perhaps contributing to a more constructive political environment within the German states. In Prussia, for instance, the government's willingness to meet the economic demands of business elites in the 1860s reduced the political complaints of hitherto fairly vocal businessmen to a minimum, even at the height of the Prussian constitutional conflict.[90]

There can be no doubt that railways played a crucial role in fostering economic integration and encouraging the creation of national markets in Germany. They therefore made a crucial contribution to the unification process. Equally, national and international rail links were invariably the first priority of German states in railway construction, because the small size of most states meant that railway construction without such connections was a pointless activity. Ultimately, however, the impact of railway construction in Germany remained ambivalent. Whilst railways clearly undermined the economic autonomy of individual states, they also provided a vital source of support for German governments and an important area of consensus between conservative regimes and their liberal opponents.

[90] See Brophy, *Capitalism, politics and railroads in Prussia*, pp. 155–62.

CHAPTER SEVEN

Imagined identities

What did it mean to be a Hanoverian, a Saxon or a Württemberger in the decades before German unification? In 1865 the *Budissiner Nachrichten*, a newspaper with close ties to the Saxon government, explained why it believed that the Saxons had no reason 'to yearn for Great Powerdom': 'We have a constitutional life, the like of which neither Austria nor Prussia enjoys even now. As a result, concord reigns between King and people. We have prosperity, low taxes and healthy finances . . . Higher political and cultural goals are not neglected here.'[1] This, in a nutshell, summed up the case made by government publicists for the continued independence of the German *Mittelstaaten*. Propaganda in the *Mittelstaaten* took many forms: newspaper articles, *Volksschule* readers, school history books, state historical museums and monarchic monuments. Ultimately, however, the message conveyed through these different media was extraordinarily consistent. Obviously, different governments tailored their propaganda to the historical and political traditions of the state in question. After all, the appeal of the *Mittelstaaten* was rooted primarily in their particularity – in the assumption that it meant something different to be a Hanoverian than a Saxon or a Württemberger. Even so, the terms in which these three governments presented their case were strikingly similar. Like the *Budissiner Nachrichten*, official publicists in all three states made much of the constitutional liberties, economic prosperity and cultural achievements of the individual German states. In this sense, government propaganda projected not merely a specifically *Mittelstaat* identity, but also a vision of the German nation that left room for these more particular identities.

The German states did not exist in a vacuum and German governments were well aware of this. They readily understood their states to be

---

[1] *Budissiner Nachrichten*, 11 June 1865. Cited after Jordan, *Die öffentliche Meinung in Sachsen*, pp. 14–15. This newspaper was edited for many years by Kunath, who had close ties with the *Dresdner Journal* and played an important role in coordinating the *Amtsblatt* initiative.

267

component parts of a collective German nation and its concomitant political form, the German Confederation. Tellingly, internal government documents in Hanover, Saxony and Württemberg seldom, if ever, used the word 'national' when referring to the state in question. In this sense, the vocabulary of statehood in these three states differed strikingly from that of Bavaria, where Max II and his advisers talked of fostering 'Bavarian national feeling'. Instead, Hanoverians, Saxons and Württembergers preferred to use the word 'vaterländisch' – literally, 'of the Fatherland' – to describe their homelands. The difference points to a surprisingly realistic assessment of independent statehood in these three states, reflecting their smaller size and more modest political aspirations. Unlike Max II of Bavaria, their monarchs and governments did not seek to compete with German identity on equal terms. Rather, propaganda in these states accepted the interdependence of German and particularist identities and interests. Consequently, the Kings of Hanover, Saxony and Württemberg saw no contradiction in sponsoring local historical societies, monuments and museums on the one hand, and in supporting fund-raising drives for nationalist initiatives like the Hermann Monument on the other. Equally, official newspapers in these states always accorded German news special status, either by presenting it as a separate section in its own right, or by placing it at the head of the foreign news section. Special treatment of this kind acknowledged the intimate relationship between domestic and national politics in Germany. Indeed, the high profile given to German news in official newspapers during the 1860s testifies to a growing awareness of the national context of domestic politics on the part of German governments, which was reflected in greater numbers of column inches and changes of format.

In many ways, however, these changes simply reinforced existing trends. Government propaganda had always assessed particularist politics and history in terms of the German context. Official newspapers habitually described their states as the most liberal *in Germany*, their inhabitants as the most prosperous, the best educated or the most loyal *in Germany*, their monarchs as the wisest and most respected *in Germany*. Typical of this phenomenon was the claim made by an official obituary of Ernst August which appeared in the *Hannoversche Zeitung*, that 'in Germany they envied the Hanoverians, who lived under the blessed sceptre of King Ernst August'.[2] Similar turns of phrase were equally

---

[2] Cited after Malortie, *König Ernst August*, pp. 198–9.

common in school books. Thus the Protestant *Volksschule* reader in Württemberg described the Münster in Ulm as the tallest church in Germany, and Lake Constance as 'the King of German lakes'.[3] Indeed, school books usually presented Germany as the primary frame of reference for studying and understanding the particular Fatherland and its past. For instance, Ludwig Uhland's poem 'The richest prince', which appeared in many Württemberg school books, told how Eberhard the Bearded successfully persuaded his fellow German rulers that he was the richest prince in Germany.[4] Moreover, school history books usually made a point of stressing the role of past monarchs in shaping national developments, as well as the history of a particular state. The only exception here was Augustus the Strong, Elector of Saxony and King of Poland, referred to in Pastor Stichart's 'The Kingdom of Saxony and its Princes' as a 'truly European' prince.[5] Clearly Stichart considered the exception to be worthy of note. By and large, the authors of particularist history books were more interested in German affairs. When the court archivist Schaumann wrote a history of Hanover and Braunschweig for use in Hanoverian schools, he presented the medieval Welf rulers as prime movers in a conflict of principle with the centralising aspirations of imperialism, describing Henry the Proud, for instance, as 'champion of the secular princes against absolute imperial power'.[6] Similarly, in his account of the reign of Elector Moritz of Saxony, Stichart wrote that it was Moritz's mission to oppose the forces of the Counter Reformation backed by the Holy Roman Emperor, 'to revive German religious and political liberty and to create a firm foundation for it'.[7] Both these assessments tacitly assumed that Germany, not Europe, provided the proper political context for patriotic state history. Interestingly, both also represented imperial power as a potential threat to German liberties, and pointed to the rulers of the smaller German states as the best defence against this.

Government propaganda in newspapers and school books did not, therefore, question the German character or vocation of the *Mittelstaaten*. Nor did propaganda question the desirability of German unity, at least in principle – quite the contrary. Patriotic school books never failed to preach the virtues of German unity or to underline the disastrous consequences

---

[3] *Lesebuch für die evangelischen Volksschulen Württembergs*, p. 153, p. 164.   [4] Ibid., p. 352.
[5] Ibid.; Stichart, *Königreich Sachsen und seine Fürsten* p. 238.
[6] Schaumann, *Geschichte der Lande Hannover und Braunschweig*, p. 78. But see the whole chapter 'Die Welfen in Deutschland bis zum Tode Heinrich des Löwen', pp. 73–104.
[7] Stichart, *Königreich Sachsen und seine Fürsten*, p. 157.

of internal strife. Typically, the two Württemberg *Volksschule* readers
taught that since Germany lacked firm geographical borders, the safety of
Germans lay 'in sticking firmly together, in their unity and in their moral
force'.[8] Indeed, the wording in both books was almost identical on this
point. Moreover, the Catholic reader went further when it provided a
graphic warning against internal divisions by describing how Napoleon
had marched on Prussia in 1806 'after he had broken up the unity of
Germany and won over the lesser German princes to his side'.[9]
Schaumann's 'History of the Lands of Hanover and Braunschweig' made
the same point when it lamented the 'prime ill of our Fatherland . . . division . . . through jealousy and enmity'.[10] Schaumann added that this
national characteristic was replicated, on a smaller scale, in the histories
of Hanover and the other German states. More concretely, government
newspapers in Saxony at least agreed that German unity was a desirable
goal and readily endorsed nationalist aspirations. In 1859, for instance, the
Leipziger Zeitung rejoiced that for the first time in years the German people
had stood 'all together as One Man'.[11] Two years later, the same newspaper acknowledged that the longing for greater German unity was in
many ways justified.[12] Yet this kind of language certainly did not amount
to unqualified support for German unity. Rather, *Mittelstaat* propaganda
consistently distinguished between the unity of the German peoples on
the one hand, and the centralisation of the German states on the other.
Whereas the former was desirable, the latter was emphatically rejected,
reflecting the official view that unity in diversity was the predominant
characteristic of German nationhood.

This vision of Germanness owed much to popular awareness of the
role of the German tribes or peoples (*Stämme*) in German history, and
their continued contemporary relevance. At this time, the belief was
widespread that the German nation consisted of various sub-national
groups, each of which claimed descent from ancient German tribes like
the Franconians and the Allemannen. These ideas provided fertile soil
for particularist propaganda in the *Mittelstaaten*, each of which was commonly identified with a particular *Stamm*. Often, these identifications
were fairly tenuous, since the boundaries of *Stamm* and state seldom
coincided. For instance, the area associated with the Franconians was

[8] *Lesebuch für die evangelischen Volksschulen Württembergs*, p. 195; *Lesebuch für die katholischen Volksschulen
Württembergs* (Stuttgart, 1862), p. 183.   [9] Ibid., p. 380.

[10] Schaumann, *Geschichte der Lande Hannover und Braunschweig*, p. 8.

[11] *Leipziger Zeitung*, No. 72, 25 March 1859, 'Rückblick auf die Landkarte von Deutschland'.

[12] *Leipziger Zeitung*, No. 164, 12 July 1861, 'Das revolutionäre und conservative Prinzip in Europa IV'.

located on the border between Bavaria and Württemberg, and the Franconians were not exclusively associated with either state. Broadly speaking, however, Württemberg was seen as the homeland of the Swabians, Hanover as that of the Lower Saxons and Saxony as that of the Saxons. In practice, the word 'Stamm' was used fairly loosely to denote either the various German peoples or the inhabitants of the various German states, depending on the context. Government propaganda readily exploited the slippage between the two ideas. An article in the Württemberg *Staats-Anzeiger* comparing the historic achievements of 'that self-same country' with those of 'the other German *Stämme*' typifies this kind of linguistic confusion.[13]

Identifying the state with a particular *Stamm* in this way enabled government propaganda to portray that state as something more than a random dynastic unit. Indeed, the *Stämme* even fulfilled this function for members of the political opposition, who sought to downplay the central role of the monarchy in these states. Thus in 1851 Franz Wilhelm Miquel, brother of the prominent National Liberal politician Johannes Miquel, called for Lower Saxon history to be taught in schools as an alternative to the kind of dynastic history children normally learnt. In fact, of course, Hanover, Saxony and Württemberg *were* random dynastic units. Ironically, therefore, the most convincing way of linking state and *Stamm* was through the dynasty itself. Tellingly, the most common adjective used to describe the German dynasties in government propaganda was 'ancestral' (*angestammt*). Equally, government propaganda sought to portray contemporary German states and their political institutions as a product of the organic development of *Stamm* and dynasty. In 1861, for instance, the Württemberg *Staats-Anzeiger* presented the sovereignty of the *Mittelstaaten* as the joint achievement of princes and people, claiming 'These governments have been supported by their people for centuries in the struggle for their independence.'[14] Similarly, the *Neue Hannoversche Zeitung* argued that the customs and laws of the different *Stämme* were firmly rooted in their own soil and had been 'reflected in the dynasties and constitutions' of the individual German states.[15] Admittedly, propaganda in Hanover, Saxony and Württemberg never claimed that the *Stämme* were actually nations. Nevertheless, propaganda did claim that the *Stämme* possessed at least some of the attributes of nationhood, since each *Stamm* was supposedly united by a shared

[13] *Staats-Anzeiger für Württemberg*, No. 167, 14 July 1850, 'Unsere Lage III'.
[14] *Staats-Anzeiger für Württemberg*, No. 30, 5 February 1861.
[15] *Neue Hannoversche Zeitung*, No. 499, 27 October 1859, 'Die deutsche Bundesreform'.

past and a historic destiny, which found expression in particular traditions and in a sense of common identity.[16]

Again and again, government newspapers picked up on this belief
when they argued that centralisation (in the shape of a unitary nation
state) was contrary to the ingrained particularities of the *Stämme* and
consequently doomed to failure. In 1850, for instance, the Württemberg
Staats-Anzeiger warned that the 'centralisation of authority' should not be
allowed to undermine the peculiarities of the *Stämme* or the traditional
institutions of the German states.[17] Equally, in 1859 the *Neue Hannoversche
Zeitung* declared the German to be an 'enemy of centralisation, he wants
to observe his own morals at home, his own customs in his towns and his
own law in his country'.[18] Like the *Staats-Anzeiger*, the *Neue Hannoversche
Zeitung* claimed that these laws and customs reflected the separate origins
of the different *Stämme*. Similarly, in 1861 the *Leipziger Zeitung* asserted the
right of every German *Stamm* to its own language, customs and 'tribal
characteristics'. In fact, government newspapers in the *Mittelstaaten*
maintained that the German question could be resolved only by endors-
ing rather than undermining the independence of the *Stämme*. Typically,
Oswald Marbach, editor of the *Leipziger Zeitung* in 1850, argued that
Germany could overcome its problems only 'if every German *Stamm* . . .
is true to itself, does not abandon its own interests and independently
unites with the greater Whole'.[19] On one level, this kind of reasoning
was simply a reformulation of well-worn conservative arguments against
radical change, which maintained that only traditional laws and institutions could fulfil the needs of a specific society and properly reflect its
organic evolution over centuries. On another level, this reasoning was
perhaps the most extreme expression of a certain kind of German
nationalism.[20] During the Napoleonic era, nationalists like Fichte had
self-consciously rejected the claims of French political thought to
provide a generally applicable model for political and social reform.
Instead, they maintained the importance of national difference, by

[16] For a discussion of these ideas with particular reference to Hanover and Lower Saxony, see
Dieter Lent's excellent article 'Das Niedersachsenbewußtsein im Wandel der Jahrhunderte' in
Carl Haase (ed.), *Niedersachsen. Territorien – Verwaltungseinheiten – geschichtliche Landschaften*
(Göttingen, 1971), pp. 27–50.

[17] *Staats-Anzeiger für Württemberg*, No. 6, 6 January 1850, 'Zur Geschichte der Verfassungsberath-
enden Versammlung III.'

[18] *Neue Hannoversche Zeitung*, No. 499, 27 October 1859, 'Die deutsche Bundesreform'.

[19] *Leipziger Zeitung*, No. 67, 8 March 1850.

[20] On the parallels between romantic nationalism and particularism in Germany, see Irmline Veit-
Brause, 'Particularism: a paradox of cultural nationalism?' in J. C. Eade (ed.), *Romantic
Nationalism in Europe* (Canberra, 1983) pp. 33–46.

arguing that only German institutions could express the unique character of the German nation because only they could reflect its cultural and
historic traditions. Similarly, after 1815 particularists rejected the claims
of German nationalists to provide an acceptable political solution to the
German question, arguing that political diversity was fundamental to
the preservation of the traditional German laws, customs and liberties
embodied in the *Stämme*. The creation of a unitary nation state was, they
believed, the first step on the road to centralisation, standardisation and
authoritarian government. As the *Staats-Anzeiger* put it in 1866: '[the
question is] whether our situation develops in a spirit of federal liberty
or unitary and despotic absorption'.[21]

Ultimately, however, the force of this argument lay not in its appeal to
the age-old traditions of the German *Stämme*, but rather in its contemporary implications. In practice, by the 1860s talk of the 'traditional' institutions and laws of the *Mittelstaaten* and their respective *Stämme* referred
above all to their constitutions, which tended to be significantly more progressive than the constitutions of Prussia or Austria. Indeed, by 1866 this
contrast was so glaring that even Hanoverian newspapers felt able to draw
it to the attention of their readers. In March 1866, for instance, the
Hildesheimer Allgemeine Zeitung argued that the Hanoverian Estates were
better off than their Prussian counterpart because 'our constitution is
thirty years older than that of the Prussians'.[22] Two months later the
Hildesheimer Zeitung claimed that the Welfs were more popular than liberals liked to think, because Hanoverians realised that 'the incorporation of
Hanover into Bismarck's Prussia would lead to no improvement in the
domestic situation, but rather to a deterioration under Prussian military
absolutism and the pressures of high taxation'.[23] By and large, however,
the coups of 1837 and 1855 made it hard for the Hanoverian press to lay
claim to a tradition of constitutional government. Consequently,
Hanoverian newspapers preferred to find fault with Prussia rather than
defend the Hanoverian situation as such. Propaganda in Saxony and
Württemberg went far further than this, arguing that the *Mittelstaaten* were
the true home of German liberty. On one level, this argument picked up
on historical traditions about the role of rulers like Henry the Proud and

[21] *Staats-Anzeiger für Württemberg*, No. 79, 4 April 1866, 'Das Interesse des Volks an der preußisch-
österreichischen Streitfragen'.
[22] *Hildesheimer Allgemeine Zeitung*, No. 60, 13 March 1866, 'Die nächste Session der Ständeversammlung'.
[23] *Hildesheimer Zeitung*, No. 123, 29 May 1866. Cited in Tagesberichte, May 1866, HSAHan Dep. 103
IX 296 (May–June 1866).

Moritz of Saxony in resisting the tyrannical urges of earlier German emperors. More immediately, however, government publicists in both states maintained that the *Mittelstaaten* had proved consistently more responsive to liberal demands than either of the two great powers. When the Württemberg *Staats-Anzeiger* maintained in 1863 that constitutionalism had now been accepted as a part of German political life, it added that 'In this respect the *Mittelstaaten* have made the greatest advances.'[24] Equally, in 1866 the *Staats-Anzeiger* claimed that the German *Mittelstaaten* enjoyed a degree of freedom second to none, because they 'are not so small as to decline into patriarchal barbarism, nor so big that they cannot do justice to individual needs and desires'.[25] Government newspapers in Saxony made very similar claims. In 1859 the *Dresdner Journal* even argued that the German Confederation was partly responsible for this happy state of affairs, since it had protected the inhabitants of the *Mittelstaaten* from the authoritarian inclinations of their more powerful neighbours: 'in the individual sovereign states political liberty developed along constitutional lines, and the great powers, which were at the time very opposed to this system, could do nothing to hamper this development'.[26] The message from official newspapers to their readers in both states was clear: abandon the cosy world of independent statehood at your peril.

In itself, this message was primarily negative, but governments in both Saxony and Württemberg also laid claim to a more positive constitutional tradition of their own. This tradition was most pronounced in Württemberg, where the origins of parliamentary government could be traced back to the concessions made by Duke Ulrich at Tübingen in 1514. The two Württemberg *Volksschule* readers made much of the Tübingen Agreement in particular and the state's relatively progressive constitutional traditions in general. Thus the Protestant *Volksschule* reader also underlined the historic liberties of the Württemberg peasantry, who had the right to be represented in the Estates, adding that this was 'something which was accorded peasants in many other countries only much later, or not at all'.[27] This claim was clearly made with the book's readership in mind, since in a predominantly rural society the *Volksschulen* were inevitably dominated by peasant children. Equally, official newspapers did not hesitate to exploit Württemberg's constitutional past for contemporary

---

[24] *Staats-Anzeiger für Württemberg*, No. 60, 13 March 1863, 'Deutschland: Zur Verständigung in der deutschen Frage II'.
[25] *Staats-Anzeiger für Württemberg*, No. 63, 15 March 1866, 'Die Aufgabe der Mittelstaaten'.
[26] *Dresdner Journal*, No. 240, 16 October 1859. 'Rückblicke auf das deutsche Kaiserthum II'.
[27] *Lesebuch für die evangelischen Volksschulen Württembergs*, p. 347.

political purposes through articles like 'A piece of Tübingen's history from the year 1514', which appeared in the *Staats-Anzeiger* in 1851.[28] More commonly, however, government propaganda focused on the state's current constitution. In 1850, for instance, the *Staats-Anzeiger* published a series of articles that provided 'A History of the Württemberg Constitution'.[29] Articles like this stressed Württemberg's unusually early commitment to constitutional government in its modern form. In another article published that year, the *Staats-Anzeiger* described Württemberg as the state which, in 1819, 'outdid the other German *Stämme* by forging ahead in creating a healthy political life'.[30]

Saxon propaganda could not tap into a similarly ancient constitutional tradition, but it did draw the attention of Saxons to the virtues and relative stability of their constitution. In schools, Saxon history books often included lengthy eulogies of the Saxon constitution and some even provided detailed summaries of its contents.[31] Elsewhere, the official *Dresdner Journal* published annual articles to mark 4 September, the anniversary of the Saxon constitution, which hammered home to the reader how lucky the Saxons were in their constitution and their political life. Typically, in 1859 the *Dresdner Journal* declared: 'Saxony can look with heart-felt satisfaction upon its constitutional situation, in comparison with other states, whose constitutions still seem so uncertain and incomplete'.[32] The newspaper made precisely the same point in 1861, enjoining its readers: '[we should] show ourselves full of deep devotion to this constitution that reflects our character so well'.[33] Boasts of this kind reinforced broader claims made in the official press during the 1860s that Saxony was in fact a relatively liberal state. In 1863 for instance, the *Dresdner Journal* asserted that the government's excellent relations with the Saxon parliament, magnanimous treatment of political dissidents and toleration of widespread associational activity proved 'irrefutably how far the government is from opposing the development of popular feeling and resisting the manifestations of public opinion'.[34] Similarly, in

---

[28] *Staats-Anzeiger für Württemberg*, No. 121, 22 May 1851, 'Württemberg: Ein Stück aus der Geschichte Tübingens vom Jahre 1514'.

[29] *Staats-Anzeiger für Württemberg*, Nos. 40–1, 15–16 February 1850, 'Die Geschichte der württembergischen Verfassung'.

[30] *Staats-Anzeiger für Württemberg*, No. 167, 14 July 1850, 'Unsere Lage III'.

[31] See Anon., *Die Geschichte Sachsens von den ältesten Zeiten bis auf unsere Tage, ein Buch für Volk, Schule und Haus*, Vol. III (Leipzig, 1851), pp. 857–74; Hingst, *Sächsischer Zeitspiegel*, pp. 264–70.

[32] *Dresdner Journal*, No. 204, 4 September 1859, 'Zum 4. September'.

[33] *Dresdner Journal*, No. 206, 4 September 1861, 'Zum 4. September'.

[34] *Dresdner Journal*, No. 236, 11 October 1863, 'Zeitungsschau. Die Constitutionelle Zeitung und die öffentliche Zustände in Sachsen'.

1866 the *Dresdner Journal* noted with satisfaction that there were now 'no inhibiting limitations' on freedom of expression in Saxony, and even press and association legislation had been applied 'liberally' here.[35]

In both Saxony and Württemberg this kind of propaganda never failed to highlight the contribution of the King and his dynasty to the state's constitutional traditions, past and present. Passages in the Württemberg *Volksschule* readers that dealt with the Tübingen agreement invariably stressed the role the dynasty had played in granting and guaranteeing the rights of the Württemberg Estates. Typically, the Catholic *Volksschule* reader described how Duke Christoph had subsequently confirmed the Tübingen agreement and so 'granted the country the right to be consulted over legislation and to authorise taxation'.[36] Other kinds of propaganda sought to portray Württemberg's more recent history of constitutional government primarily as Wilhelm's achievement. In one article published shortly before the 1861 elections, the *Staats-Anzeiger* claimed that Württembergers were luckier than their German neighbours because 'during this period of almost fifty years [since the granting of the constitution in 1819] . . . our country has been guided slowly but surely by the prudence and moderate wisdom of its prince in developing the seed, which he who so magnanimously granted the constitution established therein'.[37] Saxon school books and official newspapers also sought to present the history of the state's constitution in this light. Here, however, the task was complicated by the fact that the Saxon constitution had only been granted in response to the revolutionary upheavals of 1830. Consequently, in their approach to the 1830 revolution, Saxon history books were forced to perform a delicate balancing act.[38] On the one hand, they stressed the good intentions of King Anton in the years leading up to the revolution. On the other hand, they accepted that the people's complaints were justified and applauded the readiness with which Anton and the new King, Friedrich August II, set about responding to them. This view of the 1830 revolution contrasted starkly with accounts of 1848 in the same textbooks. After all, what possible cause for complaint could the Saxon people have, now that they had been granted such an excellent constitution? The actions of the people in 1848 were

---

[35] *Dresdner Journal*, No. 106, 10 May 1866.

[36] *Lesebuch für die katholischen Volksschulen Württembergs*, p. 190.

[37] *Staats-Anzeiger für Württemberg*, No. 296, 14 December 1861, 'Quosque tandem . . .'

[38] See Anon., *Geschichte Sachsens von den ältesten Zeiten bis auf unsere Tage*, pp. 843–57; Gräße, *Geschichte Sachsens und seiner Fürsten*, pp. 161–8; Carl August Friedrich Mohr, *Die Geschichte von Sachsen zum Unterricht in den vaterländischen Schulen* (Leipzig, 1843), pp. 79–81; Stichart, *Königreich Sachsen und seine Fürsten*, pp. 291–7.

7.1 Friedrich August II, portrayed here in Stichart's *The Kingdom of Saxony and its Princes* as constitutional monarch and citizen king. He is wearing civilian dress, but military uniform was usually *de rigueur* for this kind of portrait.
Source: By permission of the British Library 9325.d.10

therefore portrayed as misguided and ungrateful, the monarch as wronged, but generous. By and large, however, particularist history books preferred not to dwell on recent political upheavals and turned their attention instead to the monarchs themselves, and to the more distant past of the state and its ruling house.

The dynasty inevitably took centre stage in particularist history and culture because monarchy was central to *Mittelstaat* identity. Officially sponsored monuments usually depicted monarchs quite simply because the choice of alternative subject matter was so limited, since the state itself was defined primarily in relation to its rulers. Lacking a more solid foundation, patriotic history also focused on the age-old ties between prince and people. Where these age-old ties did not really exist, governments were forced to invent them. During the celebrations marking fifty years of Hanoverian rule in East Friesland, held in 1865, Georg V of Hanover spoke of the 'return' of the province to Welf hands in 1815 after centuries of foreign rule. Conversely, a petition from Duderstadt – a town regained relatively recently by the Welfs – for a railway connection referred to the town's long-standing links with that dynasty, when it claimed 'The Eichsfeld is no foundling'.[39] Likewise, the Historical Association for Franconian Württemberg expressed its gratitude for King Karl's financial support by producing a pamphlet that traced Franconia's historic links with the Württemberg dynasty. The titles of school history books also reflected this dynastic focus. Not for nothing was Stichart's history of Saxony called 'The Kingdom of Saxony and its Princes'.[40] Equally, Brackenhoff's 'History of the Lands of Hanover and Braunschweig', for many years the only history of Hanover available in schools, and Schaumann's officially commissioned work of the same title dealt with the history of both Hanover and Braunschweig – two separate states ruled by different branches of the Welf dynasty and due to be reunited under a single ruler in the forseeable future.[41] Indeed, the dynastic focus of Hanoverian history was particularly pronounced, reflecting both the long-standing presence of the Welfs in North West Germany and the relatively late emergence of the Hanoverian state itself. Tellingly, Kings of Hanover were usually described in propaganda as 'Welf' princes (*Welfenfürst*), whilst their Wettin counterparts were only ever 'Saxon' princes (*Sachsenfürst*).

In general, school history books followed the guidelines for patriotic history set out by the Württemberg Association for Fatherland Studies

[39] Wernick, Duderstadt to H. M., 22 January 1863, HSAHan Dep. 103 IX 416.

[40] J. G. Th. Gräße, *Geschichte Sachsens und seiner Fürsten, ein Lesebuch für Schule und Haus zugleich als erklärender Text zu: Sachsens Fürsten in Bildern* (Dresden, 1855) had a very similar title.

[41] H. L. Brackenhoff, *Geschichte der Hannoverschen und Braunschweig'schen Lande in 60 Erzählungen* (Einbeck, 1855). The Braunschweig line was on the point of extinction, whereupon Braunschweig would revert to the Hanoverian branch. The annexation of Hanover by Prussia in 1866 did not prevent this happening and the succession helped reintegrate the Welfs in the new German *Reich*.

in 1822, and emphasised 'the small beginning and the wonderful preservation of state and ruling house, the permanent progress of both to greater things, the indissoluble . . . ties between them'.[42] Above all, they sought to demonstrate the historic attachment of dynasty and people. Thus Stichart's history of Saxony opened with an account of 'the history of the first ancestors of our beloved royal house, whom thousands of long-dead generations of our forefathers recognised and honoured as their master many centuries ago, with whom they shared joy and sorrow, from whom they received manifold benefits'.[43] In particular, school history books, like Brackenhoff's 'History of the Lands of Hanover and Braunschweig', sought to stress the twin themes of '*princely greatness* and *popular loyalty*'.[44] In the introduction to his history book, Brackenhoff undertook to celebrate both 'those descendants of the high race of Welfs distinguished through their courage, wisdom, justice and gentleness; and the oft tried and ever proven healthy *devotion* of the people *to their princes*'. In practice, however, most patriotic history books (including Brackenhoff) dwelt primarily on rulers and their achievements. Even so, popular loyalty was a recurrent theme. Stichart's history of Saxony repeatedly drew the reader's attention to instances of Saxon love for the Wettins that demonstrated their 'unshakable devotion to their ancestral ruling house'.[45] Such loyalty was also an important motif in Ludwig Uhland's epic cycle of poems about Eberhard the Bearded, which were reproduced in both Württemberg *Volksschule* readers. The first poem in this cycle, 'The raid on Wildbad', told how a loyal subject had saved Eberhard from being ambushed whilst bathing by carrying the ageing prince up a mountain on his back.[46] Another poem, 'The richest Prince', recounts how Eberhard persuaded his fellow German monarchs that he

---

[42] *Württembergisches Jahrbuch* (1822). Cited in Schmoll, *Verewigte Nation*, p. 20.

[43] Stichart, *Königreich Sachsen und seine Fürsten*, p. 2.

[44] Brackenhoff, *Geschichte der Hannoverschen und Braunschweig'schen Lande*, p. 4.

[45] Stichart, *Königreich Sachsen und seine Fürsten*, p. 285. Here Stichart refers to the loyalty shown to Friedrich August the Just after the Battle of Leipzig. Or see his account of the travails of Friedrich I, where Stichart praises the 'the loyalty and love of the Saxon people to their ancestral ruling house which remains constant in times when danger threatens', p. 51.

[46] *Lesebuch für die evangelischen Volksschulen Württembergs*, pp. 339–41. It is worth noting that Uhland's poems were not unthinkingly included in these readers. The 1873 *Volksschule* reader supplement included the third section of Uhland's *Patriotic History*, written in defence of Württemberg's traditional constitution during the constitutional conflict immediately after Wilhelm's accession. The poem opens by asking 'But what do you lack / beloved Fatherland?' and precedes to enumerate Württemberg's many blessings. The final couplet concludes thus: 'What do you lack? – But one thing; / The good and ancient laws.' This last, crucial stanza is omitted from the 1873 supplement. A political protest poem becomes a piece of anodyne patriotism. *Anhang zum Lesebuch für die evangelischen Volksschulen Württembergs* (Stuttgart, 1873), pp. 32–3. For the full version of the poem see Uhland, *Gedichte, Dramen and Prosa*, pp. 71–2.

was the richest prince in Germany, not by virtue of his lands or wealth but rather because he could rest in the lap of any peasant as safely as in any castle.[47]

Inevitably, the history taught in these books was specific to the state in question. Nevertheless, most histories intended for *Volksschule* use were structured in the same way: as a chronologically ordered series of sections devoted to particular monarchs.[48] Each section described the political events of the monarch's reign, the various wars fought, the land lost and won, and ended with an assessment of the monarch himself. Neither Schaumann's nor Brackenhoff's history of Hanover went much beyond this. Indeed, Schaumann concentrated almost exclusively on the shifting redistribution of the Welf lands, stressing again and again the disastrous consequences of partible inheritance practices and the need for unity. History books in Saxony and Württemberg did not focus on the dynasty to quite this extent. They too described wars and the different lands which made up the state at different times, but they also demonstrated an awareness that the history of a state was more than this.

Monarch-by-monarch sections in these books repeatedly mentioned the monarch's contribution to the state's internal development: to religion, culture and learning, to trade and industry. For instance, the Protestant Württemberg reader described how Duke Christoph set about his 'life-long task . . . the consolidation of the Württemberg state and its church, the foundations of which had been laid by Eberhard'.[49] It also detailed how Christoph instituted a unified legal system; reformed forest, tariff and fire legislation; created a standing committee of the Württemberg Estates; reorganised the church; founded church and elementary schools and expanded the university at Tübingen. Similarly, Stichart's history of Saxony described the founding of towns under Konrad the Great; the fostering of trade and mining under Otto the Rich and Heinrich the Noble; the founding of Leipzig University under Friederich the Quarrelsome; the development of the constitution under Friederich the Gentle; the role of Friederich the Wise, Johann Friederich the Generous and Georg the Bearded as patrons of learning and the arts; the contribution of Moritz, 'Father August' and Christoph I to education,

---

[47] *Lesebuch für die evangelischen Volksschulen Württembergs*, p. 352.
[48] Only Württemberg's Catholic reader was differently structured. This reflected the drafting committee's recognition of the problems in writing a history, for instance, of the Reformation rulers which would also be suitable for Catholic pupils. See Bericht des K. katholischen Kirchenraths an das K. Ministerium des Kirchen- und Schulwesens betr. (i) die Bearbeitung des Lesebuchs für die vaterländischen katholischen Volksschulen, 22 March 1857, HSAStu E 200 107 (67).
[49] *Lesebuch für die evangelischen Volksschulen Württembergs*, p. 380.

justice and administration; and the flourishing of all these things under Saxony's more recent rulers, Friedrich August the Just, Anton and Friedrich August II. By contrast, Stichart dismissed the endless wars of Friedrich the Ernest as hardly suited to furthering domestic prosperity, noted that Johann Georg III was too preoccupied with fighting to attend to the internal needs of his state, and dwelt gloomily on the damage wrought by war under rulers like Johann Georg I, Augustus the Strong and his son Friedrich August II. This contrast was particularly clear in Stichart's praise for the efforts of those 'truly paternally inclined' rulers who rebuilt the Saxon state after the ravages of war and maintained peace and prosperity within its borders.[50] Typically, Stichart described how Friedrich August the Just healed the wounds of the Seven Years War 'with paternal devotion' and cultivated friendly relations with his neighbours 'for the good of his country, which was blessed with peace once more'.[51] The sub-text of Stichart's Saxon history was that wars and foreign ambitions were an unfortunate distraction from the true task of princes, which was to preserve peace and further prosperity.

In many ways, this sub-text simply reformulated an argument frequently advanced by *Mittelstaat* propaganda, namely that smaller states compensated in cultural and economic terms for their lack of political influence and military glory. In 1860, for instance, the Württemberg *Staats-Anzeiger* claimed:

[History] has demonstrated repeatedly that vitality, strength and influence on human development is manifested less often in large states than in states of a moderate size. It may well be true that the fragmentation of Germany into a myriad *Stämme* and states has hitherto prevented her from making her political power felt as it should be; it is at least equally true that precisely because of this, Germany has become a country second to none with regard to the dissemination of culture and knowledge, even among the very lowest classes of the population.[52]

The argument about the cultural superiority of the *Mittelstaaten* was seldom formulated so explicitly. Nevertheless, it was remarkably pervasive. On the one hand, articles in the official press emphasised contemporary cultural and economic achievements, portraying the present as a period of unprecedented prosperity. On the other hand, school books, historical associations, monuments and museums celebrated the state's cultural legacy and its traditional commitment to learning, education

---

[50] In this case the prince referred to is Friedrich Christian. Stichart, *Königreich Sachsen und seine Fürsten*, p. 256. [51] Ibid., p. 266, p. 265.
[52] *Staats-Anzeiger für Württemberg*, No. 154, 1 July 1860, news report from Berlin.

and the arts, as well as the great men it had produced. Very often, the emphasis on cultural rather than political history was deliberate. For instance, C. W. Hingst's history of Saxony explicitly set out to show how, under the leadership of its princes and through the industry of its inhabitants, Saxony had become 'a *cultural state (Kulturstaat)* in the fullest sense of the word, whose importance is to be measured not by the *number* of its *square miles*, but rather by the *achievements* of its *inhabitants*'.[53] Yet it is important to grasp that the new emphasis on cultural history, as opposed to political history, did not entail side-lining the monarchs themselves. Instead, school history books simply placed greater emphasis on the cultural achievements and legacies of individual monarchs.

In practice, the importance of this historic cultural legacy varied from state to state. It was natural for cultural traditions to be emphasised in Saxony, given the Wettins' grandiose activities as patrons of the arts. Indeed, Hingst's argument that Saxon school books should concentrate on Saxony's development as a *Kulturstaat* can be understood only in these terms. Equally, Saxony's great cultural tradition was central to the case made by the Association of Artists for a publicly financed Saxon Art Fund. For instance, in 1857 the Association of Artists recalled that 'Saxony rejoices in immortal glory for, in a time when the other German states were still in a state of complete barbarism regarding artistic matters, Saxony acquired art collections through the efforts of art-loving princes, which even now are undoubtedly counted among the finest collections in the world.'[54] Yet Saxon school books always portrayed the state's great cultural tradition as pre-dating the era of Augustus the Strong. For instance, Gräße's history of Saxony described how Leipzig University became 'a hothouse of European culture and civilisation' and spoke of Elector Moritz as 'the originator of that academic and classical education, which made the small country of Saxony renowned far and wide in European lands'.[55]

Official newspapers and school books made similar claims for Württemberg, perhaps with rather less justification. In 1866 for instance, the *Staats-Anzeiger* described Tübingen as one of the 'greatest seats of German learning and literature'.[56] Equally, the Protestant *Volksschule*

---

[53] C. W. Hingst, *Sächsischer Zeitspiegel, das Wichtigste aus der Staats- und Culturgeschichte des Königreichs Sachsen für Schule und Haus* (Döbeln, 1862), pp. iii–iv.

[54] Verein selbstständiger Künstler to K. Ministerium des Innern, 1 May 1857, HSADre Ministerium des Innern 17305 (28–31).

[55] Gräße, *Geschichte Sachsens und seiner Fürsten*, pp. 26–7, 84.

[56] *Staats-Anzeiger für Württemberg*, No. 110, 10 May 1866, 'Die deutschen Kultur Interessen bei der politischen Streitfrage II'.

reader described Duke Christoph's educational foundations (principally the *Volksschulen* themselves) as 'still the pride and joy of the Fatherland, a source of envy for other countries'.[57] The *Staats-Anzeiger* also described how, thanks to Christoph's efforts, 'Our country of Württemberg was ever famed for its good schools.'[58] As in Saxony, officially authorised school books were not alone in emphasising these traditions of culture and learning. One such book, Pleibel's 'Handbook of Knowledge about the Fatherland', maintained that Württemberg's cultural and scholarly achievements bore comparison with those of other lands because names like Schiller, Schelling, Hegel, Hauff, Keppler, Uhland, Schwab and Dannecker were famous far and wide.[59] Like the *Staats-Anzeiger*, Pleibel also emphasised Württemberg's tradition of *Volksschule* education, adding that whereas many in France and England could neither read nor write, in Württemberg one might reasonably ask 'Is there even one who cannot do this?' As in Saxony, Württembergers drew upon these cultural traditions to justify contemporary cultural policy. In proposing the creation of a collection of patriotic antiquities, *Kulturminister* Gäßler argued that Württemberg must 'maintain in this regard the position at the head of the German states, to which its intellectual culture has long entitled her'.[60]

By contrast, Hanoverian school books paid relatively little attention to the state's cultural heritage and concentrated almost exclusively on political history. This political bias is hardly surprising. Hanoverians themselves recognised that over a century of absentee rule had prevented Hanover from developing a distinguished cultural tradition in those areas of the arts that depended on royal patronage. The author of an 1866 tract urging greater state sponsorship of the arts readily acknowledged that Hanover could not at present hope to compete with other states in this field. 'How,' he asked, 'in the absence of its rulers, could artistic treasures and great monuments be brought to Hanover, as they came to Vienna under the Habsburgs, to Saxony under the Electors and Kings of Poland, to Bavaria under the Wittelsbachs?'[61] In a sense, therefore, Hanoverian history concentrated on the dynasty by default.

In each state, a particular contemporary monarch became the focus of government propaganda, not just in school history books but in

---

[57] *Lesebuch für die evangelischen Volksschulen Württembergs*, p. 380.

[58] *Staats-Anzeiger für Württemberg*, No. 1, 1 January 1866, 'Gute Bücher f. Gemeindebibliotheken.'

[59] Pleibel, *Handbuch der Vaterlandskunde*, p. 153.

[60] Golther, 'Anbringen des Ministeriums des Kirchen- und Schulwesen an den König betr. die Anlegung einer besonderen Sammlung vaterländischer Kunst- und Alterthumsdenkmale', 16 June 1862, HSAStu E 14 1577, 3 (8).

[61] Anon., *Das Staatsbudget und das Bedürfnis für Kunst u. Wissenschaft im Königreich Hannover*, p. 35.

newspapers, patriotic poems, obituaries and officially sanctioned biographies. In Saxony this place was occupied by Friedrich August the Just, in Hanover by Ernst August and in Württemberg by Wilhelm I.[62] Frequent popular retellings of their life stories caused these monarchs to acquire almost mythic status in the state they had ruled. Indeed, the process of mythologisation was actively encouraged by the government in question, which usually propagated an official version of the monarch's life. This official version then formed the basis for subsequent accounts, which invariably praised the same personal qualities, described the same events and even adopted the same 'catch-phrases'. The official obituary of Wilhelm of Württemberg, which was read in churches throughout the land shortly after his death, set the pattern of the Wilhelm myth. Similarly, the Ernst August myth in Hanover was defined by High Court Marshal von Malortie's official biography, which appeared in 1861 to mark the inauguration of the Ernst August Monument. What was it about these monarchs that made them so attractive to myth-makers, and what aspects of their lives did official historians like to stress?

Accounts of Friedrich August the Just of Saxony always emphasised the following elements: his peaceable inclinations and his success in restoring Saxon prosperity after years of war; the respect with which he was treated by Frederick II of Prussia and, later, Napoleon; his reluctance to enter the Napoleonic wars; his alliance with Prussia; his decision to support Napoleon in order to protect Saxony from the ravages of the French; his desire to withdraw this support before any other state in the Confederation of the Rhine had done so; the fact that he was prevented from this by Napoleon's threat of invasion and his own concern for the Saxon people; his decision to stay in Saxony during this dangerous time; an explanation of the Saxons' defection during the Battle of Leipzig; a testimony to Saxon loyalty to him when the continued existence of their state remained in doubt; his dignity in adversity; the joyful welcome he received on his return; his jubilee celebrations; and the quiet

---

[62] For the Ernst August myth see for instance: Brackenhoff, *Geschichte des Hannoverschen und Braunschweig'schen Landes*, pp. 356–60; Malortie, *König Ernst August*; articles in the *Neue Hannoversche Zeitung*, especially reports of the Ernst August Monument unveiling ceremony. For the Wilhelm myth see for instance: Zur Vorlesung in den Kirchen des Landes am Sonntag den 24 July 1864 HSAStu E 200 (508 ad24); Rector Dr. Schmid, *Gedächtnis-Rede auf des verewigten Königs Wilhelm Majestät gehalten bei der Trauerfeier im Gymnasium zu Stuttgart den 26. Juli 1864* (Stuttgart, 1864); *Lesebuch für die katholischen Volksschulen Württembergs*; and articles in the *Staats-Anzeiger für Württemberg*. For the Friedrich August the Just myth see for instance: Anon, *Geschichte Sachsens von den ältesten Zeiten bis auf unsere Tage*, pp. 700–54; Gräße, *Geschichte Sachsens und seiner Fürsten*, pp. 141–62; Hingst, *Sächsischer Zeitspiegel*, pp. 227–37; Mohr, *Die Geschichte von Sachsen*, pp. 72–9; Stichart, *Königreich Sachsen und seine Fürsten*, pp. 264–90.

last years of this 'venerable King' (*königlicher Greis*). Friedrich August himself was shown to be pious, upright, just and gentle.

Accounts of Ernst August of Hanover stressed the following elements: his early military vocation; the warm welcome he received when he liberated Hanover from the French in 1813; the joy that greeted his arrival in 1837; his promise (which he kept) to be 'a just and worthy King'; a brief mention of the 1837 constitutional coup; lengthy descriptions of his personal popularity and travels throughout the land; some reference to the 1840 constitution and its warm reception; his grief on the death of his wife Friederike; the public celebrations marking his military jubilee; the relative calm of Hanover in 1848, which was attributed to Ernst August's popularity and wise rule; finally, the wisdom and experience of the venerable King (*königlicher Greis*) in old age. Such accounts were usually peppered with variants of the phrases 'he knew what he wanted' and (in the context of 1848) 'That which I undertake, I will also fulfil'. Ernst August himself was invariably described as just, hard-working, devoted to the service of his country and close to his people.

Accounts of Wilhelm of Württemberg usually contained the following elements: his reluctance to serve under Napoleon; his military successes during the Wars of Liberation against the French; his promise (which he kept) that the 'prosperity and happiness' of his people would be his sole concern; his efforts to relieve the suffering of his people in 1816/17 in collaboration with his second wife Katharina; Katharina's tragic early death and Wilhelm's grief; his granting of the constitution (later recalled as the finest moment of his reign); the celebrations marking his silver jubilee in 1841; some mention of the 1848 revolution; his particular concern for agriculture; his dying words 'I have loved my Württemberg above all else'; a comparison of his achievements with those of the legendary Württemberg ruler Eberhard the Bearded. Variants of the phrases 'a man, fearless and true' and the 'venerable King' (*königlicher Greis*) recurred repeatedly throughout these accounts.

It is impossible to overlook the striking similarities between the portrayals of Ernst August of Hanover and Wilhelm of Württemberg in these accounts. In both cases, the story began with the protagonist's involvement in the struggle against Napoleon and his role in the liberation of his country from French oppression. Both monarchs could therefore be portrayed as military heroes – a traditional royal role. Indeed, Wilhelm was frequently described as a veteran, a label that strengthened his association with the Wars of Liberation and reinforced his nationalist credentials. The similarities did not stop here. Official accounts also credited both

7.2 Two of the bronze reliefs around the base of the Jubilee Column in Stuttgart.
(*a*) Delegates in the Württemberg parliament take an oath of loyalty to King
Wilhelm I in 1841, the year of his jubilee. Wilhelm holds the Württemberg constitution
in his hands. (*b*) One of three military scenes from the Wars of Liberation.
Photo: Gabrielle Otto

monarchs with similarly out-spoken personalities: Wilhelm was 'fearless and true', Ernst August knew his own mind and kept his word. Both made promises to rule well, which they also kept. Both lost a beloved wife and helpmeet. Finally, both lived to a ripe old age and were described affectionately as old men (*Greise*), or, more respectfully, as a 'Nestor' among contemporary monarchs. Besides this, accounts of both reigns made much of large-scale displays of popular loyalty. For instance, both monarchs celebrated an important jubilee in the 1840s and much space was usually devoted to the grandiose public festivities that marked these occasions. In fact, the contrast between these two occasions is very instructive, for whilst Ernst August was celebrating fifty years of service in the Hanoverian army, Wilhelm was celebrating twenty-five years as King. The Ernst August jubilee inevitably carried strong military associations, but the festivities marking Wilhelm's silver jubilee emphasised in particular his role in granting the Württemberg constitution. To some extent, this distinction was borne out in more lasting memorials of the two Kings. Whilst the Ernst August Monument in Hanover depicted the monarch on horseback dressed in a hussar uniform, Wilhelm's Jubilee Column in Stuttgart evoked both military and constitutional achievements. Three of the four reliefs around the base of the column showed scenes from the Napoleonic wars of 1814, but the fourth depicted Wilhelm holding the constitution as he met with the representatives of the Württemberg parliament in 1841 (see Figures 3.2, 6.1 and 7.2).

At first glance, there appear to be few parallels between these accounts of Ernst August and Wilhelm, on the one hand, and the popular portrayal of Friedrich August the Just of Saxony on the other. For one thing, Friedrich August's role in the Wars of Liberation inevitably posed serious problems for official myth-makers. Admittedly, accounts of his reign tended to stress his reluctance to support Napoleon, both in 1806 and 1813, and his unusually early desire to change sides after the retreat from Moscow. Up to a point, therefore, there was an attempt to associate Friedrich August with the nationalism of the period. On the whole, however, his image was very different to that of Ernst August or Wilhelm, because portrayals of this monarch emphasised his peaceable nature and gentle virtues, rather than the more warlike qualities of the other two. To some extent, this image reinforced the wider view presented in many school books of Saxony as a peaceful and prosperous state, whose distinguished cultural heritage more than made up for its lack of a glorious military tradition. More fundamentally perhaps, it was simply an attempt to make the best of a bad job.

Fünfte Reihe der sächsischen Fürsten.

Die Könige von Sachsen.

30. Friedrich August der Gerechte,
Kurfürst und König von Sachsen.
(1768 – 1827.)

7.3 Friedrich August the Just, as portrayed in Stichart's *The Kingdom of Saxony and its Princes*. The book was illustrated in an attempt to make it more accessible to Saxon schoolchildren.
Source: By permission of the British Library, 9325.d.10

Under these circumstances, it is worth asking why Saxon school books focused on Friedrich August the Just rather than one of his successors. If death was a necessary precondition of monarchic myth-making, in Saxony at least there were several possible choices. In some ways, both Anton and Friedrich August II. were more obvious candidates for mythothogisation, given their role in granting the Saxon constitution. Yet Grässe's 'History of Saxony and its Princes' devoted twenty pages to the reign of Friedrich August the Just, and only seven to the three reigns of Anton, Friedrich August II and Johann. Equally, Stichart devoted some twenty-five pages to Friedrich August the Just, but twenty to both Anton and Friedrich August II together. Despite his failures as a monarch, Friedrich August the Just shared several important characteristics with Ernst August of Hanover and Wilhelm of Württemberg: he had played an active part in the Napoleonic era, he reigned for many years and he lived to a ripe old age.

More importantly still, all three of these legendary monarchs were strongly associated with the origins of their state in its contemporary incarnation. This was most clearly true of Wilhelm, who by the time of his death had ruled Württemberg for almost as long as it had been a kingdom and ever since the creation of the German Confederation. It was less happily true of Friedrich August, for he had been Saxony's first King and the first to rule Saxony in its diminished form. Finally, Ernst August was the first ruling monarch for over a century to live in Hanover, and his reign had seen the rebirth of Hanover as an independent state. In a sense, therefore, all three monarchs were the founding fathers of their states. Consequently, mythologising the monarch was part of a process of objectification, whereby the aura of monarchy became detached from the actual person of the monarch and was institutional-ised in the state itself – a widespread phenomenon at this time. In Prussia, for instance, the legendary status of Frederick the Great after his death became a cornerstone of Prussian identity and the emergent state-nationalism of the Napoleonic age.[63] Similarly, celebrating the reigns of Ernst August, Friedrich August and Wilhelm in Hanover, Saxony and Württemberg was a way of celebrating the states themselves because the two were inextricably linked. This was particularly true where accounts of their reigns provided evidence of widespread popularity in the shape of festivities and publicly funded monuments. The jubilee celebrations held by all three monarchs were therefore portrayed as public demon-strations of the ties of love and loyalty that bound the King and his people, just as the monuments erected in honour of Ernst August and Wilhelm were a more concrete expression of the community of prince and people that lay at the heart of the territorial state.

Yet the appeal of propaganda in Hanover, Saxony and Württemberg was by no means exclusively rooted in the past. Patriotic history was important in validating these states as meaningful and viable political units, but it was not enough to wax lyrical over the achievements of past monarchs. Hanoverians, Saxons and Württembergers also needed to be persuaded of the virtues of their current state and its rulers. Consequently, government propaganda sought to show that nineteenth-century monarchs were worthy successors to their illustrious forebears. Contemporaries in all three states frequently drew parallels between contemporary monarchs and particularly famous former rulers. In

---

[63] On this see Eckhart Hellmuth, 'A monument to Frederick the Great: architecture, politics and the state in late eighteenth-century Prussia', in John Brewer and Eckhart Hellmuth (eds.), *Rethinking Leviathan. The eighteenth-century state in Britain and Germany* (Oxford, 1999), pp. 317–42.

Hanover, for instance, the achievements of Ernst August in particular
were often compared with those of his name-sake the first Elector, and
both these rulers were in turn associated with a third Ernst August –
Georg's son, the young crown prince.[64] Similarly, the reigns of Friedrich
August II and Johann were compared with those of other royal Saxon
brothers, Elector Moritz and 'Father August', whose reigns had seen the
zenith of Saxon influence in Germany.[65] Meanwhile, Wilhelm of
Württemberg's achievements were likened to those of Eberhard the
Bearded and (less frequently) Duke Christoph. In keeping with this rhetoric, Tübingen University marked the five hundredth anniversary of its
foundation with two new statues – one of the founder, Eberhard, and
another of the contemporary ruler, Wilhelm. Indeed, Wilhelm himself
cultivated this association when he commissioned a statue of Eberhard
for the front courtyard of his palace in Stuttgart.

Such comparisons were all very well, but they relied heavily on
popular perceptions that the achievements of modern monarchs genuinely measured up to those of their predecessors. Trumpeting their constitutional credentials was one approach to this problem and, as we have
seen, this was adopted in both Saxony and Württemberg. Equally
important, however, was the emphasis propaganda in all three states
placed on current levels of material well-being, for without exception
school books and official newspapers declared the present to be a time
of untold prosperity and content. In Hanover, this prosperity was explicitly linked with the return of the Welfs to their ancestral home. As
inhabitants of the suburbs of Celle put it in a letter to Georg V: 'with a
marvellous creative hand, the presence of our rulers has opened up the
sources of wealth in our country for us, bringing trade and transport to
an almost unimaginable bloom'.[66] Such claims drew heavily on propaganda in the official press. Every year, long articles written to mark
Georg's birthday painted in glowing colours the recent advances in
Hanoverian railway construction, the development of the coastline and
of Hanoverian shipping, the strides made by Hanoverian agriculture

[64] For instance Arnold von Weyhe-Eimke's poem, *Zum 21. September 1861. Seiner Hoheit Ernst August, Kronprinz von Hannover zu Höchstseinem Geburtstage in tiefer Ehrfurcht gewidmet* (1861). The crown prince's birthday was also the day on which the memorial to his grandfather Ernst August was unveiled in Hanover. The crown prince played an unusually important role in Hanoverian prop-aganda, perhaps in part to compensate for the blindness of his father Georg. The *Neue Hannoversche Zeitung* published homilies on the virtues of the Welf dynasty on his birthday; impor-tant ceremonies frequently took place on this day, and prayers were said in churches throughout the land after his life was supposedly endangered during a minor mishap whilst bathing off Nordeney.   [65] See for instance, Hingst, *Sächsischer Zeitspiegel*, pp. 302–3.
[66] Bewohner der beiden Vorstädte der Stadt Celle to H. M., 15 July 1862, HSAHan Dep. 103 IX 429.

and industry and the renewed vibrancy of the state capital.[67] Typically, in 1862 the *Neue Hannoversche Zeitung* drew a stark contrast between the flourishing condition of contemporary Hanover and the situation twenty-five years earlier:

[W]here . . . horses, puffing and panting, once slowly brought men and goods from one place to another, now the train thunders past in full flight . . . On the beach, where a couple of wretched fishing huts once stood . . . there are now hundreds and thousands of hands busying themselves in the port . . . Where . . . rushes and reeds were the only lifeless embellishment of wide stretches of land, now rich fields of corn blow in the wind . . . Where once a few charcoal kilns smouldered, now the smoking chimneys of newly equipped factories [can be seen].[68]

There are strong parallels between this kind of language and that used by government propaganda in Saxony and Württemberg. In 1863, for instance, the *Dresdner Journal* described Saxony thus: 'trade and industry flourishing, agriculture blooming, growing cities, newly opened sources of wealth and means of transport. The schools in almost all places adequate for their needs and often exemplary, good management of the welfare police . . . well-ordered communities, savings banks full'.[69] The newspaper [*sic*] concluded with satisfaction 'that the government has also done its bit for the happy improvement of our condition'. Likewise, Hingst's Saxon history declared that more had been done for the economy and for popular well-being under Friedrich August II and his brother Johann than ever before: 'which is why these years should be seen as years in which Saxony shone, and should be written of in glowing terms in the history books of our Fatherland'.[70] Württemberg propaganda made very similar claims for King Wilhelm. On a day-to-day basis, reports of state railway profits, new railway lines, local industrial and agricultural exhibitions, theatrical performances and art exhibitions were the staple fare of the Württemberg *Staats-Anzeiger* and testified to the state's prosperity and cultural vitality. More importantly, perhaps, Wilhelm's official obituary consciously underlined the King's personal contribution to this happy state of affairs, which it attributed to Wilhelm's acceptance of constitutional and administrative reform and to his personal enthusiasm for agricultural and industrial innovation.[71] Other commentators picked up the point. One speaker to the Stuttgart

---

[67] *Hannoversche Nachrichten*, No. 122, 27 May 1857. Or *Neue Hannoversche Zeitung*, No. 241, 27 May 1858.
[68] *Neue Hannoversche Zeitung*, No. 282, 20 June 1862, 'Der zwanzigste Juni'.
[69] *Dresdner Journal*, No. 236, 11 October 1863, 'Zeitungsschau: Die Constitutionelle Zeitung und die öffentlichen Zustände in Sachsen'. [70] Hingst, *Sächsischer Zeitspiegel*, pp. 302–3.
[71] Zur Vorlesung in den Kirchen des Landes am Sonntag den 24 July 1864, HSAStu E 200 (508 ad24)

Gymnasium claimed that 'besides politics, material interests [were] . . . above all the object of his concern. Principally thanks to his government, agriculture and trade, industry and transport took a hitherto unimaginable leap forward under his rule.'[72] Tellingly, the four female figures at the base of the Jubilee Column in Stuttgart, which reflected Wilhelm's preoccupations as monarch, represented the military, agriculture, trade and industry, learning and the arts.

Unsurprisingly perhaps, these claims of untold prosperity had much in common. Hanover, Saxony and Württemberg were all in the throes of modernisation and consequently propaganda drew on similar economic and social developments: the railway boom, the agricultural revolution, industrialisation and the flowering of culture fostered by the spread of literacy and the new trend for association formation. Equally, propaganda in all three states invariably stressed the unprecedented nature of this economic and cultural bloom. More importantly perhaps, official propaganda clearly attributed the new-found prosperity of these states to the benign influence of kings like Ernst August and Georg of Hanover, Friedrich August and Johann of Saxony, and Wilhelm of Württemberg. It is worth noting, however, that religion played no part in portrayals of contemporary well-being in any of the three states – a telling indication of the contentious nature of confessional issues.[73]

Yet despite these similarities, government propaganda also reflected the specific experience of each state. Saxons were particularly proud of the state's record in railway construction. Consequently, railways acquired a special place in Saxon identity, which reflected both the state's geographical position and its unusually advanced economy. Official historians like Stichart never forgot to mention Saxony's pioneering role in the 1830s, when the Saxon government had authorised Germany's first long-distance railway line from Leipzig to Dresden.[74] Local interest groups, eagerly lobbying for their own railway connections, were also well aware of Saxony's historic commitment to rail. In 1855, for instance, the tradesmen of Meissen praised the Saxon government for its foresight in

---

[72] Rector Dr. Schmid, *Gedächtnis-Rede auf des verewigten Königs Wilhelm Majestät*, p. 8.

[73] Religion was inevitably dealt with more extensively in school books, notably in Saxon school history books and in the Protestant Württemberg reader. The former dwelt on the role played by the Wettins in protecting Luther and in establishing and nurturing the new doctrine. Emphasis on the Wettins' earlier commitment to Protestantism distracted attention from their conversion to Catholicism in 1697. The role of the Württemberg dynasty in establishing Protestantism in Württemberg was dwelt on at similar length in the Protestant school reader, although the treatment of this subject in the Catholic reader was inevitably very different.

[74] Stichart, *Königreich Sachsen und seine Fürsten*, p. 312.

appreciating the importance of railways before anyone else, arguing that this had reinforced Saxony's central geographical location and added considerably to the state's importance: 'Saxony can be called the heart of the German railway network . . . In this way Saxony's railway network takes an honourable place as part of the greater Whole.'[75] For the tradesmen of Meissen, then, Leipzig's position at the apex of the German railway network confirmed Saxony's historic place at 'the heart of Germany'.[76]

Of course, railway construction was also a feature of government propaganda in Hanover and Württemberg – indeed, lists enumerating the blessings of Welf rule in Hanover often started with the railways. Yet in neither state did it acquire the same symbolic importance as in Saxony. Instead, Württemberg propaganda honoured Wilhelm as 'the Farmer King' (*König der Landwirthe*), and official accounts of his life made much of his efforts to improve agriculture, most successfully through his sponsorship of the *Cannstatter Volksfest*.[77] Conversely, Hanoverian propaganda emphasised Georg V's role in making the most of Hanover's unique position on the North Sea coast. In 1859, for instance, the *Neue Hannoversche Zeitung* wrote that the Hanoverian government had increased the state's prosperity 'through appropriate exploitation of this blessed geographical position'.[78] Development of the coastline brought both economic and political benefits – encouraging commerce and reinforcing the state's position in Germany and beyond. An 1864 pamphlet written by the royal archivist Grotefend, who was also president of the Historical Association for Lower Saxony, made this point very clearly. In the pamphlet, Grotefend dwelt exhaustively on the importance of Hanover's maritime position and the government's efforts 'to improve shipping and to lay the basis for overseas trade'.[79] Such developments were, he argued, merely a first step on the road to future glory. Sea power had brought England untold wealth and influence and where England led, Hanover could follow: 'Our Kingdom can also lay claim to a portion of this good fortune.'[80]

Whatever the differences between Hanover, Saxony and Württemberg, governments in all three states appealed to their inhabitants in strikingly

---

[75] Gehorsamstes Gesuch der Kaufleute von Meißen, Eisenbahnfrachtpreise betr. to Ministerium des Innern, 16 May 1855, HSADre Ministerium des Innern 103 a (120–9).

[76] As described in Petition des akademischen Raths zur Feststellung einer Summe von jährlich 5000 thaler für monumentale Kunst, 20 May 1857, HSADre Ministerium des Innern 17305 (23–7).

[77] Zur Vorlesung in den Kirchen des Landes am Sonntag den 24 July 1864, HSAStu E 200 (508 ad24). [78] *Neue Hannoversche Zeitung*, No. 243, 27 May 1859, 'Der 27. Mai 1859'.

[79] Grotefend, *Hannover, ein patriotisches Promemoria* (Hanover, 1864), pp. 20–6 (p. 23). This pamphlet was originally published in the *Deutsche Nordsee Zeitung*. [80] Ibid., p. 27.

similar terms – historic, constitutional, cultural, economic and, above all, dynastic. Propaganda sought to present the *Mittelstaaten* as valid and meaningful political units with a shared history, boasting rich cultural and political traditions that made them cradles of liberty, economic prosperity and the arts. In this context, the dynastic element of *Mittelstaat* propaganda acted as a unifying theme, for the dynasty symbolised the state's past, present and future. Its representatives embodied the particular qualities of the *Stamm* traditionally associated with the state in question and – as granters of constitutions, patrons of the arts and sponsors of industry and agriculture – they were the bearers of its political, cultural and economic heritage.

In practice, all these elements were crucial to the construction of a strong *Mittelstaat* identity. Consequently, this identity was probably weakest in Hanover, which lacked both cultural and constitutional traditions. Hanoverian propaganda sought to make good this lack by placing particular emphasis on the Welf dynasty and its historic mission in Germany, and by playing up the state's maritime vocation, which promised both material riches and political glory. Contemporaries made fun of Georg V for sponsoring a 'Welf cult' and for his grandiose rhetoric, yet in many ways he was right to try and establish a unifying basis for Hanoverian identity. In a state that lacked geographical, historical and administrative cohesion, the dynasty was the only common denominator. A healthy political tradition, based on some kind of representative government, might have proved more effective in reconciling Hanover's disparate inhabitants with the state, the government and each other. Indeed, arguably this was precisely what happened in Württemberg. Given the political inclinations of both Georg and his father Ernst August, however, this solution was simply out of the question.

By contrast, patriotic identity in Saxon and Württemberg was rooted in the cultural and constitutional traditions of these two states. True, the cultural tradition was more important in Saxony and the constitutional tradition in Württemberg; but this was a difference in emphasis, not in kind. In both cases, emphasising the state's rich cultural tradition helped to reinforce a sense of separate identity and pride in the particular Fatherland. Moreover, the stress on the cultural element played upon traditional ideas of the German nation as a cultural rather than political entity, united above all by a common language. In many ways, however, the constitutional element was more important than the cultural, because in the 1860s constitutional liberalism was the Achilles heel of *kleindeutsch* nationalism. Liberalism and nationalism had always been closely intertwined in Germany, and the relative importance of Unity and Liberty was still very much an open question. Consequently, the argument that *Mittelstaaten* like Saxony and Württemberg promised constitutional government and a liberal political environment was very powerful. A combination of liberalisation and propaganda that played up the state's constitutional credentials might well shift the balance of opinion against unification. The weakness of the *Nationalverein*, and the strength of particularism in Saxony and Württemberg during the 1860s, testifies to the success of this approach. Like German nationalism itself, particularism in the *Mittelstaaten* was rooted in a powerful combination of political and cultural identity.

To some extent, the new particularism was artificial, in that – unlike liberal nationalism – it was actively fostered by government policy. Agency of this kind was most self-conscious in Bavaria, where Max II introduced a wide range of initiatives as part of his overarching 'Policy to raise Bavarian national feeling'.[81] Nowhere else was the official response to the events of 1848 so concerted or so deliberate. Instead, changes in cultural policy, the official press and basic state education in Hanover, Saxony and Württemberg took the form of a series of disparate and unconnected measures. These measures may have lacked the conceptual cohesion of the Bavarian reforms, but in substance they were strikingly similar. Here too, the revolutions of 1848/9 prompted more active governmental support for particularist culture and heritage, in the shape of state-sponsored history, publicly funded museums, monarchic monuments and popular festivities. Here too, the revolutions of 1848 led to a reassessment of censorship policy and the official press, as governments developed a complex propaganda apparatus. This enabled them to influence public opinion through official and semi-official newspapers, polemical leading articles and more subtly biased news reporting. Here too, *Volksschule* teachers and textbooks propagated conservative and monarchic values through a contradictory mixture of religious education and the introduction of *Realien* teaching. Here too, governments reaped the benefits of economic progress and the railway boom. On the one hand, railway inauguration ceremonies and other kinds of official propaganda emphasised the role of the King and his ministers in bringing railways to the people. On the other hand, cheap and easy train travel enabled Hanoverians, Saxons and Württembergers to get to know their Fatherland. Thanks to the railways, they could visit the countryside and the capital, wonder at their historical and artistic heritage in the shape of museums, monuments and palaces, see for themselves the

[81] As discussed at length in Hanisch, *Für Fürst und Vaterland*.

forests, mountains and rivers of the Fatherland, rather than simply reading about them in the new *Volksschule* textbooks.

Yet this particularism was far more than just the artificial product of government policy or a figment of the official imagination. Indeed, government propaganda could make very little headway where it ignored popular feeling – as the Hanoverian government discovered to its cost when it sought to introduce the new state catechism in 1862. Inevitably, propaganda was at its most successful when it reinforced existing ideas and tendencies, rather than talking past them. Officially sponsored cultural activities certainly had their own conservative and royalist agenda. Historians who belonged to the royal historical associations of Hanover, Saxony and Württemberg tended to write self-consciously patriotic history, and their concerns were reflected in the collections of local antiquities on show in the new museums in state capitals. In any case, most cultural activities were overshadowed by the dominating presence of the King and the royal family. The monarchs themselves were a preferred subject for public monuments; they were inevitably the centre of major public festivities and their art collections formed the basis of the grandest of the new 'public' museums. Yet it would be wrong to dismiss particularist culture itself as monarchic propaganda, for state sponsorship of cultural activities was quite clearly a response to the growing interest in local culture manifested by many unofficial associations, clubs and societies. Historical societies were not always founded by officials, or with explicitly political goals in mind. Similarly, museums were not always the product of royal initiatives, nor did the impetus to open museums and archives to the public necessarily come from the government alone. Press policy also reflected this interplay between state and society, because changes in policy were reactive not proactive. In this sense, government press policy was policy on the hoof. Improvements to official newspapers and refinements in propaganda techniques were invariably a response to the changing political climate reflected in the excesses and successes of the opposition press. Equally, the government press could not simply impose the official view of events on the newspaper-reading classes. In order to be successful, government newspapers needed to reach a wide audience, and this was only possible if they reflected the interests and inclinations of the reading public. Up to a point, therefore, the government press had to tell its readers what they wanted to hear. Even particularist education policy reflected the modernising agenda of liberals, for whom the teaching of history and geography had very little to do with fostering patriotism. Instead, they saw the *Realien* as symbolising a commitment to higher educational standards, greater social mobility and – above all – the beginning of the end for the tyranny of priests, religion and superstition in the *Volksschulen*. Nowhere did government policy respond to popular pressure more effectively than over railway construction, an issue on which government ministers, local communities and even large sectors of the opposition press were as one in advocating a particularist agenda. Indeed, official propaganda cannily exploited this united front, emphasising the contribution of the King and his government by staging grand inauguration ceremonies for new railway lines and building monuments strategically sited by major train stations. More often than not, therefore, government policy sought to project an image of the particular Fatherland and its relationship to the greater nation, which drew on ideas that were already widely held. This image and the ideas behind it were a crucial source of legitimacy for the German states, and a powerful argument for maintaining the status quo in the face of the nationalist challenge. Government propaganda was not simply destructive. It also made a positive case for the continued independence of the German states, emphasising in particular the important role of the *Mittelstaaten* and, still more specifically, of the state in question. Crucially, however, *Mittelstaat* propaganda never sought to compete with German nationalism on its own terms. Instead, governments in the *Mittelstaaten* fostered a vision of Germany that combined the particular and the national.

This vision was attractive to the inhabitants of these states precisely because particular and national identities had always coexisted in Germany. The growth of both German nationalism and more strongly state-based particular identities in the nineteenth century did not for the most part prevent this. Particularism only very gradually came to define itself in conscious opposition to the national in these states, as political nationalism began genuinely to threaten the independence of the German states. Before this point it was not necessary to voice aggressively particularist sentiments, because particular identities and institutions did not appear to be under threat. In the same way that German nationalism intensified in the face of threats from abroad (principally France) in 1814, 1840, 1859 and 1870–1, so German particularism intensified in the face of the nationalist menace.

CHAPTER EIGHT

Nationhood

The Austro-Prussian war of 1866, and the subsequent Prussian annexations of Hanover, Hessen, Frankfurt and Schleswig-Holstein, created a hiatus in the relationship between particular states and the nation in Germany. The fear of Prussian expansionism led many Hanoverians, Saxons and Württembergers to express loyalty to the existing state and opposition to *kleindeutsch* nationalism in no uncertain terms. Nevertheless, the emergence of a French threat with the outbreak of the Franco-Prussian war in 1870 substantially altered the situation. Feelings of national community in the face of a common foe began to outweigh particularist fears of Prussian ascendancy. Ultimately, hatred of the French proved stronger and more deep-rooted than animosity towards the Prussians. Even Varnbüler, the Württemberg Prime Minister and a leading opponent of *kleindeutsch* unification, was so excited to hear of the French defeat at Sedan that he forgot himself completely. Rushing to the balcony, he announced news of the German victory to the public in Stuttgart before he had even told the King – an oversight that would cost him his position. In Württemberg, as elsewhere in Germany, the national triumph of the Franco-Prussian war therefore served to reforge the links between particular states and the emergent German nation. Yet how far did particularists in Hanover, Saxony and Württemberg really overcome their opposition to *kleindeutsch* unification? What was the legacy of pre-unification state-building in the *Mittelstaaten*? How successfully was state-based identity in Hanover, Saxony and Württemberg subsumed into a new, political nationalism focusing on the German Empire?

In 1871 the auguries were far from propitious, for the German people themselves proved strangely unmoved by national unification. Of those entitled to vote for the constituent *Reichstag* of the new Empire 49% did not bother to do so, indicating widespread political apathy.[1] Of the 51%

---

[1] See Werner Conze, 'Staatsnationale Entwicklung und Modernisierung im Deutschen Reich, 1871–1914' in Werner Conze, Gottfried Schramm and Klaus Zernack (eds.), *Modernisierung und*

who cared enough to vote, half voted for parties whose endorsement of the new nation state was luke-warm to say the least: old-fashioned Prussian conservatives, the Catholic Centre Party, left-liberals, socialists, particularists and representatives of other national minorities. In the end, only a quarter of the adult male population came out as active supporters of the new state of affairs. Even such active nationalists as these appear to have felt surprisingly ambivalent about the *kleindeutsch* German Empire. Tellingly, membership of the gymnastic associations – previously a mainstay of popular nationalism – fell off alarmingly during the 1870s. As Svenja Goltermann has argued in her excellent study of German gymnasts, this decline in popular nationalism expressed a fundamental unease about German unification.[2] Theodor Georgii, president of the gymnasts' movement, spoke for many when he drew a clear distinction between the 'German Empire of our *hopes* and *dreams*' and 'the *real* German Empire'.[3] How far did this reluctant acceptance of the new Germany give way to a genuine enthusiasm for the new nation state in the years after 1871?

Constitutionally speaking, the German Empire – largely modelled on its predecessor, the North German Confederation – was a hybrid of conflicting democratic and authoritarian, Prussian and German, unitary and federal elements. Its parliament, the *Reichstag*, was elected by near-universal manhood suffrage. Yet in practice the powers of this unusually democratic body were exceptionally limited, vis à vis both the individual German states and the imperial government. In this sense, although the *Reichstag* itself was democratic, the German Empire was not. For one thing, the vast bulk of domestic policy – education, policing, railway construction and so on – remained in the hands of individual state governments and their parliaments. Only gradually did the German Empire acquire the apparatus of central government: an Imperial Interior Ministry, an Imperial Railway Office, Post Office and so on. Initially, however, the Empire's competences were basically restricted to economic, diplomatic and military matters. Even at national level, the *Reichstag* could only approve the imperial budget and veto imperial legislation. Moreover, both the army and the foreign office remained under the direct control of the Emperor himself. Equally, the *Reichstag* had no

nationale Gesellschaft im ausgehenden 18. und im 19. Jahrhundert. Referate einer deutsch-polnischen Historiker-konferenz (Berlin, 1979) pp. 59–71 (p. 67).

[2] Svenja Goltermann, *Körper der Nation. Habitusformierung und die Politik des Turnens, 1860–1890* (Göttingen, 1998), pp. 221–4.   [3] Ibid., p. 221.

say in the appointment of imperial officials. True, the Imperial Chancellor was constitutionally responsible to the *Reichstag*. In fact, however, no procedure existed to make this responsibility anything other than theoretical. Even so, the *Reichstag* enjoyed a certain symbolic status, in that the Imperial Chancellor countersigned legislation on its behalf, alongside the Emperor who was acting on behalf of his fellow rulers. Many of these limitations on the power of the *Reichstag* reflected the fact that sovereignty in the German Empire lay not with the *Reichstag* but rather with the collectivity of German monarchs and Hansa towns represented in the *Bundesrat* (Federal Council). All this was further complicated by the role of Prussia. Prussia dominated the executive of the German Empire, since its monarch and leading minister held the key positions of Emperor and Imperial Chancellor, whilst its bureaucrats formed the backbone of the emergent imperial administration. Furthermore, the sheer size of Prussia, which made up two-thirds of the new Germany, meant that its representatives threatened to swamp both the *Reichstag* and the *Bundesrat*.

For all its limitations, the *Reichstag* represented the democratic and unitary aspects of the new Germany, since it was a national parliament elected by the people. Conversely, the *Bundesrat* stood for the federal and undemocratic aspects of the German Empire, since its members were the unelected representatives of the individual German states. Ostensibly, the *Bundesrat* acted as a safeguard that protected the smaller German states from Prussian hegemony. Of course, Prussia's presidency of the *Bundesrat* inevitably gave Prussia a certain amount of leverage. Nevertheless, voting rights within the *Bundesrat* were allocated in such a way as to ensure that the three German kingdoms (Bavaria, Saxony and Württemberg) could veto Prussian initiatives and that smaller states exercised an influence wholly disproportionate to their actual size and population. Yet despite its federal character, the *Bundesrat* was by no means the favoured option of German governments apart from Prussia. As the Württemberg Prime Minister Mittnacht commented in 1872, 'a parliamentary federal house (*Staatenhaus*) would have provided a far stronger protection for truly particular interests than the *Bundesrat*, which is largely for show'.[4] In dismissing the federalism of the *Bundesrat* as 'show' rather than substance, Mittnacht was merely stating a commonly accepted truth. By and large, the lack of unity amongst the smaller

---

[4] Cited after Manfred Rauh, *Föderalismus und Parlamentarismus im Wilhelminischen Reich* (Düsseldorf, 1983), p. 53.

German states, and the curious symbiosis between imperial institutions and the Prussian state, meant that Prussia had things very much its own way in the *Bundesrat*.

The complex constitutional structure was designed to perpetuate the importance of the German states and to minimise the role of national political structures. Bismarck, the principal architect of the new Germany, believed that a federal state was desirable in view of its 'far greater capacity to resist the republican surge, which is apparent in the [North German] *Reichstag* and all over Europe'.[5] In other words, he assumed that it would be harder for democratic forces to overcome the resistance of many state governments than that of a single national government. These considerations applied particularly forcibly in Germany, where the franchise for state parliaments remained relatively restricted. In the past, representative institutions had played an important role in state building in the German *Mittelstaaten*. After 1815 participatory politics had encouraged the inhabitants of states like Hanover, Saxony and Württemberg to take the state as their primary frame of reference and the focus of their political ambitions. The limitations placed on the power of the *Reichstag*, and the continued importance of state governments and state parliaments, ensured that this focus only shifted gradually to the nation state itself. Nevertheless, both the democratic franchise of the *Reichstag* and the inadequacy of the *Bundesrat* as an institution for defending particularist interests served to encourage a slow process of fusion between state and national politics.

Bismarck himself was always careful of the sensitivities of other German governments and tried to involve them in the decision-making process, at least informally. Subsequent Imperial Chancellors increasingly viewed the *Bundesrat* as a political irrelevance and focused instead on maintaining a majority in the *Reichstag*. This inevitably raised the prestige of the latter. Conversely, *Mittelstaat* governments began to appeal to the *Reichstag* on important matters of policy, when they had failed to impose their views within the *Bundesrat* itself – as Württemberg did over wine tax in 1893–4. In this sense, the 1890s and 1900s saw an incremental parliamentarisation of the German Empire at national level. As the national parliament grew more important, voting in *Reichstag* elections and participating in national politics became a more meaningful activity for ordinary Germans. Moreover, the fact that many Germans could vote at national but not at state level encouraged

---

[5] Cited after ibid.

them to use national politics as a vehicle for expressing their political opinions.

As a result, the pressures for democratic reform at state level began to mount during the 1900s. This was by no means a nationwide phenomenon. Crucially, the Prussian parliament continued to be elected by the system of the three-class vote, whereby the votes of a wealthy elite counted for more than the votes of the poor. Elsewhere, however, there were substantial improvements. In Württemberg, for instance, parliamentary structures had long failed to take account of social and demographic change.[6] In 1900, the number of delegates for the industrial city of Stuttgart finally increased from one to six, marking a significant step in the right direction. More importantly, in 1906 the twenty-three 'privileged [unelected] members' of the Württemberg Lower House were removed to the Upper House, and replaced by delegates elected by proportional representation. As a result the number of Social Democrats in the Württemberg parliament tripled. In Saxony, by contrast, a coalition of conservatives and liberals had introduced the three-class vote for the first time in 1896 in an attempt to keep the Social Democrats out of the Saxon parliament.[7] The immediate consequence of this was a two-thirds conservative majority in the Saxon Lower House. In the long term, however, pressures for more democratic representation – in the shape of mass demonstrations and a Socialist landslide in the *Reichstag* elections of 1903 – proved unstoppable. In 1909, with the backing of the Saxon liberals, the conservative Saxon government introduced a new electoral system which, although less democratic than the universal manhood suffrage of the *Reichstag*, was considerably more progressive than its predecessor.

These reforms were very much informed by national politics, most notably in the case of Saxony. For one thing, the conservative Saxon Prime Minister, von Metzsch, only felt able to go ahead with progressive suffrage reform when he knew that he had the backing of the Imperial

---

[6] For details of electoral reform in Württemberg see Merith Niehuss, 'Party configurations in state and municipal elections in Southern Germany, 1871–1914' in Karl Rohe (ed.), *Elections, parties and political traditions. Social foundations of German parties and party systems, 1867–1987* (New York/Oxford/London, 1990), pp. 83–107 (pp. 93–6); also Paul Sauer, *Württembergs letzter König. Das Leben Wilhelms II.* (Stuttgart, 1994), pp. 149–59.

[7] For details of electoral reform in Saxony see in particular the work of Simone Lässig. Concise accounts of her research are given in 'Wahlrechtsreformen in den deutschen Einzelstaaten: Indikatoren für Modernisierungstendenzen und Reformfähigkeit im Kaiserreich', in Simone Lässig, Karl Heinrich Pohl and James Retallack (eds.), *Modernisierung und Region im wilhelminischen Deutschland. Wahlen, Wahlrecht und politische Kultur* (Bielefeld, 1995), pp. 127–70, and 'Der "Terror der Straße" als Motor des Fortschritts? Zum Wandel der politischen Kultur im "Musterland der Reaktion"' in Lässig and Pohl (eds.), *Sachsen im Kaiserreich*, 191–239.

Chancellor, von Bülow. More importantly, the democratic nature of the *Reichstag* franchise pointed up the glaring inequalities of the franchise in Saxony: in 1903 the Social Democrats won twenty-two out of twenty-three Saxon *Reichstag* mandates, although they did not have a single representative in the Saxon parliament between 1900 and 1905. This had important implications for the continued relevance of Saxon politics within the German Empire. Metzsch described King Georg of Saxony's conversion to the cause of electoral reform on his accession to the throne in 1902 as follows:

After [I] told him that statistics gathered under the present franchise indicated that 80 percent of voters have no influence on the choice of deputies and are therefore unrepresented in the *Landtag* [Saxon parliament] – which contravenes principles of fairness – also that among this 80 percent are found not only Social Democrats but also many clergy, teachers, lower- and middle-ranking officials, etc, who are embittered because of this disadvantage; and finally that as a result of these circumstances, the *Reichstag* has been made into a forum for discussing the domestic political affairs of Saxony, which properly belong only in the *Landtag* – the King agreed that the government should proceed with electoral reform.[8]

By the early 1900s, therefore, the coexistence of democratic and regressive franchises within Germany had become problematic. Crucially, conservatives like Metzsch recognised that democratic politics lent legitimacy and meaning to state institutions and that, conversely, without democracy such institutions would become moribund. In other words, the parliamentarisation of the German Empire was not merely reflected in the shifting balance of power between *Reichstag* and *Bundesrat*. Rather, the mere existence of a democratically elected national parliament – however limited its powers – had wide-ranging implications for the nature of politics and government at state level.

In many ways, the existence of two complementary political spheres at state and national level created a schizophrenic political environment. On the one hand, the very existence of the *Reichstag* encouraged the nationalisation of politics, in the sense that *Reichstag* deputies debated national policy and won their seats in nationwide election campaigns, prompting the emergence of national political parties and political leaders. Questions like the *Kulturkampf* (Bismarck's campaign against political Catholicism), the socialist threat, social welfare legislation, the

---

[8] Cited after James Retallack, 'Liberals, Conservatives and the modernizing state: the Kaiserreich in regional perspective' in Geoff Eley, *Society, culture and the state in Germany, 1870–1930* (Ann Arbor, 1996), pp. 221–56 (p. 235).

relative advantages of protectionist tariffs and the need for both military
and naval funding were clearly national issues. Equally, there can be no
doubt that politicians like Bismarck, Windthorst (the leader of the
Catholic Centre Party), Bennigsen (the leader of the National Liberals)
and the Social Democrat August Bebel were national figures. At the
same time, the fact that *Reichstag* elections never led to a change of
government lent *Reichstag* politics a rather chimerical quality. National
politicians made speeches and struck postures, but at the end of the day
their rhetoric and electioneering had only a limited impact on national
policy.

Meanwhile, the continued existence of less democratically elected
state parliaments created a distinctive political environment at state
level. Indeed, state politics frequently bore strikingly little resemblance
to events at national level. Parties like the National Liberals, whose vote
fell dramatically when they were excluded from power nationally in
1878, often remained the party of government in individual states – as
was the case in Hesse-Darmstadt and Württemberg well into the 1890s.[9]
Conversely, as we have seen, the Social Democrats continued to be
under-represented at state level, although they did startlingly well in
national elections. These differences were reinforced by the coexistence
of two parallel and distinct systems of political parties, at national and
state level. For instance, the National Liberal faction in the *Reichstag* corresponded at state level to a number of different groupings, such as the
German Party in Württemberg and the Hessian Progressives in Hesse-
Darmstadt. Similarly, the German Conservative Party remained primarily a Prussian entity despite the affiliation of other regional
groupings, such as the Saxon conservatives, who themselves maintained
an independent organisation: the Conservative State Association for the
Kingdom of Saxony. Equally, Württemberg Catholics could vote for the
Centre Party in national elections, but they could not do so in state elections until the belated formation of the Württemberg Centre Party in
1894. Only the Social Democratic Party, with a nationwide membership
of one million by 1914, was genuinely national.

Inevitably, the political dualism of state and nation meant that the
behaviour of individual politicians varied significantly according to the
political context. One example of this was Julius Hölder, a leading
member of the German Party in Württemberg. In the *Reichstag* Hölder

---

[9] For a discussion of the continued strength of the Hessian Progressives (National Liberals) after
1878 see Dan S. White, *The splintered party. National Liberalism in Hessen and the Reich, 1867–1918*
(Cambridge, Mass./London, 1976), pp. 62–83.

took an uncompromising stand in support of Bismarck and protectionist tariffs during the 1878–81 crisis of the National Liberals, which saw the secession of more oppositionally inclined, free trading, left-wing delegates from the *Reichstag* faction. In Württemberg, however, Hölder acted to rein in pro-Bismarckian elements in the liberal *Schwäbischer Merkur*. He also adopted an emollient attitude in the Württemberg parliament, where the German Party's position was already undermined by the existence of an independent Prime-Ministerial bloc. Inconsistencies of this kind usually reflected the different balance of power at national and state level. In the Prussian province of Hanover, the robust alliance between political Catholicism and pro-Welf particularism meant that the National Liberals remained the party of government long after they had fallen from grace at national level.[10] In Saxony, the strength of the Social Democrats forced liberals and conservatives into a semi-permanent electoral alliance. Ironically, however, a liberal–conservative alliance only emerged shakily at national level in the mid-1900s, by which time it had already collapsed in Saxony. By contrast, the slow pace of industrialisation in Württemberg rendered the Social Democrats so unthreatening that the so-called 'bourgeois' parties were ready to ally with them on occasion. In return, the Württemberg Social Democrats adopted a conciliatory stance wholly out of keeping with the position of the national party. In 1907, for instance, they voted through the annual state budget in Württemberg – something that their counterparts in the *Reichstag* never did. In practice, state politics remained enormously important, both for the outcome of national elections and for national political parties. Indeed, Peter Steinbach has concluded that national events made little or no impact where they failed to interact with state politics.[11] Famously, the *Kulturkampf* was a dead letter in Württemberg, and as a result the Centre Party was not founded in this state until the early 1890s. Conversely, state political issues remained enormously important to many people. In Saxony, thousands cared enough to take to the streets in order to obtain a change to the state franchise. By and large, however, historians have neglected state politics and state parliaments as subjects for study in their own right. This neglect is particularly questionable since the continued relevance of state politics made it very hard to create coherent political

---

[10] On this, see John, 'Liberalism and society in Germany', passim.

[11] Peter Steinbach, 'Politisierung und nationalisierung der Region im 19. Jahrhundert. Regionalspezifische Politikrezeption im Spiegel historischer Wahlforschung' in Peter Steinbach (ed.), *Probleme politischer Partizipation im Modernisierungsprozeß* (Stuttgart, 1982), pp. 321–49 (pp. 339–41).

parties at national level. Even Johannes Miquel, the leading Hanoverian National Liberal, recognised that state politics often came before national politics in imperial Germany. In 1884, he claimed: 'The diversity of conditions in Germany does not admit of an absolute mechanical identity in practical questions of political conduct. Let us mutually recognise this! Let us have freedom on secondary things, and let us be united on all essential matters.'[12] Miquel's views reflected the fact that in a constituency-based political system, even national elections were fought and won at local level. On the one hand, therefore, the existence of national elections, institutions and debates helped to make the new nation state a meaningful political community. On the other hand, the continued importance of state elections, institutions and concerns perpetuated popular awareness of the individual German states – and even in some cases Prussian provinces – as meaningful units.

This dichotomy reflected another paradox in German national life after 1871, namely the coexistence of monarchy at state and national level. The dynasty had always been a central plank of state identity in Germany and the monarch had always played an important role in state politics. As we have seen, even Bismarck regarded the German dynasties as the glue that held the precarious edifice of imperial Germany together. Yet relatively little research has been done into the role of state monarchy after 1871. Instead, historians have turned their attention to the growing importance of the Emperor in the German Empire, particularly after 1890. Kaiser Wilhelm I may have remained essentially a Prussian monarch who did little to elevate his status as Emperor, but his grandson, Kaiser Wilhelm II, took a very different approach. As Isabel Hull has shown, the fusion of traditional Hohenzollern ceremonial with the trappings of empire was central to Wilhelm II's remodelling of monarchy at both national and state level.[13] In many ways, the failure of historians to study other German monarchs of this time testifies to the success of this approach, at least in retrospect. Certainly, it reflects a perception that the lesser German monarchs ceased to be important after 1871. Friedemann Schmoll, for instance, has argued that in Württemberg the cult of regional monarchy declined with time, in recognition of the partial loss of sovereignty.[14] Schmoll contrasts the monument to King

---

[12] Cited after White, *The splintered party*, p. 116.
[13] See Isabel V. Hull, 'Prussian dynastic ritual and the end of monarchy' in Carole Fink, Isabel V. Hull and MacGregor Knox (eds.), *German nationalism and the European response, 1890–1945* (Norman, Ok/ London, 1985), pp. 13–42.   [14] See Schmoll, *Verewigte Nation*, p. 117.

Wilhelm I of Württemberg in Cannstatt – a classic equestrian sculpture of the monarch holding the constitution in one hand – with the monuments put up to honour his successors, which were placed in gardens and on bridges where they could be ignored by passers-by. Schmoll argues that whereas King Wilhelm I was respected as a monarch of genuine stature who had granted Württemberg a modern constitution, his son Karl was honoured more through habit than anything else. Equally, Schmoll makes much of the relative lack of interest shown in public subscriptions for monuments to either Wilhelm or Karl after 1866.[15] In fact, however, the failure of fund-raising drives for regional monarchic monuments was by no means an isolated phenomenon. In the past, fund-raising had proved difficult for both national monuments like the Hermann Monument and particularist monuments like the Ernst August Monument in Hanover. In this respect, German unification changed little. Moreover, Reinhard Alings has stressed the financial difficulties faced at this time by high-profile national monumental initiatives, such as the Niederwald Monument.[16] Just like its forerunner the Hermann Monument, the Niederwald Monument had to be bailed out by the *Reichstag*. It would therefore be unwise to read very much into the unwillingness of Württembergers to put their hands in their pockets on behalf of Kings Wilhelm and Karl. Equally, state monarchs remained an important source of inspiration for monument builders elsewhere in Germany. In Saxony, for instance, the decades after 1871 saw a number of major dynastic monumental initiatives – notably the sumptuous restoration of the *Goldener Reiter*; the monument to King Johann in central Dresden; the transformation of the *Albrechtsburg* palace in Meissen into a monument to the Wettin dynasty replete with colourful historical frescos; the Wettin obelisk; and the *Fürstenzug*, an elaborate mural depicting Wettin rulers through the ages along one side of the royal palace in Dresden.

Certainly, it is important not to underestimate the continued strength of cults of regional monarchy, or the role that monarchic festivities played in state life after 1871. When the newly wed Princess Louisa arrived in Saxony for the first time in the early 1890s, she was welcomed by a heart-warming display of loyalty to the royal family:

---

[15] Schmoll points out that most of the money for the so-called state monument to Wilhelm in Cannstatt came from Cannstatt itself. Of the 1910 *Gemeinden* addressed, only 74 replied at all and only 4,000 *Gulden* were raised from public subscription. See ibid., p. 103. Equally, the committee for a Karl–Olga Monument in Stuttgart was forced to scale down its plans, as only 40,000 marks were raised. See ibid., pp. 121–2.   [16] See Alings, *Monument und Nation*, pp. 321–2.

From the Bohemian frontier to Dresden is three hours by rail, but all the way ... the people were massed on both sides of the line, trying to get a glimpse of me and my husband, and I could see innumerable handkerchiefs waving and hear frantic 'Hochs' as the train passed. ... [in Dresden] we were given a tremendous reception ... Although it was November ... [t]he roofs were black with people, who showered roses on us as we passed, and the lamp-posts were covered with people clinging to them, while others were seated on the iron brackets which supported the lamps.[17]

Similar popular enthusiasm greeted the silver wedding anniversary of King Wilhelm II of Württemberg and his wife Charlotte. To mark the occasion, loyal patriots purchased literally millions of carnations (Queen Charlotte's favourite flower) and raised 522,000 marks for charity in her honour. Inevitably, the celebrations in Stuttgart were particularly grand: a bouquet was thrown from an air-ship hovering above the royal palace; a procession of Württembergers in antique dress marched through the capital; special church services were held and the day culminated with a gala banquet in the royal palace, as grand fireworks exploded across the Stuttgart sky. Public festivities to mark King Wilhelm II's fiftieth and sixtieth birthdays in 1898 and 1908 were equally heartfelt. Unlike his predecessor Karl, Wilhelm II was genuinely loved by the people.[18]

The contrast between these displays of public support for Wilhelm and the celebrations marking Karl's silver jubilee highlights the role of individual rulers in maintaining the popularity of regional monarchy at state level. Karl was a weak and apathetic character, who played little part in government, suffered periodically from depression, and spent much of the year holidaying in Italy or the town of Friedrichshafen on Lake Constance. He increasingly neglected his ceremonial duties and allowed Wilhelm to deputise on his behalf. Worse still, Karl was a homosexual and did little to keep his affairs from the public eye. His devotion to an American adventurer called Woodcock caused a major scandal. By the time of his silver jubilee, Karl was so uncertain of his personal popularity that he chose to mark the occasion by erecting a statue to one of his more famous ancestors, Duke Christoph. Tellingly, a commemorative album published to mark the occasion, entitled 'Württemberg and its King 1864–1889', only included one portrait of Karl himself.[19] Even here Karl was surrounded by other, better-loved members of the royal family, whose presence (like that of Duke Christoph) lent legitimacy to

[17] Louisa of Tuscany, ex-Crown Princess of Saxony, *My own story* (London, 1911), pp. 85–7.
[18] For a biography of King Wilhelm II of Württemberg see Sauer, *Württembergs letzter König*.
[19] Anon., *Württemberg und sein König, 1864–1889. Eine Festgabe zum 25 jährigen Regierungs-Jubiläum Seiner Majestät des Königs Karl von Württemberg* (Stuttgart, 1889).

8.1 The only portrait of Karl to appear in the official commemorative album published to mark his silver jubilee in 1889. Karl's position is endorsed by the portrayal of other members of the Württemberg royal family, notably his father Wilhelm I, and his successor Prince Wilhelm of Württemberg, the future Wilhelm II.

Source: By permission of the British Library, 1764.b.18

his rule. When he died in 1891, the prestige of the Württemberg monarchy was at an all-time low – more as a consequence of Karl's failures than of the state's diminishing importance within Germany. Wilhelm, on the other hand, played an active role in governments and his support was crucial in forcing through the Württemberg constitutional reforms of the early 1900s. Unlike Karl, he spent most of the year in Stuttgart. He was a ubiquitous presence in Württemberg public life, inaugurating monuments and buildings, opening exhibitions, sponsoring charities and attending local jubilees. He was also very at ease with his people, chatting to them as he walked through Stuttgart and carrying sweets in his pockets for the children. His popularity was such that even Wilhelm Keil, leader of the Württemberg Social Democrats, agreed that he was ideally suited to be the president of a democratic republic.[20] In a speech made in 1908 to mark Wilhelm's sixtieth birthday, the Mayor of Stuttgart, Gauss, favourably contrasted Wilhelm's popularity in Württemberg with the popularity of the Emperor at national level. Gauss noted smugly that new imperial legislation designed to reduce instances of *lèse majesté* was pointless in Württemberg: 'For in Swabia there are no instances of *lèse majesté*. And if someone were to behave in this way, he would not be taken seriously.'[21]

The experience of the Saxon royal family at this time also demonstrated the extent to which the stature of the dynasty reflected the popularity and behaviour of individual royals. According to Crown Princess Louisa, her father-in-law Georg, who acceded to the Saxon throne in 1902, was 'an intolerable bigot, narrow-minded to a degree, and he could be a fanatic on occasion. I think he must have suffered from some kind of religious mania, for he would remain for hours prostrate before the altar, praying fervently to all his special saints'.[22] So violently Catholic were his prejudices that Georg reportedly accused Louisa of being 'an apostate to my religion', on one occasion when she had agreed to deputise for Queen Carola of Saxony by opening a Protestant bazaar.[23] Admittedly, Louisa was a biased observer. She loathed her father-in-law and claimed in her memoirs that he had threatened to shut her up in an asylum, thereby forcing her to flee Dresden in 1902. These claims were misleading. In fact, her elopement probably had rather more to do with her relationship with a young Belgian, André Giron. Yet Georg's religious fanaticism was widely documented and the subject of

---

[20] See Sauer, *Württembergs letzter König*, p. 178.   [21] Cited after ibid., pp. 171–2.
[22] Louisa of Tuscany, *My own story*, p. 94.   [23] Ibid.

lively criticism in the Saxon press, which believed the Saxon court to be a nest of Jesuits and ultramontanes. In a rabidly Protestant country, Georg's attitudes and behaviour were unfortunate to say the least. More generally, Louisa describes the Saxon court as excessively formal and rigid. Louisa, however, appears to have realised that the Saxon monarchy needed to change if it was to survive. As she put it: 'I took too much interest in the people to please the Court, and I did not conceal my opinion that a Protestant country like Saxony ought to have a Protestant King, and should not be ruled by a Roman Catholic.'[24]

Louisa herself was much loved by the Saxon people for her popular and human touch. The image of Louisa proudly showing off her children to a rapturous public as she walked through the streets of Dresden was etched in the memory of the patriotic Saxon author Friedrich Kracke.[25] According to one contemporary, Louisa's extraordinary popularity had two principal causes.[26] First, she would have nothing to do with the growing religious bigotry of the Saxon court. Secondly, her charitable activities went well beyond the call of duty and stories of her warm heart and personal generosity abounded.[27] Even before her exile, expressions of popular support for Louisa became a way of implicitly criticising the rest of the royal family. When the new King Georg appeared at the funeral of King Albert of Saxony, the crowd was unenthusiastic until, according to Louisa, a woman recognised her and cried '"Give our Louisa a cheer – we all love her" – and then cheering broke out on all sides, which made the King . . . furious.'[28] This criticism became explicit after Louisa's flight. The public outcry was such that the Saxon royal family was forced to remain indoors as thousands marched on the royal palace demanding an explanation. The skin of a black cat was hung at the entrance with a card carrying a warning: 'Be careful: this will be *your* fate in our hands.'[29] When Louisa returned to Dresden in 1904 in an unsuccessful attempt to see her children, her arrival brought the city to a standstill. Hostile crowds gathered in the streets, crying 'Louisa, stay with us!', 'Death to von Metzsch!' and 'Down with the Church!' In her memoirs, Louisa claimed: 'In tiny cottages far away in the country my photograph was encircled with chaplets of flowers,

---

[24] Ibid., p. 165.
[25] Friedrich Kracke, *Friedrich August III., Sachsens volkstümlichster König. Ein Bild seines Lebens und seiner Zeit* (Munich, 1964), pp. 60–1.
[26] Anon., *Die Wahrheit über das Kronprinzenpaar von Sachsen, von einem Eingeweihten* (Zurich, 1903), pp. 47–8.   [27] See for instance ibid., pp. 48–55.   [28] Louisa of Tuscany, *My own story*, p. 156.
[29] Ibid., pp. 204–5.

candles were burned before it, women wore brooches bearing my like-
ness, and although the police afterwards prohibited the sale of picture-
postcards of me, hundreds of thousands were sold in one day alone.'[30]
The Saxon establishment was so shaken by these events that it sought to
pretend that they had never taken place. An official biography of
Louisa's husband, Friedrich August III, published shortly after his accession to the Saxon throne and less than two years after her momentous
return to Dresden, only mentioned Louisa once in passing – as the
mother of his children.[31] On the one hand, all this would seem to demonstrate the failure of the Wettins and the unpopularity of the Saxon
monarchy at this time. On the other hand, however, the appropriation
of Louisa as a symbol of political dissent demonstrates the continued
glamour and relevance of royalty even in Saxony, the stronghold of
German Socialism. However personally unpopular certain members of
the Saxon royal family may have been, the cult of Saxon monarchy was
clearly very much alive.

Given the importance of state politics and state monarchs after unification, it is hardly surprising that German political culture continued to be
centrally preoccupied with the relationship between individual German
states and the greater German Fatherland, now redefined as the *kleindeutsch* German Empire. The years after 1871 saw the emergence of a
truly national political culture in Germany, reflected in the spread of
certain symbols and political practices as part of a shared political discourse. Some, like the image of Germania, were already well established. Others were variations on existing themes, like the Emperor's
regular reviews of the German troops (*Kaiserparaden*) and the new
national flag, which amalgamated the Prussian colours with the black,
red and gold tricolour of 1848. By far the most potent of these symbols
and practices derived their legitimacy through association with the
process of state-formation itself. In the decade or so after 1871, monuments commemorating the Franco-Prussian war and the fact of unifica-

---

[30] Ibid., pp. 257–8. Louisa is undoubtedly an unreliable witness, but less biased sources also testify
to her enduring popularity. Ida Kremer, a woman sent to bring back Louisa's youngest child to
Saxony, reported that she received 2,000 birthday greetings from 'Louisa maniacs' in 1906, and
that a tooth-powder maker called Bergmann had founded the 'Band of friends', a society to
defend her interests with branches all over Germany. See Ida Kremer, *The struggle for a royal child,
Anna Monica Pia Duchess of Saxony. My experiences as Governess in the household of the Countess Montignoso*
(London, 1907), pp. 128–9, 197–8.
[31] Wolf von Metzsch-Schilbart, *Friedrich August III., König von Sachsen. Ein Lebensbild* (Berlin, 1906), p.
111.

tion appeared all over Germany. Then, following the death of Emperor Wilhelm in 1887 and Bismarck's fall in 1890, both men were appropriated as national symbols by the monument builders. Meanwhile, Germans throughout the Empire regularly celebrated Sedan Day as a national holiday. As Eric Hobsbawm has argued in a highly influential article, the new German Empire asserted its claims to nation-statehood through a series of invented traditions focusing on the events and protagonists of 1870/1.[32] After all, the war with the French was the one thing that all Germans had in common. Yet how far did national political culture really displace state culture in Germany?

It would certainly be wrong to see this new political culture simply as a vehicle for official nationalism. Some monuments, like the *Siegessäule* and the National Kaiser Wilhelm Monument in Berlin, were officially instigated and publicly funded. Most, however, were the product of spontaneous citizen initiatives and financed through private donations. Some public rituals, like the *Kaiserparaden* and the annual celebrations of the Emperor's birthday, were officially orchestrated. Most, like Sedan Day, were voluntary demonstrations of popular support for the new Germany. Of course, the distinction between official and unofficial activities was less clear-cut than this implies, since many members of monument associations and Sedan Day committees had close ties with the political establishment. Ultimately, however, cultural activities of this kind were rooted in civil society, not the state. Their legitimacy derived from popular participation rather than official endorsement. Consequently, public monuments and festivities were an important way in which different groups could articulate and negotiate their relationship with the new nation state.

The annual Sedan Day celebrations held all over Germany were probably the most prominent example of this process. As the German Empire's unofficial national holiday, Sedan Day provided an ideal opportunity for nationalists to demonstrate their support for the new nation state, and for others to express their alienation from it. Ute Schneider has shown how in the Prussian Rhineland most of the Catholic population rejected a celebration that was 'seen as a tendentious institution of the liberals directed against the Catholic Church'.[33] Indeed, Schneider

---

[32] Eric Hobsbawm, 'Mass-producing traditions: Europe, 1870–1914' in Hobsbawm and Ranger, *The invention of tradition*, pp. 263–308 (pp. 273–7).

[33] Cited after Ute Schneider, *Politische Festkultur im 19. Jahrhundert. Die Rheinprovinz von der französischen Zeit bis zum Ende des Ersten Weltkrieges (1806–1918)* (Essen, 1995), p. 241; for a more general account of Sedan Day festivities in the Rhineland see pp. 238–63.

argues that only with the death of Kaiser Wilhelm I and the end of the *Kulturkampf* did Sedan Day emerge as a genuinely national holiday, celebrated by Protestants and Catholics alike.[34] Under Wilhelm II, however, the Rhineland Socialists boycotted the occasion, organising a rival Lassalle Day at the same time of year. The decision of first Catholics, then Socialists to opt out of these celebrations clearly demonstrated the limits of the nation in imperial Germany. Of course, historians have long been aware of the role of Catholics and Socialists as outsiders in the German Empire. In non-Prussian Germany, however, they were not alone in their rejection of Sedan Day and the nation state it symbolised. Alon Confino's study of Sedan Day in Württemberg shows that the holiday was celebrated primarily by the Protestant liberal bourgeoisie, who welcomed unification as the crowning achievement of German history. They formed committees to organise the festivities, using their influence as local notables and their positions in church, schools and state to invest the new Germany with legitimacy through carefully orchestrated popular participation in the celebrations. According to Confino, it was no coincidence that the heyday of Sedan Day as a national holiday coincided with the zenith of National Liberalism in Württemberg, during the German Party's years as the party of government from 1871 to 1895.[35] The politics of this period were dominated by the aftermath of unification and the persistent divisions between *großdeutsch* and *kleindeutsch* nationalists, Catholics and Protestants, anti-Prussians and Prussophiles. In Württemberg, therefore, the refusal to celebrate Sedan Day was not simply an expression of religious alienation from the political status quo. It could also be a purely political statement, symbolising either rejection of the *kleindeutsch* German Empire or loyalty to the particular state. Tellingly, Sedan Day received precious little endorsement from the Württemberg government. Although state officials were allowed to participate in the celebrations, in 1874 the Interior Ministry explicitly prohibited the flying of flags on public buildings to mark the occasion.[36] Nationalist festivals like Sedan Day were highly sensitive political statements. By contrast, regional festivities, like Wilhelm II of Württemberg's silver wedding anniversary, had a relatively wide public appeal. Celebrations like this, which focused on the individual German states, were often less contentious than their national counterparts.

Other aspects of national political culture faced similar difficulties in penetrating non-Prussian Germany. At first glance, the cult of monument

---

[34] Ibid., p. 251.   [35] See Confino, *The nation as a local metaphor*, pp. 54–5.   [36] Ibid., pp. 33–4.

construction appears to have been a nationwide phenomenon and it is usually taken as an important expression of post-unification nationalism. Closer examination, however, reveals a more differentiated picture. In fact, there was considerable resistance outside Prussia to the official cult of the German nation propagated by Kaiser Wilhelm II after 1890. This resistance was strongest in Württemberg which, as we have seen, had well-developed traditions of individual statehood and a popular ruler in the shape of its own Wilhelm II. Reinhard Alings distinguishes between three kinds of national monument in imperial Germany: those celebrating national unification itself; those built in honour of Kaiser Wilhelm; and those built in honour of Bismarck.[37] The geographical distribution of unification monuments was fairly uniform throughout Germany, although unification monuments in South Germany tended to be built slightly later.[38] By contrast, there were five times as many Kaiser Wilhelm monuments in Prussia as elsewhere in Germany, twice as many in East Prussia as in West Prussia and very few indeed in the annexed Prussian territories.[39] There were, indeed, no Kaiser Wilhelm monuments in the new Prussian province of Hanover. Bismarck monuments too were more frequent in Prussia than elsewhere in Germany, although here the ratio was only 3:2.[40] This indicates that monuments relating to national unification were meaningful throughout Germany, since all of Germany had participated. Yet Kaiser Wilhelm never became a genuinely integrative national symbol, and clearly remained strongly associated with Prussia in the eyes of most Germans. To a lesser extent, this was also true of Bismarck.

These regional variations in monument construction indicate that – for all their national symbolism – monuments tended to reflect regional rather than national concerns. This was certainly the case of the Hanoverian War Memorial, a monument to the fallen soldiers of 1870/1.[41] The idea for such a monument emerged from the liberal nationalist milieu in Hanover during the first Sedan Day celebrations held here, and the monument committee numbered Bennigsen – former President of the *Nationalverein* and leading National Liberal – among its members. In November 1873, the committee launched a public appeal for funds. This appeal and those that followed repeatedly emphasised that the monument was a genuinely regional undertaking, 'not just for

---

[37] For a general overview of national monuments in imperial Germany, see Reinhard Alings, *Monument und Nation. Das Bild vom Nationalstaat im Medium Denkmal – zum Verhältnis von Nation und Staat im deutschen Kaiserreich, 1871–1918* (Berlin/New York, 1996).
[38] For details see ibid., pp. 79–80. [39] For details see ibid., pp. 81–2.
[40] For details see ibid., p. 82. [41] For an in-depth analysis of this monument see ibid., pp. 176–84.

those from the city [of Hanover] but for all those from the Province of Hanover who fell during the last war'.[42] Indeed, the appeal made a point of addressing 'all Hanoverians'.[43] This was important because the monument expressed the commitment of Hanover as a province to the new political situation and the German nation state. At the same time, however, the provincial nature of the monument reflected the continued relevance of old political boundaries even after 1871. Thus the committee asserted that the monument, 'besides expressing our joyful recognition of the national progress made during recent developments, will also demonstrate how the Hanoverian lands feel closely bound to one another by the permanent ties created by their traditional togetherness'.[44] In practice, however, the monument did not speak for the whole of Hanover. The committee tended to focus its fund-raising efforts on reliably nationalist elements in the province. In 1874, for instance, it appealed to Sedan Day committees to make sure that they used the Sedan Day festivities to collect money for the monument. Targeting of this kind was understandable, since the popular response to the fund-raising drive was less than enthusiastic. In the end, voluntary contributions barely amounted to one-sixth of the monuments' total costs – the rest was raised through a combination of public subsidy, two lotteries and accumulating interest. Of course, these mundane realities did not stop Bennigsen and others from claiming success for the initiative. Tellingly, however, the actual form of the monument relied heavily on Hanoverian rather than national symbolism. To the front, it consisted of a three-metre-high female figure, symbolising Hannovera mourning her lost sons. The arms of the province and its various Provincial Estates were depicted at the back. The foot of the monument was covered with the names of Hanover's nineteen hundred dead, and bore an inscription reading: 'From the Province of Hanover to her sons, who fell in the war against France, 1870'. Further inscriptions referred to the most important battles of the war, especially the battle of Weissenburg, in which Hanoverian troops had participated. In other words, the Hanoverian War Memorial sought to mediate a sense of wider German nationhood by appealing to a more immediate and traditional sense of loyalty to the particular Fatherland.

National monuments in Württemberg also reflected a regionally specific attitude to the new nation state. The highly unusual Kaiser Wilhelm monument in Heilbronn is a particularly good example of this

---

[42] Cited after ibid., p. 181.   [43] Cited after ibid., p. 316.   [44] Cited after ibid., p. 315.

8.2 The Hanoverian War Memorial.
Source: Historisches Museum, Hanover

phenomenon. Here the figure of Germania – not Kaiser Wilhelm – took centre stage, depicted as a mother reconciling two young boys, symbolising North and South Germany. The Emperor himself was represented by a modest medallion showing his bust in profile, and the monument was topped by a statue of Viktoria with the imperial crown. In playing down the role of Wilhelm and highlighting the need for unity between North and South, this monument said a great deal about the scepticism with which Württembergers regarded the Prussian-dominated German Empire. More generally, the conflict between supporters of the new status quo and sceptical democratic nationalists in Württemberg was a recurrent theme in the construction and interpretation of national monuments. The monument to the great Württemberg poet Ludwig Uhland, unveiled in Tübingen in 1873, portrayed Germania with the imperial German eagle on her shield, alongside representations of Poetry and Research. During the unveiling ceremony, liberal nationalists retrospectively laid claim to Uhland as a prophet of German unification. Yet at the banquet that followed, a democrat, Wilhelm Zimmermann, asserted scathingly that 'more still than the lack of complete unity, Ludwig Uhland would miss the lack of complete freedom in the new Empire'.[45]

Somewhat similar forces were at play in the conflict over the most suitable location for a major Kaiser Wilhelm monument in Württemberg. There were two choices: either the state capital, Stuttgart, or Hohenstaufen, the historic site of the family stronghold of Germany's medieval Staufen emperors. The Stuttgart project had the backing of the Württemberg establishment, in the shape of the King, the government, and leading figures in the *kleindeutsch* German Party, such as the editor of the *Schwäbischer Merkur*, Otto Elben. Like their Hanoverian counterparts, those behind the Stuttgart project stressed the importance of a monument which 'is presented in cheerful . . . unity by the whole people of Württemberg, all the valleys, the town and the countryside, without any distinction of estate or political opinion or whatever else usually divides men from one another, each taking his part in accordance with his abilities'.[46] Conversely, they portrayed the Hohenstaufen plan, which was a local initiative based in Göppingen and the surrounding area, as the 'rallying cry of the Democrats'.[47] Arguably, however, the dispute between Stuttgart and Hohenstaufen was less about the conflict

---

[45] Cited after Schmoll, *Verewigte Nation*, p. 162. [46] Cited after ibid., p. 292.
[47] *Württembergische Landeszeitung.* Cited after ibid., p. 198.

between authoritarian and democratic nationalism than about the right of the state, in this case Württemberg, to act as mediator of the nation. There was no place for Württemberg in the plans for a Kaiser Wilhelm monument on the Hohenstaufen heights. Instead, the Göppingen committee envisaged a national enterprise in the widest sense of the word, similar perhaps to the Hermann Monument. The committee therefore declared its intention to raise funds 'not just in Württemberg, but in the Reich and all over the world, wherever Germans live'.[48] Popular nationalist initiatives of this kind, which bypassed the state, threatened to upset the delicate balance between state and nation in Germany. Tellingly, King Karl of Württemberg was very unwilling to allow the Göppingen nationalists to appropriate the powerful symbol of Hohenstaufen for their own ends. In a private letter, he stated unequivocally that 'Württemberg's King is Duke in Swabia and heir to the Staufen. Hohenstaufen is his, and it is for him to keep the memory of his great predecessors alive! Kaiser Wilhelm is and was a great man, hero and modern emperor. It is, however, unnecessary for him to repress and destroy the memory of the greatness of former times.'[49] Karl further asserted the right to mediate between his people and their Emperor during the ceremony that marked the inauguration of the new monument in Stuttgart, in which he played a central role. In this sense, the Stuttgart Kaiser Wilhelm Monument was as much an endorsement of the Württemberg monarchy and its place in the German Empire as it was an endorsement of Kaiser Wilhelm or the nation state.

Just as participating in national festivities and inaugurating national monuments reinforced the role of individual German monarchs, so their participation on these occasions helped to legitimise the nation state. Arguably the most important instance of this mutual reassurance was the *Kaiserparaden*. These were annual military manouevres held outside Prussia in up to four different regions of the Empire. As Jakob Vogel has pointed out, they were the only occasions on which the national cult was propagated in an identical ritual throughout Germany.[50] The *Kaiserparaden* transposed the cult of the Prussian army, developed by Wilhelm during the 1860s, to the rest of Germany, displaying the strength and ability of the nation in arms to a different regional audience every time. When reviewing his troops, the Emperor invariably

---

[48] Cited after ibid., p. 199.   [49] Cited after ibid., p. 203.

[50] Jakob Vogel, 'Militärfeiern in Deutschland und Frankreich als Rituale der Nation (1871–1914)' in Etienne François, Hannes Siegrist, and Jakob Vogel (eds.), *Nation und Emotion: Deutschland und Frankreich im Vergleich 19. und 20. Jahrhundert* (Göttingen, 1995), pp. 199–214.

rode alongside the relevant regional monarch, demonstrating his recognition of the latter's authority in his own state. The Emperor usually wore the regimental uniform of the state in question and awarded state honours to worthy soldiers. In so doing, he expressed his respect for the federal nature of the Empire, which was presented to onlookers as the basis of national strength and unity. On the surface, this ceremonial demonstrated the Emperor's endorsement of his fellow monarchs. In practice, however, their support for the Emperor was probably equally important. Certainly, the indigenous military traditions of formerly independent states like Hanover, Saxony and Württemberg retained considerable popular resonance after 1871. Thus, Kaiser Wilhelm II's public acknowledgement of Hanover's military achievements contributed greatly to his popularity in the new province. In 1899, he proclaimed the various Hanoverian regiments that made up the Tenth Army Corps to be the official heirs of the Hanoverian state army, declaring that in 1870/1 they had shown themselves 'worthy of their ancestors, the victors of Krefeld, Minden, Waterloo, and the gallant fighters on the Spanish peninsula'.[51] This flattering declaration was part of Wilhelm's wider policy of conciliation with Hanoverian particularism, which culminated in his daughter's marrying into the Welf family in 1913.

The cult of state monarchy and the regional reinterpretation of national political culture was partly a product of state-building policy in the *Mittelstaaten* before unification. These policies certainly did not come to an end in 1871. Nowhere was this more apparent than in the field of education, where government policy showed a remarkable continuity between the pre- and post-unification periods. Indeed, Hans-Michael Körner has argued that the efforts of the Bavarian government to promote a sense of the state as a meaningful cultural unit actually intensified over time, after an initial period of adaptation to the new national framework.[52] In the past, historians of imperial Germany have highlighted the role of education in shaping a new sense of national identity. Julian Schoeps, for instance, has argued that the *Volksschule* readers produced in the German Empire performed an important integrative function.[53] Schoeps claims

[51] Cited after Hartung, *Konservative Zivilisationskritik und regionale Identität*, p. 70.
[52] Hans-Michael Körner, 'Geschichtsunterricht im Königreich Bayern zwischen deutschem Nationalgedanken und bayerischem Staatsbewußtsein' in Karl-Ernst Jeismann (ed.), *Bildung, Staat, Gesellschaft im 19. Jahrhundert. Mobilisierung und Disziplinierung. Im Auftage der Freiherr-vom-Stein-Gesellschaft* (Stuttgart, 1989), pp. 245–55 (pp. 250–2).
[53] Schoeps, 'Die Deutschen und ihre Identität', pp. 92–6.

that *Volksschule* readers projected a classically Borussian interpretation of the German past and present, which emphasised the Hohenzollern mission in Germany and drew a laboured parallel between Frederick Barbarossa and Kaiser Wilhelm I. In fact, however, all but one of the books cited by Schoeps was Prussian in origin. The sole exception, printed in Leipzig, presented a picture of a distinctly more federal Germany: 'Instead of a Barbarossa, a red-bearded Emperor, a Barba blanca, a white-bearded Emperor, sat on the throne, to whom all Germany, the princes and the people, bowed in warm love and respect.'[54] This misguided tendency to generalise about German education on the basis of primarily Prussian experience is fairly widespread.[55] In reality, education policy remained the province of individual state governments. As Katherine Kennedy has shown, the portrayal of German history provided in South German school books was very different from that presented by Prussian counterparts.[56] Indeed, readers in Bavaria and Württemberg tended to minimise the role of Prussia in German unification and to dwell instead on the achievements of their own armies and monarchs. This encouraged pupils to identify with the particular state, rather than the nation as a whole. So children in Württemberg read about the Battle of Worth, where Württemberg troops received special commendations, and Bavarian children learnt about the role of Bavarian troops at the Battle of Weissenburg. Equally, South German school books depicted the German Empire as the creation of all the German princes rather than just Prussia. Tellingly, Bismarck did not merit a mention in Württemberg school readers until the end of the nineteenth century. Similarly, none of the *Volksschule* reader supplements produced in the aftermath of the Franco-Prussian war in Bavaria or Württemberg included a section on the life of Kaiser Wilhelm I. Accounts of the more distant past showed the same tendency to focus on the particular Fatherland and its rulers, and to ignore Prussian history. In this, they followed in the footsteps of pre-unification education policy. Admittedly, the Catholic Württemberg *Volksschule* reader included a short paragraph on

---

[54] Cited in ibid., p. 95. Citation taken from J. C. Andrä and E. Stürzer, *Grundriß der Geschichte für höhere Schulen*, 2 vols. (Leipzig, 1902).

[55] See for instance the contributions by Elizabeth Erdmann, Gerhard Schneider and Klaus Bergmann in Bergmann and Schneider (eds.) *Gesellschaft, Staat, Geschichtsunterricht* (Düsseldorf, 1982), pp. 77–103, 132–89, 190–217; Alfred Kelly, 'The Franco-Prussian war and unification in German history schoolbooks' in Walter Pape (ed.), *1870/71–1989/90. German unifications and the change of literary discourse* (Berlin/New York, 1993), pp. 37–60.

[56] Katharine D. Kennedy, 'Regionalism and nationalism in South German history lessons 1871–1914', *German Studies Review* 12 (1989), 11–33.

the rise of Prussia from 1640 to 1861, and its Protestant counterpart included several short sections on Frederick the Great. Yet this paled in comparison to the number of pages and sections devoted to Württemberg's
rulers. Interestingly, school books in Bavaria and Württemberg in the
1870s and 1880s showed a disproportionate interest in the Middle Ages in
general and the medieval German Emperors in particular. Kennedy concludes that although both Prussian and South German school readers
attempted to turn schoolchildren into German patriots, they nevertheless
sought to legitimise the German Empire in terms that drew heavily on
existing particularist and federal traditions and reinforced the prevailing
cult of regional monarchy.

It is inevitably hard to judge the impact of these initiatives on the consciousness of young Germans. Indeed, only one historian has been brave
enough to attempt to investigate the links between education policy and
political behaviour in any detail. Monica Wölk's study of the voting patterns of Prussian *Volksschule* leavers explores the impact of alternately
progressive and traditionalist trends in Prussian education policy as a
response to the challenges posed by universal suffrage in *Reichstag* elections.[57] She concludes somewhat surprisingly that the Prussian government's efforts to socialise future voters in the *Volksschulen* were actively
counter-productive. In fact, liberal education policy proved more effective in maintaining pro-government electoral habits among Prussian
voters.[58] Wölk's conclusions demonstrate the consummate failure of
Kaiser Wilhelm II's anti-socialist education policy. Clearly, learning
about the efforts of Prussian monarchs to improve the material welfare
of their subjects did not stop the rise of the Social Democrat vote. Yet it
is unclear that Wölk's conclusions also demonstrate the failure of the
education system to promote nationalism amongst Prussian pupils.
Jonathan Sperber's broader study of voting behaviour in the German
Empire demonstrates, for instance, that nationalist sentiments did not
stop Germans from voting against the government during elections
fought largely around economic issues, when they believed that the
Empire itself was not under threat.[59] This indicates that socialism and
nationalism were less absolutely incompatible than historians have
assumed, at least among the more moderate proponents of both beliefs.
If reactionary education policy could encourage the development of a

---

[57] Monika Wölk, *Der preussische Volksschulabsolvent als Reichstagswähler 1871–1912. Ein Beitrag zur historischen Wahlforschung in Deutschland* (Berlin, 1980).   [58] Ibid., p. 454.
[59] See Jonathan Sperber, *The Kaiser's voters. Electors and elections in Imperial Germany* (Cambridge, 1997),
e.g. pp. 259–60.

nationalist mindset in Prussia, then this was surely equally true elsewhere. In other words, education policy could very well have encouraged the persistence of particularist identity in the *Mittelstaaten*.

The continued relevance of the state in imperial Germany was by no
means restricted to politics, culture and education. It also had economic
ramifications. After 1871, the state railway systems of the *Mittelstaaten*
became one of the last bastions of territorial fragmentation in Germany.
In the 1870s Bismarck tried repeatedly to centralise and nationalise the
German railways. Yet state governments successfully resisted these efforts,
demonstrating the limitations of centralisation within the new German
Empire. Moreover, the need for individual states to collaborate in defending existing state railways strengthened federal forces in Germany in other
ways. For instance, Hans-Otto Binder has shown that railway policy
prompted initial diplomatic contacts between nationally inclined Baden
and the other, more particularist *Mittelstaaten* after unification.[60] More
importantly, perhaps, railways helped to shore up the financial independence of the *Mittelstaaten*, as they became more profitable. Had Bismarck
succeeded in nationalising the German railways, they could have formed
a new source of revenue for the Empire and strengthened it accordingly.
Conversely, railway revenue partially compensated for the antiquated tax
systems in many of the individual German states, and proved crucial in
the budgets of these states until 1914. This revenue enabled state governments to defend their relative independence within the German Empire
more effectively. Unsurprisingly, the dependence of state finances on
railway revenue encouraged inter-state railway competition after unification, just as it had done in the years before 1871. State railway administrations were ruthless in their efforts to maximise profits at the expense of
their neighbours. For instance, Baden and Bavaria successfully cut
Württemberg state railways out of the North–South and East–West
transit business, by introducing selective tariff reductions for freight and
by slowing down express trains before they reached Württemberg. Prussia
adopted a similar policy with regard to Saxony. Such tricks aroused a
public outcry, precisely because the implications for state finances and the
local economy were so serious. In this sense, they reinforced a sense of
identification with the individual German states. As one popular poem
put it:

---

[60] See Hans Otto Binder, *Reich und Einzelstaaten während der Kanzlerschaft Bismarcks 1871–1890. Eine Untersuchung zum Problem der bundesstaatlichen Organisation* (Tübingen, 1971), p. 24.

My Württemberg! The railway
Is nothing but a burden.
Since all the traffic passes by
Bavaria and Baden![61]

How far did the persistence of particularism in many aspects of German life impede a growing sense of nationhood after 1871, and what does this tell us about the long-term impact of state-building policies in the *Mittelstaaten?* Political developments in the German Empire undoubtedly reveal a gradual nationalisation of its citizens. As we have seen, only a quarter of all Germans voted in the first *Reichstag* elections for parties that actively endorsed the new German Empire. Of those who did not, only some voted for regional particularists. Unsurprisingly perhaps, the particularist vote was strongest in Hanover, where 46.1% voted for either the pro-Welf German Hanoverian Party or the Centre Party in 1871. The two parties worked so closely together that for decades they did not run against each other in any of the *Reichstag* constituencies.[62] As late as 1890 the two parties still attracted 35.8% of the vote. This anti-government alliance began to break down in the early 1900s. Thereafter, the Welf vote appears to have been considerably stronger than the Catholic vote, by a ratio of at least 2:1. In 1900 the German Hanoverian Party polled 20.1% of the vote; in 1912, 13.5%. Political particularism was markedly less successful in Prussian Hesse, although Hesse was also a recently annexed territory. This would appear to be a retrospective endorsement of the success of Hanoverian state-building policies before unification. Unsurprisingly, these policies were most successful in the traditional Protestant heartlands of the old Hanoverian state which, along with Catholic areas like Osnabrück, provided the strongest and most consistent support for the anti-government alliance in Hanover.

Local opposition to the new German Empire took a different form in both Saxony and Württemberg. Saxon conservatism continued to be tinged with particularism for many decades, but particularly during the early 1870s. Thus the 1871 manifesto of the conservative electoral association claimed for Saxony 'the same rights which other states in the Empire have been accorded'.[63] This relatively particularist appeal was

---

[61] Cited in Gisevius, *Vorgeschichte des preußisch-sächsischen Eisenbahnkrieges*, p. 15.

[62] On the relationship between particularism and political Catholicism in Hanover, see Hans-Georg Aschoff, *Welfische Bewegung und politischer Katholizismus 1866–1918. Die Deutsch-hannoversche Partei und das Zentrum in der Provinz Hannover während des Kaiserreiches* (Düsseldorf, 1987).

[63] Cited after Wolfgang Schröder, 'Die Genese des "Conservativen Landesvereins für das Königreich Sachsen"' in Lässig and Pohl (eds.), *Sachsen im Kaiserreich*, pp. 149–74 (p. 161). This article provides an interesting analysis of the development of Saxon conservatism in the 1870s.

unsuccessful and the conservative vote fell to 25%. Indeed, it did not pick up again until the Conservative State Association for the Kingdom of Saxony had categorically stated its commitment to the new Empire, declaring in 1875: 'Our kind of conservative has nothing to do with anti-imperial particularism.'[64] Yet the weakness of Saxon conservatism in the early 1870s may simply reflect the fact that potential conservative voters were naturally inclined to support the government. Genuinely opposi-tional Saxon particularism found an outlet instead in the Saxon People's Party and its successor, the German Social Democratic Party. There can be no doubting the extraordinary success of socialism in Saxony. By 1903 all but one of Saxony's *Reichstag* mandates were in Social Democrat hands and the party itself had a huge Saxon membership.[65] By 1914 there were 177,500 paid-up Saxon members of the Social Democratic Party – more than in France and Italy put together. To a great extent, the success of socialism in Saxony must be attributed to the very high degree of industrialisation and urbanisation in that state. Nevertheless, Siegfried Weichlein has argued that the early growth of the Social Democratic Party in Saxony was due in large measure to its uncompro-mising anti-Prussian position.[66] The Saxon People's Party had consis-tently demonstrated its opposition to the new Bismarckian political order in Germany during the late 1860s, and in 1871 it declared its oppo-sition to the Franco-Prussian war, which the Saxon socialist leader August Bebel regarded as an instrument of Prussian militarism and jun-kerdom.[67] Consequently, the socialists can be seen as the legitimate heirs of democratic and federalist opposition to *kleindeutsch* unification in Saxony.

In Württemberg this tradition was represented primarily by the dem-ocratic People's Party – a political force that bore very little resemblance to its Saxon namesake.[68] The left-liberal Württemberg People's Party

[64] Cited after ibid., p. 167.
[65] On the strength of socialism in Saxony see for instance Karsten Rudolf, 'Das "rote Königreich": die sächsische Sozialdemokratie im Wilhelminischen Deutschland', in Lässig and Pohl (eds), *Sachsen im Kaiserreich*, pp. 87–99.
[66] See Siegfried Weichlein, 'Saxons into Germans: the progress of the national idea in Saxony after 1866' in James Retallack (ed.), 'Memory, democracy, and the mediated nation. Political cultures and regional identities in Germany, 1848–1998. An international conference of the University of Toronto in collaboration with the German Historical Institute, Washington, D.C., Toronto, September 18–20, 1998' (unpublished conference reader, September 1998), p. 8.
[67] On the role of the Saxon People's Party in the unification era see Armstrong, 'The Social-Democrats and the unification of Germany'.
[68] On the history of the Württemberg People's Party in Imperial Germany see James Clark Hunt, *The People's Party in Württemberg and Southern Germany, 1890–1914. The possibilities of Democratic politics* (Stuttgart, 1975).

struggled politically during the 1870s, which were characterised by resignation to the new state of affairs and inactivity. In the early 1880s,
however, the fortunes of the People's Party began to revive. In 1890, the
People's Party won nine of the seventeen Württemberg *Reichstag* mandates, and ten in 1893. Interestingly, the appeal of the Württemberg
People's Party, like that of the German Hanoverian Party, transcended
the confessional divide. Consequently, the emergence of the
Württemberg Centre Party as a force to be reckoned with in regional
politics posed a real threat, causing the People's Party to redouble its
efforts in Catholic areas like Upper Swabia in the late 1890s. Even so,
the People's Party and the Centre Party in Württemberg worked loosely
together until 1898, when the Centre Party finally came out in opposition to proposed constitutional reforms that would have eradicated its
natural majority in the Württemberg Upper House.

Clearly, strong traditions of political opposition to the established
order in the new German Empire persisted in all three states into the
1890s and beyond. Indeed, only in Hanover is there evidence of a marked
decline in the particularist vote after 1900. The Social Democrats in
Saxony went from strength to strength, and the Württemberg People's
Party still held twenty-four seats in the Württemberg parliament after the
constitutional reforms of 1906. How then is it possible to talk of a nationalisation of the German public after 1871?

First, it is worth noting that the national issue clearly possessed enormous mobilising power for the German voter. Jonathan Sperber has
found that major leaps in political participation coincided with those
Reichstag election campaigns fought over national rather than economic
issues. Patriotic sabre-rattling was far more effective than class conflict
in bringing previous non-voters to the ballot box. Crucially, this mobilising power seems to have increased over time. The 1878 elections were
fought in the shadow of the socialist menace after several botched
attempts to assassinate the Emperor. Bismarck's anti-socialist scare-
mongering prompted a considerable increase in turnout amongst
Prussian Protestants, where the percentage of those voting rose by 10%,
from 49% in 1877 to 59% in 1878.[69] Outside Prussia, however, the
turnout of all voters actually fell. By contrast, the 1887 elections, which
were fought primarily over the issue of military funding against a background of French revanchism, prompted a 17% increase in the vote all
over Germany.[70] Finally, turnout in the 1907 elections jumped from 76%

---

[69] Sperber, *The Kaiser's voters*, p. 176.   [70] Ibid., p. 197.

in 1903 to an all-time high of 84%, after a particularly virulent election campaign in which the liberal and conservatives parties of the future Bülow Bloc aggressively denounced the unpatriotic stance of the Social Democrats and the Catholic Centre Party.[71] The contrast between the Prussian response to nationalist rhetoric in 1878 and the nationwide responses in 1887 and 1907 indicate the growing loyalty to the Empire in non-Prussian Germany.

More importantly, perhaps, the turn of the century saw significant changes in the political stance of both the German Hanoverian Party and the Württemberg People's Party. In 1899, the German Hanoverian delegates in the *Reichstag* gave their conditional approval to the proposed military budget for the first time. This, as Hans-Georg Aschoff argues, represented a significant reconciliation with the new nation state.[72] In many ways, the Württemberg People's Party underwent a very similar transition, despite the quite different nature of its political leanings. Traditionally, the Württemberg People's Party had always been sceptical of official German nationalism. People's Party politicians regarded Bismarck's periodic war scares as political manoeuvres, and railed in the 1890s against the 'boundless naval plans' and 'dynastic naval parades' of the Wilhelmine era.[73] In the *Reichstag*, its delegates were usually willing to vote the necessary funds for national defence, but tended to regard them as excessive and even unconstitutional. In the 1900s, however, the People's Party found it impossible to deny that international tensions posed genuine cause for concern. Moreover, at least some of its members became caught up in the colonial enthusiasms of the age. In 1906, therefore, the People's Party joined with National Liberals and conservatives to vote for an independent colonial office at national level. Later that year, the three People's Party *Reichstag* delegates voted additional funds for the colonial war in East Africa. Indeed, the party's new mood was such that the late 1900s and early 1910s saw the beginnings in Württemberg of an electoral alliance between the People's Party and their old enemies, the German Party. Interestingly, the 'nationalisation' of both the German Hanoverian Party and the Württemberg People's Party took place only after the collapse of their traditional alliance with political Catholicism. By and large, moreover, the Social Democrats did not undergo a similar change of heart – even though they eventually capitulated to the forces of nationalism, when they voted for war credits in 1914.

---

[71] Ibid., p. 249.   [72] See Aschoff, *Welfischer Bewegung und politischer Katholizismus*, pp. 288–90.
[73] Cited after Hunt, *The People's Party in Württemberg*, p. 152.

There can be no doubting the strength of popular nationalism in Germany by 1914. Some extremist organisations, like the Pan-German League, were relatively small. Others, like the Army League, were huge. Within six months of its foundation, the Army League had gathered some 100,000 members – making it the second largest nationalist organisation. Nevertheless, the popularity of these nationalist organisations varied considerably in geographical terms. Whereas the central belt of Germany, from Hesse through Thuringia to Saxony, was an area of particular strength, the appeal of popular nationalism in South Germany and particularly Württemberg was more limited.[74] In part, this difference was due to economic factors. Higher levels of industrialisation and urbanisation in Saxony created a more intense sense of crisis among the traditional lower middle classes, who could not adapt to the pace of economic change and feared proletarianisation. This fear was fed by the rise of the Social Democrats in Saxony, which was of course itself a product of the same socio-economic developments. Popular nationalism was one expression of this fear, since anti-socialism was a central plank of all nationalist organisations. Until the 1900s Saxon politics were polarised between the very strong Social Democrats and a 'bourgeois' cartel of conservatives and liberals. In practice, the conservatives dominated the cartel and the liberals remained a junior partner until the 1900s, when they emerged as a force to be reckoned with.[75] Led by the young Stresemann, this renaissance reflected a change of tack on the part of the liberals, who began to market themselves as the party of urban industry. They also successfully targeted the nationalist milieu represented by organisations like the Pan-German League, of which Stresemann was a leading member. This was relatively easy because popular nationalist voters, many of whom came from the crisis-ridden middle classes, had been deeply dissatisfied with the politics of the cartel. Indeed, Richard Levy argues that the fleeting strength of the anti-Semitic vote in Saxony during the 1890s was a similar expression of frustration by the lower middle class.[76] Even at state level, therefore, popular nationalism in Saxony was essentially oppositional. In Württemberg, by

---

[74] For further details see Roger Chickering, *We men who feel most German. A cultural study of the Pan-German League, 1866–1914* (Boston, Mass./London, 1984), pp. 138–9.
[75] On this see Karl Heinrich Pohl, 'Die Nationalliberalen in Sachsen vor 1914. Eine Partei der konservativen Honoratioren auf dem Wege zur Partei der Industrie', in Lothar Gall (ed.), *Liberalismus und Region. Zur Geschichte des deutschen Liberalismus im 19. Jahrhundert, Historische Zeitschrift,* Beiheft NF 19 (1985), pp. 195–217.
[76] On this see Richard S. Levy, *The downfall of the anti-Semitic political parties in Imperial Germany* (London/New Haven, Conn. 1975), pp. 98–9.

contrast, the room for socialist expansion was limited and the Social Democrats never appeared such a threat. Equally, the 'anti-national' People's Party in Württemberg had a relatively strong following among the lower middle class, which made it hard for movements like the Pan-German League to make headway there.

Recently, historians such as Geoff Eley and Roger Chickering have sought to overturn the 1960s orthodoxy that the jingoism of the Wilhelmine years was the product of political manipulation by the German Empire's pre-industrial elites, who fanned the flames of popular nationalism in the hope of quelling the forces of political and social change.[77] Instead, Eley and Chickering have identified two competing elements in the new nationalist organisations of the 1890s: the 'genuine' nationalists, who saw the primacy of the nation as absolute, and those in the German political establishment who sought to use popular nationalism for their own ends. By 1912, the connection between these two elements had become so tenuous that the former constituted a kind of national opposition to the imperial government. In some ways, this conflict between popular and official nationalism was inevitable. As Chickering argues, groups like the General German School Association, the German Colonial Society, the General German Linguistic Association and the Pan-German League shared a common preoccupation with Germans outside the borders of the new Germany and a fundamentally cultural understanding of German nationhood, which transcended the limits of the German Empire.[78] These views formalised and vocalised a greater German vision of the nation that predated unification and had never really gone away. In this context, Svenja Goltermann's findings regarding the strength of *großdeutsch* nationalism in the gymnasts' movement throughout the 1870s are highly significant. According to Goltermann, Austrian gymnasts were welcomed with open arms at the National Gymnastic Festival held in Bonn as early as 1872, when Theodor Georgii proclaimed that as long as the German Empire did not include all members of the German nation, gymnasts would 'make sure that border posts and constitutions do not divide German hearts and hands'.[79] Equally, newspaper accounts of national

---

[77] See Geoff Eley, 'The Wilhelmine Right: how it changed', in Richard J. Evans (ed.), *Society and politics in Wilhelmine Germany* (London, 1978), pp. 112–35, and *Reshaping the German right – radical nationalism and political change after Bismarck* (New Haven, Conn., 1980). Also of interest in this context are Roger Chickering, 'Der deutsche Wehrverein und die Reform der deutschen Armee, 1912–1914', *Militärgeschichtliche Mitteilungen* 25 (1979), 7–28 and *We men who feel most German*.
[78] Chickering, 'Der Deutsche Wehrverein', 28–9.   [79] Cited after Goltermann, *Körper der Nation*, p. 223.

gymnastic festivals invariably emphasised the particular enthusiasm that greeted speeches by and about the Austrian gymnasts.[80] Increasingly, moreover, the rhetoric of gymnasts at these occasions drew a clear distinction between the political nation and the ethnic people or *Volk*. This sense of a wider German nation that transcended the political borders of the new Germany demonstrates the persistence of pre-unification ideas of nationhood and the limits of official nationalism in Germany after 1871. In the popular nationalist movement, this sense of a cultural and ethnic nation that stretched beyond the borders of the German Empire fused with more overtly political demands for higher military expenditure, aggressive colonialism and intervention in Central Europe.

On one level, the growth of popular nationalist associations would appear to be a further demonstration of the nationalisation of Germans in the German Empire. In fact, however, popular nationalism had its particularist corollary in the shape of the *Heimat* movement. The *Heimat* movement was an expression of popular engagement with and interest in the characteristics and traditions of a particular locality, state or region, as a unique expression of the wider national culture.[81] This interest manifested itself in a flood of *Heimat* publications, *Heimat* museums and *Heimat* associations, whose concerns ranged from hiking, through the protection and prettification of local beauty sites and monuments, to the preservation of traditional folk culture. Like the nationalist societies of imperial Germany, the *Heimat* movement emerged during the 1890s and peaked in the 1900s. Celia Applegate and Alon Confino have both stressed the importance of the *Heimat* movement in reconciling national and local loyalties in the German Empire. Whereas Applegate stresses the role of the *Heimat* idea in mediating the nation for provincial Germans, Confino sees *Heimat* as a metaphor for the nation state itself. There is much truth in both these interpretations, but both Applegate and Confino tend to ignore the relationship between the *Heimat* movement, political particularism and pre-unification state-building in Germany.

First, there are clear links between the emergence of a *Heimat* ideology and the state-building efforts of the *Mittelstaaten* before unification.

---

[80] See ibid., pp. 243–5.
[81] There have been a number of important recent publications relating to the *Heimat* movement. Foremost among these are Celia Applegate, *A nation of provincials*; Confino, *The nation as a local metaphor*; Hartung, *Konservative Zivilisationskritik und regionale Identität*; and William H. Rollins, *A greener vision of home: cultural politics and environmental reform in the German Heimatschutz movment, 1904–1918* (Ann Arbor, 1997).

Thus Applegate connects the cultivation of a sense of cultural Pfalz identity in the Bavarian Palatinate to Wilhelm Heinrich Riehl's publication of 'The Pfälzers: a picture of a Rhenish people' in the late 1850s.[82] Riehl was the prophet of the *Heimat* movement in Germany, a figure as central to the development of *Heimat* ideology as Marx was to the socialist movement.[83] Yet Riehl's work on the Pfalz was inspired by Max II of Bavaria, as part of his wider policy of fostering Bavarian national identity. Furthermore, local historical and geographical associations of the kind sponsored by *Mittelstaat* governments in the earlier nineteenth century often paved the way for the emergence of more popular *Heimat* associations in the 1890s. Admittedly, *Heimat* activists stressed the differences between the *Heimat* movement and earlier organisations. In 1908, for instance, Georg Friedrich Konrich, editor of the Hanoverian *Heimat* periodical *Hannoverland*, expressed his contempt for local historical associations 'which number many hundreds of names in their membership lists, and whose gatherings are almost always totally deserted'.[84] By contrast, he claimed, '[The *Heimat* movement] does not wish to provide a few learned gentlemen with food for thought, but rather to appeal to all kinds of people and cultivate amongst them a true joy in and enthusiasm for the *Heimat*.' In practice, however, many of the activities central to the *Heimat* movement, such as the foundation of local museums, were identical to those pursued by earlier local historical associations. Equally, the introduction of '*Heimat* studies' into the *Volksschule* curriculum cannot be seen in isolation from the pre-unification education policy of *Mittelstaaten* like Hanover, Saxony and Württemberg. Alon Confino makes much of the gradual introduction of *Heimat* history in Württemberg school books at this time, arguing that the Wurttemberg government only felt it necessary to teach about *Heimat* identity once Württemberg had ceased to be an independent state.[85] In fact, however, the sudden appearance of sections on 'the *Heimat*' in the Württemberg *Volksschule* readers was simply a repackaging of old ideas. If anything, these ideas enabled the governments of states like Württemberg to make the particularist tone of school text books more explicit. This was true even in the Prussian province of Hanover. It was surely no accident that the leading pedagogical proponent of *Heimat* studies in the *Volksschule*, August Tecklenburg,

---

[82] See Applegate, *A nation of provincials*, pp. 34–5.
[83] On the central importance of Riehl, see Klaus Bergmann, *Agrarromantik und Großstadtfeindschaft* (Meisenheim am Glan, 1970), pp. 39–49.
[84] Cited after Hartung, *Konservative Zivilisaionskritik und reigonale Identität*, p. 73.
[85] See Confino, *The nation as local metaphor*, pp. 107–8.

was a Hanoverian. Tecklenburg was far from being a Welf particularist, but he clearly identified with the province of Hanover as a territorial unit with its own political history. Indeed, he even wrote a Hanoverian history book for schools, in which he praised Kaiser Wilhelm II's public recognition of Hanover's glorious past.[86] In his book 'The organic integration of *Heimat-* and tribal history into the history of the Empire' Tecklenburg argued that by focusing the pupil's attention on his *Heimat* one could lead him to the conclusion that 'Emperor and Princes protect my home, my *Heimat*, and do more for me than I do for them'.[87] For Tecklenburg, therefore, the introduction of *Heimat* studies into the *Volksschule* curriculum helped to legitimise his own particularism.

Second, it is impossible to ignore the anti-centralist, anti-Prussian and anti-Berlin aspects of *Heimat* ideology. Julius August Langbehn, an enormously influential thinker in the *Heimat* movement, believed that the development of Germany's new capital, Berlin, posed a great threat to the cultural well-being of the German people and maintained that 'Art needs localism and provincialism.'[88] 'One must,' he argued, 'play the provinces both politically and intellectually against the capital, let them march on it.' Other *Heimat* activists took up Langbehn's ideas. Friedrich Lienhardt, for instance, coined the slogan 'Away from Berlin' (*Los von Berlin*), which became the battlecry of the *Heimat* art movement in the 1900s. He believed that urban authors were too alienated from the people to write truly national poetry, and called for 'decentralisation' and a 'de-Berlinification of the *Zeitgeist*'.[89] It is hard not to relate this kind of rhetoric to the anti-Prussian sentiment of the pre-unification era and its immediate aftermath. In this sense at least, *Heimat* ideology appears to be in some sense the heir of both particularism and federalism. Interestingly, *Heimat* activists also emphasised the individuality and importance of the various German tribes. Indeed, Werner Hartung's study of the *Heimat* movement in Lower Saxony argues that this 'tribal ideology' became increasingly central to the *Heimat* movement.[90] Here too, there are strong similarities with the propaganda produced by *Mittelstaat* governments in the 1850s and 1860s. Maximillian Harden, for instance, a Hanoverian critic of Kaiser Wilhelm II, claimed in 1904 that

---

[86] August Tecklenburg and Karl Dageförde, *Geschichte der Provinz Hannover für Lehrer, Lehrerbildungs- und andere Lehranstalten der Provinz sowie für Schul- und Volksbibliotheken*, 2nd edn (Hanover and Berlin, 1909). See Hartung, *Konservative Zivilisatonskritik und regionale Identität*, p. 70.

[87] Cited after Schneider, 'Die Geschichtsunterricht in der Ära Wilhelms II (vornehmlich in Preußen)', p. 172.   [88] Cited after Bergmann, *Agrarromantik und Großstadtfeindschaft*, p. 106.

[89] Cited after ibid., p. 115.

[90] See Hartung, *Konservative Zivilisationskritik und regionale Identität*, pp. 120–3.

'Of all the German *Gaus*, Lower Saxony is the most specifically German and its inhabitants are the only real Germans, in that they cultivate homely [*heimisch*] ways . . . Berlin must not be allowed to become an arbitrator for the other German tribes in artistic matters.'[91] In the pre-unification era this tribal ideology was used to justify continuing political fragmentation. By the 1900s, tribal ideology had became increasingly intertwined with racist thought, without necessarily losing this political agenda.

Heimat thinkers like Langbehn and Lieden shared a common belief in the inherent value of popular culture as opposed to the elite culture of intellectuals, typified by Berlin. Yet they were uninterested in the popular culture of the urban masses and identified true popular culture with the peasantry and traditional rural life. This belief reflected a rejection of the city and all it stood for – notably industrialisation, liberalism and socialism. Recent historians of the *Heimat* movement, such as Applegate and Confino, have stressed, however, that its proponents were not exclusively anti-modern. Indeed, William Rollins concludes that the *Heimatschutz* movement was essentially a progressive, middle-class force.[92] Yet the rural preoccupations of the *Heimat* movement were undeniably deeply influenced by the anti-urban ideas of Riehl, Georg Hansen, Heinrich Sohnrey and others. Equally, there can be no doubt of the central role anti-socialism played in the *Heimat* movement. Indeed, Sohnrey, who was editor of the leading *Heimat* periodical *Das Land* and founder of the German Association for Rural Welfare and Cultivation of the *Heimat*, believed that 'folkishness is the best and strongest protection against the threat of the realisation of communist-socialist political ideals'.[93] This kind of anti-socialism had much in common with the views of the nationalist opposition in Germany. Indeed, anti-socialism was not the only preoccupation common to both the *Heimat* and nationalist activists. The *Heimat* movement also incorporated elements that were sympathetic to the racist ideas and aggressive expansionism of organisations like the Pan-German League. In Hanover, for instance, *Heimat* activists became increasingly concerned by what they perceived as the Slav threat to Lower Saxony.[94] Equally, Klaus Bergmann has shown how the desire of *Heimat* activists to preserve the German peasantry led them to favour an expansionist foreign policy that would enable the colonisation of Central and Eastern

---

[91] Cited after ibid., p. 156.   [92] See Rollins, *A greener vision of home*, pp. 151–3.
[93] Cited after Bergmann, *Agrarromantik und Großstadtfeindschaft*, p. 108.
[94] On this see Hartung, *Konservative Zivilisationskritik und regionale Identität*, pp. 156–9.

Europe by healthy German peasant stock.[95] Of course, it is important
to distinguish between the views of *Heimat* ideologues like Sohnrey and
the views of ordinary people, who bought into the *Heimat* idea by
sending *Heimat* postcards, reading *Heimat* books, purchasing *Heimat* art
and hiking through the local countryside. Even so, the *Heimat* movement
was clearly part of the wider nationalist milieu in imperial Germany, in
that both shared the same values and prejudices. This conclusion
appears surprising in the light of the particularism and anti-centralist
federalism of the *Heimat* movement. In fact, of course, popular nationalism differed from official nationalism in part because of its less political and more cultural vision of the German nation – a vision that was
inevitably more accommodating of particular identities. Crucially, both
the Heimat movement and the nationalist opposition aspired to tran-
scend party political divides. In Hanover, for instance, the *Heimat* movement was unique in bringing together National Liberals and supporters
of the German Hanoverian Party. At the Third Lower Saxon Festival in
Hanover in 1904, Julius Kettler, the founder of the Lower Saxon *Heimat*
League, declared proudly that 'once again today National Liberals as
well as Welfs have come to the Lower Saxon festival; Progressives as well
as Centrists and conservatives. Let us . . . think only of that which unites
us: *Heimat* and Fatherland.'[96] Ultimately, however, the appeal of the
Heimat movement was far greater than that of the national opposition.
Nationalist associations were relatively weak in areas like Hanover and
Württemberg, where *kleindeutsch* unification had been highly contested
and particularism remained ingrained. Yet the work of Hartung and
Confino has demonstrated the strength of the *Heimat* movement in both
areas. That *Heimat* proved a more effective rallying cry than the nation
in these places demonstrates the long-standing failure of the nation state
to displace particular and state-based loyalties in much of imperial
Germany.

Ultimately, a state-centred nationalism focused on the Prussian-
dominated German Empire put down only shallow roots in non-Prussian
Germany after 1871. Here, the assassination attempts on Kaiser Wilhelm
I in 1878 had minimal impact, Sedan Day celebrations remained contentious, and monuments to Kaiser Wilhelm and Bismarck were relatively
scarce. Outside Prussia, particularist political culture continued to inform
the culture of nationhood. In Saxony and Württemberg, which retained

---

[95] See Bergmann, *Agrarromantik und Großstadtfeindschaft*, pp. 164–73.
[96] Cited after Hartung, *Konservative Zivilisationskritik und regionale Identität*, p. 82.

their kings, the cult of regional monarchy remained vibrant, members of the royal family attracted widespread public interest, and the dynasty continued to be the focus for public celebration and monument construction. In Hanover, which lost its own ruling house, the Welfs became a focus for political dissent. In all three states, the imperial dynasty sought to deploy the strong tradition of particularist monarchy to shore up its own position. Usually this took the form of ceremonies like the *Kaiserparaden*, which combined particularist and imperial elements. In Hanover, however, the need to placate Welfist loyalties caused Kaiser Wilhelm II to acknowledge publicly Hanover's distinguished military traditions, and culminated in the marriage of his daughter to the Welf pretender's son. Similar considerations meant that nationalist monuments outside Prussia, such as the Hanoverian War Memorial and the Kaiser Wilhelm Monument in Heilbronn, often relied heavily on local rather than imperial symbolism. Such monuments showed far greater respect for both regional identity and non-Prussian traditions than their counterparts in Berlin. These traditions were actively nurtured by state governments, through education policy for instance. No research has been done into the nature of patriotic education in the Saxon *Volksschule*, but in Württemberg at least it is clear that *Volksschule* readers paid minimal attention to Prussian history and the role of Prussia in German unification. Instead, they projected a more federal and particularist vision of Germany, past and present. This vision remained meaningful in part as a consequence of the German constitution, which assigned considerable powers to state governments and parliaments. Consequently, Saxons and Württembergers remained aware of the particular interests of their own state – for instance, with regard to exploitation of the railway network. Under these circumstances, it is hardly surprising that parties opposed to *kleindeutsch* unification remained powerful forces in German politics in the early twentieth century. Opposition to the new nation state in Saxony – in the shape of the Saxon People's Party and its successor the Social Democratic Party – may not have been explicitly particularist. In Hanover and Württemberg, however, both the German-Hanoverian Party and the Württemberg People's Party were. Yet even political parties such as these became more nationally oriented over time. Among less particularist voters, this phenomenon was still more widespread, as the growth of the nationalist lobby in the 1890s and 1900s testifies.

Arguably, the military focus of some nationalist organisations, like the Navy and Army Leagues, was indeed influenced by Prussian traditions of statehood. This was less clearly true of other nationalist organisations, like the General German School Association, the German Colonial Society, the General German Linguistic Association and the Pan-German League. The nationalism of these organisations had a far wider focus than the Prussian-dominated German Empire. Whilst their preoccupations with Germans in Central Europe could be seen as an outcrop of traditional Prussian concerns, this was certainly not the case for other issues, such German colonialism in Africa. It was surely no coincidence that the main areas of strength for popular nationalism – Hessen, Thuringia and Saxony – had all been independent of Prussia before 1866. Interestingly, the 'nationalisation' of anti-Prussian parties such as the Württemberg People's Party is most clearly apparent with regard to precisely these 'non-Prussian' issues. In this sense, the conversion of leading politicians in the Württemberg People's Party to the colonial cause cannot really be seen as a sign of reconciliation with *kleindeutsch* nationhood. In many ways, it was simply a contemporary expression of the *großdeutsch* tradition of a cultural German nation that transcended political boundaries. This tradition had always been more federal than *kleindeutsch* nationalism. Consequently, it never posed any problems for political particularism. Indeed, as we have seen, the propaganda produced by *Mittelstaat* governments in the 1850s and 1860s never disputed the fact that states like Hanover, Saxony and Württemberg were German states, or that their inhabitants were culturally and nationally German at the same time as being, politically and more immediately, Hanoverians, Saxons and Württembergers. This sense of nationhood remained very much alive in Germany after 1871. It was a vision shared, in different ways, by nationalist organisations, *Heimat* activists and political particularists. In both Hanover and Württemberg, this vision accompanied a surprisingly wide-spread rejection of the Prussian-dominated German Empire, reflecting the strength of particularist traditions there. This rejection testified to the success of pre-unification state-building policies in these states. In Hanover, government propaganda had focused on the Welf dynasty, helping to create a loyalty that led many Hanoverians to reject the new Prussian ruling house. Had the Welfs remained in place, it is unlikely that Hanoverian opposition to unification would have proved so ingrained. In Württemberg, by contrast, government propaganda had emphasised the state's indigenous constitutional tradition and the role Wilhelm I of Württemberg had played in nurturing political liberty. It is surely no coincidence that Württemberg opposition to the new Germany focused on the anti-democratic traditions of the Prussian monarchy and the authoritarian constitution of the *kleindeutsch* nation state. In Saxony, the Wettin dynasty survived unification and the constitutional tradition was less pronounced. It is therefore unsurprising that political particularism was weakest in this state after 1871. Nevertheless, the strength of both socialism and the national opposition in Saxony indicates that even here Saxons rarely adopted the *kleindeutsch* tradition fostered by Kaiser Wilhelm II, and exemplified by the cult of Kaiser Wilhelm I.

Of course, shared political institutions and experiences did help to shape a shared political consciousness in Germany after 1871, just as they had done in the *Mittelstaaten* before 1866. At the same time, however, the political nationalism of imperial Germany drew heavily on pre-unification national feeling. In this sense, unification and statehood may have transformed the nature and objectives of German nationalism, but they did not shake the fundamental understanding of what it meant to be a German. In Prussia, which dominated the German Empire, this understanding combined Prussian dynastic and political traditions with German nationalism. In the rest of Germany, different indigenous traditions survived. Fundamentally, however, the underlying belief in a cultural nation that transcended political boundaries changed surprisingly little.

Conclusion

How far does this study of state-building and nationhood in Hanover, Saxony and Württemberg change our understanding of the wider process of nation formation in nineteenth-century Germany?

The growth of German nationalism and the process of nation-state formation in Germany had their counterparts at state level in the state-building policies of German governments and the emergence of state-based particularism in the *Mittelstaaten* before 1871. Superficially, these two developments appear to be fundamentally incompatible. In fact, however, both were a product of the interaction between pre-existing identities and the complex web of economic, social, cultural, institutional and political change that transformed nineteenth-century Europe, known to historians as 'modernisation'. Some aspects of this modernisation process encouraged the crystallisation of German national identity around pre-existing 'greater German' linguistic, cultural and historic traditions. This was true of association formation; the emergence of an independent cultural sphere; the growth of literacy; the exponential increase in printed books and newspapers; the growing acceptance of civil rights such as freedom of speech and assembly; and the process of economic integration engendered by technological progress and liberal economic legislation. Other aspects of modernisation counteracted these developments. Thus the transformation of German territorial states during and after the Napoleonic era – through territorial consolidation, administrative restructuring, the creation of a new and more powerful meritocratic bureaucracy and the foundation of representative political institutions at state level – fostered the emergence of strong particularist identities focusing on existing political structures.

It is tempting to explain the relationship between these two contradictory processes of identity formation at national and state level in terms of the traditional opposition between society and the state in Germany. The growth of nationalism is clearly linked to the emergence

338

of civil society in Germany, whilst particularism is to some extent a creation of the modern state. Yet such an interpretation is wide of the mark. In fact, the dynamic of particularist state-building in Prussia proved crucially important for German unification. Conversely, by the 1850s and 1860s, government state-building in Hanover, Saxony and Württemberg was working with rather than against the grain of developments within these states. Fifty years of shared experiences within a common institutional framework had created a genuine sense of political and cultural community, encouraging Hanoverians, Saxons and Württembergers to take the state as their primary frame of reference – whether they were going into politics, founding historical associations, reading newspapers, or building railways. By and large, moreover, German governments did not simply seek to impose their wishes on an indifferent populace. True, governments attempted to manipulate public opinion and to encourage particular views, but they did so only because they believed public opinion mattered in the first place. As a result, the history of state-building in the *Mittelstaaten* demonstrates not the opposition between state and society, but rather the symbiotic relationship between the two.

The revolution of 1848 marks a key turning-point in this relationship. Before 1848, many German governments had attempted to ignore the winds of change. After 1848, they demonstrated a remarkable ability to adapt to new circumstances, adopting progressive means to achieve reactionary ends. Association formation and the rise of the free press posed risks for the *Mittelstaaten*, but also presented them with opportunities. German governments appropriated the language and symbols of cultural nationalism, developed sophisticated news management techniques, fostered the growth of secular education at *Volksschule* level and set in motion ambitious programmes of railway construction as a means of fostering particularism. On the one hand, such policies were a response to new pressures and developments over which these governments had relatively little control. On the other hand, they enabled German governments to intervene in the process of cultural, political, social and economic change. Association formation, monument construction, the rise of the free press, education policy and railway construction have all been identified as harbingers of 'modernity'. Consequently historians have tended to study their role in promoting the transition from a traditional to a modern society, not least through their contribution to the process of nation-state formation and the emergence of nationalism as a powerful ideology. Conversely, historians have tended to dismiss the activities of *Mittelstaat* governments in these areas, since the territorial state is widely perceived to have become an anachronism by 1871. In fact, however, particularist monuments and festivities were not notably less successful than their nationalist counterparts – indeed, the reverse was very often the case. Equally, government newspapers were by no means less influential than their liberal rivals. Similarly, 'railway particularism' was certainly not restricted to government circles. Instead, it reflected widespread popular concern. Even primary schools could teach their pupils to be Hanoverians, Saxons and Württembergers quite as easily as they could teach them to be good little *kleindeutsch* nationalists.

In practice, the modernisation process inevitably cut both ways in Germany, since different facets of modernisation reinforced both the nation and the particular state. The strength of particularist identity in Hanover, Saxony and Württemberg was therefore more than a manifestation of anachronistic local and dynastic loyalties: it also testified to the success with which pre-existing territorial units had reinvented themselves as modern states after 1815. Inevitably, the appeal of these states drew heavily on indigenous traditions and identities – both local and national. Indeed, government propaganda repeatedly emphasised the compatibility of ancient dynastic, tribal and national ties. This made it easier for *Mittelstaat* identity to survive the trauma of German unification relatively unscathed and to merge with a new German nationalism that accepted Bismarck's German Empire as the basis for nationalist activities and concerns. Yet the Empire itself proved surprisingly ill-equipped to inspire Hanoverians, Saxons and Württembergers with a genuine enthusiasm for the new nation state and its Prussian monarch. Indeed, the officially sponsored *kleindeutsch* nationalism of the German Empire only succeeded in putting down relatively shallow roots in non-Prussian Germany. In many ways, the combination of particular and national identity that persisted in the *Mittelstaaten* after 1871 had far more in common with pre-unification nationalism than the *kleindeutsch* cult which sought to displace it.

In the long run at least, *Mittelstaat* identities proved remarkably long-lasting. German defeat in both 1918 and 1945 led to the re-emergence of political particularism and a more federal sense of nationhood in non-Prussian Germany. After the First World War, Hanoverian particularists called for the long-overdue re-establishment of their state within the Weimar Republic. Similarly, the inhabitants of Baden and Württemberg took issue with Allied plans for the new *Land* of Baden-Württemberg in the aftermath of World War II. The periodic revival of state-based rather than local or regional particularism is a testimony to the lasting achievements of *Mittelstaat* governments before 1871 and, perhaps still more strikingly, to the long arm of the modern state. Even in a climate of growing nationalism, 'artificial' dynastic states were able to shape the loyalties of their inhabitants for generations to come.

Bibliography

I. MANUSCRIPT AND ARCHIVAL SOURCES

HAUPTSTAATSARCHIV, STUTTGART

E 6: 245

E 9: 91, II; 94, I

E 10: 78–9; 121, II

E 11: 34, I; 36, I; 37, II; 41; 56; 63; 173

E 14: 30–1; 151; 461; 870–1; 1145–7; 118–2; 1184–6; 1245; 1408; 1475; 1502; 153–8; 1577; 1579; 1581; 1782–3

E 33: 153; 296; 556–60; 729–31; 895; 898; 902–3; 917–8; 923

E 40/56: 72

E 46: 220; 226; 693

E 146/1: 5930 UF3

E 146 (III): 4740, I

E 150 (IV): 758; 1588; 1599–602

E 151/01: 2936/11; 2936/21

E 200: 32; 61; 62/1–3; 66; 70–1; 107; 108/2; 118–21; 125–127/1; 143; 311–3; 370; 372; 411–2; 498; 500–1; 508; 513

E 222: 266

G 268

B 24

NIEDERSÄCHSISCHES HAUPTSTAATSARCHIV, HANOVER

Hann 26 a: 202; 210; 216; 220; 547–55; 557; 559; 2818–19

Hann 33c: 822; 843–4; 847–9; 853–6; 858–9; 878

Hann 80 I Hannover A: 675; 1062; 1064; 1069–70; 1075; 1079

Hann 108: F 5; F 6 I, II.

Hann 113 A: 37; 45; 55; 64; 84; 89; 95; 100; 109; 112–14; 218–19; 221–2; 224; 232; 282

Hann 113 B: 1; 40

Hann 113 K I: 34; 57; 98; 100; 109; 113; 118–20; 123; 228; 246; 277; 288; 294; 296–7; 308; 317; 325; 385; 387–9; 399; 411; 635; 647; 1125–7; 1129; 1132; 1460; 1521–2; 1726; 1737; 1754; 1767; 1788

Dep. 103 VII: 66; 147; 152

Dep. 103 IX: 24–5; 32; 34; 36; 38–42; 50; 52–3; 59; 61; 64; 278–96; 299–300; 302–7; 310–11; 313; 315; 391; 394; 397–8; 401–3; 409; 412–13; 415–16; 418; 423; 429; 436; 438; 442; 444; 477

Dep. 103 XI: 4; 19; 27–8; 86–7; 92

Dep. 103 XXIII: 50; 168; 174; 741

Dep. 103 XXVII: 572; 918

Dep. 103 XXVIII: 557; 566; 595; 599; 613; 616 I I, 616 I II, 616 I, III; 615 II; 617; 620 II, 620 III; 621 I; 622 III; 623; 624; 626–8; 637; 638 I; 639; 640 I; 640 II; 641–2; 644; 651; 894

SÄCHSISCHES HAUPTSTAATSARCHIV, DRESDEN

Gesammtministerium:

Loc. 7, No. 7; Loc. 13, No. 17; Loc. 13, No. 19; Loc. 22, No. 9; Loc. 27, No. 1; Loc. 33, No. 9; Loc. 37, No. 11; Loc. 39, No. 7; Loc. 44, No. 8; Loc. 61, No. 10; Loc. 63, No. 5; Loc. 66, No. 7; Loc. 69, No. 6; Loc. 94, No. 27

Ministerium der auswärtigen Angelegenheiten

4887; 7364

Ministerium des Innern

103a; 131–6; 138; 140–1; 150; 162; 165a; 166a; 3681–5; 3721; 3723; 3795; 3798–9; 3811; 3857; 9490–9495; 9501; 9510–14; 13755; 13870; 17263; 17304–5; 17305–7; 17347–9; 17390; 17403; 17470; 17493

Ministerium des Königlichen Hauses

Loc. 19   No. 5

Ministerium für Volksbildung

10284–6; 10288; 10290; 10294; 10687–8; 10782; 10802; 10831; 11201–2; 11204–6; 11482; 11504–6;11526–7; 11937;11942; 11946; 11950; 12603; 12775; 13073–5; 13089; 13091–7; 13107; 13170–2; 13188; 13194–5; 14260–1; 14299; 14310; 14318; 18792; 18995; 19226–7; 19243

Acten des General Secretairs der Landwirtschaftlichen Vereine

133

Finanzarchiv Rep. LVII, Sect. I

No. 38 a–h, Loc. 37, 416–17; No. 69, Loc. 37, 437; No. 143, Loc. 37, 481

Hausarchiv Friedrich August II., B

16, 18q

Hausarchiv Johann

No. 39 (5)

Sächsischer Kunstverein

14; 183; 185; 187

Sächsische Staatszeitung

8; 20; 43; 61–2

II. PERIODICAL SOURCES

Deutsche Nordsee Zeitung 1864–6
Dresdner Journal 1852–66
Hannoversche Nachrichten 1856–7
Hannoversche Zeitung 1848–57
Leipziger Zeitung 1848–66
Neue Hannoversche Zeitung 1858–66
Staats-Anzeiger für Württemberg 1850–66

III. PRINTED PRIMARY SOURCES

Anon., *Das Vierte Säcularfest der Erfindung der Buchdruckerkunst begangen zu Stuttgart am 24. und 25. Juni 1840* (Stuttgart, 1840)

Anon., *Einladung zu einer Redefeierlichkeit in der Nikolaischule am 26/05/1858 Vormittags 9. Uhr* (Leipzig, 1848)

Anon., *Die Verhandlungen der Volksschul-Commission in Hannover über die Ordnung der Ausbildung für das Volksschulfach* (Hanover, 1849)

Anon., *Die Geschichte Sachsens von den ältesten Zeiten bis auf unsere Tage, ein Buch für Volk, Schule und Haus*, Vol. III (Leipzig, 1851)

Anon., *Denkschrift über den Entwurf zur Erbauung einer Eisenbahn von Magdeburg nach Leipzig über Pommern, Zerbst, Roßlau, Dessau, Bitterfeld, Desitzsch* (Magdeburg, 1853)

Anon., *Fibel für die evangelischen Volksschulen Württembergs* (Stuttgart, 1854)

Anon., *Lesebuch für die evangelischen Volksschulen Württembergs* (Stuttgart, 1854)

Anon., *Die Bahnlinie Hall–Crailsheim–Ellwangen–Aalen und ihre Berechtigung in dem Württembergischen Eisenbahn-System mit Bezugnahme auf die Gaildorfer Denkschrift* (Ellwangen, 1861)

Anon., *Die Erbauung einer Eisenbahn von Ulm gegen Schaffhausen und den obern Schwarzwald auf Staatskosten, eventuell durch Privatmittel: Eine Denkschrift von den Comités von Ulm, Erbach, Blaubeuren, Ehingen, Rotehnacker, Munderlingen, Ober-*

und Untermachthal, Oberstadion, Münsingen, Riedlingen, Mengen, Ebingen, Mößkirch, Stockach, Radolfzell und Tuttlingen beschlossen den 5. Februar 1861 (Ulm, 1861)

Anon., *Ernst August Album* (Hanover, 1862)

Anon., *Erster Bericht über die Sammlungen des Königlichen Welfen-Museums im März 1862* (Hanover, 1862)

Anon., *Die Holländische Nordbahn und ihre östliche Fortsetzung, mit zwei Karten und einer Anlage* (Leer, 1862)

Anon., *Lesebuch für die katholischen Volksschulen Württembergs* (Stuttgart, 1862)

Anon., *Bitte an die hohe Stände-Versammlung von dem Central Comité der Bezirke Waiblingen, Backnang und Gaildorf um Herstellung einer Eisenbahn-Verbindung zwischen der Rems- und Kocherthal-Bahn in der Richtung von Waiblingen über Winnenden, Backnang, Murrhardt, Gaildorf mit dem Anschlusse bei Hall* (Backnang, 21 March 1864)

Anon., *Einem ostfriesischen Theologen, Die kirchliche Feier an dem Geburtstage Sr. Majestät des Königs und ihrer Majestät der Königin wie sie sein soll, mit Rücksicht auf das Inserat "Kirche und Schule" in No. 143 der Landeszeitung* (Aurich, 1864)

Anon., *Der Oberamtsbezirk Freudenstadt und sein Verhältnis zu dem in dem Gesetzes-Entwurf vom 28. April 1865 dargelegten württembergischen Eisenbahn-Netze, besonders zu den darin projectirten Schwarzwald-bahnen: Eine dringende Bitte an die K. Staats-Regierung und an die hohe Stände-Versammlung vorgelegt von dem Bezirks Gewerbe Verein und den bürgerlichen Collegien in Freudenstadt* (Freudenstadt, 8 May 1865)

Anon., *Das Staatsbudget und das Bedürfniß für Kunst u. Wissenschaft im Königreich Hannover* (Hanover, 1866)

Anon., *Anhang zum Lesebuch für die evangelischen Volksschulen Württembergs* (Stuttgart, 1873)

Anon., *Württemberg und sein König, 1864–1889. Eine Festgabe zum 25 jährigen Regierungs-Jubiläum Seiner Majestät des Königs Karl von Württemberg* (Stuttgart, 1889)

Anon., *Die Wahrheit über das Kronprinzenpaar von Sachsen. Von einem Eingeweihten* (Zürich, 1903)

Albrecht, Bruno, *Die Eheirrung der Kronprinzessin Luise v. Sachsen und ihre gemeinsame Flucht mit Erzherzog Leopold Ferdinand v. Österreich nach authentischen Quellen auf Grund eingeholter Gutachten hervorragender Kirchen- und Privatrechts-lehrer wissenschaftlich beleuctet* (Leipzig, 1903)

Beust, Friedrich Ferdinand, Graf von, *Aus drei Viertel-Jahrhunderten, Erinnerungen und Aufzeichnungen*, 2 vols. (Stuttgart, 1887)

Bismarck, Otto, Graf von, *Gesammelte Werke*, 15 vols., ed. Gerhard Ritter, and Rudolf Stadelmann, Vol. xv, *Erinnerung und Gedanke* (Nendeln-Liechtenstein, 1972, reprint)

Borchers, Otto, *Unter welfischem Szepter. Erinnerungen eines Hannoveraners* (Hof, 1882)

Boucher de Perthes, M., *Voyage en Danemarck, en Suède, en Norvège, par la Belgique et la Hollande. Retour par les villes anséatiques, le Mecklembourg, la Saxe, la Bavière, le Wurtemberg et le Grand-duché de Bade, séjour à Bade en 1854* (Paris, 1858)

Brackenhoff, H. L., *Geschichte der Hannoverschen und Braunschweig'schen Lande in 60 Erzählungen* (Einbeck, 1855)

Brandis, F. Ch., *Erstes Buch für Kinder nach der Lautir und Buchstabir Methode, einge-
     richtet und herausgegeben von K. Koch, Cantor zu Elbingerode* (Clausthal, 1866, 9th
     edn)
Bulnheim, Otto, *Die Heimath, ein Lesebuch für die Jugend der Stadt Leipzig und ihrer
     Umgegend* (Leipzig, 1854)
Calinich, C. A. E., *Neuer Kinderfreund für sächsische Volksschulen* (Leipzig, 1844)
Carlyle, Thomas, *Journey to Germany, Autumn 1858*, reissue ed. Richard Albert
     Brooks (New Haven, Conn., 1940)
Colshorn, Theodor and Münkel, Louis, *Kinderfreund, deutsches Lesebuch für
     Volksschulen* (Stade, 1851)
Comité für Herstellung einer Eisenbahn aus der südlichen Lausitz über Sebnitz
     nach Schandau an die Elbe, *An die Hohen Königl. Ministerien des Innern und der
     Finanzen zu Dresden: Die Herstellung einer Eisenbahn aus der südlichen Lausitz über
     Sebnitz nach Schandau an die Elbe betreffend* (Schandau, 14 February 1865)
Dertinger, Ernst, *Das Volksfest zu Cannstadt, Acht Erinnerungsblätter für Jedermann*
     (Stuttgart/Cannstatt, 1844)
Eckardt, Julius von, *Lebenserinnerungen*, 2 Vols. (Leipzig, 1910)
Elben, Otto, *Geschichte des Schwäbischen Merkurs, 1785–1885* (Stuttgart, 1885)
     Lebenserinnerungen, 1823–1899 (Stuttgart, 1931)
Elliott, Charles Boileau, *Letters from the North of Europe: or a journal of travels in
     Holland, Denmark, Norway, Sweden, Finland, Russia, Prussia and Saxony* (London,
     1832)
Ernst August, King of Hanover, *Letters of the King of Hanover to Viscount Strangford,
     G.C.B. now in the possession of his granddaughter Mrs. Frank Russell* (London, 1925)
     'Briefe Ernst Augusts von Hannover an König Friedrich Wilhelm IV. von
     Preußen 1849–1851, mitgeteilt von Studienrat Dr. Karl Hänchen',
     Niedersächsisches Jahrbuch für Landesgeschichte 10 (1933), 135–97
Fischer, Wolfram, Krengel, Jochen and Wietog, Jutta (eds.), *Sozialgeschichtliches
     Arbeitsbuch*, Vol. 1, *Materalien zur Statistik des Deutschen Bundes 1815–1870*
     (Munich, 1982)
Flathe, Theodor, *Die Vorzeit des sächsischen Volkes in Schilderungen aus den
     Quellenschriftstellern* (Leipzig, 1860)
Fremdling, Rainer, Federspiel, Ruth and Kunz, Andreas (eds.), *Statistik der
     Eisenbahnen in Deutschland 1835–1989* (St. Katharinen, 1995)
Friesen, Richard, Freiherr von, *Erinnerungen aus meinem Leben*, 2 Vols. (Dresden,
     1880)
Gräße, J. G. Th., *Geschichte Sachsens und seiner Fürsten. Ein Lesebuch für Schule und
     Haus zugleich als erklärender Text zu: Sachsens Fürsten in Bildern* (Dresden, 1855)
Griesinger, Theodor, *Württemberg, nach seiner Vergangenheit und Gegenwart in Land und
     Leuten gezeichnet* (Stuttgart, 1866)
Grotefend, *Hannover, ein patriotisches Promemoria* (Hanover, March 1864 –
     reprinted from *Deutsche Nordsee Zeitung*)
Grüneisen, Oberhofprediger Dr., *Trauergedächtniß Seiner Majestät König Wilhelm von
     Württemberg – Predigt, Trauergottesdienst und Beisetzung – auf vielseitigen Wunsch
     mit Höchster Genehmigung in den Druck gegeben* (Stuttgart, 1864)

Hartmann, Julius, *Meine Erlebnisse zu hannoverscher Zeit, 1839–1866* (Wiesbaden, 1912)

Hauff, Wilhelm, *Lichtenstein und Novellen* (Tübingen, 1996)

Hempel, Carl Friedrich, *Der Volksschulenfreund, ein Hülfsbuch zum Lesen, Denken und Lernen* (Leipzig, 1817, 2nd edn)

Hickel, J. C., *Festspiel zur Feier der Eröffnung der Prag–Dresdner Eisenbahn am 6. April 1851. Aufgeführt auf dem Königl. ständ. Theater zu Prag* (Prague, 1851)

Hingst, C. W., *Sächsischer Zeitspiegel, das Wichtigste aus der Staats- und Culturgeschichte des Königreichs Sachsen für Schule und Haus* (Döbeln, 1862)

Huber, Ernst Rudolf (ed.), *Dokumente zur deutschen Verfassungsgeschichte*, Vol. I, *Deutsche Verfassungsdokumente 1803–1850* (Stuttgart, 1961)

Invalide, Fr. Centrus, *Gratulations-Gedicht, zum Geburtstage Seiner Königlichen Hoheit Ernst August II., am 21. September 1853 nebst dem National-Liede vom 21. September 1845 sowie auch Willkommen und Lebewohl, gewidmet allen braven Hannoveranern* (Hildesheim, 1853)

Johann, King of Saxony, *Briefwechsel zwischen König Johann von Sachsen und den Königen Friedrich Wilhelm IV. und Wilhelm I. von Preußen*, ed. Johann Georg, Duke of Saxony (Leipzig, 1911)

Lebenserinnerungen des Königs Johann von Sachsen, ed. Hellmut Kretzschmar (Göttingen, 1958)

Keyser, Erich (ed.), *Bibliographie zur Städtegeschichte Deutschlands* (Cologne, 1969)

Kirsch, Karl, *Lese- und Lehrbuch der gemeinnützigen Kenntnisse für protestantische Volksschulen, zweiter Lehrgang für Oberclassen* (Leipzig, 1836)

Ueber den Unterricht in der sächsischen Geschichte, Bemerkungen für Volksschullehrer, als Beigabe zu der Geschichtstabelle 'das Haus Wettin' (Dresden, 1843)

Lese- und Lehrbuch der gemeinnützigen Kenntnisse für evangelische Volksschulen, erster Lehrgang, für Mittelklassen (Leipzig, 1847 – 3rd edn)

Kleist, Heinrich von, *Katechismus der Deutschen abgefasst nach dem Spanischen zum Gebrauch für Kinder und Alte* (1809)

Klopp, Wiard, 'Der Lebenslauf von Onno Klopp', *Jahrbuch der Gesellschaft für bildende Kunst und vaterländische Altertümer zu Emden* 16/21 (1907), 1–182

Köllmann, Wolfgang (ed.), *Quellen zur Bevölkerungs-, Sozial- und Wirtschaftsstatistik Deutschlands 1815–1875*, Vol. III, *Norddeutsche Staaten*; Vol. IV, *Mitteldeutsche Staaten*; Vol. V, *Süddeutsche Staaten* (Boppard am Rhein, 1994, 1995, 1995)

Kremer, Ida, *The struggle for a royal child, Anna Monica Pia, Duchess of Saxony. My experiences as Governess in the household of the Countess Montignoso* (London, 1907)

Lamby, Alfred, *Soll die Strecke Münster–Osnabrück der projectirten Paris–Hamburger Eisenbahn über Iburg oder über Lengrich führen: Eine Skizze nebst einer anliegenden Karte und einer Tabelle* (Iburg, 1865)

Landesverfassungs-Gesetz für das Königreich Hannover vom 6. August 1840

Legrelle, Arsène, *A travers la Saxe. Souvenirs et études* (Paris, 1866)

Lehrgang des Geschichtsunterrichts auf gelehrten Schulen (Dresden, Teubner'sche Officien, 1845)

Leo, Gottlob Eduard, *Zweites Lesebuch für Mittelclassen evangelisch-lutherischer Volksschulen* (Leipzig, 1861)

Louisa of Tuscany, ex-Crown Princess of Saxony, *My own story* (London, 1911)

Malortie, C. E. von, *König Ernst August* (Hanover, 1861)

Meding, Oskar, *Promemoria über die Aufgaben der deutschen conservativen Partei und die Gründung einer allgemeinen deutschen conservativen Zeitung: Als Manuscript gedruckt* (1869)

Memoiren zur Zeitgeschichte, 2 vols. (Leipzig, 1881)

Metzsch-Schilbart, Wolf von, *Friedrich August III., König von Sachsen, Ein Lebensbild* (Berlin, 1906)

Ministerium des Cultus u. öffentlichen Unterrichts, *Exposé über einige Fragen des Schulgesetzgebung, als Manuscript gedruckt* (Dresden, 1854)

Ordnung der evangelischen Schullehrerseminare im Königreiche Sachsen vom Jahre 1857 (Leipzig, 1857)

Mohl, Robert von, *Lebens-Erinnerungen von Robert von Mohl 1799–1875* (Stuttgart/Leipzig, 1902)

Mohr, Carl August Friedrich, *Die Geschichte von Sachsen zum Unterricht in den vaterländischen Schulen* (Leipzig, 1843)

Piozzi, Hester Lynch, *Observations and reflections made in the course of a journey through France, Italy, and Germany* (Ann Arbor, 1967, first published 1789)

Pleibel, August Ludwig, *Handbuch der Vaterlandskunde. Württemberg, sein Land, sein Volk und sein Fürstenhaus, für Schule und Familie bearbeitet* (Stuttgart, 1858)

Pressel, *Bahnen des Württembergischen Schwarzwaldes. Zweite Denkschrift des Ingenieurs Pressel in Wien als Entgegnung auf die gegen den Inhalt seiner ersten Denkschrift vom April 1864 erhobenen Einwürfe. Nebst einer Darstellung der volkswirtschaflichen und Verkehrs-Verhältnisse A. des Oberamtsbezirks Leonberg, B. des Oberamtsbezirks Calw, C. des Oberamtsbezirks Nagold. Vertreten durch die betreffenden Eisenbahn-Comités* (Calw, 1865)

Preuss, A. E. and Vetter, J. A., *Preußischer Kinderfreund, ein Lesebuch für deutsche Volksschulen, mit einer Sammlung zwei- und dreistimmiger Lieder* (Königsberg, 1854, 27th edn)

Quietmeyer, E., *Schul- und Hausfreund, deutsches Lesebuch für Volksschulen* (Hanover, 1850)

Schul- und Hausfreund II: deutsches Lesebuch (Hanover, 1853)

Ramshorn, Carl, *Deutsches Lesebuch für Bürgerschulen, II. Abtheilung für die oberen Classen* (Leipzig, 1858, 2nd edn)

Reichardt, F. O. W., *Rede, bei der Feier des Geburtstages Se. Majestät des Königs am 23. Mai 1853 im Königl. Schullehrer Seminar zu Friedrichstadt Dresden gehalten von Dr. F. O. W. Reichardt, Vice-Seminardirector* (Dresden, 1853)

Richter, M. Ernst Wilhelm, *Das Wichtigste aus der sächsischen Geschichte von der ältesten bis auf die neueste Zeit in chronologischer Folge, ein Leitfaden beim Unterricht in Volksschulen* (Grimma, 1839)

Rochow, Friedrich Eberhard von, *Der Kinderfreund, ein Lesebuch zum Gebrauch in Landschulen – für kleinere Schüler* (Munich, 1813, 8th edn)

Roger, Oberamtmann, *Die Gewerbe und Industrie Ausstellung des Oberamtsbezirks Böblingen eröffnet 12. September 1865 geschlossen 1. Oktober 1865* (Böblingen, 1866)

Schäffle, Albert Eberhard Friedrich, *Aus meinem Leben* (Berlin, 1905)

Schaumann, Adolf Friedrich Heinrich, *Handbuch der Geschichte der Lande Hannover und Braunschweig, zum Gebrauch beim Unterricht in den oberen Classen der höheren vaterländischen Lehranstalten* (Hanover, 1864)

Schmid, Rector Dr., *Gedächtnis-Rede auf des verewigten Königs Wilhelm Majestät gehalten bei der Trauerfeier im Gymnasium zu Stuttgart den 26. Juli 1864* (Stuttgart, 1864)

Smith, Richard Bryan, *Notes made during a tour in Denmark, Holstein, Mecklenburg-Schwerin, Pomerania, the Isle of Rügen, Prussia, Poland, Saxony, Brunswick, Hannover, the Hanseatic territories, Oldenburg, Friesland, Holland, Brabant, the Rhine country, and France* (London, 1827)

Steitz, Walter (ed.), *Quellen zur deutschen Wirtschafts- und Sozialgeschichte im 19. Jahrhundert bis zur Reichsgründung* (Darmstadt, 1980)

Stichart, Franz Otto, *Das Königreich Sachsen und seine Fürsten. Ein geschichtlicher Abriß für Schule und Haus* (Leipzig, 1854)

Stutzer, Henry Lewis, *Journal of a five weeks' tour through Hanover, Westphalia and the Netherlands. In July and August, 1818* (London, 1819)

Stüve, Johann Carl Bertram, *Briefwechsel zwischen Stüve und Detmold in den Jahren 1848 bis 1850*, ed. Gustav Stüve (Hanover/Leipzig, 1903)

 Briefe Johann Carl Bertram Stüves, Vol. II, *1848–1872*, ed. Walter Vogel (Göttingen, 1960)

Trollope, Frances, *Vienna and the Austrians; with some account of a journey through Swabia, Bavaria, the Tyrol and Salzbourg* (London, 1838)

Uhland, Ludwig, *Gedichte, Dramen und Prosa* (Tübingen, 1996)

Vogel, Karl, *Deutsches Lesebuch für Schule und Haus, zunächst zur Beförderung religiös-sittlicher Bildung in Elementar- und Bürgerschulen* (Leipzig, 1860, 14th edn)

Weyhe-Eimke, Arnold von, *Zum 21. September 1861. Seiner Hoheit Ernst August, Kronprinz von Hannover zu Höchstseinem Geburtstage in tiefer Ehrfurcht gewidmet* (1861)

White, Walter, *A July holiday in Saxony, Bohemia, and Silesia* (London, 1857)

Wilsdorf, Eduard, *Elementarbuch der deutschen Sprache oder Lesebuch zur Unterstützung des Denk- und Sprachunterrichts, I Cursus: für Unter- und Mittelclassen deutscher Volksschulen* (Glauchau, 1855)

Wilson, William Rae, *Travels in Norway, Sweden, Denmark, Hanover, Germany, Netherlands &c* (London, 1826)

Winter, Gg. A., *Allgemeines Lesebuch für deutsche Stadt- und Landschulen, erster Theil: für die Mittelklassen. Bearbeitet und zusammengestellt aus den Werken der ausgezeichnetsten, mustergültigsten ältern und neuern Jugendschriftsteller* (Leipzig, 1855, 5th edn)

Württembergischer Volksschullehrer-Verein, *Denkschrift des Württ. Volksschullehrer-Vereins, die Reform des vaterländischen Volksschulwesens betreffend* (Stuttgart, Karl Aue, 1862)

SECONDARY WORKS

Alings, Reinhard, *Monument und Nation. Das Bild vom Nationalstaat im Medium Denkmal – zum Verhältnis von Nation und Staat im deutschen Kaiserreich, 1871–1918* (Berlin/New York, 1996)

Alter, Peter, *Nationalism* (London, 1989)

Anderson, Benedict, *Imagined communities* (London, 1983)

Anderson, Margaret Lavinia, *Windthorst, a political biography* (Oxford, 1981)

'The Kulturkampf and the course of German history', *Central European History* 19:1 (1986), 82–115

'Piety and politics: recent work on German Catholicism', *Journal of Modern History* 63:4 (1991), 681–716

'Voter, Junker, Landrat, Priest: the old authorities and the new franchise in Imperial Germany', *American Historical Review* 98:5 (1993), 1448–74

Angelow, Jürgen, *Von Wien nach Königgrätz. Die Sicherheitspolitik des Deutschen Bundes im europäischen Gleichgewicht 1815–1866* (Munich, 1996)

Applegate, Celia, *A nation of provincials. The German idea of Heimat* (Berkeley, Oxford, 1990)

'Democracy or reaction? The political implications of localist ideas in Wilhelmine and Weimar Germany', in Larry Eugene Jones and James Retallack (eds.), *Elections, mass politics and social change in Modern Germany, new perspectives* (Cambridge, 1992), pp. 247–66

Aretin, Karl Ottmar, Freiherr von, *Heiliges Römisches Reich, 1776–1806. Reichsverfassung und Staatssouveränität* (Wiesbaden, 1967)

Armstrong, Sinclair W., 'The Social-Democrats and the unification of Germany, 1863–1871', *Journal of Modern History* 12:4 (1940), 485–509

Aschoff, Hans-Georg, *Das Verhältnis von Staat und katholischer Kirche im Königreich Hannover (1813–1866)* (Hildesheim, 1976)

'Die welfische Bewegung und die Deutsch-hannoversche Partei zwischen 1866 und 1914', *Niedersächsisches Jahrbuch für Landesgeschichte* 53 (1981), 41–64

Welfische Bewegung und politischer Katholizismus 1866–1918. Die Deutsch-hannoversche Partei und das Zentrum in der Provinz Hannover während des Kaiserreiches (Düsseldorf, 1987)

Assmann, Aleida, *Arbeit am nationalen Gedächtnis. Eine kurze Geschichte der deutschen Bildungsidee* (Frankfurt, 1993)

Aurig, Rainer, Herzog, Steffen and Lässig, Simone (eds.), *Landesgeschichte in Sachsen: Tradition und Innovation* (Bielefeld, 1997)

Austensen, Roy A., 'Metternich, Austria and the German question, 1848–51', *International History Review* 13 (1991), 21–37

Barclay, David E., *Frederick William IV and the Prussian monarchy 1840–1861* (Oxford, 1995)

Barkin, Kenneth, 'Social control and the *Volksschule* in *Vormärz* Prussia', *Central European History* 16:1 (1983), 31–52

Barmeyer, Heide, 'Gewerbefreiheit oder Zunftbindung? Hannover an der Schwelle des Industriezeitalters', *Niedersächsisches Jahrbuch für Landesgeschichte* 46/47 (1974/5), 231–62

'Bismarck, die Annexionen und das Welfenproblem 1866–1890. Der unvollendete nationale Verfassungssstaat in Verteidigung und Angriff', *Niedersächsisches Jahrbuch für Landesgeschichte* 48 (1976), 397–432

'Die hannoverschen Nationalliberalen 1859–1885', *Niedersächsisches Jahrbuch für Landesgeschichte* 53 (1981), 65–85

Hannovers Eingliederung in den preußischen Staat. Annexion und administrative Integration, 1866–1868 (Hildesheim, 1983)

Bartels, Gunhild, *Preußen im Urteil Hannovers, 1815–51* (Hildesheim, 1960)

Bassler, Gerhard P., 'Auswanderungsfreiheit und Auswanderfürsorge in Württemberg 1815–1855', *Zeitschrift für Württembergische Landesgeschichte* 33 (1974), 117–60

Baumgart, Franzjörg, *Zwischen Reform und Reaktion. Preußische Schulpolitik 1806–1859* (Darmstadt, 1990)

Baumgart, Peter (ed.), *Bildungspolitik in Preußen zur Zeit des Kaiserreichs* (Stuttgart, 1980)

Bazillion, Richard J., *Modernizing Germany, Karl Biedermann's career in the Kingdom of Saxony 1835–1901* (New York, 1990)

Beachy, Robert, 'Local protest and territorial reform: public debt and constitutionalism in early-nineteenth-century Saxony', *German History* 17:4 (1999), 471–88

Bentfeldt, Ludwig, *Der Deutsche Bund als nationales Band 1815–1866* (Göttingen, 1985)

Berdahl, Robert M., 'Conservative politics and aristocratic landholders in Bismarckian Germany', *Journal of Modern History* 14:1 (1972), 1–20

Berding, Helmut, 'Staatliche Identität, nationale Integration und politischer Regionalismus', *Blätter für deutsche Landesgeschichte* 121 (1985), 371–94

Bergmann, Klaus, *Agrarromantik und Großstadtfeindschaft* (Meisenheim am Glan, 1970)

Bergmann, Klaus and Schneider, Gerhard (eds.), *Gesellschaft, Staat, Geschichtsunterricht. Beiträge zu einer Geschichte der Geschichtsdidaktik und des Geschichtsunterrichts von 1500–1980* (Düsseldorf, 1982)

Berg-Schlosser, Dirk and Schissler, Jakob, *Politische Kultur in Deutschland. Bilanz und Perspektiven der Forschung* (Opladen, 1987)

Bertram, Mijndert, 'Der "Mondminister" und "General Killjoy". Ein Machtkampf im Hintergrund der Ernennung des Herzogs Adolph Friedrich von Cambridge zum Generalgouverneur von Hannover (1813–16)', *Niedersächsisches Jahrbuch für Landesgeschichte* 65 (1993), 213–62

Betteridge, H. T., 'The Romantic spirit in Germany', *German Life and Letters* 3 (1938–9), 12–24

Beyer, Peter, *Leipzig und die Anfänge des deutschen Eisenbahnbaus. Die Strecke nach Magdeburg als zweitälteste deutsche Fernbindung und das Ringen der Kaufleute um ihr Entstehen 1829–1840* (Weimar, 1978)

Biefang, Andreas, *Politisches Bürgertum in Deutschland 1857–1868. Nationale Organisationen und Eliten* (Düsseldorf, 1994)

Binder, Hans Otto, *Reich und Einzelstaaten während der Kanzlerschaft Bismarcks 1871–1890. Eine Untersuchung zum Problem der bundesstaatlichen Organisation* (Tübingen, 1971)

Bird, Anthony, *The damnable Duke of Cumberland, a character study and vindication of Ernest Augustus, Duke of Cumberland and King of Hanover* (London, 1966)

Birke, Adolf M. and Kettenacker, Lothar (eds.), *Bürgertum, Adel und Monarchie: Wandel der Lebensformen im Zeitalter des bürgerlichen Nationalismus* (Munich, 1989)

Blackbourn, David, *Class, religion and local politics in Wilhelmine Germany. The Centre Party in Württemberg before 1914* (New Haven, Conn. London, 1980)
  'The politics of demagogy in Imperial Germany', *Past and Present* 113 (1986), 152–84
Blackbourn, David (ed.), *Populists and patricians. Essays in modern German history* (London, 1987)
  The Fontana history of Germany 1780–1918. The long nineteenth century (London, 1997)
Blackbourn, David and Eley, Geoff, *The peculiarities of German history. Bourgeois society and politics in nineteenth-century Germany* (Oxford, 1984)
Blanning, T. C. W., 'The French revolution and the modernisation of Germany', *Central European History* 22:2 (1989), 109–29
Blessing, Werner K., 'Allgemeine Volksbildung und politische Indoktrination im bayerischen Vormärz. Das Leitbild des Volksschullehrers als mentales Herrschaftsinstrument', *Zeitschrift für bayerische Landesgeschichte* 37:2 (1974), 479–568
  Staat und Kirche in der Gesellschaft. Institutionelle Autorität und mentaler Wandel in Bayern während des 19. Jahrhunderts (Göttingen, 1982)
Blühm, Elger (ed.), *Presse und Geschichte, Beiträge zur historischen Kommunikationsforschung, Referate einer internationalen Fachkonferenz der Deutschen Forschungsgemeinschaft und der Deutschen Presseforschung / Universität Bremen 5.-8. Oktober 1976 in Bremen* (Munich, 1977)
Blühm, Elger and Gebhardt, Hartwig (eds.), *Presse und Geschichte II. Neue Beiträge zur historischen Kommunikationsforschung* (Munich, 1987)
Böhme, Helmut, *Deutschlands Weg zur Großmacht. Studien zum Verhältnis von Wirtschaft und Staat während der Reichsgründungszeit 1848–1881* (Cologne/Berlin, 1966)
  'Big-business pressure groups and Bismarck's turn to protectionism 1873–9', *The Historical Journal* 10:2 (1967), 218–36
Boelcke, Willi A., 'Wege und Probleme des industriellen Wachstums im Königreich Württemberg', *Zeitschrift für württembergische Landesgeschichte* 32 (1973), 436–520
Boldt, Werner, *Die württembergischen Volksvereine von 1848 bis 1852* (Stuttgart, 1970)
Bongaerts, Jan C., 'Financing railways in the German states 1840–1860. A preliminary view', *Journal of European Economic History* 14:2 (1985), 331–45
Boockmann, Hartmut, et al. (eds.), *Geschichtswissenschaft und Vereinswesen im 19. Jahrhundert. Beiträge zur Geschichte historischer Forschung in Deutschland* (Göttingen, 1972)
Borchardt, Knut (ed.), *Perspectives on modern German economic history and policy* (Cambridge, 1991)
Borkenhagen, Helene, *Ostfriesland unter der hannoverschen Herrschaft, 1815–1866* (Aurich, 1924)
Borsche, Eberhard, *Adolf Ellissen 1815–1872, Ein Vorläufer der modernen byzantinischen Literatur- und Sprachforschung, Ein Gelehrtenleben zwischen Politik und Wissenschaft* (Hildesheim, 1955)

Bosl, Karl, 'Die historische Staatlichkeit der bayerischen Lande', *Zeitschrift für bayerische Landesgeschichte* 25:1 (1962), 3–19

Boyer, John W., *Political radicalism in late imperial Vienna. Origins of the Christian Social movement, 1848–1897* (Chicago/London, 1981)

Brake, Ludwig, *Die ersten Eisenbahnen in Hessen. Eisenbahnpolitik und Eisenbahnbau in Frankfurt, Hessen-Darmstadt, Kurhessen und Nassau bis 1866* (Wiesbaden, 1991)

Brandes, Helga, *Die Zeitschriften des Jungen Deutschlands. Eine Untersuchung zur literarisch-publizistischen Öffentlichkeit im 19. Jahrhundert* (Opladen, 1991)

Brandt, Hardtwig, *Parlamentarismus in Württemberg 1819–1870. Anatomie eines deutschen Landtags* (Düsseldorf, 1987)

Breuilly, John, *Nationalism and the state* (Manchester, 1993, 2nd edn)

Breuilly, John (ed.), *The state of Germany. The national idea in the making, unmaking and remaking of a modern nation state* (London/New York, 1992)

Brockmann, Stephen, 'The politics of German history', *History and Theory* 29:2 (1990), 179–89

Brophy, James M., *Capitalism, politics and railroads in Prussia, 1830–1870* (Columbus, 1998)

Brosius, Dieter, 'Georg V. von Hannover – der König des "monarchischen Prinzips"', *Niedersächsisches Jahrbuch für Landesgeschichte* 51 (1979), 253–91

Burg, Peter, *Die Deutsche Trias in Idee und Wirklichkeit. Vom Alten Reich zum Zollverein* (Stuttgart, 1989)

Büsch, Otto and Sheehan, James J. (eds.), *Die Rolle der Nation in der deutschen Geschichte und Gegenwart. Beiträge zu einer internationalen Konferenz in Berlin (West) vom 16. bis 18. Juni 1983* (Berlin, 1985)

Buse, Dieter K., 'Urban and national identity: Bremen, 1860–1920', *Journal of Social History* 26:3 (1993), 521–38

Busshoff, Heinrich, 'Die preußische Volksschule als soziales Gebilde und politischer Bildungsfaktor in der ersten Hälfte des 19. Jahrhunderts. Ein Bericht', *Geschichte in Wissenschaft und Unterricht* 22:7 (1971), 385–95

Calhoun, Craig (ed.), *Habermas and the Public Sphere* (Cambridge, Mass., 1992)

Cannadine, David, 'The transformation of civic ritual in Modern Britain: the Colchester oyster feast', *Past and Present* 94 (February 1982), 107–30

'Introduction', in David Cannadine and Simon Price (eds.), *Rituals of royalty: power and ceremonial in traditional societies* (Cambridge, 1987), pp. 1–19

Chickering, Roger, 'Der deutsche Wehrverein und die Reform der deutschen Armee, 1912–1914', *Militärgeschichtliche Mitteilungen* 25 (1979), 7–33

We men who feel most German. A cultural study of the Pan-German League, 1866–1914 (Boston, Mass./London, 1984)

' "Casting their gaze more broadly": women's patriotic activism in Imperial Germany', *Past and Present* 118 (1988), 156–85

Chickering, Roger (ed.), *Imperial Germany: a historiographical companion* (Westport, Conn./London, 1996)

Colley, Linda, 'The apotheosis of George III: loyalty, royalty and the British nation, 1760–1820', *Past and Present* 102 (February, 1984), 94–109

Confino, Alon, *The nation as a local metaphor. Württemberg, Imperial Germany and national memory 1871–1918* (Chapel Hill/London, 1997)

Conze, Werner, 'Staatsnationale Entwicklung und Modernisierung im Deutschen Reich, 1871–1914' in Werner, Conze, Gottfried Schramm and Klaus Zernack (eds.), *Modernisierung und nationale Gesellschaft im ausgehenden 18. und im 19. Jahrhundert. Referate einer deutsch-polnischen Historikerkonferenz* (Berlin, 1979), pp. 59–70

Daniel, Ute, *Hoftheater. Zur Geschichte des Theaters und der Höfe im 18. und 19. Jahrhundert* (Stuttgart, 1995)

Dann, Otto, 'Die bürgerliche Vereinsbildung in Deutschland und ihre Erforschung', in Etienne François (ed.), *Geselligkeit, Vereinswesen und bürgerliche Gesellschaft in Frankreich, Deutschland und der Schweiz 1750–1850* (Paris, 1986), pp. 43–52

Dann, Otto (ed.), *Nationalismus und sozialer Wandel* (Hamburg, 1978), 77–128
Vereinswesen und bürgerliche Gesellschaft in Deutschland. Historische Zeitschrift, Beiheft NF9 (1984)

Demel, Walter, *Der bayerische Staatsabsolutismus 1806/08–1817. Staats- und gesellschaftspolitische Motivationen und Hintergünde der Reformära in der ersten Phase des Königreichs Bayern* (Munich, 1983)

Denecke, Bernward and Kahsnitz, Reiner (eds.), *Das kunst- und kulturgeschichtliche Museum im 19. Jahrhundert. Vorträge des Symposion im Germanischen Nationalmuseum, Nürnberg* (Munich, 1977)

'Der Dresdner Maiaufstand von 1849', *Dresdner Hefte* 43 (1995)

Diefendorf, Jeffry M., *Businessmen and politics in the Rhineland, 1789–1834* (Princeton, 1980)

Dietrich, Richard, 'Die Verwaltungsreform in Sachsen 1869–1873', *Neues Archiv für sächsische Geschichte* 61 (1940), 49–85

Dipper, Christoph, 'Die Bauernbefreiung in Deutschland, ein Überblick', *Geschichte in Wissenschaft und Unterricht* 43:1 (1992), 16–31

Ditt, Hildegard and Schöller, Peter, 'Die Entwicklung des Eisenbahnnetzes in Nordwestdeutschland', *Westfälische Forschungen* 8 (1955), 150–80

Dobbin, Frank, *Forging industrial policy. The United States, Britain, and France in the railway age* (Cambridge, 1994)

Dörner, Andreas, *Politischer Mythos und symbolische Politik. Sinnstiftung durch symbolische Formen am Beispiel des Hermannsmythos* (Opladen, 1995)

Dorpalen, Andreas, *Heinrich von Treitschke* (Port Washington/ London, 1973 – reissue)

Düding, Dieter, 'Die deutsche Nationalbewegung des 19. Jahrhunderts als Vereinsbewegung. Anmerkungen zu ihrer Struktur und Phänomenologie zwischen Befreiungskriegszeitalter und Reichsgründung', *Geschichte in Wissenschaft und Unterricht* 42:10 (1991), 601–24

Düding, Dieter, Friedemann, Peter and Münch, Paul (eds.), *Öffentliche Festkultur. Politische Feste in Deutschland von der Aufklärung bis zum Ersten Weltkrieg* (Reinbeck bei Hamburg, 1988)

Duindam, Jeroen, *Myths of power. Norbert Elias and the early modern European court* (Amsterdam, 1995)

Eade, J. C. (ed.), *Romantic Nationalism in Europe* (Canberra, 1983)

Eckert, Helmut, 'Zur Charakteristik des hannoverschen Staatsministers Heinrich Bergmann. Seine "Consideranda" vom 25.01.1855', *Niedersächsisches Jahrbuch für Landesgeschichte* 46–7 (1974–5), 345–54

Eley, Geoff, *Reshaping the German right – radical nationalism and political change after Bismarck* (New Haven, Conn., 1980)

'Nationalism and social history', *Social History* 6:1 (1981), 83–107

Society, culture and the state in Germany, 1870–1930 (Ann Arbor, 1996)

Elias, Norbert, *The court society* (Oxford, 1983)

Engelsing, Rolf, *Massenpublikum und Journalistentum im 19. Jahrhundert in Nordwestdeutschland* (Berlin, 1966)

'Zur politischen Bildung der deutschen Unterschichten 1789–1863', *Historische Zeitschrift* 206 (1968), 337–69

Analphabetentum und Lektüre. Zur Sozialgeschichte des Lesens in Deutschland zwischen feudaler und industrieller Gesellschaft (Stuttgart, 1973)

Enzweiler, Hans-Jürgen, *Staat und Eisenbahn. Bürokratie, Parlament und Arbeiterschaft beim badischen Eisenbahnbau 1833–1855* (Frankfurt, 1995)

Epstein, Klaus, 'Stein in German historiography', *History and Theory* 5:2 (1965), 241–74

Ermisch, Hubert, 'Zur Geschichte des Königlich Sächsischen Alterthumsvereins 1825–1885', *Neues Archiv für sächsische Geschichte und Alterthumskunde* 6 (1885), 1–50

Evans, Richard J. (ed.), *Society and politics in Wilhelmine Germany* (London, 1978)

Fahrmeir, Andreas Karl Otto, 'Citizenship, nationality and alien status in England and the German states, 1815–1870' (unpublished Ph.D. thesis, Cambridge, 1997)

Fairbairn, Brett, 'Authority vs. democracy: Prussian officials in the German elections of 1898 and 1903', *The Historical Journal* 33:4 (1990), 811–38

Faith, Nicholas, *The world the railways made* (London, 1990)

Faulenbach, Bernd (ed.), *Geschichtswissenschaft in Deutschland. Traditionelle Positionen und gegenwärtige Aufgaben* (Munich, 1974)

Fehrenbach, Elisabeth, 'Über die Bedeutung der politischen Symbole im Nationalstaat', *Historische Zeitschrift* 213:2 (1971), 296–357

Ferguson, Niall, 'Public finance and national security: the domestic origins of the First World War revisited', *Past and Present* 142 (1994), 141–68

Fischer, Heinz-Dietrich, *Handbuch der politischen Presse in Deutschland 1480–1980. Synopse rechtlicher, struktureller und wirtschaftlicher Grundlagen der Tendenzpublizistik im Kommunikationsfeld* (Düsseldorf, 1981)

Fischer, Heinz-Dietrich (ed.), *Deutsche Zeitungen des 17. bis 20. Jahrhunderts* (Pullach bei München, 1972)

Fischer, Wolfram (ed.), *Wirtschaft und Gesellschaft im Zeitalter der Industrialisierung. Aufsätze – Studien – Vorträge* (Göttingen, 1972)

Fischer-Frauendienst, Irene, *Bismarcks Pressepolitik* (Münster, Westf., 1963)

Flathe, Theodor, *Geschichte des Kurstaates und Königreiches Sachsen. Dritter Band: Neuere Geschichte Sachsens von 1806–1866* (Gotha, 1873)

Flockerzie, Lawrence J., 'State-building and nation-building in the "Third

Germany": Saxony after the Congress of Vienna', *Central European History* 24:3 (1991), 268–92

François, Etienne, 'Regionale Unterschiede der Lese- und Schreibfähigkeit in Deutschland im 18. und 19. Jh.', *Jahrbuch für Regionalgeschichte* 17:1 (1990), 154–72

François, Etienne, (ed.), *Geselligkeit, Vereinswesen und bürgerliche Gesellschaft in Frankreich, Deutschland und der Schweiz 1750–1850* (Paris, 1986)

François, Etienne, Siegrist, Hannes and Vogel, Jakob (eds.), *Nation und Emotion: Deutschland und Frankreich im Vergleich, 19. und 20. Jahrhundert* (Göttingen, 1995)

Franz, Günther, 'Ferdinand Cohen-Blind und sein Attentat auf Bismarck 1866', *Zeitschrift für württembergische Landesgeschichte* 40 (1981), 387–97

Fremdling, Rainer, 'Railroads and German economic growth: a leading sector analysis with a comparison in the United States and Great Britain', *Journal of Economic History* 37:3 (1977), 583–604

Fremdling, Rainer and Tilly, Richard (eds.), *Industrialisierung und Raum. Studien zur regionalen Differenzierung im Deutschland des 19. Jahrhunderts* (Stuttgart, 1979)

Frensdorff, Friedrich, *Gottlieb Planck, deutscher Jurist und Politiker* (Berlin, 1914)

Friedeburg, Ludwig von, *Bildungsreform in Deutschland. Geschichte und gesellschaftlicher Widerspruch* (Frankfurt, 1989)

Friederich, Gerd, *Die Volksschule in Württemberg im 19. Jahrhundert* (Weinheim, 1978)

Fritz, Eberhard, 'König Wilhelm und Königin Katharina von Württemberg. Studien zur höfischen Repräsentation im Spiegel der Hofdiarien', *Zeitschrift für Württembergische Landesgeschichte* 54 (1995), 157–78

Fuhrmann, Horst, 'Gelehrtenleben: Über die Monumenta Germaniae Historica und ihre Bearbeiter', *Geschichte in Wissenschaft und Unterricht* 45:9 (1994), 558–72

Gagliardo, John G., *Germany under the old regime, 1600–1790* (London/New York, 1991)

Gaida, Hans-Jürgen, *Dampf zwischen Weser und Ems. Die Geschichte der Großherzoglich Oldenburgischen Eisenbahn* (Stuttgart, 1979)

Gall, Lothar, *Der Liberalismus als regierende Partei. Das Großherzogtum Baden zwischen Restauration und Reichsgründung* (Wiesbaden, 1968)

Gall, Lothar (ed.), *Liberalismus* (Königstein/Ts, 1980)

   Bismarck, the white revolutionary, Vol. 1, *1851–1871* (London, 1986)

   'Liberalismus und Region. Zur Geschichte des deutschen Liberalismus im 19. Jahrhundert', *Historische Zeitschrift*, Beiheft NF19 (Munich, 1995)

Gall, Lothar and Pohl, Manfred (eds.), *Die Eisenbahn in Deutschland, von den Anfängen bis zur Gegenwart* (Munich, 1999)

Geertz, Clifford, 'Centers, kings, and charisma: reflections on the symbolics of power', in Joseph Ben-David and Terry Nichols Clark (eds.), *Culture and its creators. Essays in honor of Edward Shils* (Chicago/London, 1977), pp. 150–71

Gellner, Ernest, *Nations and nationalism* (Oxford, 1983)

Gestrich, Andreas, *Absolutismus und Öffentlichkeit: politische Kommunikation in Deutschland zu Beginn des 18. Jahrhunderts* (Göttingen, 1994)

Geyer, Curt, *Politische Parteien und Verfassungskämpfe in Sachsen von der Märzrevolution bis zum Ausbruch des Maiaufstands 1848–1849* (Leipzig, 1914)

Gillis, John R., 'Aristocracy and bureaucracy in nineteenth-century Prussia', *Past and Present* 41 (1968), 105–29

Gisevius, Hans-Friedrich, *Zur Vorgeschichte des preußisch-sächsischen Eisenbahnkrieges. Verkehrspolitische Differenzen zwischen Preußen und Sachsen im Deutschen Bund* (Berlin, 1971)

Goetz, Walter, 'Die baierische Geschichtsforschung im 19. Jahrhundert. Zur Erinnerung an Sigmund Riezler', *Historische Zeitschrift* 138 (1928), 255–314

Golka, Heribert and Reese, Armin, 'Soziale Strömungen der Märzrevolution von 1848 in der Landdrostei Hannover', *Niedersächsisches Jahrbuch für Landesgeschichte* 45 (1973), 275–301

Gollwitzer, Heinz, *Die Standesherren. Die politische und gesellschaftliche Stellung der Mediatisierten 1815–1918* (Göttingen, 1964, 2nd edn)

'Die politische Landschaft in der deutschen Geschichte des 19./20. Jahrhunderts. Eine Skizze zum deutschen Regionalismus', *Zeitschrift für bayerische Landesgeschichte* 27 (1964), 523–52

'Fürst und Volk, Betrachtungen zur Selbsbehauptung des bayerischen Herrscherhauses im 19. und 20. Jahrhundert', *Zeitschrift für bayerische Landesgeschichte* 50:3 (1987), 723–47

Goltermann, Svenja, *Körper der Nation. Habitusformierung und die Politik des Turnens, 1860–1890* (Göttingen, 1998)

Graff, Harvey J., *The legacies of literacy: continuities and contradictions in Western culture and society* (Bloomington, 1987)

Grasskamp, Walter, *Museumsgründer und Museumsstürmer. Zur Sozialgeschichte des Kunstmuseums* (Munich, 1981)

Grauer, Karl Johannes, *Wilhelm I., König von Württemberg. Ein Bild seines Lebens und seiner Zeit* (Stuttgart, 1960)

Griepentrog, Martin, *Kulturhistorische Museen in Westfalen (1900–1950). Geschichtsbilder, Kulturströmungen, Bildungskonzepte* (Paderborn, 1998)

Griewank, Theodor, *Württemberg und die deutsche Politik in den Jahren 1859–1861 mit einem Überblick bis zum Thron- und Regierungswechsel von 1864* (Stuttgart, 1934)

Grob, Ernst, 'Beusts Kampf gegen Bismarck' (unpublished doctoral dissertation, Zurich, 1934)

Gross, Hans, 'The Holy Roman Empire in modern times: constitutional reality and legal theory' in Steven W. Rowan and James A. Vann (eds.), *The old Reich. Essays on German political institutions, 1495–1806* (Brussels, 1974) pp. 1–30

Grotefend, Otto, '100 Jahre Historischer Verein für Niedersachsen', *Jahrbuch für Niedersächsische Landesgeschichte* 12 (1935), 1–24

Grüner, Wolf D., *Die deutsche Frage, ein Problem der europäischen Geschichte seit 1800* (Munich, 1985)

Gütersloh, Birgit, 'Die Vertretung sächsischer Interessen auf internationalem Gebiet gegenüber Reichsorganen von 1919 bis 1933' in Werner Bramke and Ulrich Hess (eds.), *Sachsen und Mitteldeutschland, Politische, wirtschaftliche und soziale Wandlungen im 20. Jahrhundert* (Weimar/Cologne/Vienna, 1995) pp. 197–214

Guhl, Wilhelm, *Johannes von Miquel, ein Vorkämpfer deutscher Einheit* (Berlin, 1928)

Haase, Carl (ed.), *Niedersachsen. Territorien – Verwaltungseinheiten – geschichtliche Landschaften* (Göttingen, 1971)

Habermas, Jürgen, *The structural transformation of the public sphere, an inquiry into a category of bourgeois society* (Oxford, 1992)

Hahn, Hans-Werner, *Wirtschaftliche Integration im 19. Jahrhundert. Die hessischen Staaten und der Deutsche Zollverein* (Göttingen, 1982)

Geschichte des Deutschen Zollvereins (Göttingen, 1984)

Halperin, William S., 'The origins of the Franco-Prussian war revisited: Bismarck and the Hohenzollern candidature for the Spanish throne', *Journal of Modern History* 45:1 (1973), 83–91

Hamann, Manfred, 'Die Gründung des Historischen Vereins für Niedersachsen 1835' in Helmut Maurer and Hans Patze (eds.), *Festschrift für Bernd Schwineköper, zu seinem siebzigsten Geburtstag* (Sigmaringen, 1982), pp. 569–82

Hamerow, Theodore S., *Restoration, revolution, reaction. Economics and politics in Germany 1815–1871* (Princeton, 1958)

'The elections to the Frankfurt Parliament', *Journal of Modern History* 33:1 (1961), 15–32

Hammer-Schenk, Harold and Kokkelink, Günther (eds.), *Laves und Hannover, niedersächsische Architektur im neunzehnten Jahrhundert* (Hanover, 1989)

Hammerton, Elizabeth and Cannadine, David, 'Conflict and consensus on a ceremonial occasion: the Diamond Jubilee in Cambridge in 1897', *The Historical Journal* 24:1 (1981), 111–46

Hanisch, Manfred, *Für Fürst und Vaterland. Legitimitätsstiftung in Bayern zwischen Revolution 1848 und deutscher Einheit* (Munich, 1991)

Harder, Klaus Peter, *Environmental factors of early railroads: a comparative study of Massachusetts and the German states of Baden and the Pfalz (Palatinate) before 1870* (New York, 1981)

Hardtwig, Wolfgang, 'Geschichtsinteresse, Geschichtsbilder und politische Symbole in der Reichsgründungsära und im Kaiserreich' in Ekkehard Mai and Stephan Waetzoldt (eds.), *Kunstverwaltung, Bau- und Denkmal-Politik im Kaiserreich* (Berlin, 1980), pp. 47–75

'Von Preussens Aufgabe in Deutschland zu Deutschlands Aufgabe in der Welt. Liberalismus und Borussianisches Geschichtsbild zwischen Revolution und Imperialismus', *Historische Zeitschrift* 231:2 (1980), 265–324

'Der bezweifelte Patriotismus – nationales Bewußtsein und Denkmal 1786 bis 1933', *Geschichte in Wissenschaft und Unterricht* 44:12 (1993), 773–85

Ausgewählte Aufsätze (Göttingen, 1994)

Harris, James F., 'Eduard Lasker: the Jew as national German politician', *Leo Baeck Institute Yearbook* 20 (1975), 151–77

Hartlieb von Wallthor, Alfred, 'Der Freiherr von Stein und Hannover', *Niedersächsisches Jahrbuch für Landesgeschichte* 66 (1994), 233–59.

Hartmann, Wolfgang, *Der historische Festzug. Seine Entstehung und Entwicklung im 19. und 20. Jahrhundert* (Munich, 1976)

Hartung, Werner, *Konservative Zivilisationskritik und regionale Identität, am Beispiel der niedersächsischen Heimatbewegung 1895 bis 1919* (Hanover, 1991)

Hassell, W. von, *Geschichte des Königreichs Hannover. Unter Benutzung bisher unbekannter Aktenstücke*, 3 Vols. (Leipzig, 1901)

Hastings, Adrian, *The construction of nationhood: ethnicity, religion and nationalism* (Cambridge, 1997)

Hauptmann, Fritz, 'Sachsens Wirtschaft und der soziale Gedanke, 1840–1850', *Neues Archiv für sächsische Geschichte* 59 (1938), 129–207

Heimpel, Hermann, 'Über Organisationsformen historischer Forschung in Deutschland' in Theodor Schieder (ed.), *Historische Zeitschrift* 189, *Hundert Jahre Historische Zeitschrift 1859–1959, Beiträge zur Geschichte der Historiographie in den deutschsprächigen Ländern* (1959), pp. 139–222

Geschichtsvereine einst und jetzt. Vortrag gehalten am Tag der 70. Wiederkehr der Gründung des Geschichtsvereins für Göttingen und Umgebung (Göttingen, 1963)

Hellmuth, Eckhart, 'A monument to Frederick the Great: architecture, politics and the state in late eighteenth-century Prussia' in John Brewer and Eckhart Hellmuth (eds.), *Rethinking Leviathan. The eighteenth-century state in Britain and Germany* (Oxford, 1999), pp. 317–42

Hellwag, Fritz E., *Varnbüler und die deutsche Frage 1864–66* (Stuttgart, 1934)

Heming, Ralf, *Öffentlichkeit, Diskurs und Gesellschaft. Zum analystischen Potential und zur Kritik des Begriffes der Öffentlichkeit bei Habermas* (Wiesbaden, 1997)

Henderson, W. O., *The state and the industrial revolution in Prussia 1740–1870* (Liverpool, 1958)

Henkel, Martin and Taubert, Rolf, *Die deutsche Presse 1848–1850, eine Bibliographie* (Munich, 1986)

Hermann, Ulrich (ed.), *Schule und Gesellschaft im 19. Jahrhundert. Sozialgeschichte der Schule im Übergang zur Industriegesellschaft* (Weinheim, 1977)

Herrigel, Gary, *Industrial constructions, the sources of German industrial power* (Cambridge, 1996)

Herrlitz, Hans-Georg, Hopf, Wulf and Titze, Hartmut, *Deutsche Schulgeschichte von 1800 bis zur Gegenwart. Eine Einführung* (Weinheim, 1993)

Herrmann, Wolfgang, *Gottfried Semper, in search of his architecture* (Cambridge, Mass., 1984)

Hettling, Manfred, 'Bürger oder Soldaten? Kriegerdenkmäler 1848 bis 1854' in Reinhart Koselleck and Michael Jeismann (eds.), *Der politische Totenkult. Kriegerdenkmäler in der Moderne* (Munich, 1994), pp. 147–95

Hettling, Manfred and Nolte, Paul (eds.), *Bürgerliche Feste, symbolische Formen politischen Handelns im 19. Jahrhundert* (Göttingen, 1993)

Hiery, Hermann, *Reichstagswahlen im Reichsland. Ein Beitrag zur Landesgeschichte von Elsaß-Lothringen und zur Wahlgeschichte des Deutschen Reichs, 1871–1918* (Düsseldorf, 1986)

Hildebrandt, Alfred, 'Die Pressepolitik der hannoverschen Regierung vom Beginn der Reaktionszeit bis zum Ende des Königreichs Hannover' (unpublished doctoral dissertation, Leipzig, 1932)

Hobsbawm, Eric, *Nations and nationalism since 1780. Programme, myth, reality* (Cambridge, 1990)

Hobsbawm, Eric and Ranger, Terence (eds.), *The invention of tradition* (Cambridge, 1983)

Hochstadt, Steve, 'Migration in preindustrial Germany', *Central European History* 16:3 (1983), 195–224.

Mobility and modernity. Migration in Germany 1820–1989 (Ann Arbor, 1999)

Höfer, Franz Thomas, *Pressepolitik und Polizeistaat Metternichs: die Überwachung von Presse und politischer Öffentlichkeit in Deutschland und den Nachbarstaaten durch das Mainzer Informationsbüro (1833–1848)* (Munich, 1983)

Hoffmann, Peter, *Die diplomatischen Beziehungen zwischen Württemberg und Bayern im Krimkrieg und bis zum Beginn der Italienischen Krise 1853–1858* (Stuttgart, 1963)

Holldack, Heinz Georg, *Untersuchungen zur Geschichte der Reaktion in Sachsen, 1849–1855* (Berlin, 1931)

Hollenberg, Gisela and Hollenberg, Günther, 'Die Katholische Kirchenpolitik der württembergischen Kultusbürokratie unter Freiherr von Wangenheim. Ein Beispiel gouvernementalen Liberalismus in deutschen Mittelstaaten nach dem Wiener Kongress ', *Zeitschrift für württembergische Landesgeschichte* 36 (1977), 114–31

Hölscher, Lucian, *Öffentlichkeit und Geheimnis. Eine begriffsgeschichtliche Untersuchung zur Entstehung der Öffentlichkeit in der frühen Neuzeit* (Stuttgart, 1979)

Hope, Nicholas Martin, *The alternative to German unification: the anti-Prussian party in Frankfurt, Nassau and the two Hessen 1859–1867* (Wiesbaden, 1973)

Hughes, Michael, *Nationalism and society. Germany 1800–1945* (London, 1988)

Hull, Isabel V., 'Prussian dynastic ritual and the end of monarchy' in Carole Fink, Isabel V. Hull and MacGregor Knox (eds.), *German nationalism and the European response, 1890–1945* (Norman, Ok/London, 1985), pp. 13–42

Hunt, James Clark, *The People's Party in Württemberg and Southern Germany, 1890–1914. The possibilities of democratic politics* (Stuttgart, 1975)

Hüsgen, Ed, *Ludwig Windthorst. Sein Leben, sein Wirken* (Cologne, 1911)

Hutchinson, John and Smith, Anthony D. (eds.), *Nationalism* (Oxford, 1994)

Hutter, Peter, 'Zur Baugeschichte des Völkerschlachtdenkmals in Leipzig' in Katrin Keller, and Hans-Dieter Schmid (eds.), *Vom Kult zur Kulisse: das Völkerschlachtsdenkmal als Gegenstand der Geschichtskultur* (Leipzig, 1995), pp. 42–61

Iggers, Georg G., *The German conception of history. The national tradition of historical thought from Herder to the present* (Middletown, Conn., 1968)

Jaeger, Hans, *Geschichte der Wirtschaftsordnung in Deutschland* (Frankfurt, 1988)

Jakobi, Franz-Josef, 'Mittelalterliches Reich und Nationalstaatsgedanke. Zur Funktion der Mittelalterrezeption und des Mittelalterbildes im 19. und 20. Jahrhundert' in Karl-Ernst Jeismann (ed.) *Einheit–Freiheit–Selbstbestimmung. Die Deutsche Frage im historisch-politischen Bewußtsein* (Frankfurt, 1988), pp. 155–78

James, Harold, 'Germans and their nation', *German History* 9:2 (1991), pp. 136–52

Jarausch, Konrad H., 'Students, sex and politics in Imperial Germany', *Journal of Contemporary History* 17:2 (1982), 285–304

Jeismann, Karl-Ernst (ed.), *Bildung, Staat, Gesellschaft im 19. Jahrhundert. Mobilisierung und Disziplinierung. Im Auftrage der Freiherr-vom-Stein-Gesellschaft* (Stuttgart, 1989)

Jeismann, Karl-Ernst and Lundgreen, Peter (eds.), *Handbuch der deutschen Bildungsgeschichte*, Vol. III, *1800–1870. Von der Neuordnung Deutschlands bis zur Gründung des deutschen Reiches* (Munich, 1987)

John, Michael, 'Liberalism and society in Germany, 1850–1880: the case of Hanover', *English Historical Review* 102:402 (1987), 579–598
'National and regional identities and the dilemmas of reform in Britain's "other province": Hanover, c.1800–c.1850' in Laurence Brockliss and David Eastwood (eds.), *A union of multiple identities: the British Isles c. 1750–c.1850* (Manchester, 1997), pp. 179–92

Jordan, Herbert, *Die öffentliche Meinung in Sachsen 1864–66* (Kamenz, 1918)

Kaemmel, Otto, *Sächsische Geschichte. Mit einem Beitrag, Sachsen im 20. Jahrhundert, von Agatha Kobuch* (Dresden, 1995)

Kaernbach, Andreas, *Bismarcks Konzepte zur Reform des Deutschen Bundes. Zur Kontinuität der Politik Bismarcks und Preußens in der deutschen Frage* (Göttingen, 1991)

Kahan, Alan, 'Liberalism and *Realpolitik* in Prussia 1830–52: The Case of David Hansemann', *German History* 9:3 (1991), 280–307.

Kaufhold, Karl Heinrich, 'Die Anfänge des Eisenbahnbaus in Niedersachsen' in Dieter Brosius and Martin Last (eds.), *Beiträge zur niedersächsischen Landesgeschichte, zum 65. Geburtstag von Hans Patze* (Hildesheim, 1984), pp. 364–87

Keller, Katrin, 'Landesgeschichte zwischen Wissenschaft und Politik: August der Starke als sächsisches "Nationalsymbol"' in Konrad H. Jarausch and Matthias Middell (eds.), *Nach dem Erdbeben. (Re-)Konstruktion ostdeutscher Geschichte und Geschichtswissenschaft* (Leipzig, 1994), pp. 195–215

Keller, Katrin (ed.), *Feste und Feiern: zum Wandel städtischer Festkultur in Leipzig* (Leipzig, 1994)

Keller, Ulrich, *Reitermonumente absolutistischer Fürsten* (Munich, 1971)

Kelly, Alfred, 'The Franco-Prussian war and unification in German history schoolbooks', in Walter Pape (ed.), *1870/71–1989/90. German unifications and the change of literary discourse* (Berlin/New York, 1993), pp. 37–60

Kennedy, Katharine D., 'Regionalism and nationalism in South German history lessons 1871–1914', *German Studies Review* 12 (1989), 11–33

Kiesewetter, Hubert, 'Economic preconditions for Germany's nation-building in the nineteenth century', in Hagen Schulze (ed.), *Nation-building in Central Europe* (Leamington Spa, 1987), pp. 81–106
Industrialisierung und Landwirtschaft. Sachsens Stellung im regionalen Industrialisierungsprozeß Deutschlands im 19. Jahrhundert (Cologne/Vienna, 1988)
Industrielle Revolution in Deutschland, 1815–1914 (Frankfurt, 1989)

Kitchen, Martin, 'The traditions of German strategic thought', *International History Review* 1:2 (1979), pp. 163–91

Klee, Wolfgang, *Preußische Eisenbahngeschichte* (Stuttgart, 1982)

Kleinknecht, Thomas, 'Mittelalterauffassung in Forschung und politischer Kontroverse. Zu den Beiträgen von James Bryce und Georg Waitz', in Heinz Dollinger, Horst Gründer and Alwin Hanschmidt (eds.), *Weltpolitik, Europagedanke, Regionalismus. Festschrift für Heinz Gollwitzer zum 65. Geburtstag am 30. Januar 1982* (Münster, 1982), 269–286

Klemm, Mathilde, 'Sachsen und das deutsche Problem 1848' (unpublished doctoral dissertation, Ruprecht-Karls Universität zu Heidelberg, Phil. Faculty, 1914)

Klenke, Dietmar, 'Nationalkriegerisches Gemeinschaftsideal als politische Religion. Zum Vereinsnationalismus der Sänger, Schützen und Turner am Vorabend der Einigungskriege', *Historische Zeitschrift* 260:2 (1995), 395–448

Klocke, Helmut, 'Die Sächsische Politik und der Norddeutsche Bund' (unpublished doctoral dissertation, Leipzig, 1927)

Kocka, Jürgen (ed.), *Bürgertum im 19. Jahrhundert. Deutschland im europäischen Vergleich*, Vol. III (Munich, 1988)

Kocka, Jürgen (ed.), *Bürger und Bürgerlichkeit im 19. Jahrhundert* (Göttingen, 1987)

Kohnen, Richard, *Pressepolitik des Deutschen Bundes. Methoden staatlicher Pressepolitik nach der Revolution von 1848* (Tübingen, 1995)

Kolb, Karlheinz and Teiwes, Jürgen, *Beiträge zur politischen Sozial- und Rechtsgeschichte der Hannoverschen Ständeversammlung von 1814–1833 und 1838–1849* (Hildesheim, 1977)

Koselleck, Reinhart, *Preußen zwischen Reform und Revolution, Allgemeines Landrecht, Verwaltung und soziale Bewegung von 1791 bis 1848* (Stuttgart, 1967)

Köster, Fredy, *Hannover und die Grundlegung der preußischen Suprematie in Deutschland, 1862–1864* (Hildesheim, 1978)

Koszyk, Kurt, *Deutsche Presse im 19. Jahrhundert. Geschichte der deutschen Presse*, Vol. II (Berlin, 1966)

Kötschke, Rudolf and Kretzschmar, Hellmut, *Sächsische Geschichte* (Augsburg, 1995, reprint)

Kracke, Friedrich, *Friedrich August III., Sachsens volkstümlichster König. Ein Bild seines Lebens und seiner Zeit* (Munich, 1964)

Kraehe, Enno E., 'Austria and the problem of reform in the German Confederation 1851–1863', *American Historical Review* 56 (1950–1), 276–94

Kramer, Margarete, *Die Zensur in Hamburg, 1819 bis 1848. Ein Beitrag zur Frage staatlicher Lenkung der Öffentlichkeit während des Deutschen Vormärz* (Hamburg, 1975)

Kraus, Andreas (ed.), *Land und Reich, Stamm und Nation. Probleme und Perspektiven bayerischer Geschichte. Festage für Max Spindler zum 90. Geburtstag*, Vol. II, *Frühe Neuzeit*; Vol. III, *Vom Vormärz bis zur Gegenwart* (Munich, 1984)

Kretzschmar, Hellmut, 'Schicksal und Anteil Sachsen auf dem Wege zum Kriege 1866', *Neues Archiv für sächsische Geschichte* 60 (1939), 66–125

Die Zeit König Johanns von Sachsen 1854–1873 (Berlin, 1960)

'Das sächsische Königtum im 19. Jahrhundert: Ein Beitrag zur Typologie der Monarchie in Deutschland', *Historische Zeitschrift* 170 (1950), 457–93.

Krieger, Leonard, *The German idea of freedom: history of a political tradition* (Chicago, 1957)

Ranke, the meaning of history (Chicago, 1977)

Kroker, Angelika, 'Niedersächsische Geschichtsforschung im 19. Jahrhundert: Zwischen Aufklärung und Historismus', *Westfälische Forschungen* 39 (1989), 83–113

Kruedener, Jürgen von, 'The Franckenstein paradox in the intergovernmental fiscal relations of Imperial Germany', in Peter-Christian Witt (ed.), *Wealth and taxation in Central Europe. The history and sociology of public finance* (Leamington Spa, 1987), pp. 111–24

Krüger, Peter (ed.), *Deutschland, deutscher Staat, deutsche Nation. Historische Erkundungen eines Spannungsverhältnisses* (Marburg, 1993)

Kuhlemann, Frank-Michael, *Modernisierung und Disziplinierung. Sozialgeschichte des preußischen Volksschulwesens 1794–1872* (Göttingen, 1992)

Lamberti, Marjorie, *State, society, and the elementary school in Imperial Germany* (Oxford, 1989)

'State, church and the politics of school reform during the Kulturkampf', *Central European History* 19:1 (1986), 63–81

'The attempt to form a Jewish Bloc: Jewish notables and politics in Wilhelmine Germany', *Central European History* 3:1–2 (1970), 79–93

Lampe, Klaus, *Oldenburg und Preußen 1815–1871* (Hildesheim, 1972)

Lange, Karl, *Die Krise des Deutschen Bundes (1866) aus der Sicht der französischen Gesandtschaft in Hannover und Braunschweig* (Hildesheim, 1978)

Langewiesche, Dieter, *Liberalismus und Demokratie in Württemberg zwischen Revolution und Reichsgründung* (Düsseldorf, 1974)

Langewiesche, Dieter, 'Julius Hölder (1819–1887). Zur Geschichte des württembergischen und deutschen Liberalismus im 19. Jahrhundert', *Zeitschrift für württembergische Landesgeschichte* 36 (1977), 150–66

'Deutschland und Österreich: Nationswerdung und Staatsbildung in Mitteleuropa im 19. Jahrhundert', *Geschichte in Wissenschaft und Unterricht* 42:12 (1991), 754–66

'Reich, Nation und Staat in der jüngeren deutschen Geschichte', *Historische Zeitschrift* 254:2 (1992), 341–81

'Die schwäbische Sängerbewegung in der Gesellschaft des 19. Jahrhunderts, ein Beitrag zur kulturellen Nationsbildung', *Zeitschrift für württembergische Landesgeschichte* 52 (1993), 257–302

'Nation, Nationalismus, Nationalstaat: Forschungsstand und Forschungsperspektiven', *Neue Politische Literatur* 40:2 (1995), 190–236

Langewiesche, Dieter (ed.), *Die Deutsche Revolution von 1848* (Darmstadt, 1983)

Laslowski, Ernst, 'Zur Entwicklungsgeschichte Onno Klopps. Ein Beitrag zum Problem Persönlichkeit und Geschichtsauffassung', *Historisches Jahrbuch* 56 (1936), 481–98

Lässig, Simone and Pohl, Karl Heinrich (eds.), *Sachsen im Kaiserreich. Politik, Wirtschaft und Gesellschaft im Umbruch* (Cologne, 1997)

Lässig, Simone, Pohl, Karl Heinrich and Retallack, James (eds.), *Modernisierung und Region im wilhelminischen Deutschland. Wahlen, Wahlrecht und politische Kultur* (Bielefeld, 1995)

Lee, W. R., 'Economic development and the state in nineteenth-century Germany', *Economic History Review*, 2nd ser., 41: 3 (1988), 346–67

Lee, W. R. (ed.), *German industry and German industrialisation: essays in German economic and business history in the nineteenth and twentieth centuries* (London, 1991)

Lehmann, Hartmut, *Pietismus and weltliche Ordnung in Württemberg vom 17. bis zum 20. Jahrhundert* (Stuttgart, 1969)

Lent, Dieter, 'Das Niedersachsenbewußtsein im Wandel der Jahrhunderte' in Carl Haase (ed.), *Niedersachsen. Territorien – Verwaltungseinheiten – geschichtliche Landschaften* (Göttingen, 1971), pp. 27–50

Leschinsky, Achim and Roeder, Peter Martin, *Schule im historischen Prozeß. Zum Wechselverhältnis von institutioneller Erziehung und gesellschaftlicher Entwicklung* (Frankfurt, 1983)

Levinger, Matthew, 'Hardenberg, Wittgenstein, and the constitutional question in Prussia 1815–22', *German History* 8:3 (1990), 257–77

Levy, Richard S., *The downfall of the anti-Semitic political parties in Imperial Germany* (London/New Haven, Conn., 1975)

von der Leyen, Alfred, *Die Eisenbahnpolitik des Fürsten Bismarck* (Berlin, 1914)

Liebl, Anton J., *Die Privateisenbahn München–Augsburg (1835–1844). Entstehung, Bau und Betrieb, ein Beitrag zur Strukturanalyse der frühen Industrialisierung Bayerns* (Munich, 1982)

Lipp, Wilfried, *Natur – Geschichte – Denkmal. Zur Entstehung des Denkmalbewußtseins der bürgerlichen Gesellschaft* (Frankfurt, 1987)

Lowenstein, Steven M., 'The rural community and the urbanization of German Jewry', *Central European History* 13:3 (1980), 218–36

Lüdtke, Alf, 'The role of state violence in the period of transition to industrial capitalism: the example of Prussia from 1815–1848', *Social History* 4:2 (1979), 175–222

Lundgreen, Peter, 'Industrialisation and the educational formation of manpower in Germany', *Journal of Social History* 9:1 (1975), 64–80

Sozialgeschichte der deutschen Schule im Überblick. Teil I: 1770–1918 (Göttingen, 1980)

Lutz, Heinrich, *Zwischen Habsburg und Preußen: Deutschland 1815–1866* (Berlin, 1985)

Lutz, Rolland Ray, 'The German revolutionary student movement 1819–1833', *Central European History* 3 (1971), 215–41

Maatz, Helmut, *Bismarck und Hannover 1866–1898* (Hildesheim, 1970)

Mages, Emma, *Eisenbahnbau. Siedlung, Wirtschaft und Gesellschaft in der südlichen Oberpfalz (1850–1920)* (Kallmünz, 1984)

Mallgrave, Harry Francis, *Gottfried Semper, architect of the nineteenth-century* (New Haven, Conn./London, 1996)

Mann, Bernhard, 'Die württembergische "Organisations Kommission" von 1848', *Zeitschrift für württembergische Landesgeschichte* 40 (1981), 519–46

Mansel, Philip, 'Monarchy, uniform and the rise of the Frac 1760–1830', *Past and Present* 96 (August, 1982), 103–32

Marquardt, Frederick D., '*Pauperismus* in Germany during the *Vormärz*', *Central European History* 2 (1969), 77–88

Martel, Gordon (ed.), *Modern Germany reconsidered, 1870–1945* (London, 1992)

Maschke, Erich, 'Landesgeschichtsschreibung und historische Vereine', *Jahrbuch für württembergisch Franken* 58 *Festschrift für Gerd Wunder* (1974), 17–34

Mattheisen, Donald J., 'Voters and parliaments in the German revolution of 1848: an analysis of the Prussian Constituent Assembly', *Central European History* 5:1 (1972), 3–22

Maurer, Hans-Martin, 'Das Haus Württemberg und Rußland', *Zeitschrift für württembergische Landesgeschichte* 48 (1989), 201–22

Maurer, Michael, 'Feste und Feiern als historischer Forschungsgegenstand', *Historische Zeitschrift* 253:1 (1991), 101–30

Megerle, Klaus, 'Der Beitrag Württembergs zur Industrialisierung Deutschlands', *Zeitschrift für württembergische Landesgeschichte* 34–5 (1975–6), 324–57

  Württemberg im Industrialisierungsprozeß Deutschlands. Ein Beitrag zur regionalen Differenzierung der Industrialisierung (Stuttgart, 1982)

  'Ökonomische Integration und politische Orientierung deutscher Mittel- und Kleinstaaten im Vorfeld der Reichsgründung', in Helmut Berding (ed.), *Wirtschaftliche und politische Integration in Europa im 19. und 20. Jahrhundert, Geschichte und Gesellschaft* Sonderheft 10 (Göttingen, 1984), pp. 102–27

Meidenbauer, Jörg, *Aufklärung und Öffentlichkeit. Studien zu den Anfängen der Vereins- und Meinungsbildung in Hessen-Kassel, 1770 bis 1860* (Darmstadt, 1991)

Meinecke, Friedrich, *Die deutsche Katastrophe. Betrachtungen und Erinnerungen* (Wiesbaden, 1965, 6th edn)

Meyer, Folkert, *Schule der Untertanen. Lehrer und Politik in Preußen* (Hamburg, 1976)

Möckl, Karl (ed.), *Hof und Hofgesellschaft in den deutschen Staaten im 19. und beginnenden 20. Jahrhundert* (Boppard am Rhein, 1990)

Moersch, Karl, 'Das Altwürttembergische bei Uhland' in Hermann Bausinger (ed.), *Ludwig Uhland. Dichter. Politiker. Gelehrter* (Tübingen, 1988), pp. 87–107.

Mögle-Hofacker, Franz, *Zur Entwicklung des Parlamentarismus in Württemberg. Der 'Parlamentarismus der Krone' unter König Wilhelm I.* (Stuttgart, 1981)

Möllney, Ulrike, *Norddeutsche Presse um 1800. Zeitschriften und Zeitungen in Flensburg, Braunschweig, Hannover und Schaumburg-Lippe im Zeitalter der Französischen Revolution* (Bielefeld, 1996)

Mommsen, Wolfgang J., 'Preußisches Staatsbewußtsein und deutsche Reichsidee. Preußen und das Deutsche Reich in der jüngeren deutschen Geschichte', *Geschichte in Wissenschaft und Unterricht* 35:10 (1984), 685–705

Morck, Gordon R., 'Bismarck and the "Capitulation" of German Liberalism', *Journal of Modern History* 43 (1971), 59–75

Mosse, George L., *The nationalisation of the masses: political symbolism and mass movements in Germany from the Napoleonic Wars, through the Third Reich* (New York, 1975)

'Friendship and nationhood: about the promise and failure of German nationalism', *Journal of Contemporary History* 17:2 (1982), 351–67

Na'aman, Shlomo, *Der Deutsche Nationalverein, die politische Konstituierung des deutschen Bürgertums 1857–1867* (Düsseldorf, 1987)

Naujoks, Eberhard, *Bismarcks auswärtige Pressepolitik und die Reichsgründung, 1865–71* (Wiesbaden, 1968)

Die parlamentarische Entstehung des Reichspressegesetzes in der Bismarckzeit (1848/74) (Düsseldorf, 1975)

'Der "Staatsanzeiger" und die württembergische Regierungspresse in der Krise der Reichsgründungszeit (1864–1871)', *Zeitschrift für württembergische Landesgeschichte* 50 (1991), 271–304

Nettl, Peter, 'The German Social Democratic Party 1890–1914 as a political model', *Past and Present* 30 (1965), 65–95

Niehuss, Merith, 'Party configurations in state and municipal elections in Southern Germany, 1871–1914', in Karl Rohe (ed.), *Elections, parties and political traditions. Social foundations of German parties and party systems, 1867–1987* (New York/Oxford/Munich, 1990), pp. 83–107

Nipperdey, Thomas, 'Mass education and modernisation: the case of Germany 1780–1850', *Transactions of the Royal Historical Society*, 5th Series, 27 (1977), 155–72

Deutsche Geschichte 1800–1866. Bürgerwelt und starker Staat (Munich, 1983)

'Der Föderalismus in der deutschen Geschichte' in Thomas Nipperdey (ed.), *Nachdenken über die deutsche Geschichte, Essays* (Munich, 1986), pp. 60–109

Deutsche Geschichte 1866–1918, Vol. II, *Machtstaat vor der Demokratie* (Munich, 1992)

Nipperdey, Thomas (ed.), *Gesellschaft, Kultur, Theorie. Gesammelte Aufsätze zur neueren Geschichte* (Göttingen, 1976)

Nolte, Paul, 'Das südwestdeutsche Frühliberalismus in der Kontinuität der Frühen Neuzeit', *Geschichte in Wissenschaft und Unterricht* 43:12 (1992), 743–56

Nonn, Christoph, 'Arbeiter, Bürger und "Agrarier": Stadt-Land-Gegensatz und Klassenkonflikt im Wilhelminischen Deutschland am Beispiel des Königreichs Sachsen', in Helga Grebing, Hans Mommsen and Karsten Rudolph (eds.), *Demokratie und Emanzipation zwischen Saale und Elbe, Beiträge zur Geschichte der sozialdemokratischen Arbeiterbewegung bis 1933* (Essen, 1993) pp. 101–13

Nöth-Greis, Gertrud, 'Das Literarische Büro als Instrument der Pressepolitik' in Jürgen Wilke (ed.), *Pressepolitik und Propaganda. Historische Studien von Vormärz bis zum Kalten Krieg* (Cologne, 1997), pp. 1–79

Nürnberger, Richard, 'Städtische Selbstverwaltung und sozialer Wandel im Königreich und in der Provinz Hannover während des 19. Jahrhunderts', *Niedersächsisches Jahrbuch für Landesgeschichte* 48 (1976), 1–15

O'Boyle, Leonore, 'Liberal political leadership in Germany, 1867–1884', *Journal of Modern History* 28:4 (1956), 339–52

Oberschelp, Reinhard, *Politische Geschichte Niedersachsens 1714–1803* (Hildesheim, 1983)
Politische Geschichte Niedersachsens 1803–1866 (Hildesheim, 1988)
Pakula, Hannah, *An uncommon woman: the Empress Frederick, daughter of Queen Victoria, wife of the Crown Prince of Prussia, mother of Kaiser Wilhelm* (London, 1996)
Pascal, Roy, 'The Frankfurt Parliament, 1848, and the *Drang nach Osten*', *Journal of Modern History* 18:2 (1946), 108–22
Penny, Glenn, 'Fashioning local identities in an age of nation-building: museums, cosmopolitan visions, and intra-German competition', *German History*, 17:4 (1999), 489–505.
Perkins, J. A., 'The agricultural revolution in Germany', *Journal of European Economic History* 10 (1981), 71–118
Pflanze, Otto, 'Bismarck and German nationalism', *American Historical Review* 60:3 (1955), 548–66
Piereth, Wolfgang, 'Propaganda im 19. Jahrhundert. Die Anfänge aktiver staatlicher Pressepolitik in Deutschland 1800–1871' in Wolfram Siemann and Ute Daniel (eds.), *Propaganda, Meinungskampf, Verführung und politische Sinnstiftung 1789–1989* (Frankfurt, 1994), pp. 21–43
Plagemann, Volker, *Das deutsche Kunstmuseum 1790–1870. Lage, Baukörper, Raumorganisation, Bildprogramm* (Munich, 1967)
Plessen, Marie-Louise von (ed.), *Die Nation und ihre Museen. Für das Deutsche Historische Museum* (Frankfurt, 1992)
Pohl, Karl Heinrich, ' "Einig", "Kraftvoll", "Machtbewusst". Überlegungen zu einer Geschichte des deutschen Liberalismus aus regionaler Perspektive', *Historische Mitteilungen* 7:1 (1994), 61–80
Pollard, Sidney (ed.), *Region und Industrialisierung. Studien zur Rolle der Region in der Wirtschaftsgeschichte der letzten zwei Jahrhunderte* (Göttingen, 1980)
Pollmann, Karl Erich, *Parlamentarismus im Norddeutschen Bund 1867–1870* (Düsseldorf, 1985)
Press, Völker, 'Österreich und Deutschland im 18. Jahrhundert', *Geschichte in Wissenschaft und Unterricht* 42:12 (1991), 737–53
'Der württembergische Landtag im Zeitalter des Umbruchs 1770–1830', *Zeitschrift für württembergische Landesgeschichte* 42 (1983), 256–81
Preuss, Erich and Preuss, Reiner, *Sächsische Staatseisenbahnen* (Berlin, 1991)
Pulzer, Peter, *Jews and the German state: the political history of a minority, 1848–1933* (Oxford, 1992)
Rapp, Adolf, *Die Württemberger und die nationale Frage, 1863–1871* (Stuttgart, 1910)
Rauh, Manfred, *Föderalismus und Parlamentarismus im Wilhelminischen Reich* (Düsseldorf, 1983)
Real, Willy, *Der deutsche Reformverein. Großdeutsche Stimmen und Kräfte zwischen Villafranca und Königgrätz* (Lübeck, 1966)
Reininghaus, Wilfried and Teppe, Karl (eds.), *Verkehr und Region im 19. und 20. Jahrhundert. Westfälische Beispiele* (Paderborn, 1999)
Requate, Jörg, *Journalismus als Beruf. Entstehung und Entwicklung des Journalistenberufs im 19. Jahrhundert. Deutschland im internationalen Vergleich* (Göttingen, 1995)

Retallack, James, *Notables of the right. The Conservative Party and political mobilization in Germany, 1876–1914* (Boston, Mass. London 1988)

'"Why can't a Saxon be more like a Prussian?" Regional identities and the birth of modern political culture in Germany, 1866–7', *Canadian Journal of History* 32:1 (1997), 26–55

'Society and politics in Saxony in the nineteenth and twentieth centuries. Reflections on recent research', *Archiv für Sozialgeschichte* 38 (1998), 396–457

'Conservatives and anti-Semites in Baden and Saxony', *German History*, 17:4 (1999) 507–526.

Retallack, James, (ed.), 'Memory, democracy, and the mediated nation. Political cultures and regional identities in Germany, 1848–1998. An international conference of the University of Toronto in collaboration with the German Historical Institute, Washington, D.C., Toronto, September 18–20, 1998' (unpublished conference reader, September 1998)

Richards, Jeffrey and MacKenzie, John M., *The railway station, a social history* (Oxford, 1986)

Richter, Julius, *Geschichte der sächsischen Volksschule* (Berlin, 1930)

Ringsdorf, Ulrich Otto, *Der Eisenbahnbau südlich Nürnbergs 1841–49. Organisatorische, technische und soziale Probleme* (Nuremberg, 1978)

Rohe, Karl, 'Konfession, Klasse und lokale Gesellschaft als Bestimmungsfaktoren des Wahlverhaltens – Überlegungen und Problematisierungen am Beispiel des historischen Ruhrgebiets' in Lothar Albertin and Werner Link (eds.), *Politische Parteien auf dem Weg zur parlamentarischen Demokratie in Deutschland. Entwicklungslinien bis zur Gegenwart* (Düsseldorf, 1981), pp. 109–26

Röhl, J. C. G., 'Higher civil servants in Germany, 1890–1900', *Journal of Contemporary History* 2:3 (1967), 101–21

Rollins, William H., *A greener vision of home: cultural politics and environmental reform in the German Heimatschutz movmeent, 1904–1918* (Ann Arbor, 1997)

Ross, Ronald J., *Beleageured tower: the dilemma of political Catholicism in Wilhelmine Germany* (London, 1976)

'Enforcing the Kulturkampf in the Bismarckian state and the limits of coercion in Imperial Germany', *Journal of Modern History* 56:3 (1984), 456–82

Roth, Ralf, *Stadt und Bürgertum in Frankfurt am Main. Ein besonderer Weg von der ständischen zur modernen Bürgergesellschaft, 1760–1914* (Munich, 1996)

Rumpler, Helmut, *Die deutsche Politik des Freiherrn von Beust 1848 bis 1850. Zur Problematik mittelstaatlicher Reformpolitik im Zeitalter der Paulskirche* (Vienna, 1972)

Rumpler, Helmut (ed.), *Deutscher Bund und deutsche Frage 1815–1866* (Munich/Vienna, 1990)

Runge, Gerlinde, *Die Volkspartei in Württemberg von 1864 bis 1871. Die Erben der 48er Revolution im Kampf gegen die preußischkleindeutsche Lösung der nationalen Frage* (Stuttgart, 1970)

Rürup, Reinhard, 'Emancipation and crisis: the 'Jewish Question' in Germany 1850–1890', *Leo Baeck Institute Yearbook* 20 (1975), 13–25

Sachsen und die Wettiner. Chancen und Realitäten. Internationale Wissenschaftliche Konferenz, Dresden vom 27. bis 29. Juni 1989 (Dresden, 1990)

Samuel, Ralph and Stedman Jones, Gareth (eds.), *Culture, ideology and politics* (London, 1982)

Sauer, Michael, *Volksschullehrerbildung in Preußen. Die Seminare und Präparandenanstalten vom 18. Jahrhundert bis zur Weimarer Republik* (Cologne, 1987)

'Zwischen Negativkontrolle und staatlichem Monopol. Zur Geschichte von Schulbuchzulassung und -einführung', *Geschichte in Wissenschaft und Unterricht* 49:3 (1998), 144–56

Sauer, Paul, *Das württembergische Heer in der Zeit des Deutschen und des Norddeutschen Bundes* (Stuttgart, 1958)

Württembergs letzter König. Das Leben Wilhelms II (Stuttgart, 1994)

Schama, Simon, 'The domestication of majesty: royal family portraiture, 1500–1850', *The Journal of Interdisciplinary History*, 17:1 (1986), 155–84

Scheel, Günter, 'Die Anfänge der Arbeiterbewegung im Königreich Hannover. Zwischen Integration und Emanzipation', *Niedersächsisches Jahrbuch für Landesgeschichte* 48 (1976), 17–70

Schieder, Theodor, *Das deutsche Kaiserreich von 1871 als Nationalstaat* (Cologne/Opladen, 1961)

Schivelbusch, Wolfgang, *The railway journey: the industrialisation and perception of time and space in the 19th century* (Leamington Spa, 1986)

Schlechte, Horst, 'Friedrich Ludwig Breuer (1786–1833). Ein Diplomat der sächsischen Biedermeier', *Neues Archiv für sächsische Geschichte* 61 (1940), 14–48

Schleunes, Karl A., *Schooling and society. The politics of education in Prussia and Bavaria 1750–1900* (Oxford, 1989)

Schmidt, Gerhard, *Die Staatsreform in Sachsen in der ersten Hälfte des 19. Jahrhunderts, eine Parallele zu den Steinischen Reformen in Preußen* (Weimar, 1966)

Reformbestrebungen in Sachsen in den ersten Jahrzehnten des 19. Jahrhunderts (Dresden, 1969)

Schmitt, Hans A., 'Count Beust and Germany, 1866–70: reconquest, realignment, or resignation?', *Central European History* 1:1 (1968), 20–34

'Prussia's last fling: the annexation of Hanover, Hesse, Frankfurt, and Nassau, June 15–October 8, 1866', *Central European History* 8:4 (1975), 316–47

'From sovereign states to Prussian provinces: Hanover and Hesse-Nassau, 1866–1871', *Journal of Modern History* 57:1 (1985), 24–56

Schmoll, Friedemann, *Verewigte Nation, Studien zur Erinnerungskultur von Reich und Einzelstaat im württembergischen Denkmalkult des 19. Jahrhunderts* (Tübingen, 1995)

Schnabel, Franz, 'Der Ursprung der vaterländischen Studien', *Blätter für deutsche Landesgeschichte* 88 (1951), 4–27

Schneider, Franz, *Pressefreiheit und politische Öffentlichkeit. Studien zur politischen Geschichte Deutschlands bis 1848* (Neuwied am Rhein/Berlin, 1966)

Schneider, Gerhard, 'Langensalza – ein hannoversches Trauma. Gefallenendenken auf dem Schlachtfeld von 1866', *Niedersächsisches Jahrbuch für Landesgeschichte* 61 (1989), 265–324

Schneider, Ute, *Politische Festkultur im 19. Jahrhundert: die Rheinprovinz von der franzö-sischen Zeit bis zum Ende des Ersten Weltkrieges (1806–1918)* (Essen, 1995)

Schridde, Rudolf, *Bismarck und Hannover, Die Gesandtenzeit 1851–62* (Hildesheim, 1963)

Schroeder, Paul W., 'Austro-German relations: divergent views of the disjointed partnership', *Central European History* 11:3 (1978), 302–12

Schübelin, Walter, *Das Zollparlament und die Politik von Baden, Bayern und Württemberg, 1866–1870* (Berlin, 1935)

Schuh, Kathrin, 'Festarchitektur. Inszenierungen des Hofarchitekten Georg Ludwig Friedrich Laves' in Hans-Dieter Schmid (ed.), *Feste und Feiern in Hannover* (Bielefeld, 1995), pp. 109–24

Schulze, Hagen, 'The "German question" and European answers', *The Historical Journal* 30:4 (1987), 1013–22

The course of German nationalism, from Frederick the Great to Bismarck 1763–1867 (Cambridge, 1991)

Seeger, Christine, 'Die Sedanfeiern in Hannover – Integration oder Ausgrenzung im Kaiserreich?', *Hannoversche Geschichtsblätter* NF 46 (1992), 121–36

Seibt, Ferdinand, 'Die bayerische "Reichshistoriographie" und die Ideologie des deutschen Nationalstaats 1806–1918', *Zeitschrift für bayerische Landesgeschichte* 28 (1965), 523–54

Seydewitz, Max, 'Sachsen und der Suezkanal', *Neues Archiv für sächsische Geschichte* 63 (1942), 80–129

Seydewitz, Ruth and Seydewitz, Max, *Das Dresdener Galeriebuch. Vierhundert Jahre Dresdener Gemäldegalerie* (Dresden, 1957)

Die Dresdener Kunstschätze. Zur Geschichte des Grünen Gewölbes und der anderen Dresdener Kunstsammlungen (Dresden, 1960)

Sheehan, James J., 'Liberalism and the city in nineteenth-century Germany', *Past and Present* 51 (1971), 116–37

'What is German history? Reflections on the role of the *Nation* in German history and historiography', *Journal of Modern History* 53 (1981), 1–23

German Liberalism in the nineteenth century (London, 1982)

German History 1770–1866 (Oxford, 1989)

Siemann, Wolfram, 'Giuseppi Mazzini in Württemberg? Ein Fall staatspolizei-licher Fahndung im Reaktionssystem des Nachmärz', *Zeitschrift für württem-bergische Landesgeschichte* 40 (1981), 547–60

Der 'Polizeiverein' deutscher Staaten: eine Dokumentation zur Überwachung der Öffentlichkeit nach der Revolution von 1848/9 (Tübingen, 1983)

'Propaganda um Napoleon in Württemberg. Die Rheinbundära unter König Friedrich I. (1806–13), *Zeitschrift für Württembergischen Landesgeschichte* 47 (1988), 359–80

Gesellschaft im Aufbruch. Deutschland 1849–1871 (Frankfurt, 1990)

Simon, Walter M., 'Variations in nationalism during the great reform period in Prussia', *American Historical Review* 59: 2 (1954), 305–321

Skopp, Douglas R., 'Auf der untersten Sprosse: Der Volksschullehrer als "Semi-

Professional" im Deutschland des 19. Jahrhunderts', *Geschichte und Gesellschaft* 6:3 (1980), 382–402

Smith, Anthony D., *The ethnic origins of nations* (Oxford, 1986)

Sperber, James, 'State and civil society in Prussia: thoughts on a new edition of Reinhart Koselleck's *Preussen zwischen Reform und Revolution*', *Journal of Modern History* 57:2 (1985), 278–96

Sperber, Jonathan, 'Echoes of the French revolution in the Rhineland 1830–1849', *Central European History* 22 (1989), 200–17

'Festivals of national unity in the German revolution of 1848', *Past and Present* 36 (1992), 114–38

The Kaiser's voters. Electors and elections in Imperial Germany (Cambridge, 1997)

Sondhaus, Lawrence, 'Schwarzenberg, Austria and the German question 1848–51', *International History Review* 13:1 (1991), 1–19

Southard, Robert, *Droysen and the Prussian school of history* (Lexington, Ky., 1995)

Staatliche Kunstsammlungen Dresden, Institut für Denkmalpflege, Arbeitsstelle Dresden, *Gottfried Semper 1803–1879. Baumeister zwischen Revolution und Historismus* (Fribourg, GDR, 1980)

Stedman Jones, Gareth, 'The mid-century crisis and the 1848 revolutions', *Theory and Society* 12 (July 1983), 505–20.

Stehlin, Stewart A., 'Guelph plans for the Franco-Prussian war', *The Historical Journal* 13:4 (1970), 789–98

Steinbach, Peter (ed.), *Probleme politischer Partizipation im Modernisierungsprozeß* (Stuttgart, 1982)

Stern, Fritz, 'Money, morals and the pillars of Bismarck's society', *Central European History* 3:1–2 (1970), 49–72

Gold and iron: Bismarck, Bleichröder and the building of the German Empire (Harmondsworth, 1987)

Storch, Dietmar, 'Die hannoversche Königskrone. Ursprung, Geschichte und Geschicke eines unbekannten monarchischen Herrschaftszeichens des 19. Jahrhunderts', *Niedersächsisches Jahrbuch für Landesgeschichte* 54 (1982), 217–50

Strauss, Gerald, 'The Holy Roman Empire revisited', *Central European History* 11:3 (1978), 290–312

Stroheker, Hans Otto, and Willmann, Günther, *Cannstatter Volksfest. Das schwäbische Landesfest im Wandel der Zeiten* (Stuttgart, 1978)

Tacke, Charlotte, *Denkmal im sozialen Raum. Nationale Symbole in Deutschland und Frankreich im 19. Jahrhundert* (Göttingen, 1995)

Tenfelde, Klaus, 'Adventus. Zur historischen Ikonologie des Festzugs', *Historische Zeitschrift* 235 (1982), 45–84

Theil, Bernhard, 'Der württembergische Konsul Karl von Kolb und die französische Intervention in Rom im Jahre 1849', *Zeitschrift für württembergische Landesgeschichte* 46 (1987), 394–402

Thieme, Wilhelm, 'Eintritt Sachsens in den Zollverein und seine wirtschaftlichen Folgen' (unpublished doctoral dissertation, Leipzig, 1914)

Tilly, Richard, 'The political economy of public finance and the industrialisation of Prussia, 1815–1866', *Journal of Economic History* 26:4 (1966), 484–97

'Popular disorders in nineteenth-century Germany: a preliminary survey',
Journal of Social History 4 (1970), 1–40

'Financing industrial enterprise in Great Britain and Germany in the nineteenth century: testing grounds for Marxist and Schumpeterian theories?'
in H.-J. Wagener and J. W. Drukker, *The economic law of motion of modern
society, a Marx–Keynes–Schumpeter centennial* (Cambridge, 1986), pp. 123–55

Trox, Eckhard, 'Heinrich Elsner: Vom Jakobinismus zum Konservatismus. Ein
Beitrag zur Entstehungsgeschichte der konservativen Partei in Württemberg', *Zeitschrift für württembergische Landesgeschichte* 52 (1993), 303–36

Ulbricht, Johann Ferdinand, *Geschichte der Königlich Sächsischen Staatseisenbahnen,
1889* (Leipzig, 1989, reprint.)

Ullmann, Hans Peter and Zimmermann, Clemens (eds.), *Restaurationssystem und
Reformpolitik. Süddeutschland und Preußen im Vergleich* (Munich, 1996)

Ullner, Rudolf, *Die Idee des Föderalismus im Jahrzehnt der deutschen Einigungskriege, dargestellt unter besonderer Berücksichtigung des Modells der amerikanischen Verfassung für
das deutsche politische Denken* (Hamburg/Lübeck, 1965)

Umbach, Maiken, 'Visual culture, scientific images, and German small-state
politics in the late Enlightenment', *Past and Present* 158 (1998), 110–45.

Vandré, Rudolf, *Schule, Lehrer und Unterricht im 19. Jahrhundert. Zur Geschichte des
Religionsunterrichts* (Göttingen, 1973)

Vann, James Allen, *The making of a state, Württemberg 1593–1793* (Ithaca, 1985)

Vieregg, Hildegard, *Vorgeschichte der Museumspädagogik, dargestellt an der
Museumsentwicklung in den Städten Berlin, Dresden, München und Hamburg bis zum
Beginn der Weimarer Republik* (Münster, 1991)

Vivarelli, Roberto, '1870 in European history and historiography', *Journal of
Modern History* 53 (June 1981), 167–88

Voigt, Rüdiger (ed.), *Symbole der Politik, Politik der Symbole* (Opladen, 1989)

La Vopa, Anthony J., 'Status and ideology: rural schoolteachers in pre-March
and revolutionary Prussia', *Journal of Social History* 12:3 (1979), 430–50
Prussian school teachers, profession and office, 1763–1848 (Chapel Hill, 1980)

Walker, Mack, *German home towns. Community, state and General Estate 1648–1871*
(Ithaca, 1971)

Weber, Eugen, *Peasants into Frenchmen: the modernisation of rural France 1870–1914*
(London, 1977)

Weber, Wolfgang (ed.), *Der Fürst, Ideen und Wirklichkeiten in der europäischen Geschichte*
(Cologne,1998)

Wegert, Karl H., 'The genesis of youthful radicalism: Hesse-Nassau, 1806–19',
Central European History 10:3 (1977), 183–205

'Patrimonial rule, popular self-interest, and Jacobinism in Germany,
1763–1800', *Journal of Modern History* 53:3 (1981), 440–67

'Contention with civility: the state and social control in the German South-
west, 1760/1850', *The Historical Journal* 34:2 (1991), 349–69

Wehler, Hans-Ulrich, 'Bismarck's imperialism 1862–1890', *Past and Present* 48 (1970), 119–55

The German Empire 1871–1918 (Leamington Spa, 1985)

Deutsche Gesellschaftsgeschichte, Vol. II, *Von der Reformära bis zur industriellen und politischen 'Deutschen Doppelrevolution' 1815–1845/9*; Vol. III, *Von der Deutschen Doppelrevolution bis zum Beginn des Ersten Weltkrieges 1849–1914* (Munich, 1987/1995)

Wehner, Norbert, *Die deutschen Mittelstaaten auf den Frankfurter Fürstentag 1863* (Frankfurt, 1993)

Weigelt, Klaus, *Heimat und Nation. Zur Geschichte und Identität der Deutschen* (Mainz, 1984)

Wertheimer, Jack, 'The "unwanted element": East European Jews in Imperial Germany', *Leo Baeck Institute Yearbook* 26 (1981), 23–46

Whaley, Joachim, 'Thinking about Germany, 1750–1815: the birth of a nation?', *Transactions of the English Goethe Society* NS 66 (1997), 53–72

White, Dan S., *The splintered party. National Liberalism in Hessen and the Reich, 1867–1918* (Cambridge, Mass./London, 1976)

Wienfort, Monika, *Monarchie in der bürgerlichen Gesellschaft. Deutschland und England von 1640 bis 1848* (Göttingen, 1993)

Wilkinson, James, 'The uses of popular culture by rival elites: the case of Alsace, 1890–1914', *History of European Ideas* 11 (1989), 605–18

Willis, Geoffrey Malden, *Ernest Augustus, Duke of Cumberland and King of Hanover* (London, 1954)

Wilson, Peter H., *War, state and society in Württemberg, 1677–1793* (Cambridge, 1995)

Windell, George G., 'The Bismarckian Empire as a federal state 1866–1880. A chronicle of failure', *Central European History* 2:4 (1969), 291–311

Winzer, Fritz, *Hannover und die deutsche Frage 1848/9* (Berlin, 1937)

Wölk, Monika, *Der preussische Volksschulabsolvent als Reichstagswähler 1871–1912. Ein Beitrag zur historischen Wahlforschung in Deutschland* (Berlin, 1980)

Wülfing, Wulf, Bruns, Karin and Parr, Rolf, *Historische Mythologie der Deutschen, 1798–1918* (Munich, 1991)

Wunder, Bernd, 'Der württembergischen Personaladel (1806–1913)', *Zeitschrift für württembergische Landesgeschichte* 40 (1981), 494–518

Ziegler, Dieter, *Eisenbahnen und Staat im Zeitalter der Industrialisierung. Die Eisenbahnpolitik der deutschen Staaten im Vergleich* (Stuttgart, 1996)

Zorn, Wolfgang, 'Die wirtschaftliche Integration Kleindeutschlands in den 1860er Jahren und die Reichsgründung', *Historische Zeitschrift* 216:2 (April 1973), 304–34

Zucker, Stanley, 'Ludwig Bamberger and the rise of anti-semitism in Germany, 1848–1903', *Central European History* 3:4 (1970), 332–52

Zug der Zeit – Zeit der Züge, deutsche Eisenbahn 1835–1985. Das offizielle Werk zur gleichnahmigen Ausstellung (Berlin, 1985)

Index

374

Lightning Source UK Ltd.
Milton Keynes UK
175575UK00001B/88/A